EXPLORATIONS IN PSYCHOHISTORY

THE WELLFLEET PAPERS

EDITED BY **ROBERT JAY LIFTON**

WITH **ERIC OLSON**

SIMON AND SCHUSTER
NEW YORK

PUBLISHED BY SIMON AND SCHUSTER
ROCKEFELLER CENTER, 630 FIFTH AVENUE
NEW YORK, NEW YORK 10020

DESIGNED BY IRVING PERKINS
MANUFACTURED IN THE UNITED STATES OF AMERICA
BY THE BOOK PRESS INC., BRATTLEBORO, VT.

1 2 3 4 5 6 7 8 9 10

LIBRARY OF CONGRESS CATALOGING IN PUBLICATION DATA

EXPLORATIONS IN PSYCHOHISTORY.
INCLUDES BIBLIOGRAPHICAL REFERENCES.
1. PSYCHOANALYSIS IN HISTORIOGRAPHY—ADDRESSES, ESSAYS, LECTURES. I. LIFTON, ROBERT JAY, 1926– ED. II. OLSON, ERIC, ED. [DNLM: 1. HISTORY. 2. PSYCHOLOGY. D16.9 L722E]
D16.E9 907'.2 74-13758
ISBN 0-671-21848-4
ISBN 0-671-21849-2 (PBK.)

Permission to reprint the following is gratefully acknowledged:

"Moses and Monotheism," from the Standard Edition of *The Complete Psychological Works of Sigmund Freud,* Vol. XXIII. Reprinted by permission of Sigmund Freud Copyrights Ltd., the Institute of Psychoanalysis, and The Hogarth Press, Ltd. The James Strachey translation is reprinted by permission of Alfred A. Knopf, Inc., the authorized publisher in the United States of *Moses and Monotheism,* by Sigmund Freud.

"On Psychohistory," by Robert Jay Lifton, © 1970 by Robert Jay Lifton. Earlier versions have appeared in *Partisan Review,* Spring 1970; *The State of American History,* ed. Herbert J. Bass, Quadrangle/The New York Times Book Co., 1970; and *Psychoanalysis and Contemporary Science,* eds. Robert R. Holt and Emanuel Peterfreund, Vol. I, 1972.

"On the Nature of Psychohistorical Evidence: In Search of Gandhi," reprinted from *Life History and History* by Erik H. Erikson, © 1975 by W. W. Norton & Company, Inc. Reprinted with the permission of W. W. Norton & Company, Inc.

"Play and Actuality," by Erik H. Erikson, reprinted from *Play and Development,* a symposium, ed. Maria W. Piers, © 1972 by W. W. Norton & Company, Inc. Reprinted with the permission of W. W. Norton & Company, Inc.

ABOUT THE CONTRIBUTORS

NORMAN BIRNBAUM is a professor of sociology at Amherst College. His main interests are sociological theory and the sociology of culture. His books include *The Crisis of Industrial Society* and *Toward a Critical Society*. He has conducted much of his recent research as a John Guggenheim Fellow.

PETER BROOKS is an associate professor of French and Comparative Literature at Yale University. He is a contributing editor of *Partisan Review*, co-author of *Man and His Fictions*, and author of *The Novel of Worldliness*.

ROBERT COLES is a child psychiatrist who has been working in various parts of the country examining how social, cultural and historical forces impinge upon the growth and development of children. He is the author of *Children of Crisis* (in three volumes).

ERIK H. ERIKSON is Professor Emeritus of Human Development at Harvard University. His writings include *Childhood and Society, Young Man Luther, Gandhi's Truth* and, most recently, *Dimensions of a New Identity*, the 1973 Jefferson Lectures in the Humanities.

STUART HAMPSHIRE is currently Warden of Wadham College, Oxford University. From 1963 to 1970 he was Chairman of the Philosophy Department at Princeton University. He is the author of *Spinoza, Thought and Action*, and *Freedom of Mind and Other Essays*.

KENNETH KENISTON is now Chairman and Director of the Carnegie Council on Children, on leave as a professor of psychology in the Department of Psychiatry at Yale Medical School. His main field of interest is the relation between youth, society and political action. His books include *The Uncommitted, The Young Radicals*, and *Youth and Dissent*.

ROBERT JAY LIFTON is Foundations' Fund for Research Professor of Psychiatry at Yale Medical School and author of *Death in Life: Survivors of Hiroshima, Home From the War: Vietnam Veterans—Neither Victims Nor Executioners*, and other books and articles dealing with psychology and history and with holocaust and social change. He has been coordinator of the Wellfleet meetings.

BRUCE MAZLISH is a professor of history at Massachusetts Institute of Technology. His interests center in modern intellectual history and psychohistory. His books include *In Search of Nixon*, *The Riddle of History* and, in collaboration with J. Bronowski, *The Western Intellectual Tradition.*

ALEXANDER MITSCHERLICH is a professor at the University of Frankfurt and Director of the Sigmund Freud Institute for Psychoanalysis. He has written extensively on post-Hitler Germany, and his translated books include *Doctors of Infamy*, *Society Without the Father*, and *The Inability to Mourn.*

MARGARETE MITSCHERLICH is a psychoanalyst practicing in Frankfurt. She is co-author of *The Inability to Mourn* and has written on changing aspects of psychoanalytic technique, aggression, perceptions of reality, and the psychology of women.

ERIC OLSON is completing his graduate studies at Harvard University. He is research assistant to Robert Lifton and co-author with him of *Living and Dying.*

PHILIP RIEFF is Benjamin Franklin Professor of Sociology at the University of Pennsylvania. His main interest is sociological theory. Two of his books are *The Triumph of the Therapeutic* and *Fellow Teachers.*

CONTENTS

PREFACE

The Wellfleet meetings began in conversations between Erik Erikson and myself in late 1964 and early 1965, but he and I had been talking together about psychology and history for ten years before that. I had embraced his work, which I saw as opening up a highly significant intellectual dimension while most of psychoanalysis seemed stagnant. I had also struggled with my own investigations and with concepts having to do with individual experience in holocaust and historical change, and was impressed by how little we still really knew about psychological interaction between "the individual" and "the collectivity."

Neither of us had anything like a sense that psychohistory was "an idea whose time had come"—indeed we hesitated then, as perhaps we should now, to use that noun form. But those twelve or fourteen of us who took part in the early Wellfleet meetings, starting in August 1966, did experience the special excitement that can accompany the combination of a beginning intellectual breakthrough with problems so formidable as to constantly challenge and defy solution. Contributing greatly to that enthusiasm was (and still is) the conviction that rigorous development of a psychohistorical perspective holds out special promise, on the one hand for addressing the extraordinary threats and confusions of our time, and on the other for generating a new conceptual and perhaps therapeutic vitality within the psychological professions. To recognize that the one promise cannot be realized independently of the other is to be no more than "psychohistorical."

More personally, I believe that Erikson and I were seeking ways to further a relationship between a mentor who did not cultivate disciples but was bent upon extending and consolidating his ideas, and a close student struggling to break sufficiently free of mentorship to explore directions that his own investigations seemed to suggest if not demand. Never having formally worked together, the Wellfleet group provided an "institutional structure" for our intellectual exchange. I was then thirty-eight and Erikson sixty-three.

Kenneth Keniston was also at the center of the Wellfleet enterprise from the beginning. We had met in Cambridge, Massachusetts, in the mid-fifties where we were members of an amorphous subculture, in which David Riesman was a key figure, concerned with a variety of stimulating combinations of psychological and social thought and ethical and political questions around war and peace. Keniston and I shared not only an immersion in Erikson's work, and a combination of involvement with and criticism of the psychoanalytic tradition, but also a strong interest in the compelling interplay of youth and history. A few years younger than I, Keniston found my struggles for autonomy relevant to his own efforts to emerge responsibly from the influence of several powerful teachers. We both moved to Yale in the early sixties, where our dialogue and friendship have continued though our interests have somewhat diverged. During the Wellfleet meetings Keniston's closely reasoned distinctions, drawn from a broad knowledge of social and political as well as psychological thought, have been a steady counterpoint—both a restraint and a stimulus—to the speculative and visionary inclinations of others (including Erikson and myself) in the group.

Over the years the three of us have been the continuous core, if that is the phrase, of the Wellfleet gatherings. We have planned and presented work at all of them. Though I have assumed responsibility for many details of agenda and organization, I have always consulted them both—the three of us frequently sitting down somewhere in New Haven, Stockbridge, or Litchfield (midway between the two) to imagine together the events of the forthcoming summer—never with the expectation that things would happen exactly as we imagined but always with the faith that *something* of value, of a more or less serendipitous nature, would occur.

That faith has had partly to do with the Wellfleet setting—the renovated hut (my summer study) in which we meet—that overlooks the magnificent Cape Cod dunes and the Atlantic Ocean beyond. As it happened, the renovation of the hut and building of the summer home coincided with the planning of the first Wellfleet meeting, which I confess I had very much in mind when I ordered the construction of the heavy oak tables that provide the main furnishings. I do not underestimate the influence of such a setting—Thoreau called it The Great Beach—on psychohistorical deliberation. Beyond encouraging imaginative freedom, I think it has done much to bring out already existing cosmic intellectual inclinations. Also affecting us, perhaps not so much as it should, has been the contrast between our own well-being in the midst of the beauty around us and the pain and horror we have frequently explored.

That contrast imposed itself upon me in very personal ways on two occasions: on returning to Wellfleet after my father's funeral in August 1966, to present my work on Hiroshima to the group; and on arriving at Wellfleet with my family directly from Vietnam in July 1967. Many have commented on the relationship between holocaust and transcendent beauty, but there are no guidelines for dealing with one's own awareness of the human imbalance. We have of course discussed many things other than holocaust, and the setting has also encouraged a conflict between an unusually intense inwardness and mental sharing that has held us powerfully to our continuing exchange and an equally intense impulse to escape the hut and the exchange and plunge physically into the pleasures of The Great Beach and the nearby ponds and tennis courts.

Very roughly, the Wellfleet meetings can be divided into two phases—a first period of about four years that could be called The Grand Illusion of Unity, and a subsequent phase of continuing Work, Play, and Struggle.

Even at the height of our early enthusiasm, none of us fully embraced the ever-present illusion of unification—inevitably based on a misleading application of a scientific model—that has long haunted sociological and psychological thought. In an organizing letter, I projected simply "a working group for the exchange of ideas on the interrelationship of psychology and history." But I also suggested the rather grandiose name, "Group for the Study of Psychohistorical Process," which we continued to use for the next three years or so (after which we have simply spoken of the "Wellfleet meetings").

Active participants during that first phase included Margaret

Brenman, Robert Coles, George Klein, and Frederick Wyatt from the psychiatric and psychological side; historians Lawrence Chisolm, Frank Manuel, and Bruce Mazlish; sociologists Kai Erikson and Philip Rieff; political scientists Harold Isaacs, Lloyd Rudolph, and Susanne Rudolph; literary critic-historian Steven Marcus; and philosopher Stuart Hampshire. We went through many experiments in style of presentation—in the extent one used texts or notes, whether or not one circulated a paper or statement of any kind in advance, etc. We sought a balance between structure and spontaneity, recognizing that, together with our emphasis on informality, a certain amount of structure was necessary for the kind of intellectual opening-up we wanted—for discussion that, at least ideally, could combine disciplined thought with far-out speculation. We always encouraged participants to present work that was both actively in progress and conceptually problematic, and they have done so often enough to provide moments when we seemed to approach that ideal. That is not to say that we have not also had our share of non-communication, posturing, and absurd soliloquy. It may be rationalization but I suspect one needs some of the latter in order to have some of the former. In any case, the sublime and the absurd moments (as well as moments that were both) emerged from a general tension in the group between the impulse toward integration—finding a basic area of conceptual agreement and making the compromises necessary for that agreement in order to create a kind of psychohistorical baseline—and an individualistic tendency to utilize the group and interact with its flow of ideas and images as a means of furthering and deepening one's own evolving work in the psychohistorical area. The first, perhaps more noble, impulse has always been present, but the second has generally prevailed. Yet, paradoxically, that individualistic process has produced something like a psychohistorical baseline—in no sense a wholly unified theory but a beginning set of working principles that echoes throughout these papers. A number of those principles are outlined in my paper, "On Psychohistory," which is meant to serve partly as an introduction to the volume.

A similar tension was expressed in our relationship with The American Academy of Arts and Sciences, which offered us generous financial support for our first three years. The Academy's representatives, John Voss and Stephen Graubard, were always considerate and sensitive to our needs, but the sponsorship inevitably brought to bear on us a certain pressure toward a more organized and integrative effort and practical products: using a particular meeting to create an issue of *Daedalus,* the Academy's journal, and a series of meetings to create an enduring institution that could coordinate, and train others in, psychohistorical work.

The suggestions had their attractions. Many of us had associations with the Academy, had written for *Daedalus,* and had been approached by young historians and psychologists searching for training programs for psychohistorical work. But in candor, we realized that we lacked a sufficient body of psychohistorical theory to form an institution around; and immersed in our individual work, we were unwilling to give the time and energy we knew such an institution would demand. Some of us felt that dependency upon the Academy, any academy, could serve to blunt our boldness and mute whatever intellectual (if not political) subversion we were capable of mounting.

By the time of what I am calling the second phase, we had resolved the matter in favor of a more limited (not necessarily easier) commitment to our own intellectual exploration. It was not so much a pulling in of horns—our meetings were still full of "great issues" and "grand visions"—as a more relaxed awareness that progress for us lay not in imposed unification, but in further probing our observations, our concepts, and ourselves. No longer thinking in terms of an organization or institution, we were free to reconstitute ourselves as a loosely assembled but intensely interacting group of individuals—the "continuous core" of Erikson, Keniston, and myself now expanded to include Norman Birnbaum and Brenman and, a bit later, Peter Brooks and Richard Sennett. Others who came together with us for varying periods have included psychoanalysts Charles Fisher, Robert Liebert, Alexander Mitscherlich, and Margarete Mitscherlich; social theorists Richard Barnet, Richard Falk, and Rosabeth Kanter; historians Leo Marx and Howard Zinn; literary critic William Phillips; and theologian Colin Williams.

We struggled with a constant dialectic between responding to the overwhelming national and international events of the late sixties and early seventies and detailed theoretical exchanges. And we held larger evening meetings, to which we invited friends from the Lower Cape summer community (academics, writers, and artists) which were devoted to such matters as university uprisings, decision-making processes of the Vietnam War, relationships between My

Lai and Nuremberg, the outer space programs, and the presidential election of 1972. We were informally addressed by such people as Noam Chomsky, Karl Deutsch, Richard Goodwin, Stanley Kunitz, Salvador Luria, Seymour Melman, and James Thomson. And we had smaller evening meetings, usually confined to participants in the working group and their guests. One of these was a Chinese dinner on those oak tables in the study. Culinary pleasures and joyous libation mingled with critical intellectual responses to a presentation I was making on psychic numbing and its relationship to the symbolizing process. At another we heard Erik Erikson read the remarkable chapter he had just completed from his book on Gandhi in which, in an imaginary letter, he "tells off" his biographical subject concerning the Mahatma's own unrecognized violence.

Throughout, there has been a significant tension in the group that includes both theoretical-psychohistorical and ethical-political questions. On one side there is a position, exemplified by Erikson, in which the Freudian vision is extended creatively to historical questions—the psychohistorian assumes a stance modeled essentially on the psychoanalyst's interpretive detachment, but modified by an active awareness of his own historical subjectivity. On the other side there is a more fundamental shift from Freudian theory—in my case toward a formative-symbolic perspective—together with a greater focus on the psychohistorian's advocacies and involvements as elements of his interpretive stance and impact. The two positions of course overlap and it is not always possible to distinguish one from the other. A lack of political involvement is not inevitably associated with adherence to the Freudian tradition—nor do advocacy and activism always go with a more heretical view toward Freud. But these combinations have more or less held at Wellfleet and, I suspect, in various pockets of American intellectual life in general. And the two positions have, at least in our discussions, extended to social theory as well—the first seeking, at least theoretically, a synthesis between Freud and Marx (an emphasis of Norman Birnbaum in particular, and also Steven Marcus and Stuart Hampshire) as a way of grappling with contemporary issues; and the second emphasizing the need for new social theory, to which psychohistory can contribute, that draws upon Freud and Marx but has considerable autonomy from both (the emphasis of Keniston, Sennett, Chisolm, and myself).

Related to these excruciating ethical and conceptual dilemmas has been our growing awareness of the problems posed by current cultural attitudes surrounding the words "psychohistorical" and "psychohistory". The words have quickly come to call forth responses either of magical enchantment or of angry-fearful taboo. No doubt those of us who come to the Wellfleet summer meetings bear some responsibility. It was Erikson who first used the term "psychohistorical" as a parallel word to "psychosocial"; and it was in reference to my Hiroshima work that the more dubious noun form first appeared (from the pen of a Yale undergraduate writer, now a historian [if not a psychohistorian], Daniel Yergin). Or so we thought—until it was pointed out to us that Isaac Asimov, some years earlier, had employed both words in his compelling science fiction trilogy, *Foundation.* Asimov's "psychohistory" is a mathematical science that predicts the future with complete accuracy. Hence, when its practitioners, the "psychohistorians," determine that an age of barbarism is about to appear, they go underground and transmit their secret teachings to a select few, a process that continues over endless generations. In that vision, the "psychohistorians" are an intellectual elite of philosopher-scientists ready to surface and disseminate what they have preserved when the more enlightened regime anticipated by their mathematical predictions actually appears.

I would worry about anyone doing psychohistorical work who is not made just a bit uneasy by Asimov's vision (parable?). Not that one need feel embarrassed by having been anticipated by science fiction—that may well be a badge of honor. What we had better examine, though, is Asimov's keen perception of the contemporary fascination with the *idea* of a transcendent combination of two ultimate domains of human experience—psychology and history. Such a transcendent combination allows at least a select few to achieve an absolute reversal of the present sense that our history is running away with us and that our psychological selves are dismembered, and can thereby seem to guarantee the perpetuation of the human civilization we feel to be so endangered. How great, then, the temptation of would-be psychohistorians to exploit that fascination, and of some critics to view *all* psychohistory as an expression of that form of *hubris.* And psychohistory becomes an incantation—either white or black magic.

Wellfleet is not like that, as I believe these essays demonstrate. Putting the volume together has meant flying in the face of the

Wellfleet ethos of process rather than product (though that ethos has not prevented participants from subsequent conversion of process to essay or book). Of the fourteen essays, all but three were presented in earlier form at Wellfleet. The exceptions are Rieff's statement on Freud, which overlapped considerably with things he did talk about at Wellfleet; the Mitscherlichs' essay on post-Hitler Germany, portions of which they discussed during a Wellfleet evening on Nuremberg and My Lai; and of course the excerpts from *Moses and Monotheism*, Freud's most important psychohistorical statement, which we see as providing a baseline for all who are involved in psychohistorical matters. (Freud never came to Wellfleet but he was always there.) About half of the papers stem from the first phase of Wellfleet—Erikson's on psychohistorical evidence, much of which literally took shape in his mind during the course of our first meeting in August 1966; Mazlish's on the Mills, Coles's on method, and Hampshire's on theory. Both of Keniston's papers span the two periods, as do my own, while the Erikson paper on play, and those of Birnbaum on critical theory and Brooks on symbolization, are entirely from the second phase. The Hampshire, Birnbaum, and Brooks presentations, along with the discussion that follows each, were taken directly from the tapes of the meetings with the minimal editing required to convert them to written form.

We have tried to include essays that represent the Wellfleet enterprise, provide a glimpse of the give-and-take of the meetings, and tell something of the state of psychohistorical work in general. That may be too much to do in one volume and the effort has required painful decisions, for which I ask forbearance.

While I bear ultimate responsibility for the choices, the volume would not have come into being—and certainly there would have been no direct presentations from the tapes—without the dedicated and sensitive work of Eric Olson. His efforts span all phases of the editing, from the smallest detail to the most delicate intellectual judgment. He has also for the past few years been recorder at Wellfleet, continuing in the fine tradition of Richard Almond and Michael Lerner. In working on the volume, I found myself leaning very heavily on the special talents and judgment of Alice Mayhew of Simon and Schuster as editor, advisor, and friend. The contributions of Lily Finn, my assistant at Yale, date back to arrangements for the first Wellfleet meeting and all of the ensuing ones, and extend right down to the last manuscript and publishing detail—to all of which she brought her extraordinary combination of skill, tact, and compassion. Betty Jean Lifton, sand dobby, comrade of the dunes, and writer in residence, has been the real source of the Wellfleet ambience and much else.

RJL
Wellfleet, Mass.
June 1974

ON PSYCHOHISTORY

ROBERT JAY LIFTON

Granted there is such a thing as a "psychohistorical approach," can we then speak of a "new psychohistory"? If so we had best be tentative. Historians know well—and psychologists should know—that anything now new will soon be old, and that we often label as new (or New) that which does not yet quite exist. As for psychohistory, it is in one sense already old, and in another hardly born.

None can deny the logic of a marriage between psychology and history. Many writers from both traditions have emphasized their common concern with narrative sequence and with the nature of man's experience in the midst of that sequence. But a certain amount of skepticism about logical marriages (and their offspring) is always in order. And the greater one's commitment to this marriage, the more convinced one becomes of the impossibility—and undesirability—of an easy union.

I

Skepticism, in fact, is as good a principle as any for approaching psychohistory. Most of us involved in the project are not only critical of traditional psychoanalytic views of history but skeptical of the kind of pristine cause and effect—and therefore of the kind of knowledge—claimed by *any* monocausal and hyperreductive approach to history. Our simple commitment to develop a psychological framework that takes historical currents seriously is itself an act of skepticism toward what I shall soon identify as the ahistorical position of most psychological thought. But this kind of skepticism must be distinguished from the automatic dismissal of all psychological approaches to history—and even from the more subtle dismissal of psychological efforts by insisting that one cannot "really know" anything significant about the minds of men (great or ordinary) of the past, or about the ways in which current individual and collective ideas and emotions connect with wider historical events.

We are dealing, then, with three levels of skepticism: immediate and total rejection (the assumption that the knowledge sought is unobtainable and the whole enterprise futile); anticipated rejection (the attitude "You have to show me," implicitly "I don't expect or wish to be shown"); and a sense (which I share with a number of colleagues in the enterprise) that the kind of knowledge we seek is extremely refractory, and our methods of seeking it highly vulnerable. This third stance turns out to be in many ways the most skeptical of all.

It is tempting, especially for those with clinical experience, to speak of those forms of skepticism that dismiss out of hand, or nearly so, as "resistance." For the term suggests the kind of psychological force and need that can accompany the rejection. But I think the temptation itself should be "resisted," because the word also implies —whether used by classical psychoanalysts or Protestant evangelists or Chinese thought-reformers—that there is a true direction or intention that is ultimately to be accepted, even embraced, once the "resistance" has been overcome. This last assumption, dubious enough when applied to the individual, could be disastrous when applied to history. Moreover, by invoking the term "resistance" one could all too readily fall into the psychologistic fallacy of explaining away criticism by examining critics' involvements and needs, thereby avoiding any consideration of the weaknesses of that which is being criticized.

Yet the psychological approach to history does cause discomfort, because it entails formidable problems in method, and because, for many working in both traditions and in other branches of social thought, it threatens to undermine explicit concepts and implicit images about how men behave, why societies change, and what constitutes an acceptable professional discipline or "field." We are all, in other words, formatively bound by our own psychohistorical "place," and by our activity in that place. And so we should be, at least to a point, if our skepticism is to be rooted as well as fertile.

But what are the impediments? Why is it so difficult for psychology and history to get together? Generally speaking, I would say that not only do the two traditions often work at cross purposes; worse, each has something of an impulse to eliminate the other. And this is so even if we limit our observations to depth psychology and to man-centered history.

For instance, there is in classical psychoanalysis an implicit assumption that the larger historical universe is *nothing but* a manifestation of the projections or emanations of the individual psyche. Or if not that, history is seen as a kind of featureless background for those projections and emanations—something "out there" which is "given," but which does not significantly influence what is "in here." The emergence, over the past few decades, of a more developed "ego psychology" has somewhat altered the situation by directing our attention to the influence of the environment on the development of the self. But, as Erikson has pointed out, the grudging and impoverished terms used in the psychoanalytic approach to the environment reveal the approach itself to have remained grudging and impoverished. Ego psychology, moreover, has had very little to say about shifts in social ethos central to historical change, especially those related to the new technological environment and its destructive capacities.

Neo-Freudian psychoanalysis has been ahistorical in other ways. More open to the influence of environment, it has for the most part failed to evolve compelling general principles in the social sphere. And where it has actively sought such principles, as in the work of Abram Kardiner, it has tended to view a culture or a society as a more or less cross-sectional entity within which one can study the relationship of social institutions and "basic personality," but not as evolving phenomena whose relationship is importantly defined by change.[1] Neo-Freudian psychoanalysis thus finds itself, as much as or at times even more than the Freudian tradition it rebelled against, bound by certain limitations of the rationalistic and mechanistic imagery of the nineteenth-century world view. And when psychoanalysis has moved in a phenomenological or existential direction, its intrapsychic insights, however valuable, have tended to be insulated from historical issues.

Historical writing, about which I can speak with considerably less authority, seems (perhaps somewhat analogously) to replace a psychological perspective with common-sense assumptions about human motivation, or else to drown psychological man—that is, the inner life of individual man—in a sea of collectivity.

And yet there is much evidence of a longing from both sides for some kind of union—of widely shared recognition that psychological man lives in a history extending beyond himself, and that history is bound up with conflicts and struggles within the minds of men. Indeed, these two simple principles form the basis for a contemporary psychohistory.

II

I have suggested that the general idea of a psychological approach to history is by no means new. But rather than attempt to document comprehensively the various efforts that have been made in the name of that idea, I would like to focus upon four models (really paradigms) of psychohistory, all of which have emerged in some relationship to the psychoanalytic tradition. Two of them are Freudian, and the other two both draw upon Freud and move away from his historical assumptions.

Freud's most fundamental historical model is not really historical at all, but is rather a *pre*historical paradigm: the primeval encounter between father and sons, in which the sons rebel against the father's authority and kill him, with the entire encounter psychologically centered on the Oedipus complex. This model was first put forward in *Totem and Taboo* (1912–1913) as an explanation for the origins of society itself; and then again in modified form toward the end of Freud's life in *Moses and Monotheism* (1934–1938), to account for the origins of Jewish religion and Jewish identity—for how, as Freud put it, the "one man, the man Moses . . . created the Jews." Freud saw Moses as a kind of foster father, an Egyptian who "chose" the Jews as his people and gave to them the gift of monotheism, only to be eventually rejected and murdered by his "chosen people," his symbolic sons.

As Philip Rieff has pointed out, the model here is that of "a certain event, or events, necessarily in remote rather than near history—indeed, at the beginning become[ing] determinative of all that must follow." Rieff suggests that Freud was influenced by certain facets of Judeo-Christian millennial thought and of German historicism, according to which one crucial Event determines and explains all subsequent, and even previous, history. The principle is that of *Kairos*, of the "decisive moment," as opposed to that of *Chronos*, the more orderly sequence of qualitatively identical units of "mathematical time." Freud's historical Event can be said to be a mythical one —the primeval murder of the father, as allegedly reenacted in the Jews' murder of Moses. But it is also individual-psychological, in the sense of being a product of the Oedipus complex, which is seen as the ultimate source of these decisive occurrences. Indeed, one could view Freud's overall historical method as a kind of apologia for the Oedipal Event.[2]

Now there are powerful insights in the two books expressed around this prehistorical encounter, insights that center upon the psychological significance of the perceived historical past for both present and future, and for the movement of history itself. And I shall soon suggest ways in which this model has nourished more recent psychohistorical approaches. But since the model is a mythic one which transcends history as such, it can be profoundly misleading when used to explain specific historical events. (I have in mind particularly a current vogue among psychoanalytic and psychoanalytically minded observers of viewing recent student rebellions as little more than a repetition of the primeval rebellion of enraged sons against their fathers, as a rebellion explained by—and reducible to—the Oedipus complex. The explanation happens to be congenial to those in authority, the symbolic [or as I prefer, formative] fathers involved. But it totally neglects the larger historical currents that so forcibly intrude upon the psyches of young and old alike, and therefore misrepresents both the individual-psychological and the group processes at play.) For within Freud's prehistoric paradigm there is bequeathed to us an iron mold of psychological repetition (or "repetition-compulsion"), enveloping indiscriminately the individual and the undifferentiated collectivity. When this principle of repetition is seen as the essence of historical experience, there can be nothing new in history; indeed, if (in Rieff's paraphrase of Freud) "history is predestination," then there is no history.

The second Freudian paradigm is perhaps the more obvious one, the one most likely to come to mind when people think of a psychoanalytic approach to history: that of individual psychopathology. The best known example here is the Freud-Bullitt biography of

Woodrow Wilson,[3] a work which Bullitt almost certainly wrote but which exemplifies the Freudian approach to history more than many present-day followers of Freud would care to admit. In language and quality of thought, the Wilson biography is a vulgarization of the Freudian paradigm—Freud himself never wrote without elegance. But the idea of interpreting the outcomes of major historical events as expressions of the individual psychopathology of a particular national leader—in this case Wilson's struggles with masculinity and his need to fail—was prefigured in Freud's own work. I have in mind not only his treatment of men like Leonardo and Dostoevsky (as great artists rather than political leaders), but also Freud's general focus upon individual psychopathology as existing more or less apart from history. When this second paradigm dominates, psychopathology becomes a substitute for the psychohistorical interface. The psychopathological idiom for individual development (so prominent in the literature of psychoanalysis) becomes extended to the point where it serves as the idiom for history, or psychohistory. When this happens there is, once more, no history.

These two Freudian paradigms—the prehistorical confrontation and the leader's individual psychopathology—come together in their assumption that, in one way or another, history represents the intrapsychic struggles of the individual writ large: the same intrapsychic struggles that can be observed by the psychoanalyst in his therapeutic work. For instance, the scenario of *Totem and Taboo* includes not only the murderous rebellion against the father and the consuming of the father in the totem feast, but the subsequent remorse and residual guilt of the sons, and of their sons and daughters ad infinitum, which then reasserts itself periodically in the phenomenon of the "return of the repressed."* The entire argument derives from an individual-psychological model; and precisely the "return of the repressed" becomes the basis for Freud's view of history as psychological recurrence. And in the individual-psychopathological model, it is the *aberration* of a specific person that is writ large as historical explanation.

No wonder, then, that Freudian models are frustrating to the historian: they interpret but avoid history. They are equally problematic for the historically minded psychologist. On the one hand

*I shall not discuss the question of *how* this guilt is transmitted through the generations, or the problems surrounding the Lamarckian position on inheritance of acquired characteristics which Freud held to throughout his work.

Freud's clinical method, as many have pointed out, is entirely historical: it works on the assumption that a man automatically reveals his personal history if he merely lets his mind wander freely, that is, if he engages in free association. And Freud's fundamental discoveries—of the significance of man's individual and collective past—provide the basis for psychohistory. Yet on the other hand these same Freudian principles, when applied with closed-system finality, tend to reduce history to *nothing but recurrence* (or "repetition-compulsion") and thereby to eliminate virtually all that is innovative, or even accumulative, in the story of man.

The Faustian intellectual temptation is to dismiss the paradox and make things simple—either by direct and uncritical application of classical Freudian terms to all manner of historical events or else by pretending that neither Freud nor the emotional turmoil he described (and himself stimulated) has ever existed. We do better, I am certain, to embrace the paradox. For it can be energizing.

III

Erik Erikson has done just that. He has retained a focus upon the individual—the great man—and upon the kinds of inner conflicts illuminated by the Freudian tradition. But he has placed the great man within a specific historical context: hence the model of *the great man in history*. With Erikson's elaboration of this paradigm something approaching a new psychohistory began to take shape.

Erikson's *Young Man Luther*,[4] a pivotal work for the psychohistorical enterprise, has a direct historical relationship to Freud's *Moses and Monotheism*. Apart from Erikson's connection as a young man with the Freudian circle in Vienna, and his continuing identification of himself as a Freudian, his title is meant to echo Freud's phrase (mentioned earlier) "the man Moses." Freud used that same phrase as his original title for the book he later called *Moses and Monotheism*. I might add that Freud's original subtitle was "A Historical Novel," which suggests an interesting element of self-irony in relationship to a historical method we must now view as highly dubious (I refer to the kind of evidence Freud used to develop his thesis that Moses was an Egyptian, and that Moses was killed by the Jews). That subtitle has also found another recent echo, probably less intentional—"History as a Novel, The Novel as History," the subtitle chosen by a promising young existentialist psychohistorian named Norman Mailer for his much awarded book *Armies of the Night.* The self-irony in juxtaposing history and fiction does not necessarily suggest that either Freud or Mailer lacked belief in his own views, but rather that each felt he was dealing with a kind of truth that took him beyond conventional historical description. Rather than truth stranger than fiction, each was suggesting a form of fictionalized truth, or perhaps fiction truer than truth.

Returning to Erikson, there are other ways in which his concept of the great man parallels Freud's. At the end of *Moses,* Freud said, "The great man influences his contemporaries in two ways: through his personality and through the idea for which he stands"—an "idea" which may "lay stress on an old group of wishes in the masses, or point to a new aim for their wishes." Freud saw Moses as having taken the Jews to a "higher level of spirituality," largely by means of the "dematerializing" of God and the prohibiting of the worship of a visible form of God. Similarly, Erikson saw as Luther's fundamental achievement his "new emphasis on man in *inner* conflict and his salvation through introspective perfection"—an achievement and an emphasis Erikson compared with Kierkegaard's existentialism and Freud's psychoanalysis. Freud and Erikson both depicted the great man as a spiritual hero, as a man who achieves an intrapsychic breakthrough.

But Erikson also took several crucial steps away from Freud. Instead of an instinctual idiom—Freud's view of the great man as appealing to instinctual wishes (particularly aggressive ones) and possessing the ability to bring about in the masses a form of "instinctual renunciation" (control of aggression and "subordina[tion of] sense perception to abstract ideas")—Erikson has sought out more specifically *historical* ground, the intersection of individual and collective histories. Luther's achievement, then, depends not so much upon instinctual renunciation as upon a quality Erikson sees Luther, Gandhi, and Freud to have all shared: "a grim willingness to do the dirty work of their ages."

That "dirty work," though clearly involved with psychological universals, is historically specific. "We cannot lift a case history out of history," Erikson also tells us. And he feels constrained to ask of himself and of his readers the kind of immersion he imagines Luther to have had in such early-sixteenth-century matters confronting the young German aspirant to the priesthood as the contradictions between ideal Catholic spirituality and the "high spiritual finance" of monetary purchase of immortality through the practice of indulgences, the influence of Occamism in Catholic theology, the prevailing child-rearing practices and standards of family (especially father–son) relationships, the discipline of monastic training, and the complexities of the Catholic response to the Renaissance. In all this we leave behind Freud's concept of the traumatic historical event, followed by repression, and then by the "return of the repressed" in the form of guilt and conflict. We concern ourselves instead with the great man's monumental struggles at the border of religion and politics, with his simultaneous effort to remake himself and his world. For Luther to emerge from his own identity crisis, he had to bring about a shift in the historical identity of his epoch. He had to engage in a desperate effort "to lift his individual patienthood to the level of the universal one, and to try to solve for all what he could not solve for himself alone."

By "patienthood" Erikson (here following Kierkegaard) means exemplar of ultimate alternatives. And one of the extraordinary qualities of Erikson's rendition of the young Luther is the book's painstaking exploration of the very tenuous psychic boundaries between identity crisis, psychosis, theological innovation, and individual and historical revitalization. What Erikson has demonstrated—in this study of Luther as in his more recent book on Gandhi—is a combination of psychoanalytic sensitivity and historical imagination. The combination has been long in coming.

IV

But the great man tends to be inaccessible, at least to direct interview, or if accessible not yet great. One must usually approach him through records, or, if he belongs to recent history, through interviews with surviving friends and followers. This does not mean that the psychohistorian cannot say useful things on the basis of careful observations from a distance. But when he is centuries removed from the individual he wishes to study in depth, problems of historical reconstruction are inevitable.

Freud faced these problems with the cavalier grandiosity of a genius—as one particularly memorable footnote in *Moses and Monotheism* makes clear:

> I am very well aware that in dealing so autocratically and arbitrarily with Biblical tradition—bringing it up to confirm my views when it suits me and unhesitatingly rejecting it when it contradicts me—I am exposing myself to serious methodological criticism and weakening the convincing force of my arguments. But this is the only way in which one can treat material of which one knows definitely that its trustworthiness has been severely impaired by the distorting influence of tendentious purposes. It is to be hoped that I shall find some degree of justification later on, when I come upon the track of these secret motives. Certainty is in any case unattainable and moreover it may be said that every other writer on the subject has adopted the same procedure.[5]

While one cannot but admire Freud's honesty and boldness, the method seems a somewhat dubious one for the aspiring psychohistorian.

Erikson is much more careful with his historical data, but he too runs into difficulties. For instance, he is forced to re-create certain psychological themes of Luther's early family life on the basis of very limited evidence. Problems have also been raised about events in Luther's adult life, notably his celebrated "fit in the choir" during which he made his dramatic statement of negation of identity: "I am *not!*" Erikson himself points out that it is not known whether "Martin roared in Latin or in German," and others have questioned whether he roared at all—that is, whether the episode actually took place.

Apart from specific problems of reconstruction, there is the larger question of the extent to which any individual, great or otherwise, can exemplify an entire historical epoch—or even (as in Erikson's treatment of Luther) its major collective psychological struggles. The question takes on special force during our unprecedentedly diverse and fickle century, no less so if raised in connection with the past.

Hence the emergence of another recent approach: that of *shared psychohistorical themes*, as observed in men and women exposed to particular kinds of individual and collective experience. Examples here are Kenneth Keniston's studies of alienated, and then activist, American students, and Robert Coles's work with children and adults in the midst of racial antagonism and social change.[6] I have been much concerned with the development of this method and ask indulgence for discussing it in relationship to my own work.

I have conducted interview studies of three specific groups of people whose historical exposures seemed to me to have bearing on important characteristics of our era: Chinese and Westerners who underwent Chinese thought reform (or "brainwashing"), Japanese university students during the early sixties, and Hiroshima survivors of the atomic bomb.[7] My focus has been upon themes, forms, and images that are in significant ways shared, rather than upon the life of a single person as such.

The shared-themes approach is based upon a psychoanalytically derived stress upon what goes on inside of people. But, as compared with Erikson's great-man paradigm, it moves still further from classical analytic tradition. That is, it moves outward from the individual in the direction of collective historical experience. It explicitly rejects the nineteenth-century scientific model of a man as a mechanism propelled by quantities of energy—energy internally generated by means of instinctual drives, partially held in check by certain defense mechanisms (notably repression), but eventually erupting in the form of various actions of the individual directed at his outer environment. This instinctual idiom (and, one may say, world view) gives way to a symbolic and formative one.

The shared-themes approach also requires considerable innovation in interview method. For more than fifteen years I have found myself struggling with modifications of the psychiatric and psychoanalytic interview, in order to approach and understand various kinds of people who have not sought therapeutic help but, on the contrary, have been sought out by me. And sought out not because of any form of psychological disturbance as such, but because of particular experiences they have undergone—experiences which may indeed be (and usually have been) disturbing, but which both they and I see as having wider significance than any individual incapacities, psychological or otherwise. I found myself developing a much freer interview style than that I was taught in my professional training. It remains probing, encouraging the widest range of associations, and includes detailed life histories and explorations of dreams. But it focuses upon the specific situation responsible for bringing the two of us (most of the interviews have been individual ones) together, and takes the form of something close to an open dialogue emerging from that situation.

The relationship we develop is neither that of doctor and patient nor of ordinary friends, though at moments it can seem to resemble either. It is more one of shared exploration—mostly of the world of the person sought out* but including a great deal of give and take, and more than a little discussion of my own attitudes and interests. It requires, in other words, a combination of humane spontaneity and professional discipline. Needless to say, one's way of combining the two is always idiosyncratic, and always less than ideal.

The method I am describing is partly empirical (in its stress upon specific data from interviews); partly phenomenological, or, as I prefer, formative (in its stress upon forms and images that are simultaneously individual and collective); and partly speculative (in its use of interview data, together with many other observations, to posit relationships between man and his history, and to suggest concepts that eliminate the artificial separation of the two). In this speculation the investigator has the advantage of beginning from concrete information that is a product of his own direct perceptions. Recognizing that subjective distortion can render the advantage a mixed one, so can it be said that exaggerated concerns with detached objectivity have too often caused us to undervalue what can be learned of history from our direct perceptions.

Within this perspective, all shared behavior is seen as simultaneously involved in a trinity of universality (that which is related to the psychobiological questions of all men in all historical epochs), specific cultural emphasis and style (as evolved by a particular people over centuries), and recent and contemporary historical influences (the part of the trinity most likely to be neglected in psychological work). My point is that any shared event is all of these. The weighting of the components may vary, but nothing is *purely* universal, or cultural-historical, or contemporary-historical; everything is all three. The overall approach, or at least my sense of it, is most

*We have no good term for the person in this situation. The traditional one, "research subject," seems increasingly unsatisfactory to me because it suggests someone merely "studied" or "investigated" in a more or less passive way. "Patient" is entirely inappropriate, and "client" is not much better. "Historical actor" and "pivotal person" come closer, but they have their own ambiguities. I believe there will be a number of new terms developed, and also new methods of investigation and interview (we already depend, to a much greater extent than my discussion indicates, upon group interviews and a host of other informal approaches) which capture, in *active ways,* lived history. I would go so far as to say that progress in psychohistory depends upon these innovations in method. Once developed in the study of contemporary matters, such innovations could also be applied to the study of the past, though mainly in relationship to the search for and interpretation of various kinds of records and documents.

fundamentally influenced by Freud and Erikson, but also by Susanne Langer and Ernst Cassirer, Otto Rank, Albert Camus, Lancelot Law Whyte, David Riesman, and R. G. Collingwood; and by Leslie Farber, Kenneth Keniston, Benjamin Schwartz, and Philip Rieff.

V

Let me describe my use of the shared-themes approach in six months of research in Hiroshima (in 1962) on the psychological effects of the atomic bomb, and in subsequent writings on that subject. The work centered mainly on intensive interviews with seventy-five atomic-bomb survivors, about half of them chosen at random from an official list, the other half specially selected because of their active involvement over the years in atomic-bomb problems. Most of the interviews were tape-recorded, and the book I wrote about the work took shape mainly from those interviews and made extensive use of direct quotations to illustrate the death-haunted responses I encountered. But in both the research and the later book I moved outward from interviews with individual survivors to groups they formed, leaders emerging from among them, and social currents in Hiroshima which they both created and were affected by. This in turn required close attention to the post-atomic-bomb history of the city, and to the relationship of that special history to the rest of Japan and to the world at large, as well as to the city's own earlier heritage. A significant part of that history consisted of creative struggles—of writers, painters, and film-makers from both within and without the city—to come to terms with Hiroshima. And these historical and creative struggles were deeply bound up with issues of memorialization and commemoration, with efforts to move beyond the bomb while remaining true to its dead.

Finally, through a detailed elaboration of the ethos of the survivor, I was in some degree able to unite the individual-psychological and historical currents I had observed. I compared survival of the atomic bomb to survival of other massive death immersions—of Nazi persecutions in our time, and of the plagues in the Middle Ages (as the latter reveal themselves through records), as well as to survival of natural disasters, and of the "ordinary" deaths of close friends and family members. I could then (in this and subsequent studies) raise questions about the general importance of the survivor ethos of our age, of the degree to which we have become historically prone to the survivor's retained death imprint, to his death guilt and his psychic numbing (or desensitization to death-dominated images), and to his struggle for significance (or what I call, after Langer, his *formulation*). These questions now intrude into virtually all of my work, and I do not think it is too much to say that they haunt the contemporary imagination.

Thus, in my more recent book, *Revolutionary Immortality*, I discuss Mao Tse-tung's relationship to the Chinese Cultural Revolution in terms of his many experiences of individual and revolutionary survival. I relate his creative use of the survivor state to his extraordinary accomplishments as a leader and consider the general relevance of death symbolism, in broadest historical perspective, to the present Chinese Cultural Revolution. By connecting certain psychological characteristics of Mao's personal and revolutionary style with the predominant themes of the Cultural Revolution, I attempt to combine the great-man and shared-themes approaches.

The central thesis of the book revolves around Mao's anticipation of his own impending death as well as his and his followers' fear of the "death of the revolution." What I see as the overwhelming threat Mao faces is not so much death itself as the suggestion that his "revolutionary works" will not endure. By revolutionary immortality, then, I mean a shared sense of participating in permanent revolutionary ferment, and of transcending individual death by "living on" indefinitely within this continuing revolution. I point out that some such vision has been present in all revolutions, and was directly expressed in Trotsky's principle of "permanent revolution"; but that it has taken on unprecedented intensity in present-day Chinese Communist experience. This quest for revolutionary immortality provides a general framework within which the political and economic struggles and antibureaucratic and antirevisionist assaults of the Cultural Revolution can be examined, without being reduced to anyone's particular psychological or psychopathological trait.

Also related to that quest is a pattern which reflects the excruciating Maoist struggles with technology. I call that pattern "psychism," by which I mean an exaggerated reliance upon psychic power as a means of controlling the external environment, an attempt to replace the requirements of technology with pure revolutionary will. Technology is desperately sought, but feelings are cultivated. In this pattern of psychism there is once more a coming together of Mao's personal-revolutionary style—including what Chinese Communist commentators themselves refer to as his "revolutionary romanticism"—and a number of larger currents surrounding the Cultural Revolution. The concept of psychism, like that of revolutionary immortality, is an attempt to say something about precisely that psychohistorical interface.

The book was not based upon the kind of detailed interview approach I described in relationship to my Hiroshima work. Rather, it is a brief, interpretive essay, which draws heavily upon documents and observations by others of the Cultural Revolution as well as upon the writings of Mao; and only upon a very limited number of interviews with participants and observers of the events described. Compared to the Hiroshima study, it is more tenuous and more vulnerable. But I wrote it because I was convinced that the themes and concepts I develop in it could shed light on a mysteriously explosive social upheaval, and because I thought it a useful experiment in the pursuit of psychohistory.

VI

Yet the post-Freudian paradigms, like the Freudian ones, do not make clear exactly what they "explain," and fall far short of providing coherent theories of historical causation. The Freudian paradigms, we recall, lean heavily upon instinctual energies and struggles, which inevitably reduce themselves to the Oedipal Event, whether in connection with a prehistorical generational conflict or with the psychopathology of a leading historical actor. Now if broadened, this principle of the Oedipal Event could be made to connect with more inclusive versions of generational impasse, in keeping with Ortega y Gasset's belief that "the concept of the generation is the most important one in the whole of history." But Ortega had in mind the "three different and vital times" (or twenty-, forty-, and sixty-year-olds) "lodged together in a single external and chronological fragment of time," which in turn provide an "internal lack of equilibrium," because of which "history moves, changes, wheels, and flows." [8] Implicit in Ortega's view, then, is an examination of the precise nature of these "three different and vital times," of precisely the historical dimension which Freudian models have tended to ignore.

Erikson's great-man paradigm looks for historical causation in the leader's singular capacity, and absolute need, so to speak, to carry history with him as he breaks out from, and transcends, his own demonic intrapsychic conflicts. Since these conflicts are rooted in the leader's historical period, and his solution affects a great collectivity of his contemporaries, as well as subsequent generations, the great-man approach is relatively more specific than the other paradigms in its causal explanations. But we still sense a theoretical gap between the individual and the collectivity which none of the paradigms has fully bridged.

The shared-themes approach is the most diffuse of the four paradigms, though in many ways the most attuned to historical complexity. Within it, effect can become virtually indistinguishable from cause. A group understood to be *created by* a particular historical event (the Hiroshima survivors) or by an evolving set of historical vicissitudes (dissident Japanese or American youth) is also seen simultaneously to *act upon* and affect history—by epitomizing, exacerbating, and suggesting something beyond the immediate conflicts and visions of large numbers of contemporaries. If this kind of explanation, strictly speaking, deals more with historical flow than cause, it at least leaves open many possibilities for more subtle theoretical explorations which relate cause and effect to evolving patterns and directions. Among these future possibilities are additional combinations of the shared-themes and great-man approach; and new ways of conceptualizing radical historical shifts—the breakdown and re-creation of the forms of human culture (biological, experiential, institutional, technological, aesthetic, and interpretive) —or what I call a New History.[9]

In both of the post-Freudian paradigms, the social theory necessary to bridge the gap between individual and collectivity remains fragmented, implicit, unclear, or nonexistent. One solution would be to graft onto either of the two paradigms such relatively established and comprehensive social theory as the neo-Marxist concepts of alienation and overspecialization. Useful as that might be, my own view is that much of the necessary theory will have to be constructed anew. When approaching intellectual traditions of all kinds, we may do better to draw upon them partially and critically—sometimes even fragmentally—as we construct new combinations of ideas from our continuing investigation of shared psychohistorical themes. Most of all, we should avoid that form of professional territoriality which insists that psychological, sociological, and historical realms remain categorically discrete, with each holding fast to an explanatory principle claimed to subsume, or exist independently of, all else.

VII

The concept of revolutionary immortality is part of a more general theory of symbolic immortality I have been attempting to develop,[10] which concerns man's need, in the face of inevitable biological death, to maintain an inner sense of continuity with what has gone on before, and what will go on after, his own individual existence. From this standpoint the *sense* of immortality is much more than mere denial of death (though it can certainly be bound up with denial). Rather, it is part of compelling, life-enhancing imagery binding each individual to significant groups and events removed from him in place and time. The sense of immortality may be expressed biologically, by living on through (or in) one's sons and daughters and their sons and daughters; theologically, in the idea of a life after death, or in other forms of spiritual conquest of death; creatively, or through "works" and influences perceived as persisting beyond biological death; through identification with nature and its infinite extension into time and space (the idea of "eternal nature"); or experientially, through a feeling-state—one I speak of as experiential transcendence—so intense that, at least temporarily, time and death are eliminated (the mode classically employed by mystics).

What I wish to suggest is that this sense of immortality serves as the individual's connection with man's general past and future, as the individual's inner perception of his involvement in what we call the historical process. Much of human history consists of the struggle to achieve, maintain, and reaffirm a shared or collective sense of immortality under constantly changing psychic and material conditions.

Generally speaking, imagery of immortality has shifted, over the course of history, from the magical, to the supernatural, to the natural and man-centered—from *literal* promise of eternal life to more *symbolic* expressions of human continuity. One must add, however, that the emerging discussion and practice of "cryonics," the freezing of bodies from the time of death in the hope of later restoring life, returns us to the most literal kind of quest for direct bodily immortality. In any case, the shifting and recombining of modes of immortality mark great turning points in human history. The Darwinian Revolution, for instance, epitomized the shift from the theological to the biological mode, and did so in relationship both to man's origins and to his destiny. A shift of this kind, of course, can be neither total nor unopposed, and we are still in the midst of its reverberations.

Hiroshima and the subsequent development of nuclear weapons can be viewed as another major shift, perhaps more in the undermining of existing modes of immortality than in any clear suggestion of new combinations. Indeed, one way of viewing our present world-wide crisis, in terms other than political, is as a form of radical psychohistorical dislocation associated with the breakdown of viable modes of symbolic immortality. What has broken down is the sense of connection men have long felt with the vital and nourishing symbols of their cultural traditions, the sense of connection with their own history. Our sense of historical continuity (or of symbolic immortality) is now being profoundly threatened: by simple historical velocity, which subverts the imagery—notably the theological imagery—in which it has been traditionally maintained; and by nuclear and other ultimate weapons which, by their very existence, call into question all modes of immortality. When we consider (more often unconsciously or preconsciously than with clear awareness) the possibility of nuclear or bacteriological warfare, we can hardly be certain of living on in our children or grandchildren, in our works or influence upon others, in some form of theological conquest of death, or even in nature, which we now know to be itself vulnerable to our weapons. The striking contemporary reliance upon the fifth mode of symbolic immortality mentioned earlier, that of experiential transcendence—whether through drugs or other forms of "turned-on" psychic states—may well be a reflection of precisely this decline in our belief in the other four modes. We hunger for both connection and transcendence, and we have need to experiment with the historical and antihistorical boundaries of both.

In America we feel this kind of dislocation profoundly, so much so that we may well be in the vanguard of two specific responses to it. The first, which can have highly malignant consequences, entails an embrace—even deification—of technology as a new mode of immortality through which we seek to perpetuate ourselves. This embrace of technology can be associated with great adventure and with other forms of imaginative transcendence, as in the case of the space program. But it takes on grotesque contours when the technology involved is that of weaponry. We then witness the development, not only in America but throughout the world, of what I call the religion of nuclearism, an attitude of worship toward weapons of destruction, and a dependence upon them to solve otherwise baffling human problems—ultimately the investment in them of the sense of immortality that has been lost.

A second response to historical dislocation is the emergence of what I call Protean man[11]—by which I mean a relatively new life style, characterized by interminable exploration and flux, by a self-process capable of relatively easy shifts in belief and identification—a life style that is postmodern and in some ways post-Freudian. Protean man has been created not only by the dislocations I have mentioned but by the revolution in mass media as well. I have in mind the flooding of imagery produced by the extraordinary flow of postmodern cultural influences over mass-communications networks, so that each individual can be touched, and at times significantly affected, by virtually everything, and presented with endless partial alternatives in every sphere of life, whether superficial messages, undigested cultural elements, or moving evocations.

These two concepts—symbolic immortality and Protean man—provide a way of returning to where we began, to psychologists and historians in the midst of a difficult struggle to create a new psychohistory.

To be sure, the theory of symbolic immortality can hardly resolve the many-sided dilemmas of historical causation. But it does seem to me a potentially useful way of looking at man in history, most specifically as a framework for the study of revolutions and a variety of related problems of historical continuity and discontinuity. The general point of view seems also to be given force by the death-dominated times in which it emerges; history does much to create the ways in which we, at any particular moment, decide to study it.

Concerning the Protean style, I bring it up not only as a way of epitomizing contemporary experience but for another reason as well. Since I believe this style in some degree inhabits us all, I assume further that it affects our relationship to ideas—the ways in which we respond to them, believe them, and attach them to our sense of self. Protean man is continuously open to new ideas and can move among them rather freely. His difficulty lies in giving lasting allegiance to any particular idea or idea system. I do not believe that scholars are immune from precisely this pattern. Hence the intellectual restlessness within most disciplines—the dissatisfaction with established concepts, together with the failure of newer concepts of equal authority to appear.

Those working in the area of psychohistory, where established concepts hardly exist, are especially likely to encounter such restlessness in both their readers and themselves. It will not be easy to discover, and then collectively maintain, the kind of authoritative conceptual principles we have come to expect and depend upon within an intellectual tradition. Moreover, there is a sense in which psychohistory adds to the burdens of a historical discipline already immersed in difficult struggles to replace no longer acceptable nineteenth-century versions of history as clear narrative or epic or inevitable destiny, struggles to come to grips with the convoluted, opaque, and deadly actualities of the twentieth century. Psychohistory, at least in the version I have been describing, tends to complexify rather than simplify, which I think is as it should be. And Protean tendencies among scholars can render them receptive to the new principles of psychohistory and yet cautious in granting them intellectual authority, which is also as it should be.

Within these uncertainties lie extraordinary possibilities. These too are Protean, and I think one can observe in contemporary man an increasing capacity for coming to what would have previously been viewed as impossible intellectual combinations and innovations. Compared with his predecessors he is not only less bound by tradition but much more fluid in his potential integration of very diverse conceptual elements. And the new psychohistory—having stated my reservations and qualifications, I think I can begin to call it that—emerges as itself a radical investigative response to a radically dislocated historical epoch.

Despite what I speak of as Protean possibilities, and what some perceive as an exotic aura surrounding the idea of psychohistory, all that I have said here and experienced in my investigations militates strongly against facile intellectual efforts or the creation of "instant psychohistorians." To the contrary, the approach seems to require not only a central commitment to one of the disciplines (or a related one) and a considerable knowledge of the other, but something more: a considerable ethical concern with the problems being investigated. Erik Erikson has hardly been neutral in his feelings about Luther's achievements or about what Gandhi's legacy may still mean for the world. Nor has Keniston been neutral about student radicals, Coles about minority-group aspirations, nor I about Hiroshima and its legacy. Rather, all of us have been struggling toward ways of acknowledging our involvements and exploring their relationship to our findings, toward making conceptual use of these very involvements.[12]

The developments I have discussed have for the most part come from the psychological direction. This is not because historians have been totally aloof from psychohistory: they have in fact produced a number of important studies within it. But at this phase, beginning with Erikson, the focus seems to be upon concepts emerging from the psychoanalytic heritage, even if in great tension with that heritage. No one knows what will happen in the future, but one can be sure that things will change. Psychohistory could be an avenue toward the revitalization of psychoanalysis itself, through which the latter might rediscover its own history and thereby transform itself. Or psychohistory could develop more autonomously and, despite (partly because of) its profound debt to psychoanalysis, separate itself decisively from the ahistorical bias of that tradition.

In the end, psychohistory may turn out to be nothing more than a minor intellectual curiosity. Or, as I confess to be my belief, it could develop into a significant body of thought whose evolving ideas will be as compelling as they are difficult to establish. However things turn out, psychohistory will benefit from the disciplined free spirits who, whatever their origin, bring their critical imaginations to bear upon it.

ON THE NATURE OF PSYCHOHISTORICAL EVIDENCE: IN SEARCH OF GANDHI

ERIK H. ERIKSON

I

About a decade ago, when I first participated in a *Daedalus* discussion, I represented one wing of the clinical arts and sciences in a symposium on Evidence and Inference.[1] I offered some observations of a "markedly personal nature," and this not only from predilection but because the only methodological certainty that I could claim for my specialty, the psychotherapeutic encounter, was "disciplined subjectivity." Of all the other fields represented in that symposium, I felt closest (so I cautiously suggested) to the historian: for he, like the clinician, must serve the curious process by which selected portions of the past impose themselves on our renewed awareness and claim continued actuality in our contemporary commitments. We clinicians, of course, work under a Hippocratic contract with our clients; and the way they submit their past to our interpretation is a special form of historicizing, dominated by their sense of fragmentation and isolation and by our method of restoring to them, through the encounter with us, a semblance of wholeness, immediacy, and mutuality. But as we, in our jargon, "take a history" with the promise of correcting it, we enter another's life, we "make history." Thus, both clinician and patient (and in psychoanalysis, at any rate, every clinician undergoes voluntary patienthood for didactic purposes) acquire more than an inkling of what Collingwood claims history is

—namely, "the life of mind" which "both lives in historical process and knows itself as so living."

Since that symposium, the former caution in the approach to each other of clinician and historian has given way to quite active efforts to find common ground. These have been confined for the most part to the joint study of the traditional affinity of case history and life history. But here the clinician is inexorably drawn into superpersonal history "itself," since he too must learn to conceive of, say, a "great" man's crises and achievements as communal events characteristic of a given historical period. On the other hand, some historians probably begin to suspect that they too are practitioners of a restorative art which transforms the fragmentation of the past and the peculiarities of those who make history into such wholeness of meaning as mankind seeks. This, in fact, may become only too clear in our time when the historian finds himself involved in ongoing history by an accelerated interplay of communication between the interpreters and the makers of history: Here, a new kind of Hippocratic Oath may become necessary. And as for him who would cure mankind from history itself—he certainly takes on the therapeutic job of jobs.

It is not my purpose, however, to blur the division between therapist and historian. Rather, I would like to try to delineate an in-between field which some of us have come to call the psychohistorical approach. Such a compound name usually designates an area in which nobody as yet is methodologically quite at home, but which someday will be settled and incorporated without a trace of border disputes and double names. The necessity to delineate it, however, becomes urgent when forward workers rush in with claims which endanger systematic exploration. Thus, today, psychoanalytic theory is sometimes applied to historical events with little clarification of the criteria for such a transfer. Such bravado can lead to brilliant insights, but also to renewed doubt in the specific fittedness and general applicability of psychological interpretation. I will, therefore, attempt to discuss here, in a manner both "markedly personal" and didactic, what parallels I have found between my clinical experience and the study of a circumscribed historical event.

Since the symposium on Evidence and Inference, my study *Young Man Luther* has also appeared[2]; and nothing could have better symbolized the methodological embarrassment on the part even of friendly critics than the stereotyped way in which editors, both in this country and in England, captioned the reviews of my book with the phrase "Luther on the Couch." Now, clinicians are in fact rather sparing in the use of the couch except in a systematic psychoanalysis; yet, "on the couch" has assumed some such popular connotation as "on the carpet." And it so happens that Luther all his life was a flamboyant free associator and in his youth certainly often talked as if he *were* "on the couch." His urbane superior von Staupitz, could we inform him of the new uses of this adaptable furniture, would gladly testify to that. He recognized in the young monk's raving insistence that his repentance had not yet convinced God a "confession compulsion" altogether out of proportion to what the father confessor was ready to receive or to absolve; wherefore he told young Luther that *he* was resisting *God,* not God him. And with the recognition of an unfunctional resistance operative within the very act of "free" self-revelation, the confessor of old was on good clinical grounds.

The recognition of an inner resistance to some memories is, in fact, the technical basis for the whole theory of defense in psychoanalysis. As such, it is one of the five conceptions which Freud in one little-known dogmatic sentence calls "the principal constituents of . . . psychoanalysis."[3] To begin on didactic home ground, I will briefly discuss these fundamental assumptions, which have remained fundamental to all modifications of psychoanalysis and to its application in other fields. A "resisting" patient, then, may find something in himself obstructing him in his very determination to communicate what "comes to his mind": Too much may come too fast, or too little too tortuously, if at all. For such *resistance,* Freud blamed the mechanism of *repression* and the fact of an *unconscious,* for what once has been repressed can reassert its right to awareness and resolution only in indirect ways: in the symbolic disguise of dreams and fantasies, or in symptoms of commission (meaning acts alien to the actor himself), or in symptoms of omission (inhibitions, avoidances).

On the basis of his Victorian data, Freud found "behind" repression and resistance primarily what he called the *aetiological significance of sexual life*—that is, the pathogenic power of repressed sexual impulses. But, of course, he included a wide assortment of impulses and affects in the definition of "sexual"; and he considered systematic attention to the *importance of infantile experiences* an intrinsic part of his method and his theory. The last two conceptions led to what has been called the Freudian revolution, although Freud has no more reason than have the fathers of other kinds of revolutions to acknowledge the "liberation" named after him.

But there is one more term, mentioned by Freud in the same study and called "neither more nor less than the mainspring of the joint work of psychoanalysis": *transference*—and for a good historical example of father transference, we again need look no further than Luther's relation to Herr von Staupitz and the Pope. How he made this, too, historical in a grand manner is, for the moment, another matter. Transference is a universal tendency active wherever human beings enter a relationship to others in such a way that the other *also* "stands for" persons as perceived in the pre-adult past. He thus serves the reenactment of infantile and juvenile wishes and fears, hopes and apprehensions; and this always with a bewildering *ambivalence*—that is, a ratio of loving and hateful tendencies which under certain conditions change radically. This plays a singularly important role in the clinical encounter and not only in the dependent patient's behavior toward the clinician. It is also part of what the clinician must observe in himself: He too can transfer on different patients a variety of unconscious strivings which come from *his* infantile past. This we call *countertransference.*

All these seeming difficulties, however, are the very tools of the psychoanalyst. To a determined believer in free will, they may all sound like weaknesses, if not dishonesties, while together they are really an intrinsic "property" of the clinical situation. Relived and resolved in each case, they are a necessary part of the evidence; and their elucidation is the only way to a cure. But are they also applicable to some aspects of historical research? Here the difficulties of a hyphenated approach become only too obvious, for in the absence of historical training I can only describe the way in which my clinical tools either hindered or proved handy in an attempt to reconstruct a historical event. Yet, it would seem that even the best-trained historical mind could not "live in the historical process" without underscoring and erasing, professing and denying, even loving and hating, and without trying to know himself as so living and so knowing. I may hope, then, that the predicaments to be described will remind the reader of his own experiences or of those recorded in the other contributions to this symposium. As for historical data proper, I can only try to introduce a psychological dimension into what would seem to be well-established rules of evidence.

II

Three times in the early sixties I visited the city of Ahmedabad in the Indian state of Gujarat. The first time I went on the invitation of some enlightened citizens in order to give a seminar on the human life cycle and to compare our modern conception of the stages of life with those of the Hindu tradition. My wife and I occupied a small house on the estate of an industrialist—the city being one of the oldest textile centers of the world. Nearby was the mill owner's marble mansion, always open for rest and work to men of the mind; in its very shadow was the simple house of his sister, a saintly woman called the Mother of Labor, in whose living room hung a portrait of Tolstoy inscribed for Gandhi. It came back to me only gradually (for I had known it when I was young) that this was the city in which Gandhi had lived for more than a decade and a half and that it was this mill owner and his sister (both now in their seventies) to whom Gandhi pays high and repeated tribute in his autobiography. They had been Gandhi's opponent and ally, respectively, in the dramatic event by which labor unionism was founded in India: the Ahmedabad textile strike in 1918.

At the age of forty-five Gandhi had returned to India "for good" in 1914, after having spent his student years in England and the years of his early manhood in South Africa. He had founded a settlement near Ahmedabad, the principal city of the province in which he had been born, and had found a liberal benefactor in the man whom we shall simply refer to as "the mill owner" (as, in general, I will endeavor not to name in this paper individuals merely used for "demonstration"). Once settled, Gandhi had immediately begun to travel extensively to become familiar with the life of the masses and to find circumscribed grievances suited to his approach: the nonviolent technique which he had developed in South Africa and had called "Satyagraha"—that is, a method of recognizing and mobilizing the forces of truth and peace in the oppressor as well as in the oppressed. In 1917 he had found an opportunity to move in on the system of indigo growing in faraway Bihar in defense of the rights of the peasants there. And now, in 1918, he accepted at the mill owner's request the mediatorship in a wage dispute in the principal industry at home, in Ahmedabad. He had studied the situation carefully and had decided to accept the leadership of ten thousand workers, a decision which brought him into public, as well as personal, conflict with the mill owner and aligned him on the side of the mill owner's sister, who had been deeply involved in "social work" in the widest sense. In the weeks of this strike Gandhi developed, in deed and in words, his full technique, including even a brief fast. The whole matter ended in a compromise which nevertheless secured to the workers, in the long run, what they had asked for.

This story, then, seemed to harbor fascinating private, as well as public, issues. And it seemed significant that Gandhi would have chosen in the cataclysmic years 1917 and 1918 opportunities to demonstrate his kind of revolution in grievances involving first peasants and then workers and that he would do so on a local and even personal scale—visualize, in contrast, the global activities of other charismatic leaders in the concluding years of World War I. At the time, in fact, the mill strike was hardly noted: "We cannot see what Mr. M. K. Gandhi can win, but we can well see that he might lose everything," wrote the leading newspaper in the area. And in his autobiography, written a decade later, the Mahatma makes relatively light of the whole event—a diffidence which he transmitted to his biographers. Yet, the very next year he would lead the first nationwide civil disobedience and become forever India's Mahatma.

Enter the psychohistorian: Having learned to esteem the mill owner and his family and having become convinced of the historical and biographic significance of the strike as well as of the "resistance" against it, I determined to study both.

First, then, a word on the record of the event as written by Gandhi himself about a decade after the strike. In a previous publication,[4] I have pointed to the general difficulties encountered in using Gandhi's autobiography for either historical or psychoanalytic purposes—not to speak of a combination of both. Maybe more so in translation than in Gandhi's native Gujarati in which it was written, the autobiography often impresses the reader as monotonous and moralistic to the point of priggishness, or, at any rate, as devoid of any indication of Gandhi's presence, described by witnesses as energetic and energizing, challenging and teasing. And, indeed, the autobiography originally was not a book at all. It was written over a number of years in the form of "columns" for a biweekly primarily addressed to youth: Each column, like our traditional homilies, had to have a moral. Furthermore, these columns were written when the Mahatmaship of India, gained in the years after the strike, seemed already forfeited both by political fortune and by approaching old age: Gandhi had been jailed and set free only to face again a politically divided India. Temporarily, as we now know, but at the time often with depressing finality, he had turned from rebel to reformer. A Hindu reformer approaching sixty must face fully what the autobiography's foreword clearly states: "What I want to achieve . . . is self-realization, to see God face to face, to attain Moksha." And Moksha in the Hindu life cycle means final renunciation and withdrawal. The autobiography is a testament, then, even though we now know that Gandhi's leadership had just begun.

One is almost embarrassed to point out what seems so obvious—namely, that in perusing a man's memoirs for the purpose of reconstructing past moments and reinterpreting pervasive motivational trends, one must first ask oneself at what age and under what general circumstances the memoirs were written, what their intended purpose was, and what form they assumed. Surely all this would have to be known before one can proceed to judge the less conscious motivations, which may have led the autobiographer to emphasize selectively some experiences and omit other equally decisive ones; to profess and reveal flamboyantly some deed or misdeed and to disguise or deny equally obvious commitments; to argue and to try to prove what seems to purify or confirm his historical role and to correct what might spoil the kind of immortality he has chosen for himself. Confessionlike remembrances often seem to be the most naïvely revealing and yet are also the most complex form of autobiography, for they attempt to prove the author's purity by the very advertisement of his impurities and, therefore, confound his honesty both as a sinner and as a braggart.

As pointed out, past events make their often abrupt and surprising appearance in the psychoanalytic hour only as part of an observational situation which includes systematic attention to the reasons why they may come to mind just then: Factuality aside, what is their actuality in the developing relation of professional observer and self-observing client? It is, therefore, hard to understand how observers trained in clinical observation can accept an event reported in an autobiography—such as, say, Gandhi's account of his father's death—both as a factual event and as a naïve confession without asking why the item came to mind in *its* autonomous setting, the autobiography; and why, indeed, a particular form of autobiography was being practiced or newly created at that moment in history. Gandhi himself states that he knew an autobiography to be a rather un-Indian phenomenon, which makes his own an all the more elemental creation comparable to the confessions of Saint Augustine and Abelard or to Rousseau's and Kierkegaard's autobiographic works.

To put this diagrammatically and didactically, a psychohistorical reviewer would have to fathom—in one intuitive configuration of thought if he can and with the help of a diagram if he must—the *complementarity* of at least four conditions under which a record emerges.

A. ***Functions of the Record***

	I MOMENT	II SEQUENCE
1. INDIVIDUAL	in the recorder's stage of life and general condition	in the recorder's life history
2. COMMUNITY	in the state of the recorder's community	in the history of the recorder's community

Under I-1, then, we would focus as if with a magnifying glass on one segment of the recorder's life as a period with a circumscribed quality. Gandhi's autobiography served the acute function of demonstrating an aging reformer's capacity to apply what he called truth to the balance sheet of his own failures and successes, in order to gain the wisdom of renunciation for himself and to promote a new level of political and spiritual awareness in his nation. But we would also have to consider the special inner conflicts and overt mood swings which aggravated these, his often withdrawn and "silent" years. Under I-2, we would consider all the acute circumstances in Indian history which would make Gandhi feel that he would find an echo for his message in those segments of India's awakening youth who could read—or be read to. Under II-1, we would remember that confession seems to have been a passion for him throughout life and that his marked concern over Moksha began in a precocious conscience development in childhood (which, in fact, he shared with other *homines religiosi*). In II-2, however, we would have to account for the fact that Gandhi's record, in both content and style, went far beyond the traditional forms of self-revelation in India and bridged such confessionalism as St. Augustine's or Tolstoy's awareness as Christians, as well as Rousseau's passionate and Freud's systematized insight into the power of infantile and juvenile experience. From the psychohistorical viewpoint, then, the question is not, or not only, whether a man like Gandhi inadvertently proves some of Freud's points (such as the power of the emotions subsumed under the term Oedipus complex), but why such items which we now recognize as universal were reenacted in different media of representation (*including* Freud's dream analyses) by particular types of men in given periods of history—and why, indeed, their time was ready for them and their medium: for only such complementarity makes a confession momentous and its historical analysis meaningful.

Our diagrammatic boxes, then, suggest the *relativity* governing any historical item—that is, the "concomitant variability" of passing moment and long-range trend, of individual life cycle and communal development.

III

Let me now turn to the autobiography's rendition of the strike of 1918—the Event, as I will call it from here on. There is besides Gandhi's retrospective reflections only one full account of it, a pamphlet of less than a hundred pages by the man who was then Gandhi's secretary.[5] Gandhi's own approach to the matter is even more casual and episodic and is, in fact, broken up by the insertion of a seemingly quite unrelated story.[6] This is the sequence: In a chapter (or installment) called "In Touch with Labor," Gandhi reports on the "delicate situation" in Ahmedabad where a sister "had to battle against her own brother." His friendly relations with both "made fighting with them the more difficult." But he considered the case of the mill hands strong, and he therefore "had to advise the laborers to go on strike." There follows a summary, less than one page long, of nearly twenty days of a strike during which he set in motion all the principles and techniques of his militant nonviolent Satyagraha—on a local scale, to be sure, but with lasting consequences for Ahmedabad, India, and beyond. Then the story of the strike is interrupted by a chapter called "A Peep into the Ashram." Here the reader is entertained with a description of the multitude of snakes which infested the land by the river to which Gandhi, at the time of the strike, had just moved his settlement. Gandhi recounts how he and his Ashramites in South Africa, as well as in India, had always avoided killing snakes and that in twenty-five years of such practice "no loss of life [had been] occasioned by snake bite."* Only then, in a further chapter, does Gandhi conclude the strike story by reporting its climax—namely, his first fast in a public issue, in spite of which (or, as we shall see, because of which) the whole strike ended with what looked like a kind of hasty compromise. What was at stake then, and what was still at stake at the writing of the autobiography, was the purity of the nonviolent method: The mill owner could (and did) consider Gandhi's fast an unfairly coercive way of making the employers give in, whereas Gandhi did (and always would) consider a fast justified only as a means of persuading weakening supporters to hold out.

The technical question that arises here is whether the chapter which interrupts the account of the strike could be shown to signify an inner resistance against the whole story, comparable to what we observe and utilize in clinical work. Again and again, one finds, for example, that a child undergoing psychotherapy will suffer what I have called "play disruption"—that is, he will interrupt his play in some anxious manner, sometimes without being able to resume it. And often the very manner of disruption or the way in which play is resumed will suggest to the experienced observer what dangerous thought had occurred to the child and had ruined his playfulness. Or an adult in psychoanalysis will embark on a seemingly easy progression of free associations only to find suddenly that he has forgotten what he was about to say next or to interrupt his own trend of thought with what appears to be a senseless image or sentence "from nowhere." A little scrutiny can soon reveal that what had thus been lost or had intruded was, in fact, an important key to the underlying meaning of the whole sequence of thoughts—a key which more often than not reveals a repressed or suppressed sense of hate against a beloved person. I will later report on Gandhi's sudden awareness of such a disruption in another part of the autobiography.

What, then, could the nonkilling of snakes have to do with the

*An old Indian friend recounted to me an event taken almost for granted in those early days—namely, how young Vinoba Bhave (the man who in all these years has come and remained closest to Gandhi in spirit, style, and stature) sat by the ashram grounds and a big and poisonous snake crawled under his shawl. He kept lovingly still, and another Ashramite quietly folded up the garment and took it to the riverbank.

Ahmedabad strike and with Gandhi's relation to the mill owner? Mere thematic play would suggest Gandhiites bent on nonviolence in the first column meet mill owners; in the second, poisonous snakes; and in the third, mill owners again. Do snakes, then, "stand for" mill owners? This could suggest to a clinician a breakthrough of Gandhi's anger against the mill owners—an anger which he had expressly forbidden himself, as well as the striking and starving workmen. If one can win over poisonous snakes by love and nonviolence, the hidden thought might be, then maybe one can reach the hearts of industrialists too. Or the suggestion might be more damaging—namely, that it would be more profitable to be kind to poisonous snakes than to industrialists—and here we remember that another Man of Peace, also using an analogy from the bestiary, once mused that big lazy camels might squeeze through where a rich man could not or would not. Was Gandhi's suppressed rage apt to be "displaced" in such a flagrant way? This would have to be seen.

There is, however, an explanation closer to historical fact and to the propagandistic purpose of the autobiography. He and the mill owner had been involved in a public scandal. Briefly, the mill owner had noted hordes of ferocious-looking dogs around his factory on the outskirts of the city and had ascertained that the municipal police, knowing how Hindus feel about killing animals, were in the habit of releasing captured stray dogs outside the city limits. Since hydrophobia had reached major proportions in the area, the mill owner had requested the police to kill these dogs, and some obliging officer, for reasons of his own, had arranged for the carcasses to be carted away through the crowded city streets. Such is the stuff that riots are made of in India. But Gandhi did not hesitate to speak up for the mill owner, saying he himself would kill a deranged man if he found him massacring other people. He wrote in *Young India:*

> The lower animals are our brethren. I include among them the lion and the tiger. We do not know how to live with these carnivorous beasts and poisonous reptiles because of our ignorance. When man learns better, he will learn to befriend even these. Today he does not even know how to befriend a man of a different religion or from a different country.[7]

In this prophetic statement we see the reptiles "associated" with carnivorous beasts; and from here it is only one step to the interpretation that Gandhi, before telling the story of how he had made concessions to the mill owner at the end of the strike, had to tell himself and his readers that his basic principles had not suffered on that other and better-known occasion when he took the mill owner's side.

Was Gandhi "conscious" of such pleading with the reader? Probably, for the whole trend of thought fits well into the professed aim of his self-revelations: to sketch his "experiments with truth." But factual explanation (and here is the psychohistorical point) should not do away with the underlying and pervasive emotional actuality. For my story, the assumption of an ambivalence toward the mill owner is inescapable. In historical fact it is an example of a mutual and manly acceptance of the Hindu dharma—that is, of the assignment to each man of a place within the world order which he must fulfill in order to have a higher chance in another life. If, as Gandhi would put it, "fasting is my business," then making money was that of the mill owner; and Gandhi could not have fulfilled his role of saintly politician (or, as he put it, "a politician who tried to be a saint") had he not had the financial support of wealthy men. This, the Marxist might say, corrupted him, while the Hindu point of view would merely call for a clean division of roles within a common search for a higher truth. The Freudian point of view, however, would suggest that such a situation might cause an unconscious "transference" of unresolved conflicts of childhood to the present.

Young Gandhi had, in varying ways, forsaken his caste and his father when he left to become an English barrister; and he had forsaken his older brother who had wanted him to join him in legal work when he had become a reformer. Such deviations from one's ancestral dharma are a grave problem in the lives of many creative Indians. At any rate, when he returned and settled down in Ahmedabad—the city in which both his native language and the mercantile spirit of his ancestors had reached a high level of cultivation—and when he again deviated grievously by taking a family of Untouchables into his ashram, the mill owner alone had continued to support him. The mill owner, thus, had become a true brother; and anyone familiar with Gandhi's life will know how desperate at times was the "Great Soul's" never requited and never fully admitted search for somebody who would sanction, guide, and, yes, mother *him*. This is a complex matter, and it will be enough to indicate here that without the assumption of such a transference of the prime actor in my story to the principal witnesses, a brother and sister, I could not have made sense of the meaning of the Event in Gandhi's life—and of his wish to "play it down."

IV

Nobody likes to be found out, not even one who has made ruthless confession a part of his profession. Any autobiographer, therefore, at least between the lines, spars with his reader and potential judge. Does the autobiographic recorder then develop a kind of transference on the potential reviewer of his record? Gandhi did, as we shall see.

But before reporting this, let me ask another question: Does not the professional reader and reviewer, who makes it his business to reveal what others do or may *not* know about themselves, also feel some uncomfortable tension in relation to them? Yes, I think that he does and that he should know that he does. There are, of course, some who would claim that, after all, they are voyeurs merely in *majorem gloriam* of history or humanity and are not otherwise "involved" with their subjects. But such denial often results only in an interpretive brashness or a superior attitude toward the self-recorder who seems to reveal himself so inadvertently or to hide his "real" motivation so clumsily. A patient offers his motivation for full inspection only under the protection of a contract and a method; and the method is not complete unless the "doctor" knows how to gauge his own hidden feelings. If it can be assumed that the reviewer of self-revelations or of self-revealing acts and statements offered in nonclinical contexts also develops some form of irrational countertransference, that too must be turned to methodological advantage not only for the sake of his work, but also for that of his friends and his family.

I hope to have aroused just enough discomfort in the professional reader to make him share the sting I felt when in the course of my study I came once again across the following passage midway through Gandhi's autobiography: "If some busybody were to cross-examine me on the chapters which I have now written, he could probably shed more light on them, and if it were a hostile critic's cross-examination, he might even flatter himself for having shown up the hollowness of many of my pretensions."[8] Here, then, we seem to have a real analogue to what I described above as "play disruption"; and, indeed, Gandhi continues with a momentary negative reaction to his whole undertaking: "I therefore wonder for a moment whether it might not be proper to stop writing these chapters altogether." After which he recovers, luckily, with a typically Gandhian form of self-sanction: "But so long as there is no prohibition from the voice within, I must continue the writing." There seems to be an awareness, however, of having given in to something akin to free association, though dictated by a higher power: "I write just as the spirit moves me at the time of writing. I do not claim to know definitely that all conscious thought and action on my part is directed by the spirit." Again, he recovers, however, and sanctions his own doings: "But on an examination of the greatest steps that I have taken in my life, as also of those that may be regarded as the least, I think it will not be improper to say all of them were directed by the spirit." Now he can dismiss his "hostile" reader: "I am not writing the autobiography to please critics. Writing it itself is one of the experiments with truth." And he can distribute the blame for writing at all: "Indeed, I started writing [the autobiography] in compliance with their [his co-workers'] wishes. If, therefore, I am wrong in writing the autobiography, they must share the blame." This concluding remark is, I think, typical of the Gandhian half-humor so easily lost in translation; and humor means recovery.

To say more about this sudden disruption, I would have to know (according to my own specifications) exactly in what period of his life Gandhi wrote this particular installment of the autobiography. Was there a real snooper and critic in his life at the time? Or was the imaginary one an externalization of a second inner voice, one temporarily at odds with the one that inspired his every effort? Much speaks for the latter assumption, for the disruption follows a chapter called "A Sacred Recollection and Penance" in which Gandhi describes an especially cruel outbreak against his wife under circumstances (there were many in his life) both sublime and ridiculous. Once, in South Africa, while cleaning her house, which had become a hostel, she had refused to empty a Christian Untouchable's chamber pot (*that* combination was too *much*), and Gandhi had literally shown her the gate. After such extreme and extremely petty moments something could cry out in him: What if all his professions of universal love, all his sacrifices of those closest to him by family ties for the sake of those furthest away (the masses, the poor, the Untouchables), were a "pretense"? So here, the reader and reviewer become an externalization of the writer's self-doubt, and I felt so directly appealed to that I began to think of how I might have explained these matters to him in the light of our clinical knowledge. Not without the sudden awareness of being older than he had been when he wrote that passage, I addressed him in an ensuing chapter, explaining that, as a student of another lover of truth, a contemporary of his on the other side of the world, I had a more charitable term than "pretense" for the psychological aspect of his dilemma: namely, "ambivalence." I confronted him with another instance of petty and righteous cruelty and attempted to formulate a pervasive ambivalence: that his marriage at the age of thirteen to a girl of the same age and fatherhood in his teens had prevented him from making a conscious decision at an informed age for or against married life; that this "fate" had been foisted on him in the traditional manner by his father, whom he never forgave. Thus, a lifelong ambivalence toward his wife and children, not to speak of sexuality in general, had perpetuated a predicament in his life as well as in that of many of his followers: Are Satyagraha and chastity inseparable? That such conflicts in the lives of saintly men are more than a matter of mental hygiene I need not emphasize here. Gandhi, I think, would have listened to me, but probably would have asked me teasingly why I had taken his outburst so personally. And, indeed, my impulsive need to answer him "in person" before I could go on with my book revealed again that all manner of countertransference can accompany our attempts to analyze others, great or ordinary.

And what, we must ask (and he might have asked), legitimizes such undertaking in clinical work? It is, of course, the mandate to help—*paired with self-analysis*. And even as we demand that he who makes a profession of "psychoanalyzing" others must have learned a certain capacity for self-analysis, so must we presuppose that the psychohistorian will have developed or acquired a certain self-analytical capacity which would give to his dealings with others, great or small, both the charity of identification and a reasonably good conscience. Ours too are "experiments with truth."

I can offer, for such an ambitious aim, only another schema which lists the minimum requirements for what a reviewer of a record and of an event should be reasonably clear about:

B. ***Functions of the Review***

	I MOMENT	II SEQUENCE
1. INDIVIDUAL	in the stage and the conditions of the reviewer's life	in the reviewer's life history
2. COMMUNITY	in the state of the reviewer's communities	in the history of the reviewer's communities

Under communities I here subsume a whole series of collective processes from which the reviewer derives identity and sanction and within which his act of reviewing has a function: there, above all, he must know himself as living in the historical process. Each community, of course, may call for a separate chart: the reviewer's nation or race, his caste or class, his religion or ideological party—and, of course, his professional field.

V

Did Freud live up to our methodological standards? His introduction to what we now know to have been the first psychohistorical essay—namely, the book on Wilson allegedly coauthored by him and William Bullitt [9]—does give an admirable approximation of what I have in mind. But not in the bulk of the book: for here he unwisely relied on Bullitt to review the record for him and to provide him with the data necessary for an application of the laws found in case histories to the life history of a public figure. In my review of this book,[10] I felt it necessary to explain the strange collaboration in this way: As a young man and before he became a doctor, so Freud himself tells us, he had wanted to be a statesman. His deep identification with Moses can be clearly read in his work. Did Bullitt awaken in the old and ailing man (who, in fact, was dying in exile when he signed the final manuscript) the fading hope that his life work, psychoanalysis, might yet be destined to become applicable to statesmanship? The task at hand, however, was obviously overshadowed by Freud's passionate feelings in regard to the joint subject, President Wilson. About this, Freud is explicit in his introduction, the only part of the book clearly written by him, all other handwritten contributions having been "lost" by Bullitt in one way or another. Freud declares that the figure of the American President, "as it rose above the horizons of Europeans, was from the beginning unsympathetic" to him and that this feeling increased "the more severely we suffered from the consequences of his intrusion into our destiny." Wilson's Fourteen Points had promised that a semblance of Christian charity, combined with political shrewdness, might yet survive the first mechanized slaughter in history. Could it be that the destruction or the dehumanization of mankind by the unrestricted use of superweaponry might be checked by the creation of a world democracy? What followed Versailles played into a pervasive trend in Freud's whole being: a Moses-like indignation at all false Christian (or other) prophecy. A proud man brought up in Judaism, I concluded, even if surrounded by the folklore and display of Catholicism, persists in the historical conviction that the Messiah has not yet appeared and persists with more grimness the more he has been inclined temporarily to give credence to the Christian hope for salvation. Such overall prejudice, however, even where clearly expressed, is methodologically meaningful only insofar as the slant thus given to the whole work is thereby clarified *and* insofar as it is vigorously counteracted by an adherence to the other criteria for evidence and inference—and for literary form. On the other hand, where a sovereign acknowledgment like Freud's introduction enters an alliance with a vindictive and tendentious case study clearly written by a chronically disappointed public servant such as Bullitt, then the whole work itself becomes a case study of a fascinating, but in its final form abortive, psychohistorical essay. The Wilson book can serve to illustrate, then, if somewhat by way of a caricature, the decisive influence on a bit of history which results from basic differences in *Weltanschauung* among actor, recorder, and reviewer—that is, a world view, a sense of existential space-time which (as a venerable physicist acknowledged in my seminar in Ahmedabad) is "in a man's bones," no matter what else he has learned.

Freud's example leads me back to the days when I first heard of Gandhi and of Ahmedabad and maybe even of the mill owner—all of which remained latent until, at the time of my visit, it "came back to me" almost sensually in the occasional splendor and the pervasive squalor of India. In my youth I belonged to the class of wandering artists who—as some alienated and neurotic youths can and must in all ages—blithely keep some vision alive in the realities of political and economic chaos, even though, by a minute slip in the scales of fate, they may find themselves among the uniformed to whom killing and being killed becomes a sacred duty, or they may perish ingloriously in some mass furor.

As Wilson's image had set in the cruel night of post-Versailles, it was Gandhi's which then "rose above the horizon"—on the other side of the world. As described to us by Romain Rolland, he seemed to have that pervasive presence, always dear to youth, which comes from the total commitment (for that very reason) to the actuality of love and reason in every fleeting moment. The Event had been contemporaneous with Wilson's Fourteen Points; and if these Points were (and with variations still are) "Western democracy's answer to Bolshevism," so was Gandhi's Satyagraha (begun so locally) the East's answer to Wilson *and* to Lenin.

As for myself, I was to spend a lifetime finding an orientation in, and making a living from, the field created by Sigmund Freud. But when I decided in advanced years to study the Event—and all I can say is that at a certain time I became aware of having made that decision—I do not think that I set out merely to "apply" to Gandhi what I had learned from Freud. Great contemporaries, in all their grandiose one-sidedness, converge as much as they diverge; and it is not enough to characterize one with the methods of the other. As Freud once fancied he might become a political leader, so Gandhi thought of going into medicine. All his life Gandhi ran a kind of health institute, and Freud founded an international organization with the ideological and economic power of a movement. But both men came to revolutionize man's awareness of his wayward instinctuality and to meet it with a combination of militant intelligence—and nonviolence. Gandhi pointed a way to the "conquest of violence" in its external and manifest aspects and, in the meantime, chose to pluck out the sexuality that offended him. Freud, in studying man's repressed sexuality, also revealed the internalized violence of self-condemnation, but thought externalized violent strife to be inevitable. And both men, being good post-Darwinians, blamed man's instinctuality on his animal ancestry—Gandhi calling man a sexual "brute" and Freud comparing his viciousness (to his own kind!) to that of wolves. Since then ethology has fully described the intrinsic discipline of animal behavior and most impressively (in this context) the pacific rituals by which some social animals—yes, even wolves—"instinctively" prevent senseless murder.[11]

When I came to Ahmedabad, it had become clear to me (for I had just come from the disarmament conference of the American Academy) that man as a species cannot afford any more to cultivate illusions either about his own "nature" or about that of other species, or about those "pseudo-species" he calls enemies—not while inventing and manufacturing arsenals capable of global destruction and relying for inner and outer peace solely on the superbrakes built into the superweaponry. And Gandhi seems to have been the only man who has visualized *and* demonstrated an overall alternative.

Less nobly, I should admit that I must have been looking for a historical figure to write about. What could be more fitting than (as my students put it) letting "Young Man Luther" be followed by "Middle-aged Mahatma"? And here I had witnesses: the survivors of a generation of then young men and women who had joined or met Gandhi in 1918, and whose life (as the saying goes) had not been the same since, as if one knew what it might have been. They included, besides the mill owner and his sister, individuals now retired or still in the forefront of national activity in industry, in the Cabinet, or in Parliament. These I set out to meet and to interview on my subsequent visits to India.

If all this sounds self-indulgently personal, it is spelled out here only far enough to remind the psychohistorian that his choice of subject often originates in early ideals or identifications and that it may be important for him to accept as well as he can some deeper bias than can be argued out on the level of verifiable fact or faultless methodology. I believe, in fact, that any man projects or comes to project on the men and the times he studies some unlived portions and often the unrealized selves of his own life, not to speak of what William James calls "the murdered self." The psychohistorian may owe it to history, as well as to himself, to be more conscious of what seems to be a *retransference* on former selves probably inescapable in any remembering, recording, or reviewing and to learn to live and to work in the light of such consciousness. This, incidentally, also calls for new forms of collaboration such as the father of psychoanalysis may have had in mind when he met the brilliant American diplomat.

To confound things a little further, there are also *crosstransferences* from one reviewer of the same subject to another. For example, in a book on Gandhi's main rivals for national leadership, *Tilak and Gokhale* (both of whom died before his ascendance),

S. A. Wolpert [12] calls Gandhi a disciple of Gokhale, and, worse, calls Gokhale Gandhi's "guru." Now, Gandhi, while comparing Tilak with the forbidding ocean and Gokhale (his elder by three years only) with the maternal Ganges and while sometimes calling Gokhale his "political guru," certainly kept *the* guruship in his life free for his own inner voice: an important step in Indian self-conception. But why should Wolpert want to call *his* Gokhale *my* Gandhi's guru with such monotonous frequency—and why should this annoy me? The italics indicate the answer which (as I would judge from my perusal of the literature on Luther) points to a pervasive aspect of a reviewer's "genealogical" identification with his subject as seen through his method, which may make history more entertaining, but rarely more enlightening unless seasoned with insight.

VI

In India, intellectual as well as political travelers could always count on being lodged with friends of means or with friends of friends, and the mill owner related the sayings of many interesting house guests—among them, Gandhi. He had offered me a terrace as a study, saying quietly, "Tagore has worked here." But to be a guest in a man's house is one thing; to be a reviewer of his place in history is another. When I returned to Ahmedabad to interview the mill owner regarding the mill strike, he became strangely distant and asked me to meet him at his office in the mill. This, he made clear, was business: What did I want?

I should say in general that the clinician turned historian must adapt himself to and utilize a new array of "resistances" before he can be sure to be encountering those he is accustomed to. There is, first of all, the often incredible or implausible loss or absence of data in the postmortem of a charismatic figure which can be variably attributed to simple carelessness or lack of awareness or of candor on the part of witnesses. Deeper difficulties, however, range from an almost cognitively ahistorical orientation—ascribed by some to Indians in general—to a highly idiosyncratic reluctance to "give up" the past. Here the myth-affirming and myth-destroying propensities of a post-charismatic period must be seen as the very stuff of which history is made. Where myth-making predominates, every item of the great man's life becomes or is reported like a parable; those who cannot commit themselves to this trend must disavow it with destructive fervor. I, for one, have almost never met anybody of whatever level of erudition or information, in India or elsewhere, who was not willing and eager to convey to me the whole measure of the Mahatma as based on one sublime or scandalous bit of hearsay. Then there are those whose lives have become part of a leader's and who have had to incorporate him in their self-image. Here it becomes especially clear that, unless a man wants to divest himself of his past in order to cure, purify, or sell himself—and there are always professions which receive and sanction such divestment—he must consider it an invested possession to be shared only according to custom and religion, personal style and stage of life. The interviewee, not being a client, does not break a contract with either himself or the interviewer in not telling the whole truth as he knows or feels it. He has, in fact, every right to be preoccupied with the intactness of his historical role rather than with fragmented details as patients and psychotherapists are—often to a fault. After all, this man had been Gandhi's counterplayer in the Event, and he had (as Gandhi knew and took for granted) used all the means at his disposal to break the strike. About this he was, in fact, rather frank, while he seemed "shy" about those episodes which had proven him to be a gallant opponent and faithful supporter. What kind of "resistance" was *that*?

Let me be diagrammatic: The old man's insistence on anonymity turned out to be a lifelong one. In old newspapers I found more than one reference to his charitable deeds which in feudal manner he had always considered his own choice and his own affair. "This is business, not charity," a union official quoted him as saying when he handed him a contribution; and it will be remembered that he did not identify himself when, as a young industrialist, he left money at the ashram gate. Here was a lifelong trend, then, possibly aggravated by some sense of Moksha, which supervenes both good deeds and misdeeds. It is not so easy to judge, then, what a man (and a foreigner) does not want to remember or does not want to say or cannot remember or cannot say.

By the same token, the old man's businesslike attitude was later clarified in its most defensive aspects as resulting from an experience with an inquisitive visitor, while in general it seemed to reflect a sense of propriety as though he wanted to delineate what in this matter was "my business" and what his. I have already indicated that this same attitude pervaded even Gandhi's sainthood. When Gandhi said to his friends who wanted to starve themselves with him, "Fasting is my business," he added, "You do yours." But then both he and the mill owner belonged to a cultural and national group referred to in India (admiringly as well as mockingly) as *banias*—that is, traders. And while the whole strike and its outcome are often considered a *bania* deal by Gandhi's many critics (Marxists, or Maharashtrians, or Bengalis), there is little doubt that Gandhi chose to unfold his whole Satyagraha technique first in a locality and with people who spoke his language and shared his brand of mercantile shrewdness. And behind such life styles there is always India and that larger framework of cosmic propriety which is called dharma—that is, a man's preordained place in the cyclic order of things and their eventual transcendence. Dharma can excuse much wickedness and laziness, as can Fate or God's Will. But it will help determine, from childhood on, what a man considers proper and what out of line; above all, it provides the framework within which the individual can knowingly take hold of the law of Karma, the ethical accounting in his round of lives.

I felt, then, literally "put in my place" by the old man's "resistance." In fact, when he asked me after our first interview what, if anything, I had learned, I could only say truthfully that I had gotten an idea of what Gandhi had been up against with him and he with Gandhi. Only afterward did I realize how right I was and that the cause of my initial annoyance had been due to a certain parallel between Gandhi's and my relationship to the mill owner. Had I not gladly accepted the wealthy man's hospitality when I was a newcomer to India so that I could venture out into the dangers and horrors of that land from an initial position of friendship and sanitary safety? And had not Gandhi gladly accepted his financial support when he came back from South Africa, in many ways a newcomer to India after twenty-five years of absence? And had not both of us, Gandhi and I, developed a certain ambivalence to our benefactor? Here a Marxist could find an opening for legitimate questions; and while he is at it, he might well consider the relationship of the social scientist to the foundations which support him. The common factor which interests us here, however, is the unconscious transference on any host—that is the attribution of a father or older-brother role to anyone in whose home one seeks safety or in whose influence one seeks security. I should add that in my case this theme seems to be anchored in the infantile experience—and, strictly speaking, this alone makes a real transference out of a mere thematic transfer—of having found a loving stepfather in an adoptive country. Every worker must decide for himself, of course, how much or how little he should make of such a connection, and how little or how much of it he should impose on his readers. But first we must become aware of it.

Now an equally brief word on the other side of the coin—namely, the often sudden and unsolicited revelation of such highly personal material as dreams, memories, and fantasies in the course of interviews. In my case, these were offered by a number of informants in the more informal settings of social get-togethers. Accepting them with gratitude, I was always determined to make use of them only as an auxiliary source of insights, not to be attributed to individuals. I do not know, of course, whether revelations of this kind are common in such work or appeared in mine because my interviewees knew me to be a psychoanalyst. If this most personal data eventually proved to have some striking themes in common, I cannot say whether these themes are typically Indian or typical for men who had followed Gandhi. Here are the themes: a *deep hurt* which the informant had inflicted on one of his parents or guardians and could never forget, and an intense wish *to take care of abandoned creatures,* people or animals, who have strayed too far from home. I had secured from each interviewee the story of how he first met Gandhi, only to learn with increasing clinical admiration how determinedly and yet cautiously Gandhi had induced his alienated young followers to cut an already frayed bond with their elders. Tentatively, then, I saw these revelations as an indirect admission of the obvious fact that followers can develop a more or less conscious sense of having vastly outdistanced their original life plan by serving a man who has the power to impose his superior dharma on his contemporaries, making a modernized use of the traditional need for a second, a spiritual, father. A resulting powerful ambivalence toward him is often overcompensated by the submissive antics of followership. And followership divides too: Gandhi's disciples had to accept what was his own family's plight—namely, that he belonged to all and to no one, like the mother in a joint family. Gandhi's was a unique maternalism, happily wedded in his case with a high degree of paternal voluntarism, but not always easily shared or tolerated by others.

Followers too deserve a diagram. Whatever motivation or conflict they may have in common as they join a leader and are joined together by him has to be studied in the full complementarity of

C.

	I MOMENT	II SEQUENCE
1. INDIVIDUAL	the stage of life when they met the leader	lifelong themes transferred to the leader
2. COMMUNITY	their generation's search for leadership	traditional and evolving patterns of followership

As to the last point, Gandhi was a master not only in the selection and acquisition of co-workers, but also in assigning them to or using them in different tasks and ways of life—from the position of elected sons and daughters in his ascetic settlement to that of revolutionary organizers all over India and of aspirants for highest political power, including the prime ministership, for which he "needed a boy from Harrow."

The monumental compilation of Gandhi's works[13] undertaken by the government of India (and now under the charge of Professor Swaminathan) permits us to follow Gandhi's acts, thoughts, and affects literally from day to day in speeches and letters, notes and even dreams (as reported in letters), and to recognize his own conflicts over being invested with that charismatic cloak, the Mahatmaship. That publication will permit us for once to see a leader in a life crisis fighting on two fronts at once: the individual past that marks every man as a defined link in the generational chain, and historical actuality. One thing is clear: On the verge of becoming the father of his nation, he did not (as he has been accused of having done) forget his sons, although the manner in which he did remember them was not without tragic overtones and consequences.

VII

The psychoanalyst, it seems, makes a family affair out of any historical event. Does anybody, we may ask, ever escape his internalized folk and learn to deal with the cast of his adult life on its own terms? The answer is yes and no. Certainly, where radical innovation depends on very special motivations and is paired with strong affect, there its impetus can be shown to draw on lifelong aspirations and involvements. It is true that the psychoanalytic method rarely contributes much to the explanation of the excellence of a man's performance—which may be just as well, for it permits the factor of grace to escape classification and prescription—but it may indicate what freed him for his own excellence or what may have inhibited or spoiled it. It so happens that the Ahmedabad Event *was* something of a family affair not only in that Gandhi's counterplayers were a brother and a sister, but also because Gandhi here tried to do what is proverbially the most difficult thing for a leader—to be a prophet in his own country. The proverb too may gain a new meaning if we can locate the difficulty in the prophet's conflicts as well as in his "country's" diffidence. The very intimacy of my story may seem inapplicable to large events; yet the way Gandhi used his local successes to establish himself firmly as his whole nation's leader—a year later he would command nationwide civil disobedience against the British government—would seem to go to the core of his style as a leader. A man's leadership is prominently characterized by his choice of the proper place, the exact moment, and the specific issue that help him to make his point momentously. Here I would like to quote from a political scientist's work which has aroused interest and on which I have been asked to comment because it uses some "classical" psychoanalytic assumptions rather determinedly.

Victor Wolfenstein, in discussing Gandhi's famous Salt-Satyagraha of 1930, asks bluntly: "But why did Gandhi choose the salt tax from among his list of grievances as the first object of *Satyagraha*?"[14] This refers to the occasion when Gandhi, after his long period of political silence, chose (of all possible actions) to lead an at first small but gradually swelling line of marchers on a "sacred pilgrimage" from Ahmedabad to the Arabian Sea in order to break the law against the tax-free use of salt. Wolfenstein's answer is threefold: First, Gandhi "believed that of all British oppressions the salt tax was the most offensive because it struck the poorest people hardest. . . . By undertaking to serve or lead the lowliest self-esteem is raised." This refers to the assumption that Gandhi and other revolutionary leaders overcome a sense of guilt by acting not for themselves, but for the exploited. Wolfenstein's second point is that "the tax on salt constituted an oral deprivation, a restriction on eating." And it is true,

Gandhi was preoccupied all his life with dietary prohibitions and dietary choices. But then Wolfenstein introduces psychoanalytic symbolism in a way which must be quoted more fully:

> Another line of interpretation, which is consonant with the view I have been developing of Gandhi's personality, is suggested by Ernest Jones' contention that one of the two basic symbolic significances of salt is human semen. If it had this unconscious meaning for Gandhi, then we may understand his depriving himself of condiments, including salt, as a form of sexual abstinence, involving a regression to an issue of the oral phase. In the context of the Salt March, Gandhi's taking of salt from the British can thus be seen as reclaiming for the Indian people the manhood and potency which was properly theirs.

The choice of issues worthy of a Satyagraha campaign must interest us in past as well as in ongoing history, and Gandhi's choice of the salt tax has always impressed me as a model of practical and symbolic action. It pointed to a foreign power's interdiction of a vast population's right to lift from the long shorelines surrounding their tropical subcontinent a cheap and nature-given substance necessary for maintaining work capacity as well as for making bland food palatable and digestible. Here Gandhi's shrewdness seemed to join his capacity to focus on the infinite meaning in finite things—a trait which is often associated with the attribution of sainthood. Wolfenstein's suggestion—that the power of this appeal is attributable to an unconscious sexual meaning of salt—while seeming somewhat ludicrous as an isolated statement, appears to have a certain probability if viewed in cultural context. Anybody acquainted with the ancient Indian preoccupation with semen as a substance which pervades the whole body and which, therefore, is released only at the expense of vitality, acuity, and spiritual power will have to admit that if there is an equation between salt and semen in the primitive mind, the Indian people more than any other could be assumed to make the most of it. I suggest, however, that we take a brief look at what E. Jones really said and what the place of his conclusions is in the history of psychoanalytic symbolism.

Jones's classical paper, "The Symbolic Significance of Salt in Folklore and Superstition," was written in 1928.[15] It really starts with the question of the meaning of superstitions that the spilling of salt at a table may bring ill luck and discord to those assembled for a meal. Jones brings together an overwhelming amount of data from folklore and folk custom which indicate that salt is used in some magic connection with or as an equivalent of semen. A peasant bridegroom may put salt in his left pocket to insure potency; tribesmen and workmen may abstain from both salt and sex during important undertakings; Christian sects may be accused of "salting" the Eucharistic bread with semen—and so on. Jones's conclusion is that to spill salt "means" to lose or spill semen as Onan did: suggesting, then, the sexual model of an antisocial act.

But before we ask how salt may come to mean semen, it is only fair to state that through the ages it has had a powerful significance as itself. When other preservatives were not known, the capacity of salt not only to give pungent taste to the blandest diet but also to keep perishable food fresh, to cleanse and cure wounds, and even to help embalm dead bodies gave it magic as well as practical value: The very word *salary* apparently comes from the fact that this clean, indestructible, and easily transportable substance could be used instead of money. That it comes from the great Sea, the mythical giver of life, makes salt also a "natural" symbol of procreation as well as of longevity and immortality, wit and wisdom, and thus of such incorruptibility as one fervently hopes will preserve the uncertain phenomena of friendship, loyalty, and hospitality. The use of salt on its own terms, then, for the ceremonial affirmation of mutual bonds would do nicely to explain the superstition concerning the unceremonious spilling.

Jones's conclusion is really rather cautious:

> The significance naturally appertaining to such an important and remarkable article of diet as salt has thus been strengthened by an accession of psychical significance derived from deeper sources. The conclusion reached, therefore, is that salt is a typical symbol for semen. There is every reason to think that the primitive mind equates the idea of salt not only with that of semen, but also with the essential constituent of urine. The idea of salt in folklore and superstition characteristically represents the male, active, fertilizing principle.

In psychoanalysis, "deeper" always seems to mean both sexual and repressed, an emphasis which made sense within Freud's libido theory—that is, his search for an "energy of dignity" in human life that would explain the fantastic vagaries of man's instinctuality and yet be comparable to the indestructible and commutable energy isolated and measured in natural science. In civilization and especially in his day, he would find pervasive evidence of the systematic repression in children of any knowledge of the uses and purposes of the sexual organs and this most particularly in any parental context —a repression which no doubt used the pathways of universal symbolization in order to disguise sexual and, above all, incestual thoughts and yet find expression for them. Among these, early psychoanalysis emphasized paternal and phallic symbolism more than maternal; yet, if sexual symbolism did play a role in helping Gandhi, as he put it, "to arouse the religious imagination of an angry people," then the Indian masses, with all their stubborn worship of mother-goddesses, surely would have been swayed as much by the idea of free access to the fecundity of the maternal sea as by the claim to male potency.

At any rate, the one-way symbolization suggested in psychoanalysis, by which the nonsexual always symbolizes the sexual, is grounded in the assumption that the erotic is more central to infantile and primitive experience than are the cognitive and the nutritional. But one wonders. Where survival is at stake, where sexuality is not so obsessive as it becomes in the midst of affluence, where sexual repression is not so marked as it became in the civilized and rational mind—could it not be that the symbolic equation of salt and semen is reciprocal? Could not the ceremonial linking of the two have the purpose of conferring on life-creating semen, a substance so easily squandered, the life-sustaining indestructibility of salt? That is, at the end, a question of determining the place of sexuality in man's whole ecology. But in the immediate context of the chronic semistarvation that has undermined the vitality of the Indian masses and considering the periodic threat of widespread death by famine, it would seem appropriate to assume, first of all, that salt means salt. In fact, the further development of psychoanalysis will have to help us understand the symbolic representation not only of repressed sexuality, but also of the ever-present and yet so blatantly denied fact of death in us and around us.[16] If reason will not suffice, then new forms of irrational violence will force us to consider the consequences of man's seeming ability to ignore not only the certainty of his own death, but also the superweaponry poised all around him to destroy the world he knows—literally at a moment's notice.

Sexual symbolism may help, I would agree, to understand superstitions and symptoms such as, say, the often self-destructive food fads Gandhi indulged in: At one time, he excluded natural salt from his diet, while at another his friends had reason to tease him over his addiction to Epsom salt. In such matters, however, he was only the all-too-willing victim of a tremendous preoccupation with diet rampant during his student days in vegetarian circles in England as well as in the tradition of his native country, although he adorned this with his own concerns over the impact of diet on sexual desire. In deciding on the Salt March, however, he was obviously in command of his political and economic as well as his psychological wits. And in any context except that of irrationality clearly attributable to sexual repression, one should take any interpretation that explains a human act by recourse to sexual symbolism with a grain of salt.

VIII

A historical moment, we have been trying to suggest, is determined by the complementarity of what witnesses, for all manner of motivation, have considered momentous enough to remember and to record and what later reviewers have considered momentous enough to review and re-record in such a way that the factuality of the event is confirmed or corrected and actuality is perceived and transmitted to posterity. For recorders and reviewers alike, however, events assume a momentous character when they seem both unprecedented and yet also mysteriously familiar—that is, if *analogous events* come to mind that combine to suggest a direction to historical recurrences, be it divine intention someday to be revealed, or an inexorable fate to which man may at least learn to adapt, or regularities which it may be man's task to regulate more engineeringly, or a repetitive delusion from which thoughtful man must "wake up." Psychoanalysis is inclined to recognize in all events not only an analogy to but also a regression to the ontogenetic and phylogenetic past. This has proven fruitful in the clinical task of treating patients who suffered from "repressed reminiscences"; but out of its habitual and dogmatic application has come what I have called the *originological fallacy,* which, in contrast to the teleological one, deals with the present as almost preempted by its own origins—a stance not conducive to the demonstration of developmental or historical probability.

The diagrammatic formula for a *historical analogy* would be that another event is considered equivalent to the one at hand because it happened.

D.

	I MOMENT	II SEQUENCE
1. INDIVIDUAL	to a comparable individual at the corresponding stage of his development	to comparable individuals throughout their lives
2. COMMUNITY	in a corresponding stage of a comparable community	at comparable moments throughout history

Let me use as a first set of examples a thematic similarity between Gandhi's autobiography and that of the most influential Chinese writer of roughly the same period, Lu Hsün (1881–1937).

The memory from Gandhi's youth most often quoted to anchor his spiritual and political style in his oedipal relation to his father is that of his father's death. This passage is often referred to as a "childhood memory," although Mohandas at the time was sixteen years old and was about to become a father himself. One night his father, whom the youth had nursed with religious passion, was fast sinking; but since a trusted uncle had just arrived, the son left the nursing care to him and went to his marital bedroom in order to satisfy his "carnal desire," and this despite his wife's being pregnant. After a while, however, somebody came to fetch him: The father had died in the uncle's arms—"a blot," Gandhi writes, "which I have never been able to efface or to forget." A few weeks later his wife aborted. This experience represents in Gandhi's life what, following Kierkegaard, I have come to call "the curse" in the lives of comparable innovators with a similarly precocious and relentless conscience. As such, it is no doubt what in clinical work we call a "cover memory"—that is, a roughly factual event that has come to symbolize in condensed form a complex of ideas, affects, and memories transmitted to adulthood, and to the next generation, as an "account to be settled."

This curse, it has been automatically concluded, must be heir to the Oedipus conflict. In Gandhi's case, the "feminine" service to the father would have served to deny the boyish wish of replacing the (aging) father in the possession of the (young) mother and the youthful intention to outdo him as a leader in later life. Thus, the pattern would be set for a style of leadership which can defeat a superior adversary only nonviolently and with the express intent of saving him as well as those whom he oppressed. Some of this interpretation corresponds to what Gandhi would have unhesitatingly acknowledged as his conscious intention.

Here is my second example: The writer Lu Hsün, often quoted with veneration by Mao, is the founding father of modern China's revolutionary literature. His famous short story "Diary of a Madman" (1918), the first literary work written in vernacular Chinese, is a masterpiece not only (we are told) in the power of its style, but (as we can see) as a very modern combination of a precise psychiatric description of paranoia (Lu Hsün had studied medicine in Japan) and a nightmarish allegory of the fiercer aspects of traditional and revolutionary China. Later, in an essay entitled "Father's Illness," Lu Hsün again mixes a historical theme—namely, the discrepancy of Western and Confucian concepts concerning a man's last moments—with the ambivalent emotions of a son. He had spent much of his adolescent years searching for herbs that might cure his father. But now death was near.

> Sometimes an idea would flash like lightning into my mind: Better to end the gasping faster. . . . And immediately I knew that the idea was improper; it was like committing a crime. But at the same time I thought this idea rather proper, for I loved my father. Even now, I still think so.[17]

This is the Western doctor speaking; but at the time a Mrs. Yen, a kind of midwife for the departing soul, had suggested a number of magic transactions and had urged the son to scream into his father's ear, so he would not stop breathing.

> "Father! Father!"
>
> His face, which had quieted down, suddenly became tense. He opened his eyes slightly as if he felt something bitter and painful.
>
> "Yell! Yell! Quick!"
>
> "Father!"
>
> "What? . . . Don't shout . . . don't . . ." he said in a low tone. Then he gasped frantically for breath. After a while, he returned to normal and calmed down.
>
> "Father!" I kept calling him until he stopped breathing. Now I can still hear my own voice at that time. Whenever I hear it, I feel that this is the gravest wrong I have done to my father.

Lu Hsün was fifteen at the time (to Gandhi's sixteen). He, like Gandhi, had come from a line of high officials, whose fortunes were on the decline during the son's adolescence. At any rate, his story clearly suggests that in the lives of both men a desperate clinging to the dying father and a mistake made at the very last moment represented a curse overshadowing both past and future.

It is not enough, however, to reduce such a curse to the "Oedipus complex" as reconstructed in thousands of case histories as the primal complex of them all. The oedipal crisis, too, must be evaluated as part of man's overall development. It appears to be a constellation of dark preoccupations in a species which must live through a period of infantile dependence and steplike learning unequaled in the animal world, which develops a sensitive self-awareness in the years of immaturity, and which becomes aware of sexuality and procreation at a stage of childhood beset with irrational guilt. For the boy, to better the father (even if it is his father's most fervent wish that he do so) unconsciously means to replace him, to survive him means to kill him, to usurp his domain means to appropriate the mother, the "house," the "throne." No wonder that mankind's Maker is often experienced in the infantile image of every man's maker. But the oedipal crisis as commonly formulated is only the infantile or neurotic version of a *generational conflict* which derives from the fact that man experiences life and death—and past and future—in terms of the turnover of generations.

It is, in fact, rather probable that a highly uncommon man experiences filial conflicts with such inescapable intensity because he senses in himself already early in childhood some kind of originality that seems to point beyond the competition with the personal father. His is also an early conscience development which makes him feel (and appear) old while still young and maybe older in single-mindedness than his conformist parents, who, in turn, may treat him somehow as their potential redeemer. Thus he grows up almost with an obligation (beset with guilt) to surpass and to originate at all cost. In adolescence this may prolong his identity confusion because he must find the one way in which he (and he alone!) can reenact the past and create a new future in the right medium at the right moment on a sufficiently large scale. His prolonged identity crisis, in turn, may invoke a premature generativity crisis that makes him accept as his concern a whole communal body, or mankind itself, and embrace as his dependents those weak in power, poor in possessions, and seemingly simple in heart. Such a deflection in life plan, however, can crowd out his chances for the enjoyment of intimacy, sexual and otherwise, wherefore the "great" are often mateless, friendless, and childless in the midst of veneration and by their example further confound the human dilemma of counterpointing the responsibility of procreation and individual existence.

But not all highly uncommon men are chosen; and the psychohistorical question is not only how such men come to experience the inescapability of an existential curse, but how it comes about that they have the pertinacity and the giftedness to reenact it in a medium communicable to their fellow men and meaningful in their stage of history. The emphasis here is on the word *reenactment*, which in such cases goes far beyond the dictates of a mere "repetition-compulsion," such as characterizes the unfreedom of symptoms and irrational acts. For the mark of a creative reenactment of a curse is that the joint experience of it all becomes a liberating event for each member of an awe-stricken audience. Some dim awareness of this must be the reason why the wielders of power in different periods of history appreciate and support the efforts of creative men to reenact the universal conflicts of mankind in the garb of the historical day, as the great dramatists have done and as the great autobiographers do. A political leader like Mao, then, may recognize a writer like Hsün not for any ideological oratory, but for his precise and ruthless presentation of the inner conflicts that must accompany the emergence of a revolutionary mind in a society as bound to filial piety as China. In a man like Gandhi the autobiographer and the leader are united in one person, but remain distinct in the differentiation of reenactments in writing and in action. In all reenactment, however, it is the transformation of an infantile curse into an adult deed that makes the man.

Common men, of course, gladly accept as saviors *pro tem* uncommon men who seem so eager to take upon themselves an accounting thus spared to others, and who by finding words for the nameless make it possible for the majority of men to live in the concreteness and safety of realities tuned to procreation, production, and periodic destruction.

All the greater, therefore, can be the chaos that "great" men leave behind and often experience in themselves in the years following their ascendance. For the new momentum which they gave to their time may now roll over them, or their power to provide further momentum may wane from fatigue and age. Uncommon men, too, ultimately can become common (and worse) by the extent to which their solution of a universal curse remains tied to its ontogenetic version. The author of "Diary of a Madman" at the end of a career as revolutionary writer himself died in paranoid isolation, as, in hindsight, one would expect of a man who, all his life, could hear his own voice yelling into his dying father's ear. And Gandhi, who could not forgive himself for having sought the warmth of his marital bed while his father was dying, in old age indulged in behavior that cost him many friends. In Lear-like fashion, he would wander through the tempest of communal riots, making local peace where nobody else could and yet knowing that he was losing the power to keep India united. It was then that the widower wanted his "daughters" close (he had never had a daughter of his own) and asked some of his women followers to warm his shivering body at night. This "weakness" the septuagenarian explained as a test of his strength of abstinence, opening himself wide to cheap gossip. This story too will have to be retold in terms of life cycle and history.

What was once united by the power of charisma cannot fall apart without exploding into destructive furor in the leader or in the masses or in both. Here life history ends, and history begins in its sociological and political aspects. How a leader survives himself and how an idea survives a man, how the community absorbs him and his idea, and how the sense of wider identity created by his presence survives the limitations of his person and of the historical moment—these are matters that the psychohistorian cannot approach without the help of the sociologist of tradition-building and institution-forming. He, in turn, may want to consider the "metabolism" of generations and the influence of a leader's or an elite's image on the life stages of the led: Kennedy's rise and sudden death certainly would provide a modern model for such a study.

To return once more to my original interest in Gandhi: I have indicated what I have learned since about his personal idiosyncrasies as well as about his power of compromise. If some say that his ascendance was unfortunate for an India in desperate need of modernization, I cannot see who else in his time could have brought the vast, backward mass of Indians closer to the tasks of this century. As for his lasting influence, I will endeavor to describe in a book his strategy (as enfolded in the Event) of challenging man's latent capacity for militant and disciplined nonviolence: In this, he will survive. In the meantime, I, for one, see no reason to decide whether he was a saint or a politician—a differentiation meaningless in the Hindu tradition of combining works and renunciation—for his life is characterized by an ability to derive existential strength, as well as political power, from the very evasion of all job specifications. In interviewing his old friends, however, I found ample affirmation of his agile and humorous presence, probably the most inclusive sign of his (or anybody's) simultaneous mastery of inner and outer events. And it is in his humor that Gandhi has been compared to Saint Francis. Luther understood such things even if he could not live them; and at least his sermons formulate unforgettably the centrality in space, the immediacy in time, and the wholeness in feeling that lead to such singular "events" as survive in parables—a form of enactment most memorable through the ages, although, or maybe just because, most effortless and least "goal-directed." Now, a man has to be dead for quite a while before one can know what parables might survive him: In Gandhi's case, one can only say that the "stuff" for parables is there. Let me, in conclusion, compare two well-known scenes from the lives of Gandhi and Saint Francis.

Teasing was a gift and a habit with Gandhi throughout his life, and elsewhere I have pointed out the affinity of teasing to nonviolence.[18] It was after the great Salt March (he had been arrested again, and while he was in jail his Satyragahis had been brutally attacked by the police) that Gandhi was invited to talks with the Viceroy. Churchill scoffed at the "seditious fakir, striding half-naked up the steps of the Viceroy's palace, to negotiate with the representative of the King-Emperor." But the Viceroy, Lord Irwin, himself described the meeting as "the most dramatic personal encounter between a Viceroy and an Indian leader." When Gandhi was handed a cup of tea, he asked to be given a cup of hot water instead, into which he poured a bit of salt (tax-free) out of a small paper bag hidden in his shawl and remarked smilingly: "To remind us of the famous Boston Tea Party."

If we choose to insist on the symbolic meaning of salt and would see in this gesture a disguised act of masculine defiance—so be it. But such meaning would be totally absorbed in the overall artfulness with which personal quirk (Gandhi would not touch tea) is used for the abstention from and yet ceremonial participation in the important act of sharing tea at the palace, and yet also for the reenactment of a historical defiance, pointedly reminding his host of the time when the British taxed another invigorating substance and lost some colonies which, in independence, did rather well.

Whatever combination of overt and hidden meanings were enacted here in unison, the analogy that comes to mind is a scene from Saint Francis' life when he was asked for dinner to his bishop's palace. A place on the bishop's right was reserved for the ethereal rebel, and the guests were seated along well-decked tables. But Brother Francesco was late. Finally he appeared with a small sack, out of which he took little pieces of dry dark bread and with his usual dancing gestures put one beside each guest's plate. To the bishop, who protested that there was plenty of food in the house, he explained that for *this* bread he had *begged* and that, therefore, it was consecrated food. Could there be a more delicate and yet finite lesson in Christianity?

The two scenes bespeak an obvious similarity in tone and artfulness; but in order to make them true analogies, comparison is not enough. Other lifelong similarities in the two men could be enumerated and their respective tasks in their respective empires compared. Gandhi was no troubadour saint, but a tough activist as well as an enactor of poetic moments; and he was a strategist as well as a prayerful man. All this only points to the psychohistorian's job of specifying in all their complementarity the inner dynamics as well as the social conditions which make history seem to repeat, to renew, or to surpass itself.[19]

FREUD AND THE AUTHORITY OF THE PAST

PHILIP RIEFF

The terrible original text *homo natura* must again be recognized. In effect to translate man back again into nature; to master the many vain and visionary interpretations and subordinate meanings which have hitherto been scratched and daubed over the eternal original text, *homo natura*: to bring it about that man shall henceforth stand before man as he now, hardened by the discipline of science, stands before the *other* forms of nature, with fearless Oedipus-eyes, and stopped Ulysses-ears, deaf to the enticements of old metaphysical bird-catchers, who have piped him far too long: "Thou art more! thou art higher! thou hast a different origin! . . ."

—NIETZSCHE

For the rationalist Freud, even sexuality is an achievement. To be achieved, it must be cut off from its profoundest complicity with the irrational, its relation to the past. Not that Freud underestimates the irrational. By his instinct theory, which posits the existence of an unresolvable warfare between erotic and aggressive instincts, Freud plainly states that the irrational component cannot be eliminated. The most that can be hoped for—and this is the aim of his therapy—is to take from irrationality the oppressive advantage it derives from its relation with the archaic, the atavistic. A healthy sexuality is one which is freed of its history.

For the Romantic Freud, sexuality when achieved means this freedom. Freud wears the face of an emancipator, physician to sick individuality in search of its abrogation in the instinctual life. Neurotics "try to make the past itself non-existent."[1] Therefore, psychoanalysis turns its patients to examine the past, to recall them to the erotic essentials of their natures. A healthy sexuality is one which can *reclaim* its history.

Freud shares the retrospective impulse of Romanticism, without, however, sharing its nostalgia; the past, for him, is condemned as permanency, burden, neurosis. His standing as a rationalist equally depends on this hatred of the past. If the Enlightenment sages left one sense sharpened, it was the sense of the past as a burden to be reexamined; whether the burden should be dropped becomes the problem of civilization set for Freud by his rationalist ancestors. Progressive rationalism, however, is not the stopping point for Freud. The past is not simply dead weight to be cast off by enlightened minds, but active and engaged, threatening to master the present.

The most energetic mutation of Enlightenment rationalism in the natural sciences, the theory of evolution, shares this antagonism toward the past. But as a counterpoise of the official optimist version of evolutionist reasoning, which hinged on the interpretation of time as a unidirectional progress from the primitive to the mature, there was an evolutionist pessimism which stressed the limits of development and the staying power of our original condition. Freudian ideas represent a climax, rather than a new departure, in a remarkable chain of reasoning about the relation between sickness and the past. Early in the nineteenth century, Carl-Gustav Carus, a lonely figure working between the then sealed borders of physiology and psychology, argued that the sickly part of the soul is really a repetition of the lowliest stuff of organic nature. During his Croonian lectures (1884) Hughlings Jackson, a great English neurologist whom Freud admired, spoke of psychoses as the dissolution of the complex system of functions and the reconstitution of the simplest and lowest elements of the nervous system. About the same time in France the psychologist T. A. Ribot used the word "regressions" to explain how memory, through some injury, might revert backward from the contemporaneous to the ancient; this he illustrated by such eruptions of spontaneity in the civilized character as automatic writing. Contemporary with Freud, Pierre Janet described a hierarchy of steps in mental functioning through which the mind could descend as well as ascend to any level. Moritz Lazarus, leader of the German school of *Völkerpsychologie,* construed mental illness as a sinking into the fantasy world of the "natural man." Freud summed up an entire movement of poetic and scientific thought when he identified the abnormal with the primitive.[2]

I

All these connections between sickness and the past depend on the idea of parallelism. Perhaps no scientific idea has found easier acceptance in both the trained and the popular mind than the "phylogenetic law": that embryonic development recapitulates racial development, that ontogeny is a short, rapid summary of phylogeny. In Viennese intellectual circles around 1900, the works of Darwin's German apostle Ernst Haeckel, especially his *The Riddle of the Universe,* were extravagantly praised. At some point in the 1870s the University of Vienna intended to have Haeckel join the faculty. When he declined, the university appointed the zoologist Carl Claus to the vacant chair, and it was under Claus, an ardent evolutionist, that the student Freud did his first serious biological research. Though Freud nowhere uses Haeckel, he was familiar with and accepted as indisputable scientific truth the phylogenetic law as it was popularized by Haeckel.

Yet Freud did not much employ this biological version of the analogy between individual and racial development; and he made scarcely more use of the psychological form of the recapitulation idea—according to which the maturing individual mind repeats the development of *mind* through the evolutionary series—than he did of the biological version. A more nearly sociological version, familiar through the variety of uses to which it was put by Herder, Herbart, Comte, and Spencer, is the one he most often employed. This idea—that the individual mind presents in its development a résumé of the stages of human *history*—reached Freud especially by way of anthropological literature. Because he was interested less in the end of the recapitulatory series than in its beginnings, he followed with special care contemporary writing on the psychology of primitives.

The first locus of the primitive which Freud found in individual mental life was the dream. Although he rightly insisted that the connection had not been scientifically developed, it was scarcely unknown. In *The Birth of Tragedy* Nietzsche remarked on how the dream, by returning us to the dark origins out of which human culture has developed, offers modern man the means of continually revising his high estimate of himself. Freud quotes Nietzsche's statement that in dreams "some primeval relic of humanity is at work which we can scarcely reach any longer by a direct path." Dreaming, in Freud's view, is an example of regression, a revival of the instinctual impulses which dominated childhood and of the methods of satisfaction which were then available to the child. Behind every childhood is revealed "a picture of a phylogenetic childhood—a picture of the development of the human race."

Dream interpretation becomes a form of archaeology in which the analyst has the task of recovering "mental antiquities." The analysis of dreams, Freud expected, would lead to a "knowledge of man's archaic heritage, of what is psychically innate in him." [3]

The second locus in which Freud found the primitive in present life was even more familiar. All the anthropological studies on which he depended—Frazer's *Golden Bough* most heavily, books by Atkinson, Lubbock, Tylor, Robertson Smith, Crawley, Marett, Lang—made free use of the analogy between the primitive and the child. It was more customary to construe the primitive era of civilization as the "childhood of the race" (cf. Rousseau, Herder) than to invert the image, making of childhood the primitive era of the individual. Nevertheless Freud was repeating a theoretical commonplace when he asserted that in the few years of childhood, "we have to traverse the immense evolutionary distance from the Stone Age to participation in modern civilization." [4] He exploited both parts of his analogy, attributing to "primeval people the same feelings and emotions that we have elucidated in the primitives of our own times, our children," [5] and attributing to "the psychic life of present-day children, the same archaic moments . . . which generally prevailed at the time of primitive civilization." [6] Thus materials on the irrational ways of primitives—Freud's point of departure in *Totem and Taboo* (1912)—were readily applied, by analogy, to the behavior of children and neurotics.

Freud did not fix wholly on the beginnings of recapitulatory development. He was especially drawn to schemes of growth on the evolutionist model. In his individual psychology there is the sexual-characterological sequence of "oral," "urethral," "anal," "phallic," and "genital" phases. Further, there is his implicit acceptance of the positivist theory of history, according to which mind evolves from animism through religion to science; this scheme not only underlies Freud's explicitly social essays, from *Totem and Taboo* to *Moses and Monotheism* (1937–1939), but was also adapted to his individual psychology. Presumably following anthropologists such as E. B. Tylor, who had been influenced by the English Comtists, Freud saw "the evolution of human views of the universe" in the inevitable three stages.[7] Psychoanalysis turned the Comtist triad to interpretative account by translating the intellectual into "the *libidinous* development of the individual." Freud asserted in *Totem and Taboo* that

> the *animistic* phase would correspond to narcissism both chronologically and in its content; the *religious* phase would correspond to the stage of object-choice of which the characteristic is a child's attachment to his parents; while the *scientific* phase would have an exact counterpart in the stage at which an individual has reached maturity, has renounced the pleasure principle, adjusted himself to reality and turned to the external world for the object of his desires.[8]

Now intellectual history is full of scientific myths, to which psychologists have contributed more than their share. The Swiss psychologist Jean Piaget internalized the liberal myth of the transformation of society from primitive collectivist tyranny to modern individualist democracy by making of it a psychology of character development from "heteronomy" to "autonomy." Thus Freud psychologized the liberal myth of growing human rationality into the theory that the individual evolves from narcissism to mature libidinal sociality. These hopes are suggestive, yet they were not the ones on which Freud elaborated. For nothing was more foreign to his mind than the optimistic temper in which the three-stage positivist theory was regularly set forth.

To be sure, it was the evolutionist faith in a more rational future which inspired Freud's late polemic on religion, *The Future of an Illusion* (1928). But his hopes for progress and reason were balanced by anxieties, fairly conventional with civilized minds of his era, about the high cost of civilization in terms of sexual vitality and the feasibility of permanent progress. His warnings in *Moses and Monotheism* against the trend whereby "the world of the senses becomes gradually mastered by spirituality"[9] echo this typically modern anxiety as to the price of civilization—the anxiety typical of psychological man. Freud feared that "the evolution of culture . . . may perhaps be leading to the extinction of the human race."[10] As a late Romantic in a world sick of romance (reality had become so much stranger), he saw the utopian possibility as the end of possibility. Hence he returned to an analysis of origins.* If the plant appears twisted, if life begins to wither away, the condition of the root becomes the inevitable question.

*G. Stanley Hall, theologian turned psychologist, who first invited Freud to America, expressed in his autobiography the aim of a psychology respectful of origins: "to conceive the whole world, material and spiritual, as an organic unity, to eliminate all breaks and supernaturalism, and to realize that everything within and without was hoary with age, so that in most experiences we were dealing with only the topmost twigs of vast but deeply buried trees."[11]

II

It was in *Totem and Taboo* (1913) that Freud linked his psychology to the study of the primitive in history. The anthropological material in the book is culled from field anecdotes cited by older authorities—Codrington, Spencer and Gillen, Frazer, Lang, Tylor. For some time Freud had been defining neurosis in terms of arrestments of psychic life—treating childhood as a literally "primitive" beginning of life, and dreams and other neurotic formations as residues of the primitive. Now, no longer content to call neurotics primitive, he drew from a growing literature on the irrationalities of primitives to illuminuate the behavior of neurotics.

To confront the author of *Three Essays on Sexuality* with *Totem and Taboo* may seem unfair. The practicing clinician ought not to be embarrassed by the armchair anthropologist. It appears, at first reading, that in *Totem and Taboo* Freud merely ornamented his science with exotic anecdote and bizarre speculation. Yet, whether right or wrong, these speculations convey the soaring and plunging quality of Freud's mind more accurately than his apparently aseptic clinical studies.* Through anthropology, Freud's psychology was able to make its first clear breakthrough to overtly social concerns—although these had always been covertly operative. Contemporary anthropology supplied Freud with a vast array of what we might call cultural symptoms. Such an ambitious (and now professionally discredited) work as Frazer's *The Golden Bough* (1890), from which Freud borrowed more than from any other, is a mine of data. With their enormous catalogues of observations, the anthropologists were

*While serviceable in expanding to the social the scope of his psychology, Freud's anthropological codifications of children's behavior seem to me otherwise to limit his perspective. Here Freud's Darwinian models certainly played his clinical intuition false. Anyone who has read the case of the precocious "little Hans" (1905) will agree that Freud does not do his masterly analysis justice by later finding in it proof of the "same archaic elements . . . which dominated human culture in primitive times" (*The Question of Lay Analysis*, p. 34). In his anthropology, indeed, we find deposited just the questionable elements in Freud's attitude toward children. He had little feeling for the autonomy of childhood. Yet his attitude shows the essential constructive ambivalence he has helped to stabilize among parents. At the same time that he deepens the parents' sense of authority, he renders more subtle and difficult to discharge the parental sense of obligation to children.

the first behaviorists of the cultural sciences. Just as he used his clinical researches to gather individual symptoms, Freud used the data of anthropology as a source book for studying the irrational. The prehistoric crises of the race illuminate, for him, the meaning of neurotic crises among historical men. At the same time, the neurotic crises of historical men reveal the original prehistoric crises.

Once upon a time, we read in *Totem and Taboo*, "psychic reality, concerning whose structure there is no doubt, . . . coincided with actual reality." It was Freud's propensity to defer to acts of violence as the original repressed substrata of all social action. Compound the recapitulation theory with this belief, add his understanding of the basic wishes of children as egoistic and murderous, and you have Freud's reasoning that later neurotic *wishes* coincide with the *deeds* of primitive men. In the beginning, thinking and doing were identical: "Men actually *did*" what now, according to clinical testimony, they only wish to do.[12] The incapacity of psychotics to distinguish between thought and reality supplied Freud with another clue to what primitive life was normally like: "There is not only *method* in madness . . . but also a fragment of historic truth." [13]

The historic truth which Freud reconstructed was based mainly on Darwin's view that "the primitive form of human society was that of a horde ruled over despotically by a powerful male."[14] To this conjecture of Darwin, Freud added the theory of the Scottish archaeologist and student of comparative religion William Robertson Smith: that sacrifice at the altar is the essential element in every primitive cult, and that such a sacrifice goes back to a killing and eating by the clan of its totem animal, which was regarded as of kin with the clan and its god, and whose killing at ordinary times was therefore strictly forbidden. Thus Freud was drawing on a modern version of euhemerism, the ancient theory that the gods were deified men, deified because they had lived heroically here on earth and were worthy to mount the heavens. But though Freud's theory of myth was euhemerist, rather than rationalizing, as in modern social science, the historical figures themselves were bound to psychological prototypes; the historical actions he inferred from neurotic fantasies were necessary—granted the nature of man.

Animated by an older and perhaps more naïve concern for the nature that drives history, Freud never ceased inquiring into prehistorical causes of events. His ante-historical research ended in a neat harmony of instinct and primordial event. Linking up his own judgment of the murderous nature of man* with the desire to kill the father which he detected in adult neurotics, in children, and in the evidence of dreams, Freud supposed that primitive man really did kill his. Men have always known, he concluded in *Moses and Monotheism,* "that once upon a time they had a primeval father and killed him." [17]

Freud did not apply this conjecture only to the violence of individual psychic impulses. Individual violence, in real life and in fantasy, points back to historical violence. Once accepted, the idea of the horde was enlarged upon by Freud as the historical model for all subsequent modes of community, and as exemplifying the tendency of all regimes today.[18] Assuming that there existed, under the original leadership of the primal father, nothing but "group feelings," it followed, for Freud, that the first act of individuality had to be rebellion, specifically the killing of the primal father by his sons. Thus individuality gains meaning in Freudian theory as an act of libidinal alienation, of antisociality.

The sons desired to kill the father, but afterward they never ceased to regret it. As they gained their freedom they missed their thralldom. Political-religious history is a record of man's irrational attempts to reinstate the primal father. The will, once free, found itself wanting also to renounce its freedom, not just from prudence—what Freud, echoing Hobbes, called "the struggle of all against all" [19]—but also from remorse and craving for authority. As children must love their parents, so did the first citizens love their ruler; his reinstatement, at least in symbolic form, as God, was as natural as his deposition.

In Freud's own origins myth all history is divided, by the act of parricide, into two stages. With this act, the political stage—submission characterized by guilt—was laid over the primal one. The primal murder signaled not merely the beginning of political society but also the beginning of all ritual. Politics and religion, understood by Freud as originally ways of reuniting the many under a single authority, came into existence together, as the profoundest expressions of the ambivalence of human will.

*From "Thoughts for the Times on War and Death," [15] and "Why War?" [16]: While man has no business to exclude himself from the animal kingdom, "that instinct which is said to restrain the other animals from killing and devouring their own species we need not attribute to him."

The surest of hands is at work sorting the rich mythic evidence, connecting, through psychoanalytic ideas, social and life history. Yet the very consistency of his selection of data exposes the weakness in Freud's reconstruction of social origins. His identification of the prototypical event with the primal *father* murder excludes other possibilities that ought not to be left unconsidered. The murder of the father is but one theme in the myth literature extant; the fratricide motif occurs quite as significantly as that of parricide. If the exemplars of the parricide motif—Oedipus and the other regicide characters that stride across the universal stage—are moving, so, to the postmythic mind equally, are the exemplars of the fratricide theme: the sons of Oedipus, Joseph and his brothers, Cain and Abel, Arthur and his knights, the Trojan peers, the *Nibelungen*, the daughters of Lear—indeed, all the brothers and sisters who have been so fatal to one another.

A third myth complicates the Freudian selection: the Abraham myth (cf. Kierkegaard, *Fear and Trembling*). Unless dismissed as "manifest" content, in the Abraham myth it is the father who would kill the son, not the son who would kill the father. Propitiatory sacrifice of a prophet (Moses, Christ) or a tragic hero (Oedipus, Hamlet), on behalf of his sinful people, is as much a son-killing as a father-killing. The fact that the death of Christ, the Son of Man, at the hands of his own brothers, the masses, is sanctioned by a more primary Father, God, may be interpreted as a sublimated solution of the fratricidal scapegoat mechanism.

The great murder myth of the Old Testament is the killing of primal brother by primal brother. The first moral question, expressed in the story of Cain and Abel, was not, as Freud implies, "Am I my father's son?" Rather, the primal question was, "Am I my brother's keeper?" *Hamlet* can be read, psychoanalytically, in a way neither Freud nor Ernest Jones* considered. After all, it is the killing of the brother that is the demiurge of the plot. Claudius instructs Hamlet, in their first scene, that nature's most "common theme is death of fathers . . . from the first corpse till he that died today." But the first corpse was a brother. The primal curse is the usurpation of the throne by fratricide. Hamlet sees the horror of brother against brother. What the ghost—the dead father who is also the dead

*Cf. *The Interpretation of Dreams*,[20] pp. 265–66; Ernest Jones, *Hamlet and Oedipus* (London, 1949; an amplified version of a paper of 1910, "The Oedipus Complex as an Explanation of Hamlet's Mystery").

brother—reveals is a fratricide; and later Hamlet kills his prospective brother-in-law, Laertes. Fratricide is what makes life rotten in the state of Denmark. Freud seems to have been deaf to the importance in myth of both sororicide and fratricide, although it fairly shouted at him in his analysis of *King Lear* and of the ninth of Grimm's fairy tales, "The Twelve Brothers," in his essay "The Theme of the Three Caskets." Instead, he writes as he rarely does, belaboring the obvious: the symbolism of death as dumbness in myth literature.

The theme of fraternal rivalry does play a decisive, if secondary, role in Freud's social theory. The civil war of the brothers, as distinct from their revolt against the tyranny of the father, is, psychologically, the original condition of political society. Freud was led to assert, finally, a "sort of social contract" theory.[21] After the rebellion of the sons, and the collective killing and devouring of the father, there followed a brief matriarchal interregnum characterized by the free disposition of erotic goods. But the "fatherless society" proved impossible in the long run. With the dissolution of the father's monopoly over the women of the horde, each of the guilty sons desired instinctual sovereignty; each envied the power of all the others. New forms of inhibition were necessary to forestall a chaos of suicidal and murderous pleasure-seeking. Failing to acquire the absolute rights possessed by the original father, each covenanted with all to submit themselves to sexual restrictions and to new patriarchal surrogates. First, then, the contract of the brothers arose out of a Malthusian calculation of the value of scarce resources and the necessity of restraint—in this case, the value of the female commodity in a scarcity situation. But even the hard light of Freud's economic sex-calculus cannot spoil the grandeur of his critical account of social origins. In the contract of the brothers there came into being "the essential element of civilization": [22] the renunciation of instinctual gratification. Equal in their renunciation as they were once equal in submission to the father, the brother-clan is able to tolerate new coercions.

All social relations, in Freud's view, are coercive. The difference between the confinements of civilization and the tyranny of nature lies in whether coercion is exercised from within or without. Now, from one point of view, we may read Freud's myth of primal origins as a parable on the futility of rebellion. For after the democratic interval of matriarchal permissiveness, the revolt against the patriarchal authority is promptly succeeded by new bondages, new sacrifices. But there is a difference. These are sacrifices self-imposed, which makes rebellion not altogether futile. Owing to a novel psychological ingredient, namely the *guilt* which the brothers feel over their supreme crime of parricide, this succeeding reign of authority is not simply a renewal of primal despotism but an advance beyond it—to civilization. Civilization begins when the paternal taboos are self-imposed, when repressions are implemented in the interest of the group. The private sexual expenditure of creative energy must be damned up and redirected toward gaining knowledge and building artifacts useful to all. Freud derived each "great cultural victory" from separate feats of instinctual renunciation. The use of tools was a mimicry of the gratifying exertion of sexual intercourse, and therefore a substitute for it; fire was secured when primitive man first denied his urge to put it out with a stream of urine (urethral eroticism); dwellings were "a substitute for the mother's womb, that first abode, in which [man] was safe and felt so content, for which he probably yearns ever after." [23] However fanciful these conjectural prototypes of work and first cultural possessions appear, Freud's basic point remains a valid one: that human culture is established through a series of renunciations. The sacrifice of self is the beginning of personality.

The act of renunciation is at once the establishment of fellowship in society and of the Father as God. The war of the generations ends in the deification of the dead father and in the socializing guilt of the brothers. Men stand, as a band of brothers, at the genesis of society when they renounce their aspirations to become, each above all, the supreme Father, and instead worship the father they have murdered (e.g., the primal father, then Moses, Christ, *et al.*) as God in heaven. God, according to Freud, is the positive projection of the act of renunciation.

Although Freud's "scientific myth" remains more myth than science, its merits lie in the judgments of value that it conceals. *Totem and Taboo, Group Psychology, Moses and Monotheism,* and allied works of Freud can no more be dismissed because the anthropology upon which they drew is now outmoded than that great polemic on the emancipation of women, *The Origin of the Family,* is refuted by citing the discredited conjectures on matriarchy and group marriage by Lewis Morgan which stimulated Engels to write his book. As illustrated propositions of value, Freud's social essays stand, even after their anthropological shorings have buckled beneath them. The evolutionist argument habitually shrank from saying a thing *is* something, and instead preferred to report that it *began* in a certain way. Freud's idea of primal history—added to his psychological Lamarckianism—gives another example of the frequently tortuous attempts in nineteenth-century evolutionary ethics to escape saying that man has a nature and that it is torn between the desire to please and the desire to be pleased. Society *begins* with a crime. Man *begins* as a killer, Freud argued. Yet not merely a killer, but a *remorseful* killer. And the primal crime is the crime to end all crimes.

If we look to the manner in which evolutionists disclose the origin of a thing in order to detect their attitude toward it, then Freud's elaborate description of the origin of society in a "primal crime" discloses his basic attitude toward the history of society as a murder mystery, and toward the main problem of humanity as that of aggression. Freud thus combined the critical aims of psychology and anthropology. His psychology sought to deflate our sentimentalizing on civilized human nature, as anthropology sought, by its revelations of the primitive, to shake our complacent sense of the progress of modern social institutions and familial customs. In anthropology Freud recognized a great polemical discipline subjoining his own, equally intent on questioning the pride of civilization. Every part of Freud's theory, from his child psychology to his political psychology, is affected by the attitude veiled in this romance of origins. The doctor living quietly in Vienna proposed a myth of human existence as terrifying as any of those he loved to read in world literature. If he was wrong, his error was a great error. Better great errors than small truths; and, perhaps, to borrow Freud's own borrowing from Polonius, his bait of falsehood snared a carp of truth.[24]

III

In Freud's parable of origins, the victories through renunciation that man has been able to achieve in the development of culture all presuppose the guilt feelings which originally followed upon the primal crime. So important an experience was the primal crime that it "must have left some permanent trace in the human soul." [25] This trace, he argues, contributed an "archaic heritage" to our psychic lives that "corresponds to the instincts of animals," but differs from animal instinct so far as it includes "not only dispositions, but also

. . . traces of the experiences of earlier generations."[26] That difference makes it, however, no less permanent. And the question remains for Freud: How are the experiences of the past transmitted? In what form does the prototypal event live on in the life of the group? To say that the primal crime must have left "something comparable to a tradition"[27] begs the question. How is tradition possible?

Of course, there is literature, and culture. But Freud rejected the conscious transmission of culture for what he considered a more profound continuity. The deepest instinctual secrets are not rationally preserved and disseminated by parents and teachers; they are remembered. Freud was Lamarckian: "What was acquired by our ancestors," he thought, "is certainly an important part of what we inherit."[28] He could not imagine social or biological science without Lamarckian hypotheses. He was of course on a well-traveled road. Nietzsche announced that the crucial inheritance was that of character, and Samuel Butler had certified instinct as "inherited memory."[29] The primitive survives in memory, the representative of the past among the faculties. Against the overconfidence of reason, representing the future, Freud asserted the ancient claim of memory to a greater power than reason had allowed. The connection between psychoanalysis and Lamarckianism cannot be overemphasized. Not only Freud, but Ferenczi, Jung, Adler, Reich—major disciples and schismatics—require the Lamarckian hypothesis. As Lamarckians, however, none presume a simple linear transmission of attitudes. Rather, the primal act must be denied, forgotten, in order to persist in the unconscious.

Finally, thus, the problem of tradition was solved. Tradition was defined as the prototypal content of the mass unconscious. Like the individual, the group, Freud boldly asserts, may "retain an impression of the past in unconscious memory traces." Jung, Freud warned, solved nothing by introducing the idea of the collective unconscious.* The "content of the unconscious is collective anyhow."[30]

*Jung's parting with Freud is over the problem of the past, rather than over the "collective unconscious." For Jung, the source of neurotic conflict is not the repression of desires but the exhaustion of the historical appropriateness of some responses to the neglect of others. This makes him, even more than Freud, an equilibrium theorist, viewing character as a response to the historical situation and that situation constantly in jeopardy of becoming obsolete—or, in Jungian terms, one-sided. In this way Jung has clarified Freud's historicist psychology by cutting away its biologistic underbrush and directing its critical animus toward

Without the hypothesis of the mass psyche, Freud found the dynamic as well as the achievements of tradition incomprehensible. Tradition is "equivalent to repressed material in the mental life of the individual." On the conscious surface of a culture, the repressed content of the past is something "vanished and overcome in the life of a people."[31] But this is just what defines the impact of memory: one's reaction to it, against it. Prototypal events—the primal crime and its repetitions, like the murder of Moses or the murder of Christ—take on the weight of tradition when they are repressed, and the reaction to them is, of course, unconscious. History, as the trail of the prototype, became for Freud a process of the "return of the repressed,"[32] distorting extensively yet eternally recapitulatory.

Freud's scientific myth of the primal father serves other, more surprising purposes when the historical argument is consigned to a proper irrelevance and the evaluative function is exhibited alone. *Totem and Taboo,* where the collective prototype is first broached, contains much on the origins of religion. Freud's myth of the primal father discloses his own left-handed admiration for monotheistic religion and offers Jewish monotheism the most pervasive of modern legitimations, that of psychological truth. (This was a subject daringly amplified in his last completed major work, *Moses and Monotheism.*) If the first father was God, then other Gods are later, and corruptions.

Freud was thus at odds with the commonly held view according to which religion begins in polytheism—the worship of vague, plural, local spirits with limited powers—and only after a long process of ethical mastery and intellection attains to the concept of a single deity. By beginning with the purest worship (of one father), from which humans regularly fall away, Freud departed from the evolu-

---

the present rather than the past. For Jung, neurosis is not, as for Freud, a failure of presentness, but rather a loss of plasticity, of potential responses which, through neglect, have been allowed to slip into unconsciousness. In the unconscious (not in reason) there is a reservoir of strength from which man ought to draw to meet the demands of the day. He must learn to see that what once was true may be true again, that what was once needful may be needful in the here and now again, that nothing old in the world of ideas is incapable of becoming novel. Jung favors therapeutic renascences as an antidote to the banalization of ruling ideas. Freud is for therapeutic reformations, which will abolish the tyranny of nostalgia that calls up renascences and gives to them a symptomatic appropriateness.

tionary optimism of both modern science and modernist religion.* *Totem and Taboo* is a thoroughly evolutionist treatise, but Freud's evolutionism was uniquely and pessimistically focused on the permanent limits of development.

Even his Lamarckianism reflects this pessimism. While Adler favored Lamarck over Darwin because the former's teleology supported his own evolutionist optimism,† Freud's version had a consistently gloomy cast. What appealed to Freud was not its teleological verve but the near-fatalism of the theory which supposes, in William James's famous definition, "the same emotions, the same habits, the same *instincts* [to be] perpetuated without variation from one generation to another."[33] Lamarck (and Darwin too) offered "serviceability" as an explanation for the persistence of certain emotional forms and accidentally produced tendencies to action. For Freud, archaic and individual memories are neither efficient nor serviceable. Once acquired, they persist in the individual (and through the generations) as the final cause of neurotic misery.

The entire evolutionist concern with "vestiges" has a pejorative implication: they are maladaptive. The thesis, stated biologically, may be found in Darwin's *Expression of the Emotions in Man and Animals,* where he argues that the movements we call expressive were once parts of practical activities—for example, baring the teeth in anger is an abbreviated expression of a formerly more complete reaction of attack. Such movements have now become "survivals,"

*A minority of scholars has, however, supported the notion of a primitive monotheistic belief antedating the Jewish or Babylonian or any recorded peoples. Trying to salvage the supremacy and priority of the monotheistic idea, the Christian anthropology of Ratzel and his pupil Frobenius discovered the towering figure of one god everywhere on the "culture horizons" of the most archaic peoples. A similar notion of a primordial monotheism, from the secular anthropological point of view, was put forward by Andrew Lang in his *Magic and Religion,* published in 1901. (Freud cites Lang's *The Secret of the Totem* [1905] frequently in *Totem and Taboo.*) And the Jesuit scholar Father Schmidt, in his massive *Origins of the Idea of God* (whose first volume was issued the same year as *Totem and Taboo*), also supports the theory of an originally pure idea of one God which, as the result of some primeval experience of guilt, had been forgotten, degenerating into the farrago of magico-authoritarian beliefs that we now understand as primitive religion.

† Cf. Adler in his *Social Interest* (London, 1938), p. 270: "Lamarck's view, which is more akin to our own [than that of Darwinism] gives us proofs of the creative energy that is inherent in every form of life. The universal fact of the creative evolution of all living things can teach us that a goal is appointed for the line of development in every species—the goal of perfection, of active adaptation to the cosmic demands."

technically purposeless, useless byproducts valuable as a sign of emotion, not as the preparation for an act. In the same way, except psychologically, not biologically, Freud showed that neurotics are beset by vestiges of their individual past. And, following out the phylogenetic analogy between the race and the individual, Freud described the individual as burdened also by psychological vestiges of the collective past. In *Moses and Monotheism* he wrote:

> In the history of the human species something happened similar to the events in the life of the individual. That is to say, mankind as a whole also passed through conflicts of a sexual-aggressive nature, which left permanent traces, but which were for the most part warded off and forgotten; later, after a long period of latency, they came to life again and created phenomena similar in structure and tendency to neurotic symptoms.[34]

The language here is big, and vague; and Freud did not become much more specific in describing the parallels. It is clear that he was interested not so much in our evolution from the past, individual and collective, as in the hazards of our reversion to it. If there are original traumas in group history as well as in the life of the individual, evolution supplies no safe distance from them. Thus Freud transformed the usually optimistic analogy of children and primitives into a grim disclosure of the power of the primitive in history and of childishness in the individual adult.

Because he understood the past as the direction of faith, it seemed to Freud that faith was a quality of one's relation to the past; or rather, of one's bondage to it. Yet, in his own way, he saw the necessity—and inevitability—of faith. Without faith—the "positive sign" of the transference—no cure is possible. The transference "clothes the physician with authority, transforms itself into faith in his findings and in his views." Neither "intellectual insight" nor "arguments" decide the outcome of the therapeutic struggle; faith is the decisive factor. And "faith repeats the history of its own origin; it is a derivative of love and at first it needed no arguments." [35] This says nothing for the historic religious faiths. On the contrary, pitting the basic mechanism of faith against the contents of the old faiths, Freud deplored the sense of dependence most people feel in regard to some higher being, as if they were still children living in a childish age. He found it "humiliating . . . to discover what a large number of those alive today, who must see that this religion is not tenable . . . try to defend it inch by inch, as if with a series of pitiful rearguard actions."[36]

Freud was not only concerned to describe the power of the past; he also hoped to prescribe a means of emancipation from it. Through his scientific myth of origins he hoped to be able to "specify the point in the mental development of mankind at which the advance from group psychology to individual psychology was achieved also by the individual members of the group."[37] Scientific myths, in contrast to religious myths, are designed to free individuals from their psychological thralldom to primal forms. Freud may have been alluding to Frazer's definition of myth as the earliest mode of scientific cognition, when somewhat facetiously he offered the scientific myth as a substitute for the prototype. "Does not every science," he asked Albert Einstein in 1932, "come in the end to a kind of mythology?"[38] But the mythology of science is radically different from other sorts. Modern scientific myths are not myths of transcendence but myths of revolt against transcendence. In Freud this revolt took curious form, as a critique of those archaic and instinctual images—the prototypes—around which our roles and perceptions of roles are organized.

IV

This heady conjectural account of social origins, these analogical encompassments of the great human leap forward into culture, turn our analysis back to the genesis of the prototypal method itself, and to some assumptions of the anthropology to which Freud was indebted.

One illuminating connection* is with Goethe. In the decade or so before 1800 Goethe was engrossed in the botanical studies out of which he formulated his theory of the metamorphosis of plants. Goethe posited a so-called ancestral plant (*Urpflanze*) which evolved into the multiformity of plants as now existing. This botanical conception, translated into psychology, describes Freud's conception of the prototype.† In Goethe's words: "With this pattern, and the key

*As Ludwig Binswanger, Fritz Wittels, and others have pointed out. See L. Binswanger, *Ausgewählte Vorträge und Aufsätze* (Bern, 1947).

†Goethe absorbed the general idea of the prototype from Diderot and Ribonet. It is worth stressing how many of the notions of Romanticism, and laterally of anthropology, originated in the French Enlightenment: not only the notion

thereto, one can still discover plants ad infinitum which must be consistent with the pattern; that is to say, they might exist even though they do not, and hence they are not merely poetic shadows and apparitions but have intrinsic truth and necessity. The same law is capable of application to all other living things." [39]

Goethe did not object when Schiller pointed out that such conceptions belong to the realm of ideas rather than of facts. The ancestral form does not appear to the sense, he replied, but to the mind. Here Goethe's theory of evolution contradicts both that of Lamarck and of Darwin. Goethe's is an idealistic morphology. No matter that there never was a first and unique instance of the plant, which then begot all other plants in all their varieties. The transformation by virtue of which the various parts of a plant—its sepals, petals, stamens, and so on—are differentiated from one primal organ, the leaf, is an ideal, not a real genesis.

As little as Goethe's *Urpflanze* was a real plant was the Freudian *Urmensch* a real person. The *Urmensch* was not a factual beginning; it is an expedient of scientific reflection and reduction. Criticism by anthropologists of Freud's ahistoric conception has been excessive, expressing, as it does, indignation at an idealism that anthropology itself has not completely abandoned, though it is hidden now behind all kinds of prefatory disclaimers. A more pertinent difficulty with psychoanalytic anthropology is that, unlike Goethe, who was less aggressive toward his imagination, Freud found the ideality of his constructs a handicap. In one place he does agree to call his account of primal events a "just-so story," intended "to lighten the darkness of prehistoric times." [40] But Darwin had professed those events as a factual beginning, and Freud could not resist the temptation to have it both ways. Elsewhere, in *Totem and Taboo,* he claimed that the murder of the primal father was a literal historical event.

This deficiency in facts is one that Freud shared with the whole of evolutionary social science, but particularly with nineteenth-century anthropology, which regularly substituted for historical documentation a logical history backward along the parallel lines or diffusional routes of cultural invention. We can better appreciate the dilemma of anthropological method by recalling that the science of man is

---

of the prototype but also the understanding of the world view of primitives as animistic. Cf. Ernst Cassirer, *The Philosophy of the Enlightenment* (Boston, 1955).

not young, nor is cultural diversity—its central problem—such a recently stated one. To go back no farther than the eighteenth century, anthropology was already flourishing then, under the significantly different name of "cosmography." In the eighteenth century cultural diversity was examined on a worldwide and history-wide scale. But in the nineteenth century, when the departmentalization of the social sciences came into being, the scope was radically curtailed. Cosmography became anthropology, withdrawing from the problem of total diversity to inspect more closely surviving primitive cultures.

This congruence of past with present feelings and social bonds allows the recovery of the nonliterate past by observing our contemporary primitives in jungle and nursery. Pre-literate and embryonically literate peoples, while offering a valuable perspective on humanity as a whole, are dangerous samples for the understanding of historic civilization. It was their history-less condition that frequently provoked anthropologists to a programmatic overvaluation of savage simplicities, and to the use of what Freud, exemplifying the practice in *Group Psychology,* called "scientific myths"[41] of the primal form of human relations. Thereby a set of events, regarded as unique and nonrecurrent, may be withdrawn from rational verification, and all subsequent (dated) history treated as repetitions of the conjectured prototype.

The appeal to conjectural history is older than Goethe and modern anthropology. In the study of language, for example, there have been particularly tenacious endeavors to discover an "original form" or "linguistic root" in the primordial past or, as in Leibniz' concept of a *lingua adamica,* in an ideal future language whose objectivity our cognition must progressively approach. But the error is particularly exposed in the social developmentalisms that flourished in the nineteenth century—the theory of descent from a common ancestry, which Freud borrowed from Darwin, being one of many instances. A method that may succeed in the natural sciences—though even one of these, geology, is said to be in historical difficulties—does not warrant confidence in the linear identities of past and present when appropriated by psychoanalysis.

Freud's appeal to a doctrine of uniformism accounts for a good part of his intellectual resistance to accelerations of historical change. Any object, event, or sequence of events can be fixed with a psychoanalytic center of gravity. The prototype or trauma may "cathect" with little regard for the context, because the object itself will stand for something else. But Freud's stress on the power of the past, while it does amount to a denial of social and historical changes in their own right, shows equally an extraordinary sensitivity on his part to the presence of prototypical motives, often in a vestigial and distorted form, in the artifacts of culture and the private art of dreams.

To detail Freud's affinities with nineteenth-century social science is not within the compass of this book. But at least one other giant of the period, Bachofen, deserves mention. What joins Freud's method to Bachofen's is their use of indirect sources in constructing conjectural history. Bachofen's notion of patriarchy as emerging from a prior matriarchal rule—which Freud rejected—is founded on a study of Aeschylus' *Oresteia*, especially the third play of the trilogy, the *Eumenides*. *King Lear* and *Faust*, Bachofen noted, show a similar "Aeschylus structure." One thinks immediately of Freud's penchant for finding the "Sophocles structure" in Ibsen, Dostoevski, Shakespeare, and practically every literary work he examined after he first translated *Oedipus Rex* as a Gymnasium student.

Bachofen's method of raiding archaeology, mythology, and poetry to discover "prehistory" has been essential to psychoanalysis in both its individual and its cultural applications. It is in myth and art that prototypes are extolled, and there Freud (like Bachofen) mined lodes that were rich in examples. By thus assimilating literary analysis to a theory of origins, Bachofen prepared the way for the elaborate and literary Freudian origins mythology.

V

Freud has no theory of gradual evolution from primal events. The earliest events stand isolated in the prehistory of individual and group, persisting unchanged alongside the latest.* Yet scarcely any-

*See *Civilization and Its Discontents*,[42] pp. 14–15: "In the realm of mind . . . the primitive type is so commonly preserved alongside the transformations which have developed out of it that it is superfluous to give instances in proof of it." Here a difference from Goethe should be noted. In Goethe's theory of the metamorphosis of plants, the ancestral leaf permutates as blossoms, filaments, and pistils, as calyx, seed, and fruit, the leaf disappearing except as a "form idea." In contrast, Freud saw in all psychological metamorphosis the reappearance of the basic form of the instincts themselves, always present as the indestructible factors in events.

thing that Freud discovered in the constitution of individual minds requires the Lamarckian hypothesis. For example, the existence of a dream symbolism uniform throughout different cultures is no reason for assuming that these symbols are "a fragment of extremely ancient inherited mental equipment." [43] First, dream symbols may not be as invariant as Freud supposed. Freud held that "the relation between a symbol and the idea symbolized is an invariable one," [44] but his own discussions provide many examples where the same symbol—for this dream, that dreamer—means different things. Second, while it is true, as Freud notes, that symbolism occurs "quite independently of direct communication and of the influence of education by example," symbols need not have been hereditarily transmitted. Freud claimed that the "ultimate meaning of the symbolic relation . . . is of a genetic character." This genetic link between sexuality and symbolism he found in a "former identity" of which the symbolism is a "relic and a mark." [45] Here Freud seems to have been following the example of Darwin. Darwin had reasoned (against the objections of Spencer) that languages arose as an adjunct of sexuality, specifically from the activity of calling the mate. Freud supported the view that "all primal words referred to sexual things" [46] and only subsequently lost their exclusively sexual significance. But we need not accept these conjectures to understand the facts of sexual symbolism. We can just as well suppose that the symbols testify to the presence of a general prerational, or unconscious, method of apprehending the peculiarity and connection of things—a method which each of us has at his command, though it is overlaid by the knowledge achieved by rational culture.*

If Freud's recourse to the convention of a prehistoric past may be considered a flaw in his individual psychology, it is equally so in his collective psychology. His chief contribution to the study of myth is his description of a *psychological* process out of which myth develops.† Yet Freud clings to a euhemerist explanation as well—the idea that all myths record historic events or figures (e.g., Moses, Jesus) that can eventually be traced back to an actual protomythic

*Georg Groddeck in his *Book of the It* (1922) early summarized the "naturalness" of symbols without historical surmise: "Symbols are not invented, they are there, and belong to the inalienable estate of man; indeed, one might say that all conscious thought and action are the unavoidable consequence of unconscious symbolization, that mankind is animated by the symbol" (pp. 43–44).

† Thus his account of the dream work as analogous to the folk work in myth, including such operations as "splitting," "multiplication," and "displacement."

person, the primal father, and a literal protomythic event, his murder by the sons. The same dual motif appears in his religious anthropology, where he holds both the psychological and euhemerist positions—that is, he maintains that monotheism was both original and historical. In *Moses and Monotheism* he tells us that the Aton religion is "the first case in the history of mankind, and perhaps the purest, of a monotheistic religion." But he also says that "when Moses gave to his people the conception of an Only God it was not an altogether new idea, for it meant the reanimation of a primeval experience in the human family that had long ago faded from the conscious memory of mankind." [47] All mankind lives in the shadow of the same primeval trauma. In consequence, there are specialized historical traumas—such as the murder of Moses.

A similar dualism emerges in Freud's reconstruction of the Moses story. From behind the historical Moses of the Jews, Freud draws the image of the personal Moses of his own private religion; the greatest Jew becomes marginal even to Jewry, having been born an Egyptian nobleman. The historical Moses emerges as a variation on the prototype of all founding fathers. An important source of Freud's reconstruction was the myth of infant exposure* as it appeared in the life stories of Moses, Cyrus, Romulus, Oedipus, Perseus, Hercules, and Christ. Because of its aptness for the myth, Freud's conjecture is that Moses did not die naturally but was killed by his adopted people, the Jews. Such reasonings on the basis of "psychological necessity" underlie his historical argument. This experiment in psychohistory remains novel and daring, but has accomplished little except to ruffle historians and offend some of Freud's fellow Jews.

VI

With Nietzsche, Freud proclaimed the master science of the future to be not history but psychology. History becomes *mass* psychology. For the historical phenomena of religion, "the only really satisfactory analogy," Freud thought, was to be found "in psychopathology, in the genesis of human neurosis; that is to say, in a discipline belonging to individual psychology, whereas religious phenomena must

* Cf. Otto Rank, *The Myth of the Birth of the Hero* (New York, 1952).

of course be regarded as a part of mass psychology." [48] Freud looked to find such an analogy to any historical phenomenon—any manifestations of mass psychology—in the mental life of an individual. The parallel relation between individual and group was "rather in the nature of an axiom." [49]

Freud applied the axiom to every kind of historical and individual experience. For example, anthropology was of use to him because he saw an analogy between the taboo customs of primitive groups and the compulsion neurosis of modern individuals. This analogy was supported by such parallels as that in both taboo and obsessional symptoms "the prohibitions lack any assignable motive," that both are "maintained by an internal necessity," that they are both "easily displaceable," and that they both "give rise to injunctions for the performance of ceremonial acts" which emancipate from the forbidden.[50]

A more subtle analogy is advanced in Freud's interpretation of the history of Judaism and Christianity. Between "the problem of the traumatic neurosis [the psychological event] and that of Jewish monotheism [the historical event]" he saw a complete series of correspondences. As individual neurosis is precipitated by a trauma, so Jewish monotheism begins with the traumatic event of the killing of Moses. Further, there is in common between traumatic neurosis and Jewish monotheism the feature Freud termed "latency." For the trauma is made dynamic by the latency period it must serve.* The

*Freud referred to a supposititious disjunction in primitive biological continuity, in order to explain the intervention of what he called a period of "latency" between childhood sexuality and the onset of mature sexuality at puberty. While Hall gave for this period the ages of eight to twelve, Freud included the years from five to twelve. (See, for example, *Moses and Monotheism*,[51] p. 118, where he discusses "the beginning twice over of sexual life," and *The Ego and the Id*,[52] p. 46.)

Hall interpreted most of the nonvolitional movements of infancy as rudimentary impulses to perform acts which must have been of importance in some prehuman stage of life. He understood children as rehearsing in adumbrated ways the social life of their ancestors—a conception which, although no longer directly influential, still finds echoes in the child psychology of Piaget, where even in play forms the evolution from primitive magical obedience to democratic consensus is supposed to be repeated. Accelerations and retardations in the rate of growth of individual children were read by Hall as traces of ancient fluctuations in the development of the race. Adolescence recapitulates some prehistoric period of storm and stress, while the characteristics of children from the ages of eight to twelve, Hall conjectures, represent the culmination of one stage of life—probably maturity—in some remote and perhaps pigmoid stage of racial evolution. For the most part, however, such biological and historical correspondences repression of Mosaic doctrine at the time of the killing of Moses (the traumatic crime that formed the Jewish character) is understood as "the latency period in the history of Jewish religion." [53] But collective repression does not, any less than individual repression, "disappear without leaving any trace." It lives on as a potential in the inherited biological structure of man, as "dormant tradition," [54] later coming to the surface again and creating the historical character of the Jews.

Freud's analogy between individual psychology and social history received its most famous development, however, in his theory of religion and obsessional neurosis. After *Totem and Taboo* (1912) Freud never doubted that the correct model for understanding religious experience was the neurotic symptoms of the individual. Obsessional neurosis is private religion, and religion is mass obsessional neurosis. The pious are the neurotics of another culture epoch. Penance is analogized to obsessional acts. Freud reports that his insights into the "origin of neurotic ceremonial" and into "the psychological processes" of religious ceremonial depend entirely upon the inferences his analogical method has emboldened him to draw about the latter from its resemblances to the former.[55] He required no other evidence, certainly not the study of cult or ritual in terms meaningful to the religious. Take, as an example, two actions: a nun tells her rosary, a neurotic counts the buttons on his shirt. Although the conscious intention and social contexts of course differ, the underlying psychological mechanism might be judged the same. Viewed in terms of their unconscious motivations, both nun and neurotic are engaged in compulsive or obsessional actions. While in older moral psychologies it is the act that transforms the compulsion, from the psychoanalytic view it is the compulsion that transforms the act. The manifest purpose of the nun's action is dimissed as superficial. Freud's method of analogy allows the observer to understand the psychological mechanism informing the nun's and the neurotic's action as identical. Thus piety is translated, all too easily, into neurosis.

Freud's analogical method often led him to an arbitrary selection of criteria, and to hidden shifts from one criterion (the psychological)

---

are ignored in Freud's writings. He preferred to state the analogy between primitive and child—and, further, between the sexual evolution of the mind and the evolution of culture—in more psychological terms. Cf. G. Stanley Hall, *Adolescence* (New York, 1905), Vol. I, pp. viii–x, xiii, 48, 160, 202, 215–16, 264, 356, 366; Vol. II, pp. 70 ff., 192–94, 212–19.

to another (the historical). However, it is important to notice not only the construction of the basic Freudian analogy but also the evaluative position that underlay that construction.

By this enticing analogy between individual neurotic behavior and that of whole social groups, and by the related reading of "primitive" motives into present actions, Freud suggests a way out of the inconclusiveness of historical study. History was conflated into symptom, its bewildering clutter arranged into grand sequences of progress and regress. Finally, the Freudian analysis permits an arbitrary devaluation of the social contexts within which given psychological processes operate. Events may be sifted into two layers: behind the ostensible variety of social acts (the manifest content) lies the more profound variety of latent psychological motive. What is definitive for the public and the social is the private and the pathological. All psychologistic social theories are dependent on such a translation of the public into the private.

Hegel announced just the opposite relation between the latent psychological and the manifest historical. If Freud hinged meanings on the private psychological motive, Hegel hinged them on the public historical context. Public contexts are autonomous and supreme as systems of social causation. Hegel decided that the world spirit has its own immanent purposes, to which private psychological constellations are secondary. The world spirit uses Napoleon's personality; Napoleon's personality does not use the world spirit. His own mode of considering personality, Hegel concluded, "excludes the so-called psychological view." [56]

Marx followed Hegel in his antipsychological orientation. Capitalism elicits certain personality types; personality types do not first elicit capitalism. It is impossible, in Marxist terms, to discover capitalist-personality types in primitive society. The capitalist personality is "personified capital." Marx would never have said capital was a "personification" of a certain character type, as Freudians view the parsimonious businessman as an elaboration of the "anal character." For Marx, "except as personified capital, the capitalist [as a personality] has no historical value, and no right to . . . historical existence." [57] As the stages of capitalist development evolve, so will the personality types evolve within that historical process. Thus an ascetic character structure is the psychological referent at one point, when abstinence is required by the objective process of capital accumulation. In later stages, "a conventional degree of prodigality" may be the historical demand placed upon the psychological material.

For both Hegel and Marx, psychological direction can be meaningful only when understood as a response elicited by the action-demand implicit in a given period of historical evolution. For both, in contrast to Freud, "nature" is merely a variable of the historical process, and therefore irrelevant as a motivational explanation of historical processes. Freud, however, has regular recourse to "nature" as the constant of social analysis. Historical processes, according to Marx, are characterized by change. But, for Freud, the more things change the more they remain the same. Society, as a psychological process, is what it has always been. Freud the social theorist, so far as he was identical with Freud the natural scientist, showed the traditional positivist eagerness to eliminate the challenge of history by finding lawfulness in nature. As a positivist, Freud managed to reduce time to a developmental sequence in which man, by virtue of his rational adaptability, can always be what he ought to be—his appropriate self. Individual history recapitulates racial history, and each historic stage is proper to man's developmental situation.

The popularity of psychoanalysis, in an age suffering vertigo from the acceleration of historical events, may be partly ascribed to Freud's rehabilitation of the constant nature underlying history. Among the educated, and more especially the educated adolescents, now so thoroughly persuaded of the naturalness of their needs, the rejection of both Christianity and Marxism testifies to the general disappointment with all constructions subordinating nature to history. It is in this sense that the sociologist Karl Mannheim understood both Christianity and Marxism as utopian doctrines. Indeed, Mannheim awarded Marxism the honor of having been the last utopianism of Western culture,* before the sociogenetic analysis of sociology and psychoanalysis together closed off the future to all illusions.

VII

History, to the late nineteenth century, was the specter that haunted European culture, the spirit in which all things had to be explained. Twentieth-century psychological ethics has seen through the camouflage of historical argument. For Freud, psychological

*Cf. *Ideology and Utopia* (New York, 1936).

knowledge was the only necessary data; history was not evidence but exemplification, as in theological argument. Indeed, Freudianism's interpretative habits are similar to those of religious historiography, with its one tremendous period of which all else that is good or bad are exemplifications, and this is perhaps an element of its appeal to those in quest of a religiosity that will at the same time debunk all revelations. However different, Jacobins and Communists are both radicals, and radicals can be considered as "radical personality types" before they are considered as Frenchmen or Germans, ancients or moderns, of this party or that. The situations studied by the Freudian natural historian are thus recurrent. That the repetitions are not exact but proximate—Hitler is, after all, not Christ, though both share the common psychological function of being "father images"—is due to disguises put on by nature to cover the identity of its repetitions. But the psychological functions remain the same.*

Freud did not distinguish human purpose from natural development. History did not begin with civilization, with self-consciousness; prehistory was by far the most significant of any historical process, Freud implied in *Totem and Taboo.* Every case history was really a prehistory, from the point of view of the consciousness of the patient.

For the very reason that Hegel thought Africa no proper subject for the historian, Freud would consider it most proper. The eruption of Vesuvius was as natural to Freud as the eruption of the unconscious in a political revolution. A historical event was at the same time a natural one, a challenge to which the personality, like any organism, tried to offer the response of conformity. What was given in time past became thereafter pregnant with future. Every pathogenic experience implied an earlier one, the later one "endowed"

*As another example of the repetition of psychological roles in widely different historical and ethical circumstances, see Freud's analysis, in a letter to Thomas Mann (Nov. 29, 1936), of Napoleon as a figure modeled after the Biblical Joseph. Napoleon had an elder brother named Joseph whom the young Napoleon hated intensely. He later identified himself with Joseph and this hatred changed into an intense love, his hostility toward other innocent persons being simultaneously displaced. Napoleon also loved his mother very much and tried to take the place of his father in caring for the siblings. He married a young widow named "Josephine" and was never able to turn against her even though she treated him badly. The Egyptian expedition may have expressed a desire for the realization of the Joseph fantasy which was later fulfilled in Europe: "He takes care of the brothers by raising them to princes and kings. The good-for-nothing Jerome is perhaps his Benjamin" (*Int. Zeitschrift für Psychoanalyse und Imago,* Vol. XXVI [1941], pp. 217–20).

with the earlier's pathogenic qualities, however inappropriate these qualities were to the present. For Marx, the past is pregnant with the future, with the proletariat as the midwife of history. For Freud, the future is pregnant with the past, a burden of which only the physician, and luck, can deliver us.

Thus, in Freud, change becomes constancy, history nature, development repetition. It is not simply that psychoanalysis can explain nothing current without referring to something past. All theories of organic causation agree to so much. Psychoanalysis adds that not all the incidents of the past, whether of individuals or groups, persist; not all past events are equivalent. For Freud, the past that lives, that is so difficult to expunge, is that which is farthest from the present. It is the "remoteness of time" that is the "really decisive factor." [58] A certain event, or events, necessarily in remote rather than recent history—indeed, at the beginning—becomes determinative of all that follows. The sickness of the present lies in the determination of origins to reassert themselves. But the persistence of the past in the present also gives the present its multiple levels of meaning, and psychology its depth.

Freud took development for granted. That children become adults, that the lower becomes higher, the simple complex, the unknown known—such optimistic commonplaces he shunned. His desire was always to find, in emergence, sameness; in the dynamic, the static; in the present, latent pasts. The analogy between individual and society was one way of stabilizing the evolutionary scheme, by viewing it structurally. Through the conception of the prototype he read the same permanence into temporal relations. Given Freud's disrespect for history, the therapist is granted a vast interpretative latitude. Although the material of therapy appears successively (as the patient relates it in the analytic sessions), and can be plotted along the lines of the patient's own life history, Freud's concern is to develop modes of transposing events and attitudes, to make them conform with his essential fiction of the timeless unconscious. The unlimited harvest of memories, associations, and symbols are to be collated *thematically,* independent of their time sequence. Freud practices the same liberty in his social analysis. For instance, as we have seen, he linked religious phenomena not merely to unique historical events but, analogically, to perennial family emotions—like the Oedipus complex—whose form persists even through changes of social context.

Of course, Freud's attitude is not all of a piece. By pointing out in both individual and society the immutable strife of the instincts and the ineffaceable influence of past events, he proclaimed the repetitiveness of human life and the constancy of nature-history. On the other hand, by analogizing society to the individual, who plainly does mature and change, Freud presumed the evolution of society. In one attitude, implemented by the method of analogy, time is a unilinear, unidirectional line of progress. In the other, exemplified by the conception of the prototype, time is unchanging. The symbolic relation of feminine to masculine, the images of the circle and the ascending line, the moods of pessimism and optimism—these express Freud's basic attitudes and embody his rich contradictions.

If any one of these attitudes prevailed over any other, it was pessimism. Through psychiatric treatment an individual can mature and acquire a permanent overlay of rationality; but it remains doubtful that society as a whole progresses or, if it does, that the achievements of progress can be maintained. Freud's primary image is horizontal and conservative. He saw equally at work in nature "two kinds of processes . . . operating in contrary directions, one constructive or assimilatory and the other destructive or dissimilatory." [59] But he found no consolation in this "oscillating rhythm," this eternal recurrence. As there was no progress in nature, there could be nothing new in history—humans are still killers, and war is part of the circular movement of social development. Analogously, "the experiences of the first five years of childhood exert a decisive influence on our life [and] resist all efforts of more mature years to modify them." [60]

Even the one hope, the primacy of intellect, was intimately derived from the "death instinct"; here the positivist evolutionist coincided with the Romantic conservative. The straight line of evolution, if drawn far enough, ends in the same place as the circle of origins. Freud's evolutionary history is as unfree as his idea of nature-history. Ethically the two aspects of the Freudian method (analogy and prototype) end in identity: both constructs are doctrines of fatalism. I have said that Freud was a Romantic conservative; perhaps the essential fact that united Romantic conservatives across the eighteenth century and into the nineteenth was that they did not fancy revolutions. Revolution could only repeat the prototypal rebellion against the father, and in every case, like it, be doomed to failure.

This is not to say that Freud venerated the past. A certain type of past, however, did attract him—not the ages of order so much as the ages of heroes; Greeks, not Latins or Catholics; Semites, not Jews. In collaboration with William C. Bullitt, Freud wrote a psychography of Woodrow Wilson, but his interest was not in contemporaries, heroic or not. More often he uses heroic figures of the antique past (such as Moses and Hannibal) to illustrate his values and doctrine. Indeed, for Freud, to view the present as autonomous would be an illusion. It would be to "experience the present naïvely, so to speak, without being able to estimate its content." [61]

Freud's well-known pessimism as a social theorist must be seen in terms of his conception of time as repetition. No future is open, no past closed. Anticipating the failure of the future to be anything except a past yet to reassert itself, Freud shares in the great gibe of all anti-utopians; not "I told you so!" but, more quietly, "I could have told you so." All observable presents point to the past. Memory is a temptation, offering greater delights than the present. There is no permanent relief either in succumbing to the temptation or in subduing it. Catharsis can only be transitory. The lot of rational humans is to face up to the comfortless world as it was, is, and will be.

This is not, of course, to disavow the prophetic element in Freud's teaching. Rather, the prophet compounded the Stoic. Both prophet and Stoic have as their chief duty the maintenance of self-identity in the face of permanent crisis. The Stoic function of Freud's crisis psychology is the day-to-day maintenance of self-identity. This maintenance function of depth psychology takes on special moral import in a culture where man is considered an actor of roles rather than an enactor of either soul or instinct.

Freud's orientation was in another way close to the prophetic. The function of a crisis psychology, as of prophets, is to heighten the sense of threat and fear in the face of losses of self-identity, and to offer a control: hope, as the psychic state supplied by adhering to tradition, with the prophet as instructor. Freud, in this sense, was on the side of tradition. For him the past constituted the most dynamic part of the present. Tradition was never remote, but continually in the process of reasserting itself. He sought to remind people of it, and of its importance.

But Freud's prophetic temper must not be labored too far. To be a prophet is to assert that there is no way out of tradition, not to try systematically to circumvent it. Freud's end, processionally and valuationally, was to outwit tradition for the sake of a personality type unknown to history thus far, the psychological man—man emancipated by rational analysis from commitments to the prototypal past. Because tradition and the repressions have failed him, psychological man must now admit that he can be all things to himself, as well as to all other men. His identity is for him to choose; none can choose him, as in the days of living gods and imposing fathers.

PLAY AND ACTUALITY

ERIK H. ERIKSON

I

I welcome the opportunity to turn once more to the play of children—an infinite resource of what is potential in man. I will begin with a discussion of a certain form of child's play and then turn to related phenomena throughout the course of life, reflecting throughout on what has been said in these symposia.

In the last few years Peggy Penn, Joan Erikson, and I have begun to collect play constructions of four- and five-year-old children of different backgrounds and in different settings, in a metropolitan school and in rural districts, in this country and abroad. Peggy Penn acts as the play hostess, inviting the children, one at a time, to leave their play group and to come to a room where a low table and a set of blocks and toys await them. Sitting on the floor with them, she asks each child to "build something" and to "tell a story" about it. Joan Erikson occupies a corner and records what is going on, while I, on occasion, replace her or (where the available space permits) sit in the background watching.

It is a common experience, and yet always astounding, that all but the most inhibited children go at such a task with a peculiar eagerness. I have described this in a number of clinical and research settings: after a brief period of orientation when the child may draw the observer into conversation, handle some toys exploratively, or scan the possibilities of the set of toys provided, there follows an absorption in the selection of toys, in the placement of blocks, and in the grouping of dolls, which soon seems to follow some imperative theme and some firm sense of style until the construction is suddenly declared finished. At that moment, there is often an expression on the child's face which seems to say that *this* is *it*—and it is good.[1] And if you have enough data on a given child's life you recognize the astonishing fact that one child after another will use a few toys and ten to twenty minutes' time to let some disturbing fact of his life, or some life task, become the basis for a performance characterized by a unique style of representation. A number of play constructions done by the same child over a period of time show an impressive variation as well as a continuity of themes. And if I ever doubted that such continuity is a witness of unifying trends close to the core of a person's development, I learned better when quite recently I had an opportunity to compare the play constructions done in the manner just described thirty years ago by children in their early teens with the dominant themes in their subsequent lives.* History, of course, assigned unexpected roles to many of these persons who are now in their early forties; and yet many of these constructions decades later can be clearly seen as a condensed statement of a theme dominant in a person's destiny.

In studying such specimens, such condensed bits of life, the observer is loath to fit them into the theories to which he and others at different times and under other conditions have subordinated related phenomena. True, the themes presented betray some repetitiveness such as we recognize as the "working through" of a *traumatic* experience: but they also express a playful *renewal.* If they seem to be governed by some need to *communicate,* or even to *confess,* they certainly also seem to serve the joy of *self-expression.* If they seem dedicated to the *exercise* of growing faculties, they also seem to serve the *mastery* of a complex life situation. As I would not settle for any one of these explanations alone, I would not wish to do without any one of them.

Declaring that he is an "interactionist," Piaget has said: "What interests me is the creation of new things that are not preformed, nor predetermined by nervous system maturation alone, and not predetermined by the nature of the encounters with the environ-

*As recorded in the Child Guidance Study of the Institute of Human Development of the University of California.

ment, but are constructed within the individual himself." Piaget concluded by suggesting a liberating methodology in all teaching. "Children," he said, "should be able to do their own experimenting and their own research." Such experimenting, however (as I felt strongly when watching Bärbel Inhelder in Geneva induce children to be experimental), relies on some playfulness and, in fact, on an interplay of the child's inner resources with the nature of the task and the suggestiveness of interviewers who are "game." "In order for a child to understand something," Piaget concluded, "he must *construct it himself*, he must *reinvent* it."

Piaget, of course, spoke of cognitive gains. But let me suggest in passing that such play procedures as the one described may well facilitate in a child an impulse to recapitulate and, as it were, to reinvent his own experience in order to learn where it might lead. If there is something to this, then we may entertain the dim hope that some such play procedure may become an adjunct to early education rather than remain a method in the service of the clinic or of research only.

But what seems to be the *function of playfulness* in the children's responses both to Piaget's cognitive challenge and to our expressive one? The most general answer necessarily points to a quality of all things alive, namely the restoration and creation of a *leeway of mastery* in a set of developments or circumstances. The German language has a word for it: *Spielraum,* which is not conveyed in a literal translation such as "playroom." The word connotes something common also for the "play" of mechanical things, namely *free movement* within *prescribed limits.* This at least establishes the boundaries of the phenomenon: where the freedom is gone, *or* the limits, play ends. Such a polarity also seems to adhere to the linguistic origins of the word "play," which connotes both carefree oscillation and a quality of being engaged, committed. Language, furthermore, conveys any number of destructive and self-destructive nuances such as playing *at* something or *with* somebody, or playing oneself *out:* all these and other kinds of play connote the limits which end all play.

But if I should now make the first of a number of comparative leaps and ask where I would look for the closest analogy to our play constructions in adult life, I would point to the dramatist's job. If, in a child's life, the classroom and the home setting are an early equivalent of the sphere of adult actuality with its interplay of persons and institutions, then his solitary construction is the infantile model of the playwright's work: he too condenses into scenes of unitary place and time, marked by a "set" and populated by a cast, the tragic (and comic) dilemma of representative individuals caught in the role conflicts of their time.

II

Before turning to the sphere of human playfulness in later life, let me touch on some of its fundamentals in man's ontogenetic beginnings. Here I can point to René Spitz's discussion of "basic education." He, who has given us classical studies of the tragic consequences of a restriction of sensory *Spielraum* in early childhood, now has returned to specify what that deprivation consists of. He tells us that it is the gift of *vision* which first serves to integrate the "unconnected discrete stimulations" of taste, audition, smell, and touch. To him, the maternal person, visually comprehended, is both the earliest environment and the earliest educator, who "enables the child—all other things being equal—to achieve the capacity to learn." She seems to do so by truly letting her face shine upon the newborn's searching eyes, and by letting herself be thus verified as one "totality." I would prefer to speak of wholeness rather than of totality, in order to indicate the very special Gestalt quality of that visual integration which permits the infant to extend what I have called his *autosphere,* and to include the inclined human face and the maternal presence in it. As Joan Erikson puts it in her essay "Eye to Eye"[2]: "We began life with this relatedness to eyes. . . . It is with the eyes that (maternal) concern and love are communicated, and distance and anger as well. Growing maturity does not alter this eye-centeredness, for all through life our visual intercourse with others is eye-focused: the eye that blesses and curses."

Spitz now ascribes to organized vision the role of a first ego nucleus, anchored "in a special sector of man's central nervous system, which permits a first integration of experience." It will be obvious that a certain playfulness must endow visual scanning and rescanning, which leads to significant interplay as it is responded to by the mother with playful encouragement. This, in turn, confirms a sense of mutuality in both partners. It is such *interplay,* I would believe, which is the prime facilitator of that "ego nucleus."

If these matters are reminiscent of religious images such as the inclined face of the Madonna and the aura of her oneness with the Christ child, I also believe that the phenomena which René Spitz (and Joan Erikson) refer to *are* the ontogenetic basis of faith, a fact which remains both elemental and fateful in man's whole development. Let me illustrate this theme with an example from art history.

In our seminar on Life History and History at Harvard, Professor Helmut Wohl enlarged on some autobiographic notes left by Michelangelo. The great sculptor right after birth had been given a wet nurse because his mother was too sick to take care of him. To farm an infant out to wet nurses was, it seems, not atypical in the lives of men and women of that time. The "other woman" in Michelangelo's case was the daughter and wife of stonemasons; and his first environment, being adjacent to a stone quarry in Settignano, must have had an inescapable auditory quality. At any rate, Michelangelo acknowledged that while his mother had given him life itself, the wet nurse ("perhaps joking or perhaps in earnest") gave him "delight in the chisel, for it is well known that nurse's milk has such power in us . . . by changing the temperature of the body."[3] That chisel eventually (and under the protectorate of a fatherly patron, Lorenzo de' Medici) became for him the executive tool of his very identity. When he created young David, Michelangelo equated "David with the sling" and "I with the chisel."[4]

But if Michelangelo had two mothers, he, alas, lost both early. He was separated from the wet nurse when he returned to his mother, and then his mother died when he was six years old. Wohl presented to us the sequence of Madonna images that Michelangelo sketched, painted, or sculptured, the first in his late teens and the last in his late eighties. His Madonnas always show a marked distance between mother and child, beyond the Renaissance theme of the willful boy Jesus straining away from his mother's arms: here the Madonna herself is looking away from her child, her eyes remaining inward, distant and almost sightless. Only the very last of Michelangelo's preserved sketches of the Madonna portrays, in Wohl's word, a neatly "conflictless" image of mother and child. The Madonna holds the child close to her face and he turns to her fully, attempting to embrace her with his small arms. So it took the closeness of death for Michelangelo to recover what he had lost early in life, and one cannot help connecting this, the old man's refound hope, with Saint Paul's saying, "For now we see through a glass, darkly; but then face to face: now I know in part; but then shall I know even as also I am known." [5]

This, of course, would seem to be only a subsidiary theme in Michelangelo's gigantic confrontations. He not only hammered away at his strangely tortured sculptures, sovereignly transcended by irate Moses; he also painted his own vision of Adam and the Creator and of Christ at the Last Judgment in the Sistine Chapel. In a sonnet, he describes how, at the crippling expense of his whole physique, he gazed up at the ceiling, lifting arm and brush: "my beard toward Heaven, I feel the back of my brain upon my neck." [6] But whether or not a mighty compensatory force intensified Michelangelo's creative furor, we may well pause to wonder at the very fact of the singular fascination which these artistically created visual worlds painted on hallowed halls hold for us. Could all this be ontologically related to the singular importance of that playfully structured visual field in the beginnings of childhood?

As we proceed, I will refer to other visualized spheres endowed with a special aura. I already have mentioned the theater. The dictionary says that the root of the word is *thea*, a sight, which, in turn, is related to *thauma*, that which compels the gaze. Maybe the "legitimate" theater is only a special case, a condensed version of all the imagined, depicted, and theorized spheres (yes, there is *thea* in *theory* too) by which we attempt to create coherencies and continuities in the complexity and affectivity of existence.* And we will not forget that the late Bertram Lewin spoke of a "dream screen" on which we experience our nightly visions.

*I owe to Gerald Holton a number of suggestive references to Einstein's meditations on the nature of his mathematical inspiration. It is said that Einstein was not yet able to speak when he was three years old. He preferred communing with building blocks and jigsaw pieces. Later (in 1945) he wrote to Jacques Hadamard: "Taken from a psychological viewpoint, this combinatory play seems to be the essential feature in productive thought—before there is any connection with logical construction in words or other kinds of signs which can be communicated to others." [7] And, again: "Man seeks to form for himself, in whatever manner is suitable for him, a simplified and lucid image of the world (*Bild der Welt*), and so to overcome the world of experience by striving to replace it to some extent by this image. That is what the painter does, and the poet, the speculative philosopher, the natural scientist, each in his own way. Into this image and its formation he places the center of gravity of his emotional life, in order to attain the peace and serenity that he cannot find within the narrow confines of swirling personal experience." [8]

III

But I must now ask a theoretical and terminological question. If, as we are apt to say, the maternal caretaker is the first "object" playfully engaged by the scanning eyes, who are the "objects" in later stages, up to Saint Paul's finite recognition? Are they, as some of us would be all too ready to say, "mother substitutes"?

First a word about the term "object." Within a theory of cognition it makes sense to speak of object constancy as the goal of the newborn child's gradual comprehension of the coherence and the continuity of what he perceives. It makes sense within a theory of sexual energy called libido to speak of a growing capacity to "cathex" the image of a comprehensively perceived person and thus to become able to love. And it makes sense to describe with clinical shorthand as "object loss" the various deficiencies or regressions which make it impossible for a person to maintain either a cognitive sense of another person's wholeness or the capacity to wholly love and accept the love of other persons. All this describes the conditions for, but neither explains nor guarantees, that interplay by which the growing person and those attending him are capable of maintaining and expanding the mutuality of "basic education." *

Today, I think we would agree on three points. Cognitively seen, the first *object wholeness* experienced by the infant must somehow coincide with the first *subject wholeness.* This means that the coherence and the continuity of the object world is a condition for the coherence and continuity of the "I" as observer. This joint sense

*The questioning of terms easily becomes part of a wider concern about conceptual habituation. What we have now heard of the importance of vision must make us wonder to what extent the "classical" psychoanalytic technique itself may have helped to shape some of our concepts. For if vision is, indeed, the basic organizer of the sensory universe and if the beholding of one person's face by another is the first basis of a sense of mutuality, then the classical psychoanalytic treatment situation is an exquisite deprivation experiment. It may be the genius of this clinical invention that it systematically provokes the patient's "free" verbal associations at the expense of a visual word, which, in turn, invites the rushing in of old images seeking a healing mutuality with the therapist. But sooner or later every field must become aware of the extent to which its principal procedure codetermines the assumed nature of the observed and the terms decreed most appropriate to conceptualize that nature.

of being both subject and object becomes the root of a sense of identity.

Secondly, if for its very "basic education" the child depended on a mothering supported by a family and a community, so will it, all through life, depend on *equivalents* (and not on *substitutes*) of the constituents of that early mutuality. I would emphatically agree with Peter Wolff that on each stage of development a child is "identified by the totality of operations he is capable of"; and I would conclude that the early mother's equivalent in each later stage must always be the sum of all the persons and institutions which are significant for his wholeness in an expanding arena of interplay. As the radius of physical reach and of cognitive comprehension, of libidinal attachment and of responsible action—as all these expand, there will, of course, always be persons who are substitutes for the original mother. But that, as we know, can be a hindrance as well as a help, unless they themselves become part of that wider sphere of interaction which is essential for the increasing scope of what once was basic education. In a five-year-old's play construction we saw reflected, in addition to impulses, fantasies and familial themes, the teacher and the school environment in the widest sense of an encounter with what can be learned. But so will, in adolescence, the peer generation and the ideological universe become part of the arena which is the equivalent of the early mother. In adulthood the work world and all the institutions which comprise the procreative and productive actuality are part of the arena within which a person must have scope and leeway or suffer severely in his ego-functioning. Thus on each step what had been "in part" will now be recognized and interacted with in its wholeness, even as the person comes to feel recognized as an actor with a circumscribed identity within a life plan. In fact, unless his gifts and his society have on each step provided the adult with a semblance of an arena of free interplay, no man can hope to reach the potential maturity of (presenile) old age when, indeed, only the wholeness of existence bounded by death can, on occasion, dimly recall to him the quality of that earliest sensory matrix.

IV

What we so far have vaguely called interplay can be made more specific by linking it with the problem of ritualization which was discussed on the last occasion when Konrad Lorenz and I served together on a symposium.[9] His subject then was the ontogeny of ritualization in animals, and mine that in man. Julian Huxley, the chairman of that symposium, had years ago described as ritualization in animals such instinctive performances as the exuberant greeting ceremonials of bird couples, who, after a lengthy separation, must reassure each other that they belong not only to the same species but also to the same nest. This is a "bonding" procedure which, Huxley suggested, functions so as to *exclude ambiguity* and to facilitate unimpaired *instinctive* interplay. Lorenz, in turn, concentrated on the ritualizations by which some animals of the same species given to fighting matches make peace before they seriously harm each other. It was my task to point to the ontogeny of analogous phenomena in man. But with us, so I suggested, ritualization also has the burden of *overcoming ambivalence* in situations which have strong *instinctual* components (that is, drives not limited to "natural" survival), as is true for all important encounters in man's life. Thus the ontologically earliest ritualizations in man, the greeting of mother and baby, adds to the minimum facial stimulation required to attract a baby's fascination (and eventually his smile) such motions, sounds, words, and smells as are characteristic of the culture, the class, and the family as well as of the mothering person.

Konrad Lorenz, the foster mother of the goose child Martina, has rightly gained fame for his ability to greet animals as well as humans in a bonding manner. Lorenz describes the lost-and-found game which in German is called guck-guck da-da and in English peek-a-boo. Let me call all these and similar phenomena in man *ritualized interplay*. This extends from the simplest habitual interaction to elaborate games, and, finally, to ornate rituals.* Today when so many ritualizations so rapidly lose their convincing power, it is especially important to remember that in this whole area of ritualized interplay the most horrible dread can live right next to the most reassuring playfulness. Little Martina was running and falling all over herself for dear survival when she pursued Konrad Lorenz, and any accidental interruption of the ritualized behavior by which

*It specifically excludes, of course, the symptomatic "rituals" of isolated neurotics, as well as all derisive uses of the word "ritualization" as synonymous with repetitiveness and rigidification. All these, in fact, connote symptoms of deritualizations in our sense.

animals do away with ambiguity can lead to murder. As to man, we need only to visualize again small children who cannot smile, or old persons who have lost all faith, to comprehend both the singular power and the vulnerability of ritualized reassurance in the human situation.

Yet, what constitutes or what limits playful ritualization in man is as hard to define as play itself: maybe such phenomena as playfulness or youthfulness or aliveness are defined by the very fact that they cannot be wholly defined. There is a reconciliation of the irreconcilable in all ritualizations, from the meeting of lovers to all manner of get-togethers, in which there is a sense of choice and ease and yet also one of driving necessity: of a highly personalized and yet also a traditional pattern; of improvisation in all formalization; of surprise in the very reassurance of familiarity; and of some leeway for innovation in what must be repeated over and over again. Only these and other polarities assure that *mutual fusion* of the participants and yet also a simultaneous *gain in distinctiveness* for each.

Before moving on to adolescence, let me stop, in passing, to recount an experience which illustrates the relevance of all this for the school age. We recently visited a Head Start school in Mississippi, in an area where sniping night riders and arson were then still expectable occurrences whenever blacks consolidated a new kind of community life with outside help. As visitors, we were called upon to concentrate on how and by whom the children were taught and what they were learning. But we were equally struck by how these people had ritualized both "school" and "learning." With our academic eyes it was, in fact, not quite easy to know to what extent they were playing at being a school or actually were one. Obviously the arrangements for learning and singing together, but also those for eating and conversing, constituted new roles under new conditions: to grow into the spirit of these roles seemed to be the heart of the matter. This, then, was ritualized interplay in the making; and only the whole milieu, the whole combination of building and equipment and of teaching mothers and of motherly teachers, of learning children and of helpful fathers and neighbors were a collective guarantee of the survival of what was being learned—whether, at this beginning, it was much or little. We could not help thinking of other schools, more easily certified on the basis of grim accomplishment, where much is learned by inexorable method but often with little spirit. And yet, the final assimilation of what has been learned would always seem to depend on any "school's" cultural coherence with a growing environment.

The life of all schooling depends on all this; but so does the fate of the children who soon will enter the stage of adolescence—the stage when the young themselves must begin to offer each other traditional ritualizations in the form of spontaneous improvisations and of games—and this often on the borderline of what adults would consider the license of youth: will they then have learned to be playful and to anticipate some leeway of personal and social development?

V

Children cannot be said or judged to be "acting" in a systematic and irreversible way, even though they may, on occasion, display a sense of responsibility and a comprehension of adult responsibility which astonishes us. Young people, on the other hand (as we realize in our time more than ever before), are apt to continue to play and to play-act in ways which may suddenly prove to have been irreversible action—even action of a kind which endangers safety, violates legality, and, all too often, forfeits the actor's future. And, in recent years, youth closer to adulthood has begun on a large scale to usurp responsibility and even revolutionary status in the arena of public action. This has resulted in lasting consequences even where the action itself may not have been much more than a dare or a prank on a stage of imagined power. Never before, then, has it been more important to understand what is happening in that wide area where juvenile play-acting and historical action meet.

The return in adolescence of childlike and childish behavior in the midst of an increasing anticipation of and participation in adulthood has been treated in innumerable textbooks. They point to the impulsivity of sexual maturation and of the power of the aggressive equipment and yet also to the vastly expanded cognitive horizon. There is the intensity of peer-group involvement at all costs, a search for inspiration (now often forfeited to drugs), and yet also the desperate need (yes, an ego need) for an ideologically unified universe sanctioned by leaders who would make both freedom and discipline meaningful. To all this, I have added the discussion of identity—and of fidelity. In my book such postadolescent "virtue" is meant to represent a minimum evolutionary requirement rather than a maximized ideal.* Actually the formulation of such successive virtues was intended to follow the clinical formula of our lamented friend Donald Hargreaves: "What is the normal survival function of the process here disturbed?" In other words, I have emphasized fidelity because I think I have observed the fateful deficit in ego-strength resulting from the absence of such commitments as would permit youth to anchor its readiness for loyalty in social reality; and the equally fateful deficit in meaningful social interplay resulting from a state of society in which old fidelities are being eroded. I would, therefore, follow Konrad Lorenz in asserting that all through man's sociogenetic development, rites and rituals have attempted to attract and to invest that fidelity. Where and when both generations can participate in them with affective and cognitive commitment, these rites, indeed, are performing "functions analogous to those which the mechanisms of inheritance perform in the preservation of the species." Today, as we all agree, a deep and worldwide disturbance exists in this central area of ritualized interplay between the generations.

But let me again take recourse in an observation which every reader can match with variations from his own experience. A few years ago I was invited to attend a confrontation between the trustees and the students of a great university which, months before, had been one of the first to undergo what for a while became obligatory crises on a number of campuses: occupation of the administration's citadel and "liberation" of captive documents; brutally effective police intervention followed by a rapidly spreading student strike; a confused arousal of the faculty; and finally a widespread bewilderment and depression on the part of almost all concerned, including the most learned and the most politically adept minds.

At this meeting there were old and wealthy men, the trustees; there were learned men and guests like me; there were some students (however selected); and there were specialists in group meetings who lent a certain technical expertise to what could have been a natural mixture of reticence and spontaneous confrontation. After

*I must repeat this in view of such well-meant pictorial presentations of my stages of life as that of the Sunday *Times* of New York, where the successive virtues were posed by models who, indeed, look "virtuous" in a class-determined and even racist way: blond and blue-eyed, healthy and well kempt, and obviously brought up on mental health food.

a few days of plenary speeches and more or less strained small group discussions, the students decided to present their case in their own way and to confront the trustees with an improvisation. The setting was a kind of amphitheater. One young man with long blond hair played a leading part; he had the words "Jesus Saves" printed in strong colors on his sweatshirt. He exhorted the elders to "give in gracefully" to certain nonnegotiable demands. Another young man, having embraced the first in brotherliness, took him by the arm and led him, one by one, before some of the men of the Establishment. Pointing to the flaming motto on his friend's sweatshirt, he asked these men whether the inscription meant anything to them—and what had they done recently for their neighbors? Now, there are probably few groups of men who (in the light of their community's standards of charity) have done more for their "neighbors," both openly or privately, than have some trustees of our colleges. But, of course, the students had intended to confront them with their sins against the university's actual neighbors in the poor housing areas surrounding the campus and owned by the university. And they made it clear that they did not expect answers other than confessions of guilt. The old men, in turn, tried desperately to understand, because that was what they had come for. The situation became extremely tense, some students themselves (as they said later) beginning to feel like "freaks." Some faculty and some visitors began to show bitter annoyance.

A scene such as this leaves the viewer in doubt as to whether he is witnessing a theatrical improvisation, a mocking demonstration, or, indeed, an act of religious ritualization. To me, it was all of this, and I said so: there were ceremonial fragments assembled in a manner half mocking and half deadly serious, flaunting as well as protesting such themes as brotherly love, charity, and sacrifice. But what had kept the performance from coming off was a failure of ethical nerve: the students had, with total righteousness, demanded that everyone should admit his sins except themselves, thus using Jesus to mock the elders; a mere turnabout of punitiveness, however, could never lead to a meaningful covenant.

I saw in this act (even/and) just where it failed, a combination of themes for which our time must find new forms, whether or not the leaders and organizers of such events consciously intend such renewal. The students, in fact, had succeeded (at the price of taking chances with their own credibility) to elucidate an overweening problem: they had played with a ritual fire which youth alone cannot possibly contain in a new universal form, and which in changing times can emerge only from a joint adulthood willing to take chances with new roles and that means: to play where it counts.

VI

Let me now turn to a historical example. One of the most noteworthy revolutionary ritualizations of recent times has been the founding of the Black Panther Party—noteworthy in our context as an illustration of youthful political imagination on the very border of disaster. Such ritualization can go to the core of history, whether it "succeeds" or not: it is successful if it makes an unforgettable point and if it has the flexibility to go on from there.

Much of the Panthers' history has happened in the dark of the ghetto as well as in that legal twilight which confuses and scares the "law-abiding." Yet, there is no denial of a certain genius in the translation of values which Huey P. Newton (he was twenty-two years old at the time) and Bobby Seale displayed when they cast themselves and other young blacks in totally new roles, and this at a time when black youth in this country needed new images of dignity and of heroism. The fact that this new image included gun-carrying in public seemed revolting to many, while it is, in fact, a traditional historical stance in formerly exploited and belittled minorities: the autonomous man with his own gun, a man ready to use it both as a symbol and as a weapon for the defense of his and his people's dignity—this stance has been true of the first American revolutionaries as well as in the radically different contexts of the modern Jews and the Diaspora,* and the erstwhile British Indians, all youths whom successful revolutions are apt to forget. Sometimes, there is a book involved as well as a gun: a book which testifies both to tradition and to the power of literacy. In Newton's case, it was a lawbook such as that found on the street on the night in Oakland when a policeman (himself only twenty-three years old) lost his life in a scuffle never clearly reconstructed. Newton survived and prevailed through years of solitary confinement with a healthy body

*Eldridge Cleaver at one time acknowledged this parallel by saying that "psychologically" black people in America had "precisely the same outlook" as Eastern European Jews had under Theodor Herzl (*New Outlook,* December 1970).

and with undaunted stature. The image he created was based on the usurpation of the black American of the oldest right of all (other) Americans (a right engraved on the imaginations of our young and the young abroad by way of Western movies), namely to bear arms in the creation of a semblance of legality in an area not yet defined in its traditionalities.

Originally young Newton not only insisted on the traditional legality of the arming of citizens, but also attempted to sanction it with a new uniform and a discipline which, I think, even Gandhi might have acknowledged (if with some sadness) as a necessary step toward a nonviolent approach—necessary for the simple reason that he who would not know how to use a gun both well and with restraint would not know how and when not to use it. But Newton, in addition to protesting dramatically the negative identity of his own people as the meek and helpless victims of the lynch law and its daily ramifications, established as the enemy of his people the very uniformed men who had become to them representatives of a lawless law employed to protect usurped privilege rather than legality and to punish powerlessness as much as illegality. Thus he attempted to turn the very image of the protectors of such law into a negative identity, namely that of victimizers of the poor. The Black Panthers, then, are of interest precisely because, according to Newton's intent, this original "violence" was to be contained in a new code of discipline.

Revolutionary activity, however, is always beset with the dilemma of defining who and what is the law, and what disruptive act, when, and where, is political rather than criminal. There may be also the proud and mocking creation of a new "species," as attested to by the very party name, which, in the case of the Panthers, is that of an animal said to be ferocious primarily in defense, and the relentless and publicist verbal weapon of calling men of the "legitimate" police force "pigs." Such debasement of the opponent is a moral violence which not only arouses murderous hate in the defamed, but can also become a retrogressive stance in the defamer. In the American black, of course, such defamation is grounded more than in any other social group, both in a common history of daily and total defenselessness (or what Newton refers to as the "truly oppressed") and in an explosive folk language long the only outlet for inturned aggression—and in fact used with mocking as well as murderous abandon against other blacks. The original imagery of the young leaders of the Black Panther movement (and I am talking about these origins of the movement and not about the tedious stance of its propagandistic habituation) surely contained, therefore, the possibility of creating a new set of roles, which often may have appeared to be all too grandiosely staged, but which did link past and future by recapitulating historical images in a radically new setting. True, certain titles of command seemed rather florid in the absence of an assured body of followers; but it must be remembered that revolutionary language—at total risk to itself—always challenges history to confirm what has already been claimed as certain. This is, of course, compounded where the revolutionaries are young, for youth and revolution both play with that theater of action where personal conversion and radical rejuvenation confirm each other, to the point where history's agreement is taken for granted. And sometimes history assents. Our black revolutionaries differ from others in that they are not rebelling against a father generation. Their symbol of the Establishment is "the man"; yet, both examples given remind us to look for the adult counterplayers in attempted ritualizations demanding new kinds of generational transfer. And there we often find glaring vacancies in the cast required for the fulfillment of the script—vacancies impossible to fill by excitable police or by uncomfortable judges.

VII

This is the "gap," then; Konrad Lorenz would convince us that it exists not only because of a combination of historical and technological changes, but because of a misdevelopment of evolutionary proportions. He reminds us of the pseudo-tribal character of much of the present-day rebellion; and to him the widespread and truly "bizarre distortions of cultural behavior" represent a new "infantilism" and a regression to a primitivity which he considers analogous to a "disturbance of the genetic blueprint." Looking at revolutionary youth from the point of view of an evolutionary ethologist, apparently he feels that humanity has reached a critical point when the changes in social norms necessary within the period between generations have begun to "exceed the capacity of the pubertal adapting mechanisms."

Lorenz introduces into the discussion a term which I used at the London symposium where I drew attention to the phenomenon of cultural *pseudo-speciation*—meaning the tendency of human groups to behave as if they were *the* chosen species. Lorenz discusses the matter vividly:

> In itself, it is a perfectly normal process and even a desirable one. . . . there is, however, a very serious negative side to it: pseudo-speciation is the cause of war. . . . If the divergence of cultural development has gone far enough, it inevitably leads to the horrible consequence that one group does not regard the other as quite human. In many primitive languages, the name of the tribe is synonymous with that of man—and from this point of view it is not really cannibalism if you eat the fallen warriors of the hostile tribe! Pseudo-speciation suppresses the instinctive mechanisms normally preventing the killing of fellow members of the species while, diabolically, it does not inhibit intra-specific aggression in the least.

Before coming to the implications of pseudo-speciation for youth and adulthood, however, let me ask what importance it may have for the problem of play. In the animal world, obviously the play of the young is linked with the adaptation of the species to a section of the natural environment. The play of the human child, however, must orient him within the possibilities and the boundaries first of what is imaginable and possible, and then to what is most effective and most permissible in a cultural setting. One of the playing child's tasks, then, is to try out some role pretensions within what he gradually learns is his society's version of reality and to become himself within the roles and techniques at his disposal. No wonder, then, that man's play takes place on the border of dangerous alternatives and is always beset both with burdening conflicts and with liberating choices.

At the same time, however, human play as well as adult ritualizations and rituals seem to serve the function of adaptation to the "pseudo" aspects of human "reality": for, as I will point out in some detail later, man, in addition to making gigantic strides in learning to know nature and the uses it can be put to, has yet also striven to maintain prejudged assumptions concerning the ordained excellence of particular versions of man. Thus, his playful imagination does not only serve all that is and could be, it also is forced to endow that which, so he is clearly taught, must be if he is to be judged sane and worthy. Youthful rebellion always attempts to create new leeway for new and potential roles in such assumed realities; but the very condition of pseudo-speciation has made man's playfulness a matter both of freedom and of bondage, both of enhanced life and of multiplied death.

I have attempted to illustrate the way in which youthful play-acting and the assumption or usurpation of historical roles can border on each other. But we must now account for the fact that new ritualizations are, indeed, apt to miscarry because of the "horrible fact that the hate which the young bear us is tribal hate." And, indeed, it seems that the shift in the overall ecological and technological conditions of mankind has led, at least within the orbit of the American industrial world culture (which includes the World War II enemies of the United States), to a new grouping of pseudo-species: on one side all the young people across the borders of former empires and on the other the whole "old" generation.

It is obvious enough that the young reject, above all, the insignia and the attitudes which have marked their victimization and heroification as soldiers serving one of the pseudo-species extant now. Because they carry this protest literally on the sleeve, we can now add to the subjects to be reviewed the ritual importance of human *display,* for we are reminded of the prominence, in all of classical warfare, of the resplendent uniforms, topped by animal plumage, which was intended to unite and divide the young men of the world into warriors serving either the right and godly or the wrong and evil species: that the display of physical insignia signifying human pseudo-speciation imitates those of animal speciation is only too obvious. And it begins to make sense that the rebellious youth of today is displaying, instead, an impressive array of self-contradicting insignia, often mocking all uniformity by mixing fragments of military uniforms (and even of flags) with the ornaments of relaxed brotherhood. For youth attempts to create not only new arenas for involvements and commitments, but also such new types of heroes as are essential to the emergence of a whole "human being" representative of mankind itself—if and when the old have abrogated their pseudo-species, or have been destroyed. In the meantime, youth often seems to feel that it can enforce basic changes only by mockingly insisting on a moratorium without end and an unlimited arena of its own, and it is often only with drugs that it can aver the remaining boundaries and simulate a free territory within. This is a state of affairs open to all kinds of group retrogressions as well as personal regressions.* But then, adolescent regressions always have been, to some

*In a paper on dissent, I have offered a topology of such semideliberate retrogression, relating them to the stages of life and thus indicating both their potentially prophetic and their potentially dangerous significance for the individuals involved.[10]

extent, semideliberate recapitulations of childhood fantasy serving the adaptive purpose of reviving what infantile playfulness was sacrificed to the established order for use on new ideological frontiers. Similarly, large-scale historical retrogressions often seem to be semideliberate attempts to invoke the revolutions of the past in the name of a future revolution as yet neither defined nor localized nor fixed in time. But the extremes noted here may be necessary aspects of a shift, the outcome of which can be appraised only when it will be clear where such playful trends combine with the discipline and the competence necessary for sustained change.

If one accepts the theory of a shift from the pseudo-species mentality to an all-human one (and this is the hopeful aspect on which Konrad Lorenz and I would agree), one may well see in the radical display of youth an upheaval necessary for an elemental regrouping which transvaluates past ideals of excellence and heroism in the service of a more universal speciation. To be sure, much horrible hate and much resultant paralysis is thus transferred to the intergenerational struggle where it appears to be hopelessly raw and untrained in comparison to the age-old stance and stamina of uniformed and disciplined military behavior. This probably is the cause of occasional enactments of totally "senseless" cruelty and of dramatic murder for the sake of a vindictive illusion of extinguishing the established.

But we may well remind ourselves of two momentous developments characteristic of the other, the adult side of playing history. The first is the fact that adult man, with the help of the most creative expansion of scientific and organizational leeway (remember Einstein's playfulness), has created a world technically ready to eliminate mankind in one instant for the sake of one nation or another that cannot stop playing empire. Is it any wonder that some of the most romantic and the most destructive behavior in modern youth seems to mock us by anticipating the day when the nuclear holocaust *has* occurred?

The second fact is the disintegration of paternalistic dominance, both in familial relations and in the "minds of man." For this again we blame primarily the antipaternal attitude of the young. Following Freud, we have obediently persisted in referring to the origins of the rebellious complex in childhood as the Oedipus complex. But we have thus immortalized as inescapable only the behavior of the son Oedipus, who unknowingly slew his father as the oracle had predicted, while we have paid little attention to the fact that this father had such faith in the oracle's opaque announcement and in his own interpretation of it that he was willing to dispose of his son. But maybe Laius did only more openly and more dramatically what may be implicit in circumcisions, puberty rites, and "confirmations" of many kinds. As a prize for certified adulthood, the fathers all limit and forestall some frightening potentialities of development dangerous to "the system." And they all strive to appropriate the new individual for the pseudo-species, marking and branding him as potentially dangerous, initiating him into the prescribed limits of activities, inducting him into a preferred service, and preparing him for being sacrificed in holy wars. Maybe they only underscore ritually what human development and the structure of human society accomplish anyway. For after having played at a variety of choices, most adults submit to so-called reality—that is, a consolidation of established facts, of acquired methods, of defined roles, and of overweening values. Such consolidation is deemed necessary not only for a style of acting and interacting, but, above all, for the bringing up of the next generation of children. They, it is hoped, will, from their childhood play and their juvenile role experimentation, move right into the dominant means of production and will invest their playfulness and their search for identity in the daily necessity to work for the higher glory of the pseudo-species.

Today, Laius and Oedipus face one another in a different confrontation. For even as the youth of divergent countries begin to look, talk, and feel alike—and this whether they are rebelling against industrial civilization or are, in fact, rapidly learning the prerequisite skills—so does the older generation appear to become more and more alike and stereotyped. For they impersonate a new and universal type, the efficient member of an organized occupation or a profession, playing free and equal while being at the mercy of mass-produced roles, of standardized consumership, and of rampant bureaucratization. But all these are developments which, in fact, take the play out of work—and this not (or not only) because of a Calvinistic choice to separate the two for the sake of righteousness, but because it can't be helped. And this seems to be the message of much of the mockery of the young, that if there must be defined roles, it may be better to go on playing at choosing them than to become their ready puppets.

VIII

A concluding section on play in adulthood can only be an opening section for another, a future essay. For here we enter both the twilight of what is called "reality" and the ambiguities of the word "play"—and these two assuredly are related to each other. Even as man protests the pure truth just because he is the animal who can lie—and pretend to be natural—so he strives to be in tune with hard reality just because he so easily falls for illusions and abstractions. And both truth and reality are at issue when man must define what he means when he says he is playing—or not playing.

The poet has it that man is never more human than when he plays. But what must he do and be, and in what context, to be both adult and playful: must he do something in which he feels again as if he were a playing child, or a youth in a game? Must he step outside of his most serious and most fateful concerns? Or must he transcend his everyday condition and be "beside himself" in fantasy, ecstasy, or "togetherness"?

Maybe an epigenetic view makes it unnecessary to categorize so sharply. The adult once was a child and a youth. He will never be either again: but neither will he ever be without the heritage of those former states. In fact, I would postulate that, in order to be truly adult, he must on each level renew some of the playfulness of childhood and some of the sportiveness of the young. As we have seen, the child in his play and games as well as the young person in his pranks and sports and forays into politics, protected as they both are, up to a point, from having their play-acting "count" as irreversible action, nevertheless are dealing with central concerns both of settling the past and of anticipating the future. So must the adult, beyond playful and sportive activities specified as such, remain playful in the center of his concerns and concerned with opportunities to renew and increase the leeway and scope of his and his fellow man's activities. Whatever the precursors of a specifically adult playfulness, it must grow with and through the adult stages even as these stages can come about only by such renewal. But here we are faced with a threefold dilemma: the adult's marked inner separation (repression and all) from much of his childhood; the limitations of adolescent identity development in terms of available roles; and a certain intrinsic intolerance in adult institutions to the renewal of the identity crisis. Adult institutions want to ban the turmoil of youth even as they want to banish the thought of decline and death. This leaves adulthood in a position of double defensiveness and with a need to bolster the boundaries of what to a given generation of adults seems "real."

"Creative" people know this, and the poet Frost said it. In an encounter with two tramps who see him chopping away at some wood and remind him of the fateful division of work and play, he intones:

> But yield who will to their separation
> My object in living is to unite
> My avocation and my vocation
> As my two eyes make one in sight.
> Only where love and need are one,
> And the play is work for mortal stakes,
> Is the deed ever really done
> For heaven and the future's sakes.[11]

We may for the moment ignore the fact that the men thus addressed were looking for work; we know that one man's play and work may be another's unemployment. But taking Frost's creativity as a measure, we may add to his formulation the postulate that the adult, in combining vocation and avocation, creates leeway for himself while creating leeway for those within his scope of mutuality.

At the beginning of this essay, I compared a child's solitary play construction with the function of a dramatic performance in adulthood: in both, a theme and a conflict, dominant in the "big" world, are meaningfully condensed into a microsphere and into a spectacle and a speculum, a mirror of inner and outer conditions. (The stage play is a tragedy, where a representative person is shown as one who can envisage greater freedom for his time and age but finds that he has forfeited it for lack of inner and outer *Spielraum*.) The dimly lit theater thus deals with the reflection in individual fate of all those areas of public action which occur in "all the world," in the light of day. But if man, as pointed out, calls these spheres "theaters," "spectacles," and "scenarios," one wonders sometimes which is metaphorical for what. For man endows such spheres of highest reality, too, with a ceremonial and procedural aura which permits him to get engaged with a certain abandon, with intensified loyalty, and often with increased energy and efficiency, but also with a definite sacrifice of plain good judgment. Some of these special spheres are endowed with rituals in superreal halls, be they cathedrals, courts, or castles. But their hypnotic power as a visionary sphere transcends all locality and institutionalization: we may think here of the monarchy or the presidency, of the law courts or the seats of government: all these, while denoting an obligation of superhuman excellence, are also apt to cover, with everybody's connivance, a multitude of contradictions and pretenses accepted as the "rules of the game." Any observing visitor to a legislative chamber or a chief executive's mansion will not escape an occasional eerie sense of unreality in such factories of decision which must determine irreversible shifts in what will seem compellingly real to so many, and in what to generations to come will seem worth living, dying, and killing for—remember the Iron Curtain! Most fateful for mankind as a species (we cannot say this too often) is the tendency to redivide the political scene in such a way that those "on the other side" suddenly appear to be changed in quality, reduced to statistical items and worthy only of "body counts." However, the aura of some (if not all) of these spheres is being diminished in our very time by the production through the media of new spheres of vision, with their strange interplay of service, truth, and business. Some such spheres, as the "national scene," or the "forum of public opinion," or the "arena of politics," are also being studied in their major dimensions by social science; but we know as yet little about their dynamic influences on personality, on identity, and, indeed, on sanity—either in individuals or in cliques, in organized groups or in the masses. The fact is that such phenomena, in turn, can only be studied by "fields" of approach and "schools" of thought and by theoretical systems which themselves fascinate by their ability to organize appearances and to make visible the factual truth. But science, at least, perseveres in an inbuilt critique of science itself as well as of the scientist; and this in terms increasingly accessible to all "species" of men. If factuality is the soul of all search for reality, then mankind is on the way to agreeing to a joint reality; and if truth can emerge only from an all-human actuality, all men may, someday soon, be "in touch" with each other.

I am suggesting for a future occasion, then, that we take a new good look not only at those occasions when adults claim that they are playing like children, or play-acting on the legitimate stage, but also other occasions when they insist with deadly righteousness that they are playing for "real" stakes and yet, sooner or later, appear to have been role-playing puppets in imaginary spheres of "necessity."

If at the beginning of this paper I made a "leap" from play construction to theater, let me now make one back from adult reality to infancy. Could it not be that all these spheres have a place in adult man's life equivalent to that visual sphere which in the very first year of life provides, all at once, an integrated sensory universe, a mutuality with a maternal person, and a beginning of inner order, and thus provides the basic leeway for growth, action, and interaction? I do not wish to overdo this: in adulthood such visualized spheres obviously overlap with concrete areas of established power and organized technique which have their own rationale of continuity and growth. Yet they all share in that quality of vision which not only renders experience vastly more comprehendible, but also provides man with collective and individual affirmations of an emotional kind. And, indeed, the vision is often attended to by some kind of goddess (made visible as Nike in graceful flight, or Freedom baring her breast to the storm of revolution, "blind" Justice, or somber and selfless Truth, not to speak of "smiling" Success) which, indeed, gives recognition in turn for having been recognized. These visions, it must be repeated, can bring out the best in man as they encourage, with a greater leeway, courage and solidarity, imagination and invention. The human tragedy has been and is that the highest of these goddesses are overshadowed by the demands of the pseudo-species, which eventually employs even the most heroic deeds and the most sincere gains in knowledge, for the exploitation and enslavement, the denigration and annihilation, or, at any rate, the checkmating of other "kinds" of men. As any visual order must always discriminate as well as abstract, it is hard for man not to make himself more real and his world more comprehensible without envisaging others as expendable or nonexistent—even eight hundred million Chinese behind a bamboo curtain.

IX

And then there are the great adults who are adult and are called great precisely because their sense of identity vastly surpasses the roles foisted upon them, their vision opens up new realities, and their gift of communication revitalizes actuality. In freeing themselves from rigidities and inhibitions they create new freedoms for some oppressed categories of men, find a new leeway for suppressed energies, and give new scope to followers who, in turn, feel more adult for being sanctioned and encouraged. The great, we say, are "gifted" with genius; but, of course, they often must destroy too, and will seem evil to those whom they endanger, or whom they exclude.

Freud, in freeing the neurotics of his repressed era from the onus of degeneracy, invented a method of playful communication called "free association" which has taught man (way beyond the clinical setting) to play back and forth between what is most conscious to him and what has remained unverbalized or become repressed. And he has taught man to give freer play to fantasies and impulses which, if not realized in sexual foreplay or "sublimated" in actuality, help only to narrow his *Spielraum* to the point of explosions in symptomatic actions.

But as Freud "took morality for granted," he also treated adulthood and reality as matters on which all enlightened man would agree. Yet, I think, he made the point that only when man has faced his neurotic isolation and stagnation is he free to let his imagination and his sense of truth come up against the existential dilemmas which transcend passing realities.

Marx, it is interesting to recall, spoke of a *coming* adulthood of the species. At the celebration of Marx's 150th birthday in Trier, Robert Tucker pointed out that "self-realization, or becoming fully human, was not for Marx a problem that an individual person could solve on his own. It could only be solved within the framework of the self-realization of the species at the end of history." [12] Marx referred to history both as an *Entfremdungsgeschichte* that made of man an alienated creature and as a *growth process of the human race,* an *Entstehungsakt:* only a kind of rebirth could overcome the submersion of the aesthetic production "according to the laws of beauty" and the deadening of all playfulness by unfree labor. Tucker suggested that we may today well be in a final "maturation crisis." "If so," he added, "the most serious aspect of the crisis is the . . . tendency of most people and even the leaders of nations to assume that no great change is called for, that we immature humans are already grown up."

Now, a few years later, it is obvious that this awareness, while maybe not yet accessible to "most people" and their leaders, has spread at least to the point where the young people deny that the older ones have grown up. In fact, there is a pervasive suspicion of the whole idea of growing up; and there is also an increased awareness of history, which among other things teaches that the revolutionary leeway gained yesterday can become the obsession and the suppression of today, and this for reasons immanent in greatness itself as well as in adulthood itself. If great men inspire vast changes with a creative playfulness both driven and (necessarily) destructive, their followers must consolidate change, which means to take the risk out of it. Neither the task of a Marxian critique of unconscious "historical" motivation nor the Freudian one of an inner enslavement to the immaturity both of impulse and of conscience can be said to be accomplished in any foreseeable future.

But the method of yesterday can also become part of a wider consciousness today. Psychoanalysis can go about defining its own place in history and yet continue to observe its traditional subject matter, namely the symptoms of repressions and suppressions—including their denial. It can study successive re-repressions in relation to historical change: there can be little doubt but that our enlightened age has set out to prove Freud wrong by doing openly and with a vengeance what he said were secret desires, warded off by inhibitions. We can learn to find out how we have contributed to such developments by our exclusive reliance (also culturally and historically determined) on the "dominance of the intellect" which often made the acceptance of psychoanalytic theory and vocabulary the measure of a man's adaptation. We know now (and the study of play confirms us in this) that the comprehension of Freud's *Wirklichkeit* must go beyond one of its meanings, namely reality, and include that of actuality.[13] For if reality is the structure of facts consensually agreed upon in a given stage of knowledge, actuality is the leeway created by new forms of interplay. Without actuality, reality becomes a prison of stereotypy, while actuality always must retest reality to remain truly playful. To fully understand this we must study for each stage of life the interpenetration of the cognitive and the affective as well as the moral and the instinctual. We may then realize that in adulthood an individual gains leeway for himself, as he creates it for others: here is the soul of adult play.

In conclusion, we must take note of another "gap" in our civilization which only partly coincides with the generational one. It is that between a grim determination to play out established and divisive roles, functions, and competencies to their bitter ends and, on the other hand, new kinds of group life characterized by a total playfulness, which simulates vast imagination (often drug-induced), sexual and sensual freedom, and a verbal openness often way beyond the integrative means of individuals, not to speak of technological and economic realities. In the first area, that of habituated pragmatism, leading individuals make a grim effort at pretending that they are in full command of the facts and by no means role-playing—a claim which in fact gives them a vanishing credibility. The playful crowd, on the other hand, often seem to play all too hard at playing and at pretending that they are already sharing a common humanity, bypassing those technical and political developments which must provide the material basis for "one world." But man is a tricky animal; and adults playing all too hard at role-playing or at simulating naturalness, honesty, and intimacy may end up being everybody and yet nobody, in touch with all and yet not close to anybody.

Yet, there are also signs that man may indeed be getting ready to renounce his claims on the ancient prerogatives of special pseudospecies, such as the abuse of others and the waste of resources in the environment and in inner life. Psychoanalysis, at this juncture, must remain vigilant in regard to the anxieties and rages aroused where a wider identity will endanger existing styles of instinctuality and identity and traditional visions of morality and reality.

But we must always also be receptive to new forms of interplay; and we must always come back to the children and learn to recognize the signs of unknown resources which might yet flourish in the vision of one mankind on one earth and its outer reaches.

THE MILLS: FATHER AND SON

BRUCE MAZLISH

One of the great pedagogic sagas of all time is the education of John Stuart by his father, James Mill. Even those who have not actually read John Stuart's *Autobiography* have heard how he learned to read Greek at three and prattled in Latin at eight. At the latter age, he tells us, he had read "a number of Greek prose authors, among whom I remember the whole of Herodotus, and of Xenophon's Cyropaedia and Memorials of Socrates; some of the lives of the philosophers by Diogenes Laertius; part of Lucian, and Isocrates' ad Demonicum and ad Nicoclem. I also read, in 1813, the first six dialogues (in the common arrangement) of Plato, from the Euthyphron to the Theaetetus inclusive: which last dialogue, I venture to think, would have been better omitted, as it was totally impossible I should understand it." So, too, by twelve, having worked through arithmetic, and having read through much of history and literature, he was given a rigorous training by his father in logic and political economy (Ricardo's principles were expounded to John Stuart during his father's early morning walks!). With such an education—or possibly in spite of it—the child prodigy became the eminent Victorian sage and social theorist, writing imperishable books on logic, political economy, and, of course, the classic *On Liberty*. If ever a man seemed the successful product of a careful and caring education, designed to produce the epitome of the rational man, it is John Stuart Mill. And credit for this achievement must go to his father, James

Mill, who, famous in his own time, has slipped into obscurity today partly as a result of standing in the shadow of the son whom he educated so successfully.

There is another way, however, of looking at the Mills. It places less emphasis on the "rational" and more on the "irrational" aspects of the relationship. It takes the chapter in John Stuart's *Autobiography* called "A Crisis in My Mental History" and attempts to understand it at least as much as an emotional crisis. Seen in this light, the "Crisis" becomes the dramatic moment in a father–son relationship whose elements come increasingly to dominate the existence and consciousness of modern man. By the end of the nineteenth century, where Marx had talked of class conflict as central to historical evolution, Freud spoke of Oedipal conflict. Now generational change was made to stand at the heart of social change.

Before Freud, of course, there had been father–son conflicts. In slowly changing societies, however, where sons merely replaced in the fullness of time their more powerful and knowing fathers, the revolts tended to fizzle out into filial submission. With the coming of the age of revolutions—both industrial and political—fathers were often no longer perceived as figures of authority but rather as anachronistic elders to be *displaced* rather than *replaced*. A glance at Turgenev's *Fathers and Sons* tells us what happened. Freud merely put into "scientific" language what was present and growing in the Western literary consciousness. His real achievement was to show that generational strife was rooted in the unconscious.

With this insight, Freud could then say:

> The freeing of an individual, as he grows up, from the authority of his parents is one of the most necessary though one of the most painful results brought about by the course of his development. It is quite essential that that liberation should occur and it may be presumed that it has been to some extent achieved by everyone who has reached a normal state. *Indeed, the whole progress of society rests upon the opposition between successive generations* [my italics].

Later, Freud added:

> In the second half of childhood a change sets in in the boy's relation to his father . . . He finds that his father is no longer the mightiest, wisest and richest of beings; he grows dissatisfied with him, he learns to criticize him and to estimate his place in society; and then, as a rule, he makes him pay heavily for the disappointment that has been caused by him. Everything that is hopeful, as well as everything that is un-

welcome, in the new generation is determined by this detachment from the father.

This last statement is rather sweeping, but to our present generation, racked as it is by a revolt of the young, it carries a good deal of conviction. We seem to be paying "heavily" for the "disappointment" of sons in their fathers (and mothers). Thus, a reexamination of the father–son relationship of the Mills might have a topical appeal that it lacked, say, a generation ago. There is a nice irony, too, in looking at the Mills with the aid of Freudian insight. It was Freud who translated the twelfth volume of John Stuart Mill's collected works into German, a volume composed of essays on the labor question, socialism, Plato, and the enfranchisement of women. Apropos of the last essay (which, in fact, many commentators presume to have been written by Harriet, with John Stuart merely rewriting, or editing, it) Freud remarked: ". . . the relationship between the sexes. That is altogether a point with Mill where one simply cannot find him human. His autobiography is so prudish or so ethereal that one could never gather from it that human beings consist of men and women and that this distinction is the most significant one that exists."

If we are to evaluate Freud's harsh judgment, we need to look for ourselves at the Mills, father as well as son. We might pause for a moment, however, to examine a part of the social setting for this generational relationship. In the early nineteenth century (John Stuart was born in 1806), population was growing by leaps and bounds; France, for example, went from twenty million in 1750 to twenty-nine million in 1820: a one-third growth. Much of this increase was attributable to a decline in infant mortality (though there was also a prolongation of adult life, especially in the childbearing years). One obvious result was a large increase in the number of young people (and in their political activism—one need only think of Mazzini's Young Italy). Thus, it is estimated that in France in 1789 the ratio of youths of fifteen to twenty-nine to persons thirty years and over was almost 61 percent (compared with 38 percent in 1964!). In Great Britain, when John Stuart was himself thirty-four, the percentage was 77 percent (which declined in 1965 to about 37 percent).

While it is true that children matured more slowly in the early and middle nineteenth century than they do today—the menarcheal age of girls is estimated to have been between sixteen and seventeen then, as compared to around thirteen now (largely due to diet)—it is obvious that so many young people were bound to constitute a potentially explosive force. If we remember that these young people were competing in a society in which the industrial and political revolutions had opened up new avenues of social mobility and career opportunities, we can see the possibilities. Yet two factors held the potential rebellion in harness. One was open migration to underdeveloped areas, which drained off many of the most energetic and rebellious youths; the other was the relatively heavy hand of traditional and paternal authority. In the nineteenth century, then, the real fight had just begun, marked by what was still a heavy heart on the part of the young. It is with this in mind that we might profitably examine John Stuart's relationship with his father, James.

Besides Greek and Latin, what did James Mill give his son? Initially, he provided him with a perfect model of the "mightiest, wisest" being in the world; only in young manhood did John Stuart come to acknowledge the flaws. Even then he was still under his father's spell to such an extent that he claimed, "In the power of influencing by mere force of mind and character, the convictions and purposes of others . . . he left, as far as my knowledge extends, no equal among men . . ." As a renowned author in his sixties, John Stuart still felt "acutely sensible of my own inferiority" in these matters.

Well he might, for the father who spent four or five hours a day coaching the son in his lessons was, indeed, a powerful figure of a self-made man. James Mill had been born the son of poor parents in Scotland, his mother originally being a servant girl and his father a shoemaker. Spurred on by his mother, who was ambitious for him, helped by the parish minister, who recognized his natural talents, James Mill had the good fortune to come to the attention of the leading local gentry family, the Stuarts. Indeed, it was only the fortunate intervention of Sir John Stuart, as his patron, that lifted James from obscurity, eventually sent him at the Stuarts' expense to the University of Edinburgh, and ultimately provided him with the means to get to London. Once in London, James Mill struck out on his own as a journalist and writer. He worked enormously hard, and his unusual abilities brought their reward: by the time his first son, John Stuart, was twelve years old, James Mill had become decently rich, famous, and powerful. He never told his son about his humble Scottish origins, and John Stuart grew up, it seems, under the impression that his father had sprung fully formed from his own loins.

The father might appear self-made, but it was clear to the son that he, John Stuart, had been "made" by his father. Alas, it was also clear to the boy that the father had had poor material with which to work. In an early draft of his *Autobiography* John Stuart gave way to his feelings:

> I was utterly unobservant: I was, *as my father continually told me,* like a person who had not the organs of sense . . . My father was the extreme opposite in all these particulars: his senses and his mental faculties were always on the alert . . . both as a boy and as a youth *I was incessantly smarting* under his severe admonitions on the subject. He could not endure stupidity, nor feeble and lax habits . . . and I was perpetually exciting his *anger* by manifestations of them. *From the earliest time I can remember* he used to reproach me, and most truly, with a general habit of inattention; owing to which, he said, I was constantly acquiring bad habits, and never breaking myself of them; was constantly forgetting what I ought to remember, and judging and acting like a person devoid of common sense; and which would make me, he said, *grow up a mere oddity,* looked down upon by everybody, and unfit for all the common purposes of life [my italics].

It is not a pretty picture. Rationally, the education was splendid; emotionally, it was debilitating. On one hand, the father showered extraordinary attention on the boy, calculated to appeal to his narcissistic tendencies. On the other, he mercilessly disparaged him, even to the point of mocking and caricaturing his reading of sentences. In one way the father offered a splendid picture of a self-made man with whom John Stuart could proudly identify. In another way James Mill made his son feel a failure—who had also failed his father—without any hope of growing up to be *like* his father. James Mill's basic problem appears to have involved the typical threat to the self-made man: the need to accept his own desire to be passive and dependent, to be given to and taken care of, as in the case of a helpless child. (The threat is that the source of supply may disappear; as the psychoanalyst Otto Fenichel puts it, "the fear that the external means of satisfaction might possibly fail to arrive. It is the 'fear over loss of love' or rather loss of help and protection.") John Stuart's problem was quite different: a desperate need to assert his autonomy, without losing a grip on his earlier life and training.

Now, the extraordinary thing is that in his early years John Stuart did not blame his father. Rather, he seems to have transferred his negative feelings to his mother. In this he was led by his father. Three years after his arrival in London James Mill married Harriet Burrow in a love match; she was higher in the social scale than he, and she brought him a small dowry. A year or two later, however, and shortly after the birth of John Stuart, James seems to have fallen out of love with his wife (not that this prevented him from having eight more children by her; children, it is interesting to note, who were initially taught by John and who were then expected to teach the next in age beneath them). She was a stupid *Hausfrau*, he now complained, and on her he let loose the irritability that he so carefully controlled in public.

John Stuart, himself disparaged by his father, identified with the father's disparagement of the mother. He did this to such an extent that in the published *Autobiography* he never *once* mentions his mother. Instead, he announces proudly: "I was born in London, on the 20th of May, 1806, and was the eldest son of James Mill, the author of the History of British India." Only in the draft of the *Autobiography* did John Stuart belie this new version of a miraculous conception and pen a paragraph about his mother (deleted in the published version). Admitting that his father was unloving and unloved by his children, John Stuart shifts the blame to the mother.

> A really warm-hearted mother [he explains] would in the first place have made my father a totally different being and in the second have made the children grow up loving and loved. But my mother with the very best of intentions only knew how to pass her life in drudging for them. . . . I thus grew up in the absence of love and in the presence of fear, and many and indelible are the effects of this bringing-up in the stunting of my moral growth.

At this point it is necessary to state that impartial outside observers did not all share John Stuart and his father's view of Mrs. Mill.

One curious aftermath is that while James Mill was a tyrant toward his own wife, and carried this into the political arena by denying women the right to vote, his son, sharing the attitude toward the mother, became a leading advocate of women's rights. The psychodynamics are too complicated for us to unravel here, but we can guess that they are crucial. They are also crucial to John Stuart's own love and sexual life. In 1830 John Stuart was introduced to the wife of John Taylor. Harriet Taylor was already the mother of two children and was shortly to have a third. Yet, with her and John Stuart, it was almost love at first sight. Within a short time, to the scandal of all their friends, John Stuart and the Taylors were living in a rather awkward *ménage à trois*.

The attraction seems to have been basically intellectual, or else the sexual was sublimated in the intellectual. In any case the evidence seems strong that Harriet and John Stuart never had sexual relations, though they claimed the freedom to have them, and merely joined together on the whole question of women's rights and independence. Whereas John Stuart had scorned his mother, he now lavished extravagant praise on Harriet Taylor, who, after the death of her husband in 1849, became Mrs. John Stuart Mill (the relationship still remained unsexual, as far as we can tell, though this conclusion is more hazardous). In the *Autobiography* he calls the chapter to her "The Most Valuable Friendship of My Life," and describes her as possessing "in combination, the qualities which in all other persons whom I had known I had been only too happy to find singly." On her death, in 1858, John Stuart bought a cottage as close as possible to the place where she was buried, and lived out his life, he tells us, solely to fulfill the objects in life that were hers. The highest praise he offered Harriet, however, was to compare her as the equal of—his father. James Mill had shaped his son's model not only of a man but, it seems, of a woman, too.

When James Mill first came to London, he began to earn his living as a journalist-editor. But he knew that he would not have his valued independence unless he established a more solid basis for his fame and fortune. With this in mind, he began to write a *History of British India,* expecting to finish it in about three years. Conceived at almost the same time as John Stuart, the book did not appear in three years but only at the end of twelve long, arduous years of overwork. Boy and book, it seems, developed into maturity together. The book made James Mill's reputation, and on the basis of this success, also secured for him the well-paid post of examiner at the East India Company. At this point, then, James Mill had made the move from the precarious life of an intellectual, a man of letters, to the established position of a high civil servant.

In making his own career James Mill also made a career for his son. In 1823, at the age of seventeen, John Stuart entered the East India Company as a junior clerk, working in his father's office. His advancement there followed his father's advancements. Even in final illness and death the father opened the way for John Stuart: it was James's death that cleared the way for John Stuart's appointment as third examiner, at a salary of £1,200. (James Mill had also paved the way for two other sons in the East India Company: James Bentham Mill actually went to India for the company, and George Grote Mill entered India House as a clerk in 1844.) John Stuart spent the rest of his "working" life in the East India Company.

The "work" identification of the son with the father extended, of course, beyond the East India Company to the intellectual sphere. No one today would remember John Stuart for his Indian activities (although James Mill made his mark there, strongly influencing British policy in India), but we do remember him for his philosophical achievements. And these, too, as we shall now see, emerged from his relationship with his father.

What James Mill gave his son was an ideology, fully formed: utilitarianism. The utilitarian creed, as summarized by John Stuart Mill, meant:

> In politics, an almost unbounded confidence in the efficacy of two things: representative government, and complete freedom of discussion. . . . In psychology . . . the formation of all human character by circumstances, through the universal Principle of Association, and the consequent unlimited possibility of improving the moral and intellectual condition of mankind by education.

Expressed also in terms of economic belief (basically laissez-faire) and as a scheme for legal reform, utilitarianism dominated English intellectual life in the early nineteenth century, helping to bring about a series of major changes in the public arena, including the Reform Bill of 1832.

James Mill himself had acquired his ideological conviction in the course of *his* "discipleship" to Jeremy Bentham. Together, he and Bentham then coached the young John Stuart, who imbibed the utilitarian doctrines along with the first words he learned. The danger, of course, was that, acquired under these conditions, the doctrines would be lifeless. But when John Stuart was fifteen, he read Bentham's treatise on legislation for himself:

> My previous education had been, in a certain sense, already a course of Benthamism. . . . When I laid down the last volume of the Traité, I had become a different being. . . . I now had opinions; a creed, a doctrine, a philosophy; in one among the best senses of the word, a religion . . .

We are in the presence of a "conversion" episode. In adolescence John Stuart acquired an ideology of his "own" that went along with his identification with his father, and instead of rebellion, we have a reaffirmation at this crucial stage in his life of his father's way of life.

The issue, however, was not settled. In a delayed reaction, at the age of twenty, John Stuart struck out, though blindly, for his independence as a separate being from his father. The "Crisis" at this time allowed him to modify both his identification and his ideology; yet the reaction did not preclude a return to his beginnings, and the unexpected result was a reaffirmation of his earlier life that allowed for development. It is time now to look at John Stuart's mental crisis.

James Mill, as we have seen, gave much to his son. The difficulty was that he could not let him go, but attempted always to keep him for himself. According to John Stuart, he "carefully kept me from any great amount of intercourse with other boys." There were, of course, no young women. However, when John Stuart was eighteen, he formed a close friendship with two young men, John Arthur Roebuck and George John Graham. James Mill fought back: when John Stuart introduced his friends to his home, there was a row and Roebuck and Graham indignantly left. John Stuart threatened to leave, too, but after a heated discussion, decided to stay on. A few years later, however, he "left" his father in a different way, through his mental crisis.

In the autumn of 1826, John Stuart tells us in the chapter of his *Autobiography* devoted to this experience,

> I was in a dull state of nerves . . . In this frame of mind it occurred to me to put the question directly to myself: "Suppose that all your objects in life were realized; that all the changes in institutions and opinions which you are looking forward to, could be completely effected at this very instant: would this be a great joy and happiness to you?" And an irrepressible self-consciousness distinctly answered, "No!" . . . I seemed to have nothing left to live for.

In this state of dejection—he even contemplated suicide—John Stuart had no one to whom he could turn. "My father, to whom it would have been natural to me to have recourse in any practical difficulties, was the last person to whom, in such a case as this, I looked for help." John Stuart knew, unconsciously, whereof he spoke. The situation was, indeed, Oedipal, and the father its object. This becomes clear as John Stuart tells us how, after the "melancholy winter of 1826–7," the resolution of his crisis took place. It is a strange experience, which he seems not to have tried to explain to himself.

> I was reading [he tells us], accidentally, Marmontel's "Mémoires," and came to the passage which relates his father's death, the distressed position of the family, and the sudden inspiration by which he, then a

> mere boy, felt and made them feel that he would be everything to them . . . A vivid conception of the scene and its feelings came over me, and I was moved to tears. From this moment my burthen grew lighter . . . I was no longer hopeless: I was not a stock or a stone. I had still, it seemed, some of the material out of which all worth of character, and all capacity for happiness, are made. . . . Thus the cloud gradually drew off, and I again enjoyed life: and though I had several relapses, some of which lasted many months, I never again was as miserable as I had been.

Intellectually, John Stuart explained his crisis (though not the Marmontel episode) as a realization that the cold, dry analysis offered by utilitarianism was not enough; it needed to be supplemented by "the internal culture of the individual," the "passive susceptibilities"—in short, the life of emotion. In his "new way of thinking" John Stuart turned to Wordsworth, who showed him "a source of inward joy, of sympathetic and imaginative pleasure, which could be shared in by all human beings." Thus, John Stuart had grown past his father, broadening his beliefs to include convictions and *feelings* outside his father's narrow purview.

What, in fact, had gone on emotionally in the Marmontel episode that allowed John Stuart to move forward intellectually? The evidence indicates that by experiencing the death of his father imaginatively and by displacement to Marmontel's father, John Stuart was able to "work through" his ambivalent and hitherto unexpressed feelings of love and hate for his father. On one side, we may conjecture that John Stuart could face the possibility of his father's death as the loss of the loved object on whom he most depended, by means of an imagined period of mourning and melancholy. On the other side, we can see rather clearly that John Stuart came to terms with his rivalrous feelings toward his father by vicariously killing him and then replacing him.

In this strange and "accidental" way John Stuart was able to assert his independence. He passed not only through a reawakened Oedipal crisis but also through a work and career crisis. His identity as a reformer—the utilitarian's pursuit of "changes in institutions and opinions"—was challenged and shaken; in the end, however, it was not destroyed but broadened and made more humane. The identification with his father's career, both as an intellectual and a civil servant, was also eventually reaffirmed, but in the new terms.

We can see John Stuart's own awareness of what had happened in his articles of 1831, collectively entitled "The Spirit of the Age," which marked his new identity (though he was still shadowed by James Mill's character; out of respect for his father, John Stuart published them anonymously). Here, John Stuart illustrates for us how developments in identity and ideology go hand in hand and, together, make up generational change: "The first of the leading peculiarities of the present age is, that it is an age of transition. Mankind have outgrown old institutions and old doctrines, and have not yet acquired new ones. . . . A man may not be either better or happier at six-and-twenty, than he was at six years of age: but the same jacket which fitted him then, will not fit him now."

In tailoring his own jacket, so to speak, John Stuart still kept to the patterns of his father. He continued to be a utilitarian to the end of his days. Nevertheless, he made a number of significant changes in the received doctrine. For one thing John Stuart moved from his father's intransigent espousal of laissez-faire economics to a mild tolerance of socialist notions. James Mill had announced that "If a man preaches this doctrine [socialism] without seeing what it is, he is below being treated with argument; if he preaches it, knowing what it is, hanging a thousand times repeated, would be too small a punishment for him." John Stuart, in later editions of his *Principles of Political Economy,* came to hold the view that "We are too ignorant either of what individual agency [i.e., laissez-faire economics] in its best form, or Socialism in its best form, can accomplish, to be qualified to decide which of the two will be the ultimate form of human society." To tolerate ideas about what we have come to call the "Welfare State" meant first, it would seem, tolerating feelings of "dependency"; these feelings, intolerable to James Mill, were acceptable to his son.

John Stuart's acceptance of dependency wishes reflected, I suspect, his views on women. Although he was unable to deal with his feelings toward his own mother and sisters, John Stuart could "love" women in a general and abstract way without feeling threatened in his independence as a man by their equality. The position here is obviously complicated and problematic, but one has the feeling that the price John Stuart paid for treating women as equals was, unfortunately, to "desex" them. This he seems to have done with Harriet Taylor, and it is perhaps what Freud had in mind when he accused John Stuart of not being able to make the distinction between men and women. Whatever the emotional underpinnings, however, we can say surely that John Stuart extended the equalitarian aspects of utilitarianism to women, transcending thereby his father's limitations.

John Stuart also went beyond his father by integrating feelings and intellect. Although I am not convinced that he did this successfully in his life, it is clear that he achieved this integration in terms of doctrine. The cold, unfeeling utilitarian of the early ideology gave way to the philosophical radical (the new term for utilitarian) of heart and mind, to imaginative pleasure and rational happiness combined. Poetry could take its place next to political economy.

Lastly, John Stuart transcended his father's commitment to independence by perceiving that independence had to be indissolubly linked to personal development. In the immortal *On Liberty* John Stuart was able to transmute his own quest for autonomy into an ideology that defended the freedom of all individuals in society to *grow* in their own way, as long as they did not harm their neighbors. Surely personal experience is behind his plea that

> If it were felt that the free development of individuality is one of the leading essentials of well-being; that it is not only a co-ordinate element with all that is designated by the terms civilization, instruction, education, culture, but is itself a necessary part and condition of all those things, there would be no danger that liberty should be undervalued, and the adjustment of the boundaries between it and social control would present no extraordinary difficulty.

And the personal is made sharper in his lament:

> Spontaneity forms no part of the ideal of the majority of moral and social reformers, but is rather looked on with jealousy, as a troublesome and perhaps rebellious obstruction to the general acceptance of what these reformers, in their own judgment, think would be best for mankind.

It is John Stuart's own educational experience, where spontaneity and free development were not allowed by his reforming, and thus "forming," father, that gives power and passion to his rational ideas on liberty.

The extraordinary thing is that with all the modifications he applied to his father's utilitarian doctrines, and even way of life, John Stuart did not need to reject his father totally. Their father–son conflict did not have to be murderous (except in fantasy; and perhaps because successfully handled in fantasy, not necessary otherwise). In a strange and tortuous way John Stuart was able to come to terms with both his love and his hate for his father, and thus to retain and extend the intellectual and social legacy handed on to him. Generational conflict, in this case, had become a vehicle for peaceful social change.

In many ways the absence of revolution in nineteenth-century England, and the presence of reform, find their familial counterpart in the father–son relationship of James and John Stuart Mill. By now we know well that the way in which generational change takes place in the family affects the way in which it takes place in the larger society (and, of course, vice versa; we are dealing with an oscillating cause and effect relation, only one part of which we have been able to explore here). We may not be clear as to the exact mechanism, but we can recognize the ticking when we hear it. Generational conflict can blow up a society, or it can provide a means by which society may renew itself and proceed peacefully, though differently, into the future. In the case of James and John Stuart Mill we have a prototype of how a member of one generation, in an age of transition, was able to come successfully to terms with himself by coming to terms with the generation before him, in the person of his father.

PSYCHOLOGICAL DEVELOPMENT AND HISTORICAL CHANGE

KENNETH KENISTON

Most efforts to marry psychology and history have ended in divorce or outright cannibalism. In the hands of psychologists and psychiatrists, psychohistorical works have traditionally concentrated upon the psychopathology of great men. Those few historians influenced by psychoanalysis have sometimes insisted that historical movements were "nothing but" repetitive reenactments of the basic themes of *Totem and Taboo*. For their part, the majority of historians and depth psychologists have been rightly skeptical of the usefulness of an approach that left one unable to understand how great men differed from psychiatric patients and did scant justice to historical events of interest primarily because they were *not* literal repetitions of the past. Until the last decade, most psychohistorical inquiries must be judged a failure from both a psychological and a historical point of view; despite the advocacy of distinguished historians like Langer, the union of history and depth psychology languished.[1]

In the last decade, inspired largely by the work of Erikson, new and potentially more fruitful kinds of psychohistorical inquiry have opened up.[2] Erikson's studies of Gandhi and Luther have shown that some of the insights of psychoanalysis can be applied to great men without reducing them to bundles of neurotic urges. In the works of psychiatrists like Lifton, Coles, and others, we see a new interest in the unifying psychological themes that unite historical movements as different as Southern school desegregation and the atomic bombing of Hiroshima. In the studies of younger historians like Demos or Hunt, we find a new sophistication in applying modern psychodynamic insights to the study of childhood and the family in other epochs.[3] To be sure, no one, least of all the authors of these works, would claim that a final psychohistorical "synthesis" has been achieved, much less that there exists a solid body of method or theory that can be taught to the novice psychiatrist, historian, or psychologist. Psychohistory is more than anything else a series of questions that cannot be answered by psychology or history alone. But the possibilities of fruitful psychohistorical collaborations seem brighter today than ever before.

The relationship between historical and psychological change is one of the problems that has most frequently attracted those interested in a collaboration between these fields. In the theoretical work of men like Reich, Fromm, and Riesman, as in anthropological studies of culture contact between nonliterate and "advanced" societies, we find a growing body of observation and theory concerning the relationship of historical and psychological change.[4] It is now clear, for example, that when so-called "primitive" peoples come into contact with more technologically advanced societies, there generally results not merely the adoption of new mores and technologies, but the erosion of the traditional culture and the demoralization of a whole people. From such studies have come the concepts of national character, social character, or modal personality—concepts which, whatever their limitations and imprecision, help us understand and explain the observable and regular differences between men in distinct cultures and distinct historical eras.[5]

Most theories of national character or modal personality originated in the effort to understand psychological and cultural change—be it the rise of fascism or the impact of modernization upon primitive societies.[6] But, paradoxically, these theories turned out to be far more useful in explaining historical inertia and cultural stability than in clarifying the mechanisms of change. For theories of national character have depended almost entirely upon the related concepts of socialization and acculturation. These concepts in turn attempt to explain how it is that social norms and cultural symbols are transmitted from generation to generation through the family, educational institutions, and other institutions of cultural transmission.

Since a "well-functioning" society is defined as one in which the young are "successfully" socialized and acculturated, the observable facts of social, cultural, and psychological change prove difficult to explain except as a consequence of "failures" in a key set of social institutions.

Stated differently, theories of national character and modal personality have tended to have an implicitly conservative bias, both ideologically and theoretically. As a result, they have proved particularly useful in explaining such phenomena as cultural disintegration, social anomie, and psychological disorientation. These concepts help us understand the high incidence of addiction, apathy, and retreatism among nonliterate peoples confronted with cultures that are more technologically advanced. They help illumine the messianic cults that appear to flourish at just that point when an old culture is becoming moribund. But they have proved less useful in understanding those social and historical changes which, all things taken together, seem more constructive than destructive, more synthetic than disintegrative. They help little in understanding the undeniable advances in the human condition brought about by the Industrial Revolution, in explaining how men could make constructive political revolutions, or, for that matter, in clarifying *any* nondegenerative historical change.

But the intertwined concepts of socialization, acculturation, and modal personality do not exhaust the potential contribution of psychology in explaining historical change. Largely ignored so far in the study of historical change have been the emerging concepts of developmental psychology—a small but rapidly growing body of theories about the sequences of stages of human development, the conditions that foster or inhibit development in children, and the consequences of early development for adult roles, symbolizations, and values. I will here argue that, in the long run, developmental concepts are likely to prove more useful than concepts of socialization, acculturation, and national character in explaining historical change, and that the relationship between historical context and psychological development is far more intimate than we have heretofore suspected. Collaboration between developmental psychology and history will clearly require major accommodations from the practitioners of both fields, but the results should be a better understanding of both historical and psychological change.

Current Views of Human Development

Every epoch tends to freeze its own unique experience into an ahistorical vision of Life-in-General. Modern developmental psychology witnesses this universal trend. Despite recent advances in our understanding of human development, our psychological concepts have generally suffered from a historical parochialism that takes the patterns, timetables, and sequences of development prevalent among middle-class children in contemporary Western societies as the norm of human development. For example, many developmental psychologists, like most laymen, consider it fairly obvious that human life falls naturally into a set of stages that can properly be labeled infancy, the preschool years, childhood, adolescence, early adulthood, middle age, and old age—for these are the stages which we recognize and institutionalize in Western society, and virtually all research on human development has been conducted in America or Western Europe.

Historians or anthropologists, however, quickly note that these segmentations of the life cycle bear little if any relationship to the definitions of life stages in other eras or cultures. During almost any previous historical era in Western societies, the life cycle has been thought to consist of different stages than those we now acknowledge; in virtually every other contemporary culture, as well, the stages of life are quite differently defined. To attend seriously to these facts requires us to reexamine the assumptions of developmental psychology, and, in so doing, to open the door to a new possibility of collaboration between historians and developmental psychologists.

The reasons for the relative neglect of historical and cultural evidence in the study of development must be understood if this neglect is to be remedied. First among these reasons, of course, is the traditional excuse of psychology: It is a new field. It has in fact proven extraordinarily difficult to understand the complexities of human development even in one subculture of one society: understanding the development of upper-middle-class American, French, Swiss, German, and English children is far from complete. How much more difficult, then, it is to study development in non-Western societies, much less in other historical eras.

Yet in addition to the infancy of developmental psychology, there are conceptual and ideological factors that have prevented our attending to historical and anthropological data. First is the generally unspoken assumption that we really *need* not examine development in any other place or time than our own, since the laws, sequences, and stages of human development transcend both culture and history in their universality.* Once this assumption is openly stated, it is revealed as parochially acultural and ahistorical. But it is often simply taken for granted in many developmental theories. It is further supported by the widespread psychological assumption that the innate "thrust" of human development cannot be stopped by any "merely" cultural or historical factor. This assumption, in turn, is bolstered by the widespread conceptual confusion between biologically determined physiological maturation, socially defined age-grading, and real psychological development—all of which are considered equally inevitable. To open the way for a closer connection between developmental psychology and historical inquiry, we must therefore engage, however briefly, in an analysis of concepts that will challenge this presumption of the inevitability of development.

If we ask what we mean by psychological development, we clearly do not mean simply the accumulation of new facts, the strengthening or weakening of preexisting characteristics, or the repetition of previous attainment. What we can loosely call "quantitative" changes in human behavior are not necessarily developmental. The facts that old people often become more rigid with age, that American girls learn to skip rope more rapidly in the early school years, or that children's vocabulary enlarges with age are not truly developmental changes.

Nor is psychological development equivalent to physical growth or physiological development—that is, to maturation. Maturational changes are indeed virtually universal and inevitable, barring the grossest of insults to the organism. In all cultures, the brain of the child develops rapidly during the first two years of life, although gross malnutrition may slow or impair that development. The historical milieu may influence the age of menarche, but it does not

*Sigmund Freud's uncompromising views about the biologically based universality of the developmental sequences are well known. Jean Piaget's acknowledgment that environmental factors play a role in determining the rate of development has always been largely *pro forma,* since he has never defined or studied these environmental differences.

prevent the onset of menstruation. In all societies, children pass through puberty, with important changes in their appearance, capacities, and general behavior. Maximal skeletal size is everywhere reached in the early twenties. And, in all eras, the vitality of early adulthood is followed by a progressive decline in physical strength that culminates in old age and death. Yet no one of these changes automatically *entails* developmental change. Maturation may, indeed perhaps usually does, promote or permit psychological development, but it need not. Both folk wisdom and clinical studies indicate that there are physically mature individuals with the psychology of children, and precocious biological children who possess adult developmental characteristics. In a phrase: Maturation and development are empirically correlated, but not *necessarily* related. The virtual inevitability of physiological maturation therefore does not demonstrate the inevitability of psychological development.

A second universal is socially defined age-grading. A few societies or subsocieties have been or are rigidly age-graded [7]: e.g., classical Spartan society, some modern East African and Melanesian societies, or modern Western school systems. In most other societies, age-grading is somewhat looser: Age cohorts are less sharply demarcated. But, in all societies there are socially defined differences in what is expected of the young and the old, the infant and the adult, the adult and the elder. In every known society the special status of the dependent and nursing infant is somehow acknowledged. It is also probably universal that societies distinguish the infant-child under the age of six or seven from the older child and/or adult. Every society, too, acknowledges that there is a stage or stages of life which are those of the fullness of life. The blessings and/or curses of old age are recognized. Admittedly, all societies do not divide up the life cycle in precisely the *same* way: On the contrary, they differ enormously in their definition of life stages, of the ages at which new stages begin, and in the substance of their expectations about age-appropriate behavior. But all societies do segment the life cycle in *some* way, and all societies apply formal and informal sanctions to ensure that people will "act their age." Thus, although the content of age-graded expectations varies with culture and history, the general process of age-grading is universal.

But neither maturation nor age-grading is equivalent to psychological development in the precise sense in which I will define this term. It is clearly possible to possess the social status of an adult but the mentality of a child. It is equally possible to have the body of an adult but the psychological development of a child. Psychological development, then, is related to both maturation and socialization, both of which may at times stimulate or prevent development, but neither of which is identical to development.

What do we mean by psychological development?[8] It can be defined as a process of qualitative change in functioning, in relationship to the world, or to oneself. To qualify as true development, this change must be age-correlated and synthetic—that is, it must involve moving to a progressively "higher" level of functioning, to a new level of organization that in general does not completely negate lower levels but tends to incorporate them. For example, the child who apprehends the grammar and vocabulary of his language, and thus learns to speak, does not lose his capacity to babble and imitate. The adolescent who moves beyond primitive identification with his parents to the more complex syntheses of identity formation described by Erikson still retains the capacity for identification.[9] The child who moves from the world of concrete operations to the hypothetical-deductive world of formal operations still remains capable of concrete operations.[10] Genitality, as defined by Freud, does not entail the disappearance of pregenital sexuality, but rather its inclusion and subordination in a genital orientation. In each case, lower levels of development tend to be subsumed as "special cases" in the next higher level of organization.

Psychological development is also essentially irreversible. This does not mean that regressions, recapitulations, reenactments, and reversions to earlier stages cannot occur in the course of development. On the contrary, most developmental theories find a place for such regressions within their theory. But *essential* irreversibility means that regression to a level is in some sense different from the first experience of that level: e.g., "regressed" behavior tends to be identifiably different; after regression (but not before) it is possible to "leapfrog" levels so as to resume development at the point from which one regressed, and so on. By stressing the sequentiality and essential irreversibility of development, we merely stress that development proceeds in a regular way through stages, each of which constitutes a prerequisite for the next. Stated schematically, Stage B cannot occur before Stage A, while Stage B is in turn a prerequisite for Stage C. Each level thus builds upon the preceding one and is the building block for the one that follows it.

To define further the concept of development or the precise sequences of development would involve controversies and complexities irrelevant to this discussion. What is important is that psychological development as here defined is closely related to social age-grading and physiological maturation, but is not identical to either. In the study of socialization to age-grades we find valuable understanding of the matrix within which development occurs, the catalysts that tend to spur it, and the obstacles that may obstruct it. But an account of social expectations about age-appropriate behavior is not an account of development. Similarly, physiological maturation may be a prerequisite for developmental change or it may be a catalyst for development. But it does not automatically produce psychological development.

The Contingency of Human Development

These distinctions between socialization to age-grades, maturation, and development enable us to focus more sharply upon the *contingency* of human development. Most developmental theorists have tended to take for granted—or even to allege—that human development is virtually inevitable, barring any but the most traumatic insults to the individual's personality. This assumption springs partly from blurring the distinctions I have just made. For since maturation and socialization are indeed virtually inevitable, if development is not distinguished from them, their development, too, must be inevitable. Thus, despite an accumulating body of research that demonstrates the possibility of irreversible retardations, slowings, arrests, fixations, lags, or foreclosures in development, the logical conclusion has not been drawn, nor have its implications been explored.

In fact, our present understanding suggests that the *extent* of human development is dependent upon the bio-social-historical matrix within which the child grows up; some developmental matrices may demonstrably retard, slow, or stop development; others may speed, accelerate, or stimulate it. We have traditionally seen the human life cycle as an escalator onto which the infant steps at birth and along which he is carried until his death. The view I am proposing here is that human development is instead a very rough road, pitted with obstructions, interspersed with blind alleys, and dotted with seductive stopping places. It can be traversed only with the greatest of support and under the most optimal conditions.

In order to carry the discussion further with any precision, it is now necessary to distinguish between "development-in-general" and development within specific "lines" or sectors of growth. Developmental theories can be roughly grouped on the basis of this distinction: some deal primarily with development in general or broad life stages (Freud, Erikson, Sullivan), while others deal with developmental changes in precisely defined areas of functioning (Piaget, Kohlberg, Perry).[11] It was Anna Freud who first pointed out that what we loosely call "development" in fact consists of a series of changes within distinguishable "developmental lines" or sectors of functioning.[12] Today developmental diagnosticians of childhood define separately the levels attained by each child in a variety of distinct sectors: e.g., fine motor, cognitive, gross motor, interpersonal, affective, defensive-adaptive, verbal-speech, etc.[13] Any global judgment of overall developmental level is based upon a profile derived from sector-specific evaluations. Thus, if we are to speak precisely about the factors that promote an individual's development, we must specify which sectors or lines of development we are talking about.

This apparently technical point is especially relevant to the cross-cultural and historical study of development. For historical or cultural conditions which may stimulate development in one sector of life may well fail to stimulate it or actually retard it in other sectors. For example, many social critics today argue that a narrow kind of cognitive development is overstimulated in modern Western societies at the expense of affective and interpersonal development, which are in turn retarded. Freud believed that precocious sexual development tended to retard intellectual development. And it is probably possible to stimulate or overstimulate some sectors of growth but to understimulate, neglect, or suppress others. The "intellectually precocious, emotionally immature" child in Western societies is a case in point.

Thus, if we are to compare different historical epochs or different cultures from a developmental perspective, we must not merely compare how they define the overall stage of life and study the extent to which individuals actually pass through these global stages, but we must examine specifically how a given cultural and historical context affects each of many specific subsectors of human development.

Furthermore, only when we have distinguished between sectors of development does the precise influence of the environmental matrix upon development become truly clear. For example, during the past two decades, the study of children in extreme situations has shown that they may "fail to develop" unless defined environmental conditions are present. The most dramatic examples of developmental failure come from studies of infants institutionalized in antiseptic, hygienic, but impersonal "children's homes." The conditions of infant care in such institutions—multiple mothering, unresponsiveness to the child's indications of distress and pleasure, lack of sensory stimulation, and so on—produce specific developmental arrests or retardations in virtually all children subjected to these conditions. Some such children die of extreme reactions to minor physical illnesses; others develop a lethal apathy called marasmus. Those who survive physically are often grossly retarded. And those who live to adulthood tend to be diagnosed as amoral sociopaths.

Until recently, the blame for these developmental failures was laid at the door of heredity: The children who ended up in foundling homes were considered constitutionally defective. But research has made clear that the damage is done not by constitution, but by environment. And research by Provence and Lipton, which carefully distinguishes between development in distinct sectors, has helped pinpoint the areas in which early developmental arrest appears to be irreversible.[14] If the children in question are placed in normal foster homes at approximately the age of two, they soon make up most of the lost ground with regard to cognitive development, speech, and gross motor development. But, in other areas, retardation appears enduring: Such children seem never to develop the full capacity for deep personal relationships, for imaginative fantasy, or for the physical grace characteristic of children brought up from birth in natural or foster homes. Each of these fundamental qualities appears to be contingent upon a certain kind of environmental matrix in early life.

The barbarity of "modern" foundling homes is so extreme that if such conditions were societally universal, they would probably produce psychological deformations so extreme that no society could survive for long. In any enduring society, infants can take for granted most of the conditions they need in order to develop. Indeed, as a preliminary hypothesis, we might suggest that until about the age of six or seven, society has relatively little leeway in what it provides children: If the society is to survive, it must provide adequate stimulation—adequate "emotional and cognitive nutriments"—for the infant to become a child. Thereafter, however, we can speculate that the relative contingency of development upon the matrix in which it occurs seems to increase, and we begin to discover a series of truly developmental changes that may or may not occur. For example, Inhelder and Piaget have described at length the development of the capacity for formal operations: i.e., the ability to generate hypotheses and deduce their conclusions regardless of whether or not these conclusions are empirically true.[15] The capacity for formal operations is the capacity for logical-deductive thought. With this capacity, the intellect breaks free from the concrete world into the realm of hypotheses, ideals, and contrafactual conjectures. Upon this cognitive capacity, Piaget insists, philosophies, systems of scientific thought, utopias, and man's awareness of his historicity are based.

With Piaget's well-bred middle-class Swiss youths, the capacity for formal operations emerges at around the age of puberty. And, despite Piaget's *pro forma* acknowledgment that environment plays a role in the development of this capacity, he has associated formal operations firmly with early adolescence. But other studies have questioned this association. In some subcultures and in some societies, including our own, numerous adults seem to lack this capacity.[16] One study of American adolescents from "culturally deprived" backgrounds found that when the capacity for formal operations developed at all, it generally emerged well after puberty.[17] One may further question whether this capacity is likely to emerge at all in nonliterate societies. In brief, here is a specific human potential which appears *not* to be actualized in certain environments, but to be crucially dependent upon the catalysts of the surrounding matrix.

Kohlberg's studies of moral development give a still more unequivocal example of developmental levels that are *not* reached by most men and women in American society, or for that matter in any society that has been studied.[18] Kohlberg argues that moral development may proceed from what he calls the preconventional and conventional levels, occurring during childhood and early adolescence, to postconventional levels. These postconventional levels are developmental in the precise sense defined above: They are essentially irreversible, sequential, age-related, and synthetic. But Kohlberg's empirical work indicates that the great majority of young Americans, like their parents, do not in fact pass beyond the conventional stage of moral reasoning. The precise psychological and cultural matrix that promotes the development of postconventional moral reasoning remains largely a matter for speculation.[19] But what seems clear is that Kohlberg has identified measurable stages of moral development which the great majority of Americans do not reach. Research in other cultures suggests that elsewhere these stages are reached even less frequently.[20]

We as yet know very little about the precise sequences of development in each of the areas of human growth that can be distinguished.[21] It will doubtless take decades before we have begun to fill in the chart of human development, much less to understand the impacts of different environmental matrices upon distinct sectors of development. But what we do now know consistently supports the hypothesis that human development, from infancy onward, is contingent upon the characteristics of the environmental matrix.

Life Stages and Developmental Profiles

This hypothesis, if correct, has important implications for the study of historical change. For, in general, members of any given society in any given historical epoch tend to share a highly similar developmental matrix. It follows that, despite the variations in human development generated by constitutional and idiosyncratic differences, there should be important constancies in the *modal developmental profile* of adults. Put differently, people in any given society or subsociety tend to resemble each other not only because they have internalized the same roles (socialization) and the same symbols and values (acculturation), but also because they have "leveled off" at approximately the same point in their development in each of the sectors of human growth.

In the past, we have learned to analyze how children internalize shared social roles and how they incorporate common cultural symbols and values. Now we should begin to examine the environments of children, adolescents, and adults in terms of their selective impact on the unfolding of development potentials. We may discover, for example, that certain societies like our own place immense stress upon some kinds of cognitive and intellectual development, while they deemphasize other sectors of development—for example, motoric development and the early development of responsibility. If this is true, then we will require a concept like "modal developmental profile" to characterize the developmental attainments of the average individual in any subculture, society, or historical epoch.

If these hypotheses and concepts prove useful, they may open the possibility of new ways of examining the family, the life cycle, and the phenomenology of human experience in other historical eras. My argument implies that we have been too quick to assume that human development in other societies and other historical eras proceeds in a manner essentially similar to developments in our own society. In our rush to reject the arrogance of the nineteenth century vis-à-vis the "savage native," we have been too quick to assume a complete identity of experience between modern man and ancient man, technological man and pre-literate man. In our acceptance of cultural relativism in the realm of values, we may have confused values with facts, generating a twentieth-century pseudo-egalitarianism which is little more than the ethnocentric assumption that all men are "basically" like Western industrialized men. Developmental psychologists have helped us to remember how profoundly different from our own are the mental processes and conceptual maps with which the small child approaches the world. Working together, developmental psychologists, historians, and anthropologists may now help us to recall how profoundly different has been the human experience of growing up in other societies and other times—and how different, as a result, was the inner experience and mind-set of adults in other places and eras.

It may clarify the view I am proposing to consider several problems which might be illumined by this approach. Consider, for one, the observation by anthropologists studying some pre-literate societies and by historians studying earlier eras that the life stage of adolescence has not always been formally recognized or acknowledged. Since puberty obviously occurs in all societies, these same scholars have generally assumed that adolescence as a psychological stage has also occurred, and have devoted their main investigative effort to explaining why so obvious a milestone in human development was not formally noted. But the point of view introduced here suggests a different interpretation. It may well be that adolescence as a stage of psychological development occurs only under specific conditions like those which obtain in modern Western societies. In other societies or historical eras, puberty is therefore not followed by anything like what we consider an adolescent experience.[22]

To state this general hypothesis in its most extreme and provocative form: Some societies may "stop" human development in some sectors far earlier than other societies "choose" to do so. If, therefore, a given stage of life or developmental change is not recognized in a given society, we should seriously entertain the possibility that it simply does not occur in that society. And, if this is the case, then in societies where adolescence does not occur many of the psychological characteristics which we consider the results of an adolescent experience should be extremely rare: For example, a high degree of emancipation from family, a well-developed self-identity, a belief system based upon a reexamination of the cultural assumptions learned in childhood, and, perhaps, the cognitive capacity for formal operation.

Let us consider a second example. Elkins has drawn an analogy between what he terms the "Sambo" mentality prevalent until recently among black American slaves and their nominally free descendants and the particular mentality observed amongst the inmates of concentration camps.[23] Elkins' hypothesis focuses upon the impact of extreme and traumatic degradation upon adult personality; he disregards almost completely the possible effects upon children of growing up under the conditions prevalent in slave quarters on North American plantations. As a result, the major intellectual problem in Elkins' formulation is how to explain why the trauma of the middle passage was communicated from generation to generation over so many centuries.

Even with our present limited knowledge of the effects of gross cultural deprivation, illiteracy, discontinuity of mothering, lack of sensory stimulation, and so on, we can readily supplement Elkins' theory by informed speculations about the catastrophic effects upon child development (and, therefore, upon adult personality) of the conditions in which children born into slavery were reared. Such conditions should predictably lead to a dulling of adult cognitive capacities, to resignation, apathy, and indifference, and to a "survival mentality" which stresses manifest acquiescence and covert resistance.

An even more speculative example of the possible connection between developmental and historical concepts may follow from the observations of Ariès, qualified by the later studies of Hunt, concerning the characteristics of child development in sixteenth- and seventeenth-century France.[24] Ariès argues that the concept of childhood as a separate stage of life was unknown during the Middle Ages. Only in the sixteenth and seventeenth centuries, and, initially, only for a small elite, was a separate stage that followed infancy but preceded adulthood socially acknowledged and sanctioned in age-graded schools. If we leap from this datum to the theories of Erikson concerning childhood as a stage of life, we find that the developmental "task" of childhood in Erikson's terms is the achievement of a sense of "industry," which Erikson relates to such human qualities as skill, a sense of workmanship, an absence of feelings of inferiority, and a sense of vocational competence. We might argue that in the absence of a stage of childhood, the psychological quality of industry simply did not develop on a mass scale, and that its absence thus helps to explain the absence of the motivations necessary for an entrepreneurial, capitalistic-industrial society. Perhaps only as childhood was recognized on a mass scale and as a large proportion of the population therefore developed a sense of industry could capitalism and large-scale industrialization proceed. Such an explanation might help us define the developmental component in the complex relationship between capitalism, Protestantism, and the work ethic.

A variety of other topics might be illumined by the application of developmental concepts. We might ask, for example, how the historical extension of literacy changes the cognitive development and social behavior of those who can read. Does it enable them to deal more effectively with complex political questions? Does it make them more susceptible to mass totalitarian movements? Does literacy help the individual attain that detachment from admired but defeated political figures which is necessary in a democracy if the opposition is gracefully to concede defeat? Or does it lay the groundwork for the ideologization of political and social controversy? Or we might ask whether, after the fall of the Roman Empire, the matrix of child development changed so that children of succeeding generations attained a less advanced cognitive level than that which characterized the aristocracy in Rome, with the result that original thought ceased for several centuries throughout most of Western Europe and the Mediterranean.

Finally, turning to our own era, I have elsewhere argued at greater length[25] that a good part of the untoward restiveness of affluent, educated young people today must be understood as a consequence of a massive historical change in the developmental matrix. Among other things, this new matrix promotes the individualization of moral judgments and the relativization of truth. One consequence is that a large minority of a youthful generation is unable, for better and for worse, to accept on faith previous moral evaluations or uncritically to accept traditional ways of viewing the world. These new mind-sets are not simply matters of the recurrence of perennial generational conflict. On the contrary, to understand fully the emergence of an oppositional youthful counterculture in the most technologically advanced nations of the world, we must begin to examine how the drastically altered historical conditions of the twentieth century (extended mass education, widespread affluence, exposure to other cultures, threat of holocaust) have in turn changed the modal matrix of human development, "producing" on a mass scale a kind of questioning, restless youth who, if he existed at all in the past, was always part of a tiny and exceptional minority.

In urging that we examine the psychological effects of wide-scale historical changes in the developmental matrix, I am not proposing that we abandon more familiar and traditional modes of psychological and historical inquiry. The concept of national character or modal personality, for example, has emerged from scathing criticism scarred but still useful in the understanding of historical continuity and change. Developmental concepts are in no sense a panacea to either the psychologist or the historian. My only claim is that they may help us understand better the processes by which sociohistorical change produces psychological change, and by which psychological change on a mass scale may in turn generate social and political transformations. And, if developmental psychology and historical inquiry can move toward a closer accommodation, we may be less inclined to impose our own culturally ethnocentric and historically parochial world views and mind-sets upon the experience of those in other cultures and historical eras.

THE METHOD

ROBERT COLES

This study* contains several elements: first, the words of others, their ideas and feelings, their statements, their assertions, their exclamations; second, my own effort to put in words what I have observed and considered important, whether inspiring, troubling, confusing, or merely worth quiet interest and reflection; and, finally, some discussion and analysis—I suppose those are the two words—of the sharpness of vision and the coherence of mind I have seen and heard others demonstrate. All three elements work together to convey not only *what is* (itself rather a daunting task) but how men and women and children, *who are,* deal with the things of this world, the "reality" or "environment" one hears so many psychiatrists talk about.

I speak as a physician and as a child psychiatrist, and as one who has tried to study not only the illnesses and problems that people have, but also their *lives.* The lives described in this book certainly are ill-favored and maybe misshapen; they must on occasion have to be acknowledged as forbidding or grotesque or ruined almost beyond repair; but they may also give cause for wonder, for more admiration than sorrow. Lives, as opposed to problems, may puzzle the fixed notions of theorists, while at the same time adding confirmation to what has been revealed by such keenly sensitive (if

*Exploration of the lives of migrants, sharecroppers and mountaineers.

"methodologically untrained") observers as Dostoevsky or Zola, Orwell or Agee, who have managed, regardless of time and place, to set down something both comprehensible and enduring about human beings the rest of us have merely pigeonholed as "peasants" or "the rural proletariat" or "the lower class" or, more recently, "the culturally deprived" or "the disadvantaged"—or, here and now, "migrants, sharecroppers and mountaineers." [1]

We hunger after certainty. We want "orientations" and "conceptual frameworks" and carefully spelled-out "methodological approaches." We want things "clarified"; we want a "theoretical structure," so that life's inconsistencies and paradoxes will somehow yield to man's need for a scrupulous kind of "order." For some it is a matter of so-called "objectivity": man's behavior at some "level" can be made utterly straightforward, can be submitted to the linear workings of a particular psychological or sociological theory. For others there may be different reasons to prune things down, forget this fact and emphasize that line of thinking; I refer, of course, to the needs of the politically active person, who wants changes and works for those changes, and who requires all "data," pure though they may be, to pass the muster of a given set of purposes and "objectives." (The resemblance to "objective" is one more irony in our path.) We want to do things *for* people, *with* them, even, alas, *to* them. Therefore, we see what we want to see, and find important. We then justify in any number of ways our reason for not looking at a particular side of a problem: it is "irrelevant," or a waste of time, or politically inexpedient, or not the business of a social scientist or of a doctor. What *really* matters, each of us insists, is one or another emphasis, one or another truth.

Meanwhile, as American Southern writers like William Faulkner and Flannery O'Connor and James Agee [2] almost drove themselves and their readers crazy trying to say, there are many truths—so many that no one mind or viewpoint or discipline or profession can possibly encompass and comprehend them all, nor do justice to them in words, even intricate and specialized ones, or "neutral" ones.

I mention all of this, none of it new or especially startling, because I want to make it very clear, as clear as I possibly can, how I have gone about doing the work described in this study—which means with what purposes in my mind and what ideas or assumptions as guides. Most especially I want to say, loud and clear, what I have not done, what this book does not lay claim to be, does not make a pretense of offering to its readers. I would suggest that some reasonably representative and suggestive voices are to be found in these pages. The voices are those of migrant farm workers and sharecroppers or tenant farmers and mountaineers—though theirs are not the only voices—and the hopes and fears expressed are also theirs. My own voice is constantly present, even when others speak, and so are some of my own hopes and fears.

Now, why do I have to intrude upon this narrative at all? Why not let the people speak for themselves? Why interrupt them? Again, during the more general and analytic sections of the book, why let these people interrupt the author? My answer is that as a child psychiatrist I had to learn how important it is not only to "detect" something going on in a child's mind, but to go through certain experiences *with* the child in order to be of help. The doctor does not investigate a case out of scientific curiosity only; he is there to *help*. Clinical "experiences," like a game of tennis, amount to an exchange, a back-and-forth movement of ideas and impressions, a shared earnestness and eagerness. And often on both sides of the net those "experiences," hard to corral in the confines of a particular kind of technical language, happen simultaneously to both physician and patient: a lump in the throat, a moment of vehemence, an outburst of apprehension, a spell of silence, a passionate conviction that must be given utterance, an increasing persuasion that "things" are going well between the doctor and the patient, the little him or little her and "the man who's still a baby and has toys all over his office," as I once heard a child psychiatrist described.

Increasingly these past years psychiatrists and psychoanalysts (some of them, at least) have learned to look upon people as citizens of a nation, as members of a given society, and *particular* members at that, not merely as members of an Oedipal family. That is to say, we become irate, hurt, worried, murderously worked up, decisively bored, or tired and sad because of events that actually take place in the economic market or the political arena. The exchanges we once had with our parents, or continue to have with ourselves in the form of fantasies or nightmares, are not the only things that upset the mind, or drive it to distraction. It is one thing, however, to ask that the windows of clinical offices be opened, so as to be rid of stale, musty air; it is quite another thing to abandon what offices in hospitals and clinics all over the world have furnished us: countless hours of experience, the pursuit of a method of observation, the acquisition of a special if limited kind of coherence—the acquisition, also, of a sensibility the doctor must work for in himself and hopefully bring about in his patients. Although I myself have in a physical sense for the most part left those offices, yet in all the work described in this book I have been working as a clinician. Not as a clinician alone, but perhaps more desperately than ever, trying to do what I have learned to do, been trained to do, in the course of studying medicine and psychiatry.[3]

I take pains to mention all of that because I do not wish to set my kind of work up against more traditional forms of psychiatry in a polemical way; nor do I wish to use the people in this book as a foil or a means of assault on other people—in this case the thousands and thousands of patients who seek psychiatric help in child-guidance clinics or outpatient clinics throughout the nation.[4] The crying needs of one group of people do not make any less real the thoroughly different needs of another group. If one argues that priorities must be established, I would agree; but I am wary of those (perhaps on occasion myself included) who would use a migrant farmer's distress as an excuse to attack and bully and abuse another worried, fearful human being who happens to come from the "middle class" and might consider himself or herself persistently "neurotic." Suffering knows no barriers of color or class. Suffering—real, substantial, hard to bear—can be found among all people, everywhere. This may sound banal, but there is a peculiar arrogance practiced by some of us who talk so proudly about our "work" with "the poor": we praise them to high heaven, and denounce everyone else either casually or mercilessly. There are, I fear, many kinds of exploitation. Certain people in this study—plantation owners or sheriffs—betray by their words the economic and political kind. It may be considerably harder for some of the rest of us to see other forms of inhumanity; it may even be hard for some of us to see what is nearest at hand—our smugness, our blind spots, our self-importance, our presumptuousness, our condescension toward people whose cause we claim to support, our bustling energetic self-righteousness.

I am taking a long time at all this, I know; but it is not an easy subject to explore, at least not for me. Long ago Freud urged all of us who would know how others think and feel to look at our own reactions and responses and styles of thought or feeling. I am not writing an autobiography, nor do I wish this chapter to become an exercise in "self-analysis" or an examination of the "countertransference" at work under particular professional circumstances. I am, however, trying to alert myself and those who read these pages to a danger I certainly do not feel any of us (myself emphatically included) can escape when we spend long stretches of time with people who at once make us feel sad, indignant, giving, resentful, and God knows how many other emotions. What are we to *do?* we begin to ask. All well and good that we feel so inclined; a lot of people had better start asking such a question if there is to be an end to political and economic injustices.

The trouble is that we don't only start asking questions. Something else begins to take place, also. The resentment and outrage we feel for the sake of the people whose lives we have come to witness spills over. The first targets are sheriffs and growers and plantation owners, but soon those individuals are not enough. Then the entire nation gets criticized, and, more specifically, a "power structure" is blamed, and not once in a while, but incessantly. There are, to be sure, many "power structures," all over the world, and many of them deserve criticism and more criticism, the strongest possible kind that an aroused and indignant public can mobilize. That said, one has to turn inward, and ask oneself whether the suffering a migrant farmer experiences justifies a refusal to look at the various "conditions" that tie others down and prevent them from knowing or caring about migrant farmers—conditions that also allow cruelty to flow not only from the "power structure" on downward, but from all of us to each other, from migrants to migrants, from sharecroppers to sharecroppers, from mountaineers to mountaineers.

Yes, one has to add quickly, even if such things are true, even if men are cursed by their "nature," there is an explicit political and economic "evil" that accounts for the way a sharecropper lives, say, in the Mississippi Delta. Still, I have to ask myself whether the situation in the Delta and my desire to see sweeping changes take place there require of me unequivocal bitterness and contempt toward those who do not happen to share my particular concerns.

Maybe it comes to this: as a citizen I am appalled by the injustice I see about, injustice that is consolidated, injustice that is handed down as a birthright over the generations, injustice whose continuing presence disgraces all human beings everywhere; but as an observer intent on seeing what exactly goes into making up those lives (uprooted lives, brutally exploited lives, dazed lives, unfamiliar lives so far as most of us are concerned) I would only be adding to the injustice just mentioned, were I to translate clear-cut economic and political wrongs into the same kind of psychological alternatives, and paint for you portraits of brutalized and desperate workers, set upon daily and viciously by rich, savage, heartless plunderers or their lackeys. There have been times when I have thought that to be the case, or at least wanted to think so; and I do not now bring up doubts and reservations in order to gloss over the misery and the exploitation one finds in the United States. No, I find it an awful disgrace that men and women whom I have known for so long, and their children, whom I have seen born, helped to be born, who belong to my children's generation—that these children, and *their* children, will live (I have no reason to doubt it) a similarly vulnerable, harsh, humiliating existence.

Nevertheless, faced with the most dreary circumstances imaginable, with the humiliating day-to-day existence I just spoke of, not a few individuals, more of them certainly than I once believed, manage to find for themselves moments of satisfaction, accomplishment and self-respect. Those moments can become stabilized in a lasting kind of wry detachment or a plucky feeling of confidence that not only is not fatuous or self-deluding but justifies itself all the time through deeds done, statements made, unfavorable odds at least confronted if not overcome. If the work I do has any justification whatever, it comes, I believe, from the capacity a clinician must have to distinguish between the objective conditions that constitute a disease and the range of subjective responses to a disease that particular men, women and children make. In so doing, they, of course, affect the way they perceive and manage their symptoms. There is no point saying that things aren't really so bad because people under great stress, involved in one crisis after another, summon incredible resources of mind and heart and spirit, and emerge finally, in spite of it all, as undestroyed, even if terribly wounded. There is no reason, either, to insist, because things are very, very bad, that any reparative and even redemptive efforts an observer may find are utterly beside the real point, namely that *more* is needed: more bread, more running water, more electricity, more jobs that offer decent wages.

Somehow we all must learn to know one another. I should imagine that a number of the people who speak out in this book feel that they are misunderstood by their friends and supporters and natural allies as well as by their obvious or thinly disguised enemies. Certainly I ought to say that I myself have been gently and on occasion firmly or sternly reminded how absurd some of my questions have been, how misleading or smug were the assumptions they convey. The fact is that again and again I have seen a poor, a lowly, an illiterate migrant worker wince a little at something I have said or done, smile a little nervously, glare and pout, wonder a little in his eyes about me and my purposes, and through his grimace let me know the disapproval he surely has felt; and, yes, the criticism he also feels, the sober, thought-out criticism, perhaps not easily put into words—though eventually that will happen, too.

What I have just been discussing has to do with my "method," which I feel inside me, after all, maybe in my bones rather than my head. The work itself is, thank God, easier to describe without a lot of sweaty, worried, and twisted declarations, retractions and qualifications. In 1958 I lived in Mississippi, and it was then that I began the first part of this research. I started making trips to the Delta, at first sight-seeing trips; later on, as racial conflict became more open and prominent in the state, I found it harder and harder not to notice something else besides large, pleasant plantations or cotton growing as far as the eye could reach or levees holding back the great river. In the first volume of *Children of Crisis*[5] I have described what eventually happened, the intersection, really, of my professional life and my personal life with the social and political changes that had come upon the South in the late 1950s. Here it is important to stress that when I started seeing particular black and white people caught up in a phase of historical change I also became determined to do something else as well: observe not only how people participate in a social revolution or how others oppose such changes, but also observe how people live and conduct their affairs and try to make do—those who live out from day to day their own version of history by trying to deal with particular burdens; historical, social, political, and awful economic burdens.

As I indicated in the preface to the first volume of *Children of Crisis,* it was almost inevitable that I would ask myself how sharecroppers and tenant farmers and migrant workers *live.* The families I first knew and studied in New Orleans in the early 1960s, families whose children pioneered school desegregation against fierce and unremitting opposition, had come to the city from rural Louisiana and Mississippi. In each family's case there were relatives who worked the land, who "sharecropped," who rented a few acres and tried to survive on what they grew each year—grew to sell and grew to eat. In some instances a brother or a cousin had left altogether, left not for New Orleans, but left for Florida, to which large numbers of field hands from all over the rural South have gone in search of work and money. I would hear about it: the gradual collapse of yet another small farm; the gradual mechanization of a plantation in this or that parish of Louisiana or county of Mississippi; the gradual loss of what little sharecroppers or tenant farmers can fall back upon; their increasingly urgent need to move someplace; and the choice various sharecroppers or tenant farmers made—such as to "try Florida, try harvesting the crops over there, and maybe moving around some, to where the crops are, standing and waiting on people to take them all in, like the beans that are there, and cukes, I guess, and like that." There, in fact, word for word, was the first description I ever heard of the migrant life; it was offered to me in New Orleans, in February of 1960, now over a decade ago. A mother and housewife was talking about her sister. I never met that particular woman, but I did make my first trip to Belle Glade, Florida (and nearby towns) in 1963, there to see where thousands of migrant workers live in the winter and work as harvesters. By that time I had come to know a good deal of what such people leave behind, the rural landscape of the "Black Belt." By that time I had started visiting with particular frequency (two, maybe three times a week) some ten families, four sharecroppers, six tenant farmers.

I would in 1963 begin to do the same with migrant families, start visiting over the months and the years ten families; and eventually start following them up the coast, up North: all through Georgia and through the Carolinas and all through Virginia, and Maryland and New Jersey and Delaware, and finally through New York or Connecticut or even Massachusetts or Maine—through, it so happens, most of the original thirteen colonies.[6] I would in 1963 also start the third part of this study by making several visits to Asheville, and Burnsville, North Carolina, at first in order to find out how school desegregation took place in a small city and rural community of the South in contrast to large cities like New Orleans and Atlanta, and later in order to meet families in the hills of western North Carolina, whose lives in many respects both resembled and were a contrast to the lives of those sharecropper and migrant families I was getting to know.

In 1965 I extended my work in Appalachia further. I started going to eastern Kentucky and West Virginia as a consultant to the Appalachian Volunteers, a group of young activists who for years have tried to make political dents that are hard to make in the region.[7] In a sense my association with the Appalachian Volunteers very much resembles the work I did during the early sixties in Mississippi and Georgia with the students who staged one sit-in after another, rode on "freedom rides" and eventually initiated the well-known Mississippi Summer Project of 1964. I have taken up and analyzed all that work in the first volume of *Children of Crisis* and have no wish here to discuss the most recent turns and twists of the South's (not only the black man's but the white man's) thoroughly unfinished racial struggle. I will simply say that in the course of my work with the AV's, as they have come to be called up the hollows, I attempted to be an observer, a student, a doctor and a child psychiatrist trying to learn a little; but at times I very much wanted to stand beside those who cannot tolerate what goes on in many of those Appalachian counties. I have also written at length in the first volume of *Children of Crisis* (and elsewhere) about "participant observation," and there is no need to go over all of that here. I can only add that for me to work with the Appalachian Volunteers, or in a different way with the National Sharecroppers Fund, the National Advisory Committee on Farm Labor, the South Florida Migrant Legal Services, Inc., has been at once to learn things and to try to change things.[8] If there is one single fact all the people described in this book share it is the fact of vulnerability, of powerlessness; and so it is the duty of people like me, who would claim some knowledge of how certain people feel way down in the lowest possible "layers" of their unconscious minds, to witness at first hand the effort made by mountaineers or tenant farmers or migrants to achieve a kinder, more decent world, and to witness also the defeats they suffer, the frustrations they have to meet, the constant insults and intimidations of all kinds that take place anywhere that a field hand tries to challenge entrenched power, change the way a given world is run, or merely assert his claim to be an American citizen, a human being, a *person.*

What sounds like a series of random and unrelated studies or explorations has over a decade gained enough coherence for me to feel I can set down on paper some descriptions of particular lives and some discussions and observations that are tied to those lives and others very much like them. I have used years of conversations and experiences in many counties of many states. The heart of the work has been the thirty families I have visited and worked with and watched and come at times to feel almost joined to—as a doctor, a companion in travel, a friend. Ten of the thirty families belong to the rural South's diminishing but still very active system of sharecropping and farm tenantry; ten other families pursue migrant lives; the final ten live up in the hollows of eastern Kentucky, western North Carolina and in several areas of West Virginia. I have divided up the years with these families. I have spent three or four months with one group, an additional season with another group, and on and on over the years. No family have I now, as I write, known less than six years; some I have known over a decade, and the great majority from seven to nine years. I have, additionally, talked with many, many others whose lives touch upon, bear upon, connect up with, have to do with the people in these thirty families: teachers, employers, merchants, county officials, sheriffs, so-called community organizers—and of course they range from advocates to opponents, from helpers to completely unsympathetic onlookers.

So, what has accumulated in ten years' time can be called thousands of "interviews," done with parents, done with children, done in cabins, done out in fields, done in buses or cars or trucks, done in packing houses, done in schools, done in the offices of growers, the homes of plantation owners, the stores that grocers run or the places that gasoline station owners use. I have used a tape recorder consistently but not always. I realize that in the twentieth century an observer who merely listens and tries to write down in somewhat understandable sentences what he has heard and seen cannot in some circles be considered "objective" or even "scientific." I am sick and tired of calling the interviews I have done "taped" and knowing thereby that they automatically gain a large-size boost in respect and worth so far as certain people are concerned. I want to make this very clear: I use a tape recorder so that I can later have with me the exact voices of the people I have known—their words, their expressions, the moods and the tone that came across in particular conversations. I do not, I hope, go running around the countryside forcing gadgetry on people who are already the victims of various technological "revolutions." I have not, I hope, felt compelled to record every breath and word of every exchange that has been pursued by me these past years. I do not feel it is up to me to judge how I have used those three tape recorders I have at different times used since 1959; rather, it has been up to the people I work with to make an assessment—and they have done so, by showing themselves frightened, amused, beguiled or bored by the machine, or indifferent to it, or utterly oblivious of it, or suspicious of it, or annoyed by it.

For my part, I have tried to be discreet; I have tried to respect the desires and attitudes of the individual families concerned. I have asked them (only after I have known them for months, I hasten to add) whether I might record some of our talks, so that I can have them, as it were, and keep them and go over them—oh, not only to analyze themes and interpret meanings and motives and "goals" and "attitudes," but because after a while a person can get to know another person, feel more and more in touch with him or her, more and more sure why certain words are spoken and with what intent, with what inner conviction. It does help, too—by God it does—to listen to the sounds of those voices, the rhythms and cadences, the pauses, the hesitations that suddenly are overcome, the hurry that is shown, followed by a relaxed stretch. I also take photographs of the people I visit, obviously not to use here, but, like the tapes, to hold near me and help guide my mind (and I hope my heart) a little nearer to what I guess has to be called the essence (words simply fail here) of particular lives. And there does come a time, after a few years of visits and more visits, talks and more talks, good talks and rather dismal ones, when something seems to have happened, "clicked," come about, developed; when, that is, on both sides some reasonably reliable and trustworthy impressions begin to congeal and become something else, so that a mountaineer can say: "Well, I guess I know you a small bit and you know me the same, and I sure hope you go and tell those people out over beyond those hills what we're *really* like. But the funny thing is, I don't believe I know myself what it is we're really like, and I don't believe you'll ever know, either, to be frank with you."

So, there it is, the tension and the mystery of things, the beginning of certainty that evaporates in a flash, the confusion that suddenly gives way to a genuinely luminous moment. Though, God knows, it may be an impossible wish, I have wanted all along to remain true to something I can only try to get at, something I can only try to describe with a series of warnings to myself: do not come up with a lot of brittle, pretentious generalizations that explain everything and anything; do not smother with sticky sentiment lives already weak and open to attack; do not refuse those lives their tenacity or shirk from pointing out the price that has to be paid for just such tenacity, for all that goes into remaining, bearing up, continuing and lasting. They have lasted, the families I have known and others who share a similar fate; they have lasted and lasted, endured as Faulkner said they will, prevailed even, if not over their many oppressors, at least over odds like disease, malnutrition, and the extreme hardships that, again, are not only their fate but also their almost inescapable destiny as American citizens. I have gradually found myself more welcome with these families, and at the same time steadily more confused by the stubborn individuality of human beings who might well have been destroyed altogether or at the very least turned into the rural equivalent of "mass men."

The names of the particular people I have known and the specific plantations or hollows or migrant camps obviously must not be given nor can the people I have known in any way at all be revealed. Accordingly, as I mentioned in the introduction, I have changed the names of counties and states, and changed dozens and dozens of other details. Often I have drawn composite pictures; that is, I have combined two or three people into one to make the particular individuals I know unrecognizable, and also to emphasize and highlight the issues for the reader. I suppose I am asking for the writer's privilege to concentrate things, combine meanings, subdue distractions, sharpen what seems central and determining. But I can and should list the "areas" within a reasonable compass: for the sharecroppers and tenant farmers, the Delta of Mississippi, and, across the river, two parishes of Louisiana that face the Delta, and two counties in south-central Alabama, and two counties in South Carolina, one to the west of the state, one in the lowlands, and also two counties in North Carolina, both coastal counties. For migrants, camps all over Florida, particularly Palm Beach and Collier counties —it is practically impossible to disguise the locations of those camps because they are well known, maybe notorious is the way to put it— and then, with migrant camps located all the way up the Atlantic seaboard, I managed to spend most of my time in upstate New York, lower New Jersey and Massachusetts, and visit more briefly places in the Carolinas and Virginia's eastern shore. Finally, so far as Appalachia is concerned, the families I know best there live in one county in western North Carolina, two in eastern Kentucky and one in West Virginia. A typical recent year was divided into thirds, and visits were devoted in that way to one group after another—mountaineers, say in a summer and early autumn, followed by sharecroppers in late autumn and winter, and then, in the spring and early summer, migrant farm workers.

If one easily justifies a decision to scramble names and locations, one has a harder time knowing how to present what some speak of as "material" or "data" or sections of "protocols"—"write-ups about people" is what I call them. I have once more decided to do what I did in the first volume of *Children of Crisis*—that is, by and large put the remarks of the people interviewed into what I suppose has to be called the middle-class, grammatical language many Americans and perhaps most book readers learn to use. Part of me has wanted to transcribe those tapes and present them directly, with only minor editing; but three groups of people are involved, and in any case it is hard to set forth all that is to be heard without constantly explaining particular words and expressions and in a way distracting the reader (and becoming distracted oneself) by dialects, slang, and the strong and suggestive vernacular of uneducated but very perceptive people. Even as I am not writing a history of Appalachia or a sociological description of a rural sharecropping community or an anthropological analysis of life among migrants or a political discussion of the rights given and denied agricultural workers, so I am not presenting here a series of appreciative or critical linguistic essays, or a footnote to the history of "folk music." My job, at least as I see it, is to bring alive to the extent I possibly can a number of lives, and especially to bring alive the "innerness" in those lives: the expectations and assumptions, the vacillations and misgivings and scruples, the rhythm—as it engages with the outside world, with social and political events, with our nation's history; as it takes place in thoughts and feelings, in a child's drawings or games, in a man's imprecations, his casual remarks, his offhand jokes, his private beliefs that are, finally, entrusted to a person like me, an outsider, a stranger, a listener, an observer, a doctor, a curious (in several senses of the word) fellow whom one mountaineer described as "always coming back and not seeming to know exactly what he wants to hear or know."

The words, then, belong to the people I have met and heard use them; but the order of the words, of whole sentences and paragraphs and days and days and days of conversation, has definitely been my doing, at times I think for the better, certainly so far as pointedness goes, so far as clear-cut, distilled, comprehensible English goes. Whether the loss of many emphatic, even brutal expressions (unfamiliar or obscure to most Americans) is a sacrifice worth making, I cannot judge, having already made the sacrifice. This study is long; were I to offer more and more of the styles of speech I heard, apart from the content expressed, I fear twice this present number of pages might not be enough.[9] I have, though, tried to get across some of the contrasting rhythms to be heard in conversation, for example, in West Virginia, or in Alabama.

In time one's literal-minded, detail-conscious eagerness can be seen for the nervousness it is, the obtuse, pedantic scholasticism it can become, and the condescension it conveys and betrays to others. In time one also begins to learn—maybe the most important thing one *can* learn, that all over the place, in Immokalee, Florida, or Ebenezer, Mississippi, or Stella, North Carolina, or Grassy, West Virginia, people voice the deepest, the most urgent and essential things on their minds in ways that are remarkably similar, that almost seem to transcend not only particular dialects, but even speech itself. I refer not only to gestures and sighs and inarticulate but unmistakable shouts and cries; I refer to the simplicity and directness of words used in cabin after cabin, words that ignore race and caste and section and region, words like *I fear, I love, I hate, I need, I want, I don't*—don't see why and don't understand—and words like *them,* used to signify all those others who are not to be trusted, only feared for their power and influence. Perhaps the narratives I have put together tell something of what prompts those words; if so, the long and perplexing task of editing tapes, of arranging and rearranging sequences of talk, of adding sentences spoken on one or another occasion and noted by me on scraps of paper, has been somewhat successful.

And one more thing: I, the author, keep interrupting, keep on intruding, it seems, with comments and summarizing accounts and various "interpretations," especially when I am writing about children or calling attention to their drawings or paintings. My job has required a meeting of people, if not of worlds, a meeting of me and a migrant child or a sharecropper child or a tall, quiet mountaineer, who teaches me by what he chooses to deliver from himself to me in the way of words. There *is* a clinical dimension to this work, a give and take any doctor knows when he talks with a patient and finds himself learning not only from what he hears, but from what he feels, what he hears within himself. I am saying again what I mentioned earlier in this chapter: some weaving in and out by me is required, so that the sense of an encounter is given, one between individuals who get to talk about what certain kinds of living can be like.

Why not, then, devote some chapters to myself, go explicitly and at length into all of the personal reactions and doubts and problems that must have arisen and appeared and loomed heavily indeed over the horizon of such work? I have asked that of myself many times—and been asked that. It may be that I have in a deliberately scattered way done so, here and elsewhere.[10] I do not wish to ignore the obvious fact that an exchange took place, that people were "out there," were come upon, repeatedly called upon, and that their responses reached me, touched me, changed me, even as my visits no doubt changed a number of the people about to speak in this book. Here a chapter given the title "method" ought to turn into one that concerns itself with "purpose." I have attempted to indicate some of the dilemmas that this kind of work inevitably produces, in the people "studied" and also in the observer who calls himself a "student," if not some more high-sounding and pretentious thing. The aim of all these trips and visits can be put like this: to approach certain lives, not to pin them down, not to confine them with labels, not to limit them with heavily intellectualized speculations but again to approach, to describe, to transmit as directly and sensibly as possible what has been seen, heard, grasped, felt by an observer who is also being constantly observed himself—not only by himself but by others, who watch and doubt and fear and resent him, and also, yes, show him kindness and generosity and tenderness and affection. The aim, once again, then, is to approach, then describe what there is that seems to *matter*. If all of this sounds increasingly vague and murky and doubtful, I apologize. Perhaps what develops over the course of the study itself will clear things up somewhat.

I do have a few more negatives, though. (Perhaps if I come up with enough of them, *that* will clarify what I positively have wanted to do.) This is not an "attitudinal study." I do not pretend that any assertions made here, by the people quoted or by me, have any "statistical significance," and general or large-scale "validity." I have used no questionnaires. I have not tried to determine whether the people I met and grow to know are in any way accurate reflections of this or that "group" or "segment" of the population. It is all impressionistic, this kind of work, all tied to one person's mind and body; even the tape recorder can only record the answers to the questions I asked, can only convey the trust that can develop between two people over those much advertised and dwelled-upon "cross-cultural" barriers. I certainly do sound "defensive" here; but then, there are too many in my profession who get "defensive" by calling others names like "defensive." Once upon a time (a long time ago, it now seems) I desperately wanted to make sure that I was doing the respectable and approved thing, the most "scientific" thing possible; and now I have learned, chiefly I believe from these people in this book, that it is enough of a challenge to spend some years with them and come out of it all with some observations and considerations that keep coming up, over and over again—until, I swear, they seem to have the ring of truth to them. I do not know how that ring will sound to others, but its sound after a while gets to be distinct and unforgettable to me. Near one of the towns I just mentioned, near Grassy, West Virginia, I heard it all said as satisfactorily as my wordy attempts will ever manage: "When I hear something that strikes me to be right, it sounds loud and clear to me; when it's a lot of talk, I find my head shutting up, like a flower does when it gets cold, because I know it's just a lot of noise, and it'll put you to sleep as much as it'll bother you."

I have known the mountaineer who spoke those words for seven years, and I keep going to see him and his wife and his eight children and his five brothers and his one sister and his father and his mother and his one little granddaughter and his many, many cousins. I go to visit them all, him and his kin, every single year. I try to find out "how it goes," how the children are, what is coming of them as they steadily grow bigger and feel more sure of themselves, if not so confident about their future in that town, that little hollow near the town. I try, most of all, to *be* there; for all the self-consciousness bound to come with my presence I still try for that, for as much naturalness as we all can manage while we talk. Of course it can be hard getting along, especially on the first few days of each visit. Yet, one can also become self-conscious about self-consciousness, so to speak. The point is that after a while a visitor may not be forgotten, but he at least can be taken for granted somewhat; he can be asked to help out a little with chores, asked to go for a walk, go to church, go to the store, go to a neighbor's. And he can be taught, he can be shown something up the hollow, a new patch of herbs, a dam being built by beavers, a spot that almost guarantees a good catch of fish, a place with a commanding view. Later, when it is time to say goodbye, there still may be plenty of "gaps" around, a "cultural" gap, a "generational" one, a "socioeconomic" one; but there is also in visitor and visited a touch of sadness, a feeling that attachments have taken place, that separations are painful, that letters ought to be written, and time declared not only an enemy but a friend, because there will be a next visit (won't there?). Another visit means, of course, the promise of yet another occasion for all of us to be courteous and friendly and even enthusiastic, to feel quizzical and perplexed, to ask questions or look interested, to answer questions and appear tired or bored or indifferent, or feel compelled to conceal one's state of mind, one's "attitude."

I cannot put such developments down on paper; they defy words, thank God, because they are the spontaneous, unaffected, unstudied stuff of life. I can only say that they are there, those mountaineers in Grassy, West Virginia, and the sharecroppers or migrants I continue to visit in colorfully named and sad, very sad towns and hamlets and camps and tiny clusters of a house or two. They are there, out on the land. They are always there, as if put there by Nature's very order of things. They are men and women and children whose job it is to take on that land, and who, in so doing, become the people they are.

CRITICAL THEORY AND PSYCHOHISTORY

NORMAN BIRNBAUM

Edited reconstruction of taped presentation at Wellfleet meetings, August 25, 1972

PARTICIPANTS: Norman Birnbaum, Margaret Brenman-Gibson, Peter Brooks, Erik H. Erikson, Kenneth Keniston, Robert Liebert, Robert Jay Lifton, Steven Marcus, Alexander Mitscherlich, William Phillips, Richard Sennett

Freud held that domination and compliance were reflections of that repressiveness without which civilization would dissolve and which was, indeed, the price of such progress as we could claim. He hoped for an ultimate alliance of Eros and reason, an extension of the psychoanalytic project to society at large. In the indeterminate historical interim, however, he resigned himself to a rational acceptance of Eros' defeat.

A Promethean Marx saw in humanity's temporary regressions injuries which would hasten its self-fulfillment. The Promethean aspects of humanity were, for the time being, objectified in the development of its productive powers, in the mastery of nature. That triumph, however, was highly equivocal. It was won precisely by developing a structure of domination and exploitation. This, however, was infused with a particular psychic content, in which human substance was distorted and fragmented. That very distortion and fragmentation, the self-alienation originating in the labor process, was a potential source of a gigantic future reversal of the historical process. The replacement of self-alienation by a conscious and free praxis, in which humanity would realize itself, was the ultimate meaning of socialist revolution. Marx's view of human fulfillment no doubt goes back to the Greek idea of *telos*. The revolution, alas, appears to have been delayed until the Greek kalends.

The failure of Marxist prophecy, the verification of the Freudian one, are the elements of a dreadful secular eschatology. We are parts of a humanity caught in an unending cycle of exploitation, domination, repression and pain. Therewith my despair—and the beginning point of the talk.

This presentation draws upon my own recent work,* but is relatively self-contained. It does rest, as I indicated last night, on an effort to extricate myself from a certain metaphysical or metahistorical despair. Despite the recent reappearance of an American left, this country still has a long way to go before we even attain an institutionalized opposition like the working-class parties of Western Europe. These countries, of course, have their own problems. Domination and exploitation seem to recur eternally, whatever new forms they may take. All attempts to concretize utopia have been defeated, and much reform is derisory. I wonder whether certain kinds of existential despair are not more appropriate responses to the problem of psychohistory—understood as the inner history of humanity—than our efforts to develop a critical theory of society which claims to be an instrument of liberation. Nevertheless, I would like to explore the problems of a critical theory. I do so, obviously, from the disciplinary bias—if it can be called that—of a social scientist, and not as a practicing clinician.

In the first place, we have to take up the idea of critical theory and its relationship to practice, or praxis as it sometimes is called in a more technical sense (as a human project conceived and executed in a dialectical relationship to theory). Then I want to look at the origins of critical theory in the Marxist theory of alienation (and its counterpart, a less developed theory of disalienation, the overcoming of alienation). I'll continue by considering the complications introduced into (or for) critical theory by the present development of society. Finally, I'll turn to the present tasks of critical theory, particularly in its relationship to psychohistory.

*I give further references to work of mine in which some of these themes are developed: "The Crisis of Marxist Sociology," in Norman Birnbaum, *Toward a Critical Sociology*, Oxford University Press, New York, 1971; "Sociology: Discontents Present and Perennial," *Social Research*, Vol. 38, No. 4, Winter 1971; "Beyond Marx in the Sociology of Religion?", Chas. Glock and Philip Hammond (Editors), *Beyond the Classics*, Harper and Row, New York, 1973.

This is a program which may claim a substantial publisher's advance, and, to be realistic, I wonder how much of it I'll get through. With all respect to the conference, I do not think it matters. These ideas are cumulative, but also to some degree repetitive, and when I've gone on for an hour, I'll simply stop so that we can have ample time for discussion.

The idea of a critical theory does go back a long way, but I think that the best (or most typical) early modern expression of it was *The Encyclopedia,* the eighteenth-century *Encyclopedia* which intellectually preceded (and anticipated) the French Revolution. *The Encyclopedia* treated knowledge as liberating—knowledge, of course, including science. (It is interesting in this connection that the Institute for Policy Studies in Washington has been thinking of a new *Encyclopedia,* which it tentatively terms *Encyclopedia of Social Reconstruction, Plans and Practices for a New Society.*) The notion of science as a liberating force underwent or was subjected to what I call a positivistic degradation. That is to say, first, as a reflection and continuation of the division of labor in the larger process of social production, science itself became a specialized activity. Secondly, no longer within the capacity of the informed citizen (to whom the eighteenth-century *Encyclopedia* was addressed) to understand, it was the domain of an esoteric specialist. More importantly, science was detached from moral and political purposes. This detachment in turn served to attach it again to other moral and political purposes than those of the citizenry as a whole, namely, those which for want of a better term I designate as the technocratic utilization of science. This I understand as the utilization of science by those with power in society for the purposes of administration and domination.

In this context, critical theory is a project. It is not a scientific theory as described in commonplace textbooks on scientific method (which themselves may be now be out of date) or methodological discourse in the prevalent schools of behavioral science in the United States. It is not a theory which claims, or pretends, to be a value-free reproduction of a segment of external reality. As I look for the correct formulation, I'd say that critical theory is not simply an expression of the human capacity for making maps, images, or models of the world. It has something to do with the truth *of* and the truth *for* a higher notion of humanity, an unrealized or utopian notion of humanity. That is, critical theory contains (or entails) a metahistorical notion of the transcendence of the conditions it describes. Naturally, there is an extremely complicated relationship (which has to be specified for each use of critical theory) between this notion or component of transcendence and the empirical or theoretic description of the immanent developmental tendencies in each segment of social process. I think you understand, however, that critical theory as a project has philosophical ambitions which go well beyond the description of reality: these ambitions intend the alteration of reality.

It is important to exemplify this by showing what critical theory is not. It is not, let us say, advocacy social science. Advocacy social science has been much discussed of late in this country. Think of the journal *Social Policy* and of a certain idea of the uses of knowledge developed by the American New Left. Knowledge is to be put at the disposal of hitherto underprivileged groups, disenfranchised by the technocratic oligopolies. There is certainly something noble, and politically justifiable, about the idea of knowledge serving new groups, new publics. But I do not think that this is necessarily connected with the conception of a critical theory. Critical theory goes beyond the expression of the partial interests of segments of the community, to the vision of a truer or more authentic and profound community. That community would be constituted by a transformed, a fulfilled humanity.

Now, I think that the Marxist origins of critical theory are clear, and I'll sketch these briefly in a moment. But I also insist on the curious fact that it was some of the idealistic opponents of Marxism at the turn of the century, working in neo-Kantian or neo-Hegelian idiom, who contributed (unintendedly) to the development of a contemporary critical theory. They insisted on the existence of a plurality of value universes, on the role of human choice in shaping these universes, and on the absolutely irreconcilable nature of value conflict. The view that values are not simply naturalistic derivations of historical process, mechanical derivations, but that they can be imposed upon history by human beings in itself can also contribute to a critical theory. It seems to me that the roots of critical theory in two of the very great Western traditions strengthen rather than weaken it.

Obviously, these ideas of critical theory swim in air, or float in classrooms, unless some kind of connection with social practice or praxis can be found. I'm one of the editors (there are twenty or so) of the Yugoslav international journal *Praxis*. This journal, like other journals which bear names like *Telos, Konkret* and so on, have one central characteristic, namely, an absurd degree of abstraction and remoteness from any concrete human activity. That is to say, praxis as a theoretic idea has become the ideology of a group of Marxist thinkers discontented with every known regime. However, the idea of a higher human practice infused by theory, or praxis, still retains a certain dignity, because I think it can be shown that it can be used to control or to criticize actual efforts at social reform, change and even (as the Yugoslav case indeed shows) revolution. If we look at some of the roots of this notion of praxis, we come closer not only to its philosophical sources but to some of its potential for guiding our own activity. These roots are found, I think, in a chain of thought that goes back from Marx and Hegel to Aristotle. Praxis is the expression of specifically human properties, so that the correct praxis consists of determining the highest human capacities and developing these. On these grounds, the kind of praxis connected with or advocated by a truly critical theory is not simply a step-by-step, pragmatic, empirical practice. Praxis entails an element of realization or liberation of human potential. On this account of the matter, the one thing indispensable to successful social practice would be a correct theory, or at least a theory with a large measure of truth about humanity and its potential. Inasmuch as pragmatic, empirical experiment is necessary, experiment with new social forms (or new styles of life, as they are sometimes called) can never generate a permanent community—unless it filters back, is referred to an assimilated, to a continuously evolving, self-critical body of theory which can shed light on the empirical paths to follow.

I do not need to carry on at length before this group on the divergences between philosophical assumptions of this kind and the kinds of ideas received favorably in doctoral oral examinations in the social sciences in most universities—particularly in the English-speaking world, and, above all, the United States. I learned these things myself, after graduate school in sociology in the Department of Social Relations at Harvard, by a process of negation—and in the course of living in Europe. These assumptions require, of course, not only a rejection of what is called the behavioral approach to the social sciences, but, much more profoundly, a rejection of the idea of a value-free social science. There is no absolute demarcation or split between the social sciences, on the one hand, and let us say the moral sciences, or philosophy, on the other. At the same time, it seems to me, there is nothing in these methodological (really, metahistorical) canons which precludes and much that encourages the rigorous examination of evidence. The construction of partial theories, the day-by-day, hard and binding work of social and psychological analysis, is imperative—as long as theories of this sort are recognized as limited.

The roots of critical theory, if we look more closely at them, do lie to a considerable degree in the Marxist theory of alienation and in the tentative Marxist sketches about what I term disalienation (termed by Marx and the Marxists the dissolution or overcoming or transforming [*Aufhebung*] of alienation). Apart from the conceptual structure derived from Hegel's *Phenomenology of the Spirit,* in which the self-alienation of the spirit is expressly dealt with, the sources of the Marxist theory are three. A Romantic aesthetics, in which human beings function as creators of values, was generalized to include the highest creative capacities of humanity. The second source is clearly the Enlightenment criticism of philosophical obscurantism and of the institutional tyranny brought about by an alliance of priests and kings. Third, we find the idea of the realization of heaven on earth, this time put in the language of a humanity transformed and in the rhetoric of the elimination or, more precisely, supersession of religion.

Now, the Marxist conception of alienation, composed from these sources, is curiously obsolescent. That is, whatever efforts we may make to connect it with modern psychoanalytic theory, we have to recognize that the psychology on which it rests is not in its content plausible to us. Its intention, its moral intention, its concept of a holistic humanity or of a mankind healed or restored, may please us; its concrete content can help us very little—a fact which is sometimes overlooked by large numbers of contemporary Marxists and sympathizers with Marxism, who suppose that the concept can be translated immediately into the language of social science. I find this deficiency the reason for the enormous disparity between the theoretic and philosophical promise of contemporary Marxism and its relatively low degree of, let us say, critical performance with respect to contemporary institutions (with certain conspicuous exceptions).

The concept of alienation in Marxism involved a unitary or integral human substance, fragmented and violated by the division of labor. The structures of domination and exchange deprived humanity of direct, primary or expressive relations between human beings. Under these conditions, human activity in the form of work and production itself contributed—paradoxically—to the inhumanity of the human world. Only the fundamental alteration, therefore, of these relationships would free humanity to become itself. In this sense, the view that an economic-interest theory (or an interest theory of any kind) is basic to Marxism strikes me as false. It is under the conditions of alienation that humanity follows, or is obliged to follow, its interests. This occurs in a labor-divided and class-divided society. In the post-alienated, or disalienated, state human beings would be free to do what is most human: express themselves. At times, then, the notion of alienation rests not on Promethean conceptions of humanity as creative but also on Dionysian modes: the expression of human impulse as the substance of humanity. I suppose that in this sense Wilhelm Reich is in the Marxist tradition.

ALEXANDER MITSCHERLICH: He [Reich] is not in the Marxist tradition?

BIRNBAUM: No, very much in the Marxist tradition, even in his treatment of the instinctual life, amongst other things. We can think of Norman Mailer's famous essay on the white Negro as to some extent the ideological manifesto of the counterculture many years in advance of the counterculture. Mailer wrote this essay (if I'm correctly informed) at a time when he was directly under the influence of Reichian psychoanalysis. I do not know whether he was in therapy or not, but it is not relevant.

PHILLIPS: Is his theory of the orgasm Marxist?

BIRNBAUM: It's compatible with the Marxist theory. Surprisingly enough, the theory of orgasm seems to me, to put it minimally, not incompatible with certain ideas found in the *Economic-Philosophical Manuscripts of 1844*.

But what about the roles of disalienation in the Marxist canon: what do they entail? In the first place, the canon argues that humanity comes to consciousness of itself through blockage, deprivation and frustration. Awareness of its potential is not simply a notion that certain needs are to be satisfied, but a view that its stature has to be altered. That is to say, under the conditions of a labor-divided society, humanity is diminished. From this point of view, revolutionary activity is in itself a form of activity therapy, or praxis. Praxis is a form of the reclamation of humanity by itself. The relationship of this process to knowledge recapitulates some of the themes of critical theory: knowledge and correct practice, or praxis, meet. Because there is a unity of human truth, it is not alone the truth about mankind, or humankind, not alone the truth about humanity, but the truth *for* humanity, the truth lived by humanity in the process of self-development. It is not an abstract theory or a positivistic conception of the truth.

In this view of disalienation, the proletariat functions as a surrogate for all of humanity. It is the most human class because the most suffering, and therefore precisely the class with the greatest capacity to develop the realization of a new human potential. In the disalienated state or postalienated society, as sketched in the *German Ideology,* we do find a utopian vision of human development: a world without the constraint of scarcity, a world in which personalities are free to develop, to exchange roles, as we should say today—an interesting connection with some of the discussion by Ken Keniston and others on the potentiality of a so-called postindustrial society. In this utopian vision of development, then, humanity is free to develop its aesthetic and intellectual, indeed its technical, capacities without the constraints of scarcity and without the division of labor. I should add that Marx asserts that it is not private property which causes the division of labor, but the division of labor which causes private property. This, of course, implies that a certain level of the development of the productive forces is necessary as a precondition of a communist or utopian society.

Now, of course, in the later Marx some of these themes were—so to speak—sublimated. This is an enormous discussion, which I do not think it really pays to recapitulate. The young Marx versus the old Marx, or was the old Marx truer, who was the real Marx, and so on. There is no doubt that what everyone says is true: as Marx grew older, he did turn to political economy and left philosophy, explicit philosophy and metahistory behind. On the other hand, the categories for the description of the working of capitalism are directly derived from the early work. Here I bow to Steven Marcus, who has taken upon himself the perverse, not to mention masochistic, task of reading everything Engels wrote. Surely, the old Engels did in fact convert Marxism from a form of Hegelian metacritique of human historical existence to something resembling evolutionist and positivist doctrine. This, however, was not necessarily true to many of the components of authentic Marxism. Our problem is, I think, not one in the textual analysis of the Marxist tradition. It is, instead, a serious historical problem, a conceptual problem. By default, Marxism remains the one critical, social theory (along with Freudianism, which deals with other domains of human existence). Marxism in its entirety clearly does not work any longer, despite all kinds of efforts to save it. I myself project a series of works under the general rubric the Marxist legacy. We have had a legacy, and like many heirs we are faced with the embarrassing task of spending or liquidating the legacy and yet remaining true to the intentions of the persons who willed it to us. But if we look at the historical problems facing a contemporary critical theory, we are overwhelmed. We are simply incapable of subsuming them under one theory; the division of labor has itself been altered (as we shall see, not least due to the role of what Marx called the "scientific power" in the production process), and a key concept like alienation no longer can function as a key to the riddle of history. Let's look at these problems in a rather concrete way, and then go on to consider some of our present analytical dilemmas.

I want to discuss four problems which a contemporary critical theory has to confront. The first is the failure of the proletariat.

MARCUS: As if Marx and Engels had disgraced themselves again.

BIRNBAUM: The failure of the proletariat may well be connected with the fact that in the Western European societies and the United States, the proletariat, as depicted by Marx in the middle of the nineteenth century, became less proletarian. That in itself was a possibility that Marx as well as Engels envisaged. They themselves tended to what might be termed reformist politics toward the end of Marx's life. This process (deproletarianization) had the effect of socially integrating the proletariat as part of a national community. Marx and Engels, I think, despite their own fierce German nationalism, curiously underestimated the appeal or the cohesiveness of national ideologies as opposed to the force of class interests. At the same time, the proletariat underwent a number of transformations. It became, not a proletariat, but a working class. It was subjected to the winds or tides of nationalism, even chauvinism; it became an accomplice in the imperial domination of other peoples. And as it was integrated socially into the national community, paradoxically it developed its own counterculture. I use the term advisedly. The parties and movements which originally intended to prepare the revolutionary transformation of capitalist society became vehicles for the adaptation of the working class to it. They formed enclaves within the national communities. This was certainly true of pre-1914 German Social Democracy; it is true today of the French and Italian Communist Parties. Both are powers in their societies incapable of assuming the leadership of those societies even if it would be very difficult to dislodge them from an important share in, let's say, the distributive process (not the administrative process) in their countries. What is at issue is more than the political integration of the working-class movements in Europe: it is, equally, a form of parallel society or culture possessed by that class and organized by its parties. That seems to me to be the first, and certainly a very critical, problem for a Marxist theory which—after all—did predict that working-class organization and culture would lead to the opposite of integration, revolution.

The second problem is what I would term the problem of the wrong revolution in the wrong place. The revolution occurred not in the industrially advanced but in the industrially backward countries, first in Russia, later in agrarian China, more recently in certain Third World countries. These are countries which had the peculiarity, as well, of being outside the Western cultural and philosophical tradition. And since they are outside that tradition I wonder whether the conceptual argument, the conceptual apparatus, involved in the doctrines of alienation and disalienation can be directly applied to these revolutions. When I speak of the wrong revolution, I also mean wrong from the viewpoint of having educative or model functions for the advanced societies. I think that they do not have those functions. I also note that with the possible exception of Yugoslavia and certain experiments connected with the Cultural Revolution in China none of these revolutions has followed what we may call explicit and purposeful disalienating policies. The notion of a policy aimed at overcoming certain forms of human alienation has more or less tacitly (at times more or less explicitly) been dropped in these revolutions.

Of more importance for us, I think, have been the structural changes in capitalism. This I would cite as the third major issue which contemporary critical theory has to confront. And here I would point to three kinds of structural changes in capitalism which I think it is important for us to consider.

The first of these is the pervasive process of bureaucratization which stems from the massive interpenetration of state and society. It is impossible to separate state and economy even in so-called free-enterprise societies. The economic role which the state adopts as a means of distribution and economic control is simply enormous. Modern capitalism is unthinkable as a free-enterprise system. Modern capitalistic interests need, above all, to control the modern capitalist state. At the same time, the scale of capitalist enterprise—national and multinational—is such that bureaucratic forms of hierarchical organization, administration and production in the private sector parallel those in the public sector.

Bureaucratization is a mode of organization of the social forms of late capitalism. That is to say, it is impossible to have a high degree of monopoly capitalism without using a bureaucratic apparatus. This was not foreseen by Marx. It was discussed already by the turn of the century among World War I Marxists of the generation of Hilferding and Rosa Luxemburg, and others. They were attempting to bridge the unbridgeable or reconcile the irreconcilable, namely, to interpret changes in capitalism with a certain fidelity to the original model. But it seems to me that the dynamics of this structural change in capitalism are to be found in what has been called social imperialism.

Here I come to the second point I want to adduce about structural change in capitalism, the development of an entire nation as an imperial community. The phenomenon is old in a country like Britain, perhaps even in this country. It has recently been subjected to an acute or heightened degree of critical consciousness. Social imperialism entails a considerable degree of integration of the working class in the imperialist enterprise or project, making it an accomplice in the exploitation of other nations, the emergence of a global proletariat. And, of course, the organization of the competing capitalist nations for imperialist purposes almost guarantees a perennial situation of international conflict, providing an economic and political dynamism for the system.

The third structural change in capitalism, and one of equal importance to our understanding of the mechanisms of integration of the working class in modern society, is the industrialization of culture. The prime source of our insight into this development can be found in the famous chapter on the cultural industry in Horkheimer's and Adorno's *Dialectics of Enlightenment,* recently available in English but first published in 1947. Cultural industry is the industrial production of a culture for mass consumption. It reproduces, uncritically, the surface of daily life. The cultural sphere, the general sphere of symbolic reflection and image-making, becomes not a protected area in which society and its institutions can be criticized, but a means of ideological consolidation of the status quo.

PHILLIPS: How are you disagreeing with Marcuse at this point?

BIRNBAUM: I'm not really disagreeing with Marcuse, the more so as the ideas found in *One Dimensional Man* and (less so, perhaps) in *Eros and Civilization* directly follow from the *Dialectics of Enlightenment.* Marcuse is, in a sense, the American representative of the Frankfurt School.

Curiously, the fourth point about capitalism is the political effect of what I would term tyrannical socialism, which seems incapable (in our societies, at least) of engendering world historical enthusiasm as a model for transformation. The Soviet Union is, perhaps, the chief example of a terroristic industrialization, with horrors that rivaled and at times exceeded those of primitive accumulation in nineteenth-century Europe. It also has a bureaucratized and centralized administration with absolutely no libertarian or pluralistic component. It manifests a degree of cultural standardization, not to mention philistinism, which makes the American TV networks seem to be functioning in some postrevolutionary utopia. Under these conditions, the absence of a really compelling counterforce, the cultural and political consolidation of capitalism was easier to accomplish.

I have been attempting to give an account, perhaps a litany, of our woes. And we may ask at this point whether, faced with the historical situation as it is, critical theory is able to offer any solutions. Must it not simply lapse, may not its components have to be separated? On the one hand, we have a moral and political critique of existing institutions, with morally motivated political action to overcome these. On the other hand, we have a more or less empirical and historical description of these institutions, descriptions compiled in the hope that in some unsystematic way the information and insight accumulated by the operations of intelligence will be used for moral and political purposes. An alternative or different system would be constructed on the basis of knowledge. If this were the case, this would indeed force us back to a situation not unlike the situation imagined to be true by most of our colleagues in the moral and social sciences. That is a situation in which there is an absolute distinction of spheres, a distinction of discourse between a social science, or a social theory, and a politics—a politics taken in the generic sense of an attempt to shape a human community. Before reconciling ourselves so easily to this situation of fragmentation and ordinary despair, we ought to see whether something can be made in fact of the legacy of critical theory. In particular, I'd ask whether an infusion (and I use the term with real hesitation, since it is so imprecise) of the Freudian legacy cannot save the Marxist one by revivifying it.

First, we must deal with a difficulty in the Freudian legacy itself. There are two somewhat contradictory, or at least very different, moral philosophies explicit in the work of Freud. Freud once praised his small group of early collaborators (those to whom he gave that set of rings) by saying of them that they had learned to bear a piece of reality.

ALEXANDER MITSCHERLICH: *Ein Stück Wirklichkeit ertragen.*

BIRNBAUM: Now, here is what has been called, I think earlier by Ken, the stoical dimension in Freud. Psychoanalysis has an Old Testament–like, awful, moral lesson: that all humans suffer, that life is hard and unremitting, and that health consists in the ability to comprehend and understand that these blows are inevitable. There is a harsh moral quality to this, some of which was expressed in that remarkable letter of what only can be termed no consolation Freud sent to the widow of Karl Abraham after the latter's death. He said that he'd had difficulty in writing the letter, had delayed doing so, but that when he sat down to write, it was not any easier. There was nothing he could tell her. This was an absolute confrontation of pain and the abyss, an almost metaphysical renunciation of hope. Yet we can find at the same time in Freud's hopes for psychoanalysis, for its cultural consequences, an idea of a liberating therapy—not just for individual patients, but for a reeducated humanity. Freud situated psychoanalysis, in other words, not only in the tradition of Copernicus and Darwin, who confronted a narcissistic humanity with hard truths, but in the tradition of the Enlightenment. That is a tradition which certainly included or includes Marx. I say this despite the anecdote reported by Sachs. At the beginning of the Soviet Revolution, the Bolsheviks were not unfriendly to psychoanalysis, and Freud had patients from the Soviet Union—including a high official. This person told Freud that Lenin had declared that the first fifty years of the Revolution would be unremitting toil, suffering, deprivation, disappointment. The next fifty, however, would be splendid. Freud, with his characteristic irony, said something like "Well, I'll give you the first half."

Freud was skeptical and wrote skeptically of Marxism, and yet in the notion of a liberating, an experienced and lived knowledge, there are obviously not alone spiritual resemblances between Freudianism and Marxism but also structural connections. Finding these structural connections is enormously difficult. This is not the place, and we lack the time to review the large, very large, Marx-Freud literature—the best of which doesn't appear in English. There were very interesting discussions in the late 1920s in Weimar, Germany (now again in the German Federal Republic), discussions participated in by persons like Bernfeld and Fenichel, some of whom came here and did rather different things, in different *personae*.

I do think that we can say that it is extremely difficult to recognize any direct relationship of a one-to-one kind between the pervasive kinds of character disorders now favored in psychoanalytical treatment (now favored in the sense that they seem to make up many of the clinical reports in the clinical literature), the disorders which introspection and observation combine to suggest also dominate our culture, and the symptomatology of alienation as depicted in the Marxist tradition. The concentration of some kinds of explicit suffering amongst patients from the middle class indeed would make the connection even more remarkable, could it be established. It is frequently middle-class persons who have the most autonomy at work, the most expressiveness in their work and their lives, who in their work enjoy considerable amounts of freedom. Yet this group is most pervaded by psychic malaise and misery, in many of its forms. I am aware that Marx did not locate alienation exclusively in work or in market and exchange relationships; it was, for him, also the consequence of the absence of an authentic human community. Nevertheless, at first glance at least, it is impossible to crystallize, or concretize, or localize, the sources of the psychic malaise we know in any one sector of the society. Familial and sexual relations; work and economic relations; politics and the organization of the larger society; culture and aesthetic expression: the malaise appears equally intense, equally pervasive. We are obviously able to establish (or diagnose) interconnections between these spheres. At the same time it is extremely difficult, even for a skilled Marxist or a dialectically supple neo-Marxist, to insist upon the priority of one or the other sphere. It is this failure of diagnostic success, a failure of causal analysis, which appears, despite promising beginnings, to have prevented the development of a theoretically enriched or articulated relationship between Marxism and the classical Freudian tradition.

This theoretical failure has led, at least in this country and perhaps elsewhere as well, to a new form of disalienating politics—the politics of the counterculture. A theoretical account of the interconnection between character disorder and alienation in the political community is absent. Present, however, are the lessons of both the Freudian and Marxist traditions—lessons read as schematized directives to go out and liberate yourselves. The counterculture has emerged as what might be described as an artificial, a willed utopia. It has obviously encountered serious institutional resistance, some of it taking the form of encapsulation and exploitation. It is interesting that the original notions of the counterculture as devised by Mailer, and later to some degree popularized or vulgarized by minor prophets like Hoffman and Rubin, has made use of extremely blunt, extremely superficial, notions of impulse expression as the *via regis* of attack on authority. There is even in Jerry Rubin's *Do It!* a parody of the Communist Manifesto, as if instinctual rebellion were all that mattered. Instinctual rebellion or impulse rebellion would in fact serve as a new Joshua's trumpet and blow down the walls of an institutional Jericho. The evidence is not all in, but it does appear that despite the counterculture and whatever long-term undermining effect it may yet have, the institutions of late-capitalist society are still able to function; they work rather well.

Brigette and Peter Berger, our colleagues in sociology, have argued that there are always replacements, that for every middle-class counterculture dropout there is a blue-collar person ready to rise in the hierarchy. This seems to me not to be true. The counterculture is intrinsically a consumer item, and can be consumed to some degree by the working class as well.

The counterculture rests on the notion that administration and production are gratuitous, that distribution is the problem, and that the problem of distribution can be solved by a parody of liberalism, by an absolutely random distribution. People will then seize upon what they need from this distributive cornucopia and use it for their own free and high purposes. That seems to make the counterculture a system heavily involved in consumption and which has nothing, or very little, to say about the institutions of administration and production. Secondly, it is a consumer item in a very specific market sense, that is to say it is sold or vended. Its heroes, meanwhile, sometimes fairly ephemeral ones, are available for the cultural industry. And the society seems to have integrated, or capitalism seems to have integrated, this challenge which was supposed to have undermined it, by undermining amongst other things the will to work, deference to any kind of authority and the like.

KENISTON: I agree with you in the short run. In the long run, however, it may be different.

BIRNBAUM: Yes, it may be. I'm reminded that an old friend of William's and mine has said recently in *Partisan Review* that the great thing about the contemporary counterculture is that people insist on having fun. This was Clement Greenberg, a profound critic of mass culture. There is something to it, and I may well be underestimating it. It seems to me that the theory of the counterculture is a curious parody of a fused and undigested Freudo-Marxism. It is almost as if all the hard work, the hard thought, the conceptual apparatus, the slow labor against the real external and intrinsic intellectual difficulties involved in the rapprochement of these two theories had been set aside in favor of a few simplified injunctions, to go out and do it or to live it up. The very frenzy of the injunction suggests the uncertainty of the directive.

LIFTON: Would you distinguish between the Jerry Rubin type of counterculture, which much that you said describes, and something a dimension removed, which is more amorphous, doesn't have a name, which adopts a lot of the experimental so-called life styles that have been talked about in association with the counterculture and that includes many very serious people? The countercultural elements of which I am speaking might be as critical of Jerry Rubin as you are. (Though a good case could be made for Jerry Rubin's seriousness too.) What I am getting at is the danger of seeing only a caricature of something that involves much more underneath and has much greater potential, although still many conflicts.

BIRNBAUM: I agree, with reservations. It may be that for the moment the truest answer is the simplest one. There is an autonomy of spheres, and we have been unable to make (with some significant exceptions) important connections and interconnections between economic-political processes, on the one hand, and the intrapsychic processes, on the other. Freud's long-term educative hopes for psychoanalysis remain unrealized. If we look for new possibilities of a revolution or human transcendence, we may have to revert for the time being to the sphere of political work in social institutions. If we look, however, at the possibilities of what we might term political mobilization, as we seek new modes of organizing new agents of social transformation, new social groupings, new sectors of the labor force, of reactivating consciousness in the working class, of devising real counterinstitutions, of devising forms of institutional and participatory democracy for wider sectors of our public life, including the economy—if we look at all of these matters and seriously pose the question of historical agency, two very great difficulties appear, the first philosophic and the second psychohistorical.

The philosophical one is more easily described than dealt with. Quite apart from our difficulty in putting together the elements of modern society for purposes of analysis, we lack a vision of our ends. We have no conception of the dimensions and structures of a fulfilled or even a viable political community. It may be that only such a conception of our ends can in turn generate the elements of an analysis of our present situation. In other words, a metahistorical idea of community may be the most effective guarantor of an empirically adequate and concrete historical analysis.

The second, or psychohistorical, difficulty is best rephrased as a difficulty in or with psychohistory. Clearly, no idea of a community can dispense with an idea of a fulfilled humanity—of a psychologically matured or developed humanity, its potential realized (or, at least, a good deal of it unblocked), relatively at one with itself. Psychohistory, as practiced up to now, does not quite escape what I would term an empiricist temptation. It offers us a series of discrete images of human development, in several historical situations, some of them very disparate. The elements are always combined and recombined in different ways, historically. Not one humanity emerges; several do.

That is one side of the difficulty. The other is no less problematical. The concept of identity and renewed attention to symbolization as a defense against the idea of death and recurrent problems of the life cycle point to the psychohistorical search for universals in the human situation. Psychohistory is, then, not alone a record of the working of these universals in specific historical epochs and structures. It is a record of human fate, of a struggle within and against history. Let us put it another way: psychohistory uses the psychoanalytic tradition and our awareness of human historicity in a new search for a human essence.

In its present phase of development, psychohistory's boundaries are difficult to circumscribe. Indeed, there seems to be no particular need to do so. Psychohistory is not only a mode for the understanding of history, but possibly a modern version or interpretation of the task of a critical theory. In that sense the pursuit of psychohistorical explanation and analysis may very well be an authentic derivative of what I depicted as the Marxist legacy.

BRENMAN-GIBSON: Or a marriage of the two?

BIRNBAUM: I wouldn't say that, because it may be just a long-term alliance, or a heated if constructive conflict. In any case a marriage takes two viable partners. Increasingly, we can see a conception of, or a project for, a critical sociological theory which would be more viable than nineteenth-century Marxism. Marriage between this and psychoanalysis is not quite the right term. Eventually, perhaps, a synthesis might be possible. For the moment, nothing so definite obtains. I think that the liberating intent of what's been done in psychohistory does coincide with the intentions of a critical social theory. There is too much connection for this not to be so.

PHILLIPS: The term "critical theory," as I understand it, means a kind of unified theoretical investigation and moral inquiry. In other words, you unite value judgments with objective observations. Retrospectively it is possible to recognize that there are activities which are morally impelled and activities which are impelled by some more purely scientific ethos. But how can you plan to combine those in advance? It's like Einstein's unified-field theory: how can you plan such unified theory, how would you go about planning it?

BIRNBAUM: Perhaps I gave too totalistic an idea of critical theory, too finished an idea. What I thought of was the infusion of particular activities, clinical and theoretical psychoanalysis, empirical and theoretical sociology, political economy, and aesthetic inquiry, but not so much a finished critical theory as the search for one. The dominant assumption is that we can never completely establish a critical theory as an articulated, finished, much less dogmatic system. But it functions as a set of moral intentions, a set of moral intentions about the world and a set of methodological assumptions about the way certain things, certain institutions, certain attitudes, certain characterological developments are put together. It involves the possibilities of reeducation. It is not a matter of the immediate conversion of *Partisan Review* into an organ for the promulgation of a critical social theory. It is that already, clearly, but it is that because a number of contributors and editors are beginning to share a certain perspective.

LIFTON: Norman, let me raise a general question that may lead to ways of discussing the really exquisite statement you made. In a way I'm struck, as I'm sure others are, by the difference in our styles —yours and mine—in groping toward critical theory. My own way has to do with certain impressions derived mostly from immediate psychological encounters with certain groups of people, and then some extension of that, calling upon Freudian and other psychological theory in a critical way. Yours has to do with starting from descriptions of Freudian and, more to the point here, Marxian theory in terms of what it tried to do as a critical theory, what it did do, where it failed and where we are now. There are obviously problems and attainments in both of these styles, leaving aside any simple judgment that one is better than the other, which isn't what I'm trying to say.

BIRNBAUM: What we may expect of critical theory is to absorb energies from contemporary experiments, but also to assimilate the lessons of the past, not alone our American but other pasts. I conceive of the task of critical theory, therefore, as also being able to situate these experiments. This isn't the first time in America that communes have been developed.

LIFTON: It may well be that what we call the counterculture may have relatively little to do with Freud and Marx beyond being a parody of a kind of fused Freudo-Marxism. It may be more fundamentally an expression of unmanageable, rapid historical and technological change, for instance, about which Freud and Marx have only relatively tangential things to say. But they did not have, you know, a precise analytic grasp of this kind of situation. I am not questioning the need to go back to Freud and Marx, but maybe one has to go back after taking a more careful look at the human struggles that a critical theory has to direct itself to, rather than critical theory being a continuation of that critical tradition of Freud and Marx. There is a kind of different emphasis.

MARCUS: How would the statements you made differ from the general thesis about Freud held by Marcuse in *One Dimensional Man?* My point is I think that that's the last critical breakthrough of critical theory, the last plateau reached by critical theory.

BIRNBAUM: I have doubts about the originality of *One Dimensional Man* (although the critique of positivistic language was somewhat new). I think that *Eros and Civilization* was the last breakthrough. *One Dimensional Man* made more news, but it was conceptually more derivative. I recall that when I spoke to Berlin students at the Free University in 1965 about some of these themes, I was criticized for having advanced a program for research rather than for action—a fate suffered by Marcuse himself some years later. The maintenance of a critical social theory in hard times, times of encapsulation and integration, let alone oppression, is in fact an act of political defiance—or an act of political hope or faith. The active pursuit of a critical theory in a so-called knowledge-based society is in itself a political act because a knowledge-based society depends on the production and strict demarcation of technically utilizable knowledge, not critical knowledge. It gets critical knowledge without intending it. It depends for functioning upon an educated labor force, a strictly technical education. The mastery of technique presupposes a general education, and that in turn brings students (and the public, addressed by those who work in universities and the contiguous sectors of the knowledge industry) in contact with critical ideas.

KENISTON: The emergence of a kind of knowledge-based society, which requires millions of highly educated, technically trained people, also tends to generate (as it were) its own contradiction in that these people do have to have, at least at the highest levels, some kind of critical capacity. So even though for the moment the counterculture, the student movement and so on are relatively quiet, there are very powerful forces in a technocratic society that serve to generate a progressively growing group of people who have some kind of individualization of their world view. Furthermore, it is possible for many of us in America and in other post-scarcity societies in Western Europe to take production and administration for granted. That is generating another long-term reaction of indifference to the Protestant work ethic. Yankelovich's repeated polling suggests that even if the heyday of political radicalism crested around 1969–70 and has declined rapidly since, one sees thereafter a progressively greater rejection of Protestant-ethic statements amongst similar groups of college students. In my optimistic moments, at least, I would reject your notion of the counterculture as simply a kind of erratic spasm. I would argue that it is indeed one form of a new consciousness. It is an orientation which a few people have always had, but which we are now producing in more people through higher education, the mass media, new kinds of childhood education, and so on.

BRENMAN-GIBSON: Not to speak of a worldwide historical crisis.

KENISTON: Yes, that's what we talked about yesterday, the relativization of all knowledge and the fact that, increasingly, to be parochial one has to be reactionary. This also speaks to a question in socialist and radical thought about whether people have to be changed in advance in order to live in a socialist society. The relativized mindset has its own terrible dangers. Still, one can argue that it may require a large group of people who have this way of looking at the world in order to create a social contract where people come together in voluntary units. If that were the case, in some distant time, one could imagine a society which was rather different, not because human nature was fundamentally different, but because human potentials which had traditionally been by and large suppressed or not needed were urgently required and deliberately encouraged through education and so on. The point is that I think there is another way of looking at what we call loosely the counterculture, or the student movement, which would be more optimistic about it.

BIRNBAUM: I think that there are two points to be made. One is that there seems to be a kind of telescoping or fusing of possibility and achievement. It is true that the productive capacity of advanced industrial societies is such that administration and production are not matters of life or death. But they are matters of political life or death. That is to say, the conquest of power depends upon controlling the mechanisms of administration and production, and turning them to more humane, more just, newer ends, what you call a new social contract. It seems to me that from this point of view, and this is without doubt an old Marxist or old political position, if we look at the emergence and consolidation of the counterculture, the guarantee of the new human existence would have to be the control of these posts. That would call for a different kind of political strategy.

PHILLIPS: It's the old argument about whether you can develop a new man without a new society.

BIRNBAUM: Marx attacked the mid-nineteenth-century equivalent of the communal movement as an illusion.

KENISTON: I'm a little less critical than you are of the communal movement of today, for example. But I think that we all agree that the movement between new men and new societies is more complicated than saying, "We have to have a new man first and then a new society" or the reverse.

LIFTON: On this issue it is interesting to look at Marcuse and his psychology. To me, Marcuse has always been a kind of enigma in his psychological perspective, because he maintains a more or less instinctual, Freudian position in his large projection of society and his notion of repression and surplus repression. Then, in *One Dimensional Man,* he reverts to an almost nonpsychological method in order to make a very strong psychological statement. That is, a society of such rigidly fixed and functional institutions in advanced capitalism, our present society, creates men and women who are mirror images of their institutions. My impression of the way things are happening in this country is rather the reverse, in which not only is man much more Protean, but even those who are constricted, and who come closest to Marcuse's definition, are in a kind of despair and conflict. They're far from being one-dimensional. Marcuse has recently perhaps slightly extricated himself from this false box he put himself into.

Increasingly, he appears to value the aesthetic dimension. He's always been drawn to the aesthetic dimension in his own personal style, but he is now theoretically recognizing this strand in himself as he responds to some of the student movement, including (despite his strictures about the counterculture and his argument with Norman O. Brown) some of the countercultural experiments insofar as they seem to be an aesthetic form of liberation. This seems to me an example of the ease with which we misuse our psychologies, or don't use them, or somehow fail to bring a certain sophistication and complexity to our application of them.

PHILLIPS: My reading is the opposite of yours, Bob. It seems to me that he looks at the counterculture in a way that might seem to be sympathetic because he's looking at a symptom, and he discusses the symptomatology. He's thoroughly critical of it; in fact, he says it's a copout.

LIFTON: We're getting mixed up by the meaning of "counterculture."

LIEBERT: The counterculture is a unit that consists of many subcultures which I think of in terms of whether they tend to be alloplastic or autoplastic. The mystical movements, the Zen and Eastern freaks, those who are into drugs, are people who have turned into themselves to transcend the pain of their existence. Another group, which I would call alloplastic, directs their energies at the social structure through activity in the New Left or the radical feminist movement or the gay movement, or other political movements. They consist of very different people who come into the movement because of very different intrapsychic conflicts and different programs. And I think it gets very confusing to speak of the counterculture.

PHILLIPS: But the only part of this large entity which has many components that Marcuse was sympathetic with was that part which was political and radical in a Marxist sense.

LIFTON: I think he's somewhere in between. He's obviously much more sympathetic to the alloplastic side of the counterculture, that which is reaching out and therefore taking on a more or less political coloring. But I heard him emphasize in a lecture at Yale three or four years ago the radical significance of aesthetic experimentation.

For instance, he made a point of the importance of the color and pageantry of some of the student rebellion which should not be minimized in its revolutionary import. That isn't going as far as to embrace the autoplastic dimension of the counterculture. That he isn't doing. But it at least has the virtue of having his psychology connect with his eyes and ears as opposed to the fairly strict, classical, cerebral psychology he applied earlier (in *One Dimensional Man*), which was wrong for the situation, it seemed to me.

ERIKSON: What we're now calling "aesthetic" is related to what the Germans call *Spielraum:* space to *play* in. Now, any worthwhile critical theory in its origins had this, too, but it loses it somewhere. I can't see how one can look at anything which has lived for a century without asking, What *Spielraum* did it have originally, what *Spielraum* did it create? Only then one can ask what proved to be forever true afterward. And one could ask, psychohistorically speaking, What type of person wanted that critical theory originally, and in what period, and who was responsible for and responsive to what was developing? And then, where is that *Spielraum* in this Marx–Freud dialogue now?

Freud once said that education can only underline what is given, what is developing. I don't think theory can do anything else, either. I can well imagine that the counterculture today attempts to introduce some playful elements which critical theory introduced in its time. At least it gives people a chance to rethink things, whatever else it does. We have to ask what is the function of a utopia at a given time, not whether it will prove true afterward. Regardless of what happens to it later, it wasn't expendable when it occurred.

BIRNBAUM: What has critical theory produced? If we understand critical theory to be the Western Marxist tradition, I think it has produced, very roughly, two things. It has produced institutionalized opposition in Western society, in the form of working-class-based political movements, unions and the like. These have become increasingly detached from the remote aim of revolution and increasingly adapted to the modes of class division in Western society, even constitutive of it. Spiritually, it has produced an oppositional set of intellectuals like some of the people Freud went to school with for whom critical theory was an expression of a longing for a better life, an aesthetically and morally gratifying life, hopes which for a time they placed in the working-class movement. At other times, they withdrew those hopes from it. It is interesting that the discussion of the counterculture today was picked up, rather than other things. It seemed to me almost as if we were collectively searching for a newer historical agency for this transformation or liberation, with youth in the place of the proletariat.

LIFTON: Last night we came to some sense that the style of theory-making may have changed. The capacity of people to make and respond to a theory might have changed. That is why this becomes a point quite beyond the entity of the counterculture *per se*.

BROOKS: In terms of your call for a critical theory, what do you make of someone like Cohn-Bendit explicitly rejecting critical theory, and saying that what you have to do is to push action to the point at which you open what he called "the glimpse of a possibility"? In other words, create a concrete situation which can serve as a model of possible future developments.

SENNETT: Cohn-Bendit would hate what Norman said, because Norman doesn't have a theory of power. Cohn-Bendit pushes for a locus of graspable power, and searches for a place where one can act. One of the reasons why critical theory has a new task is that power has mystified itself, and we can no longer isolate it.

The idea that the person who defines the place to act has any responsibility to go there himself—neither of the Cohn-Bendits believed that. They're totally uprooted, *déraciné*, there is no sense that by identifying the place to act they have any further responsibility. In that sense they're not critical theorists, you know, and it is very explicit.

BIRNBAUM: It is interesting that the failure as well as the success of the 1968 uprising in France has had a lot of derivatives. Among the most interesting is the turn of the French Socialist Party to the left, the emergence of a strong new body of French trade-union doctrine (particularly in the ex-Catholic or left union, the CFDT, to the left of the Communist-led CGT). That is, it has led to some revivification of French socialism, with the Cohn-Bendits completely out.

BROOKS: Revivification, but not social theory so much as forms of organization which ought to lead to the renewal of theory or the renewal of action.

SENNETT: What I hear you saying which I find very exciting is that power is in the act of mystifying itself in our time. And one of the reasons why a critical theory comes to an impasse is that there is no adequate theory of power.

PHILLIPS: There is such a theory, it is Marxism.

SENNETT: We can't even make a class analysis. The idea of class itself is reduced to the point where it's no longer possible to think about change in a kind of dialectic, because power itself has lost its capacity to be intellectually isolated, so that we know X controls Y controls Z and so on. They exist in much more perverse and convoluted kinds of relationships with each other.

BIRNBAUM: I spoke, as other people certainly have spoken, of the difficulty of disengaging causal chains. Family, work, the state, communities—the difficulty is real enough, but certain causal chains probably do exist. There are probably certain nodal points and connections. The point that seems important is that, to a degree not dreamt of by Marx, populations have become instruments of their own subjugation, or have internalized, to use a familiar phrase, domination and exercise domination over themselves.

SENNETT: Then you have isolated what the first task of critical theory would be, which is to find out the ways in which we can isolate those chains, if they exist.

BIRNBAUM: That is why I spoke of psychohistory as a legitimate derivative of critical theory, why I confer legitimacy as a critical theory upon psychohistory.

SENNETT: Let's take that one step further. What you're saying now is that to find out the way in which we have a dialectic of power now what we need to do is use psychohistorical, life-cycle techniques and analyses. Now, why is that? Why should we learn anything more about power by using for instance Erik's idea of crises in the stages of development; what is that going to tell us about the power, the Nixon power, in this society?

BIRNBAUM: I think it's important to answer, or to attempt to answer, that question. I think that the reason one may conceive of power this way was also mentioned last night, if you remember Dr. Mitscherlich's remark about the persistence of the superego and the need for a three-generational context to give it some kind of coherence or shape. Things fall apart, the center does not hold. But in fact we live in a period in which there are historical legacies or historical processes working themselves out in which the generations are not simply the mute bearers of history but are very actively reenacting past histories which may be in part obsolete, in part viable. The psychohistorical contribution would certainly be the way to clarify this psychic inheritance and disinheritance.

SENNETT: And I want to know why doing that, with psychohistorical analysis, tells us more about what power is, meaning, who or what has the capacity to coerce other people to act against their will? That's much harder for us to find than it was for Marx or Engels. What does an analysis of the life cycle in terms of stages, where each stage is marked by a new crisis, help us to uncover about that kind of coercion? What's it telling us?

PHILLIPS: Norman, by "power" you mean state power, don't you? You mean political and economic power?

BIRNBAUM: Yes, political and economic power.

LIFTON: Especially as internalized against one's own interests.

PHILLIPS: Why is it more difficult to recognize right now?

BIRNBAUM: It's easy enough to recognize it. The Pentagon disposes of a budget that is a certain proportion of the national product. There is a cycle that keeps going, that's difficult to break. What's hardest to deal with is that you have a politician, a Presidential candidate who says, "I'm going to end this. We're going to spend the money for other things."

PHILLIPS: That's demagoguery and stupidity.

BIRNBAUM: It's exceedingly difficult to get this message across, and if we make an examination of, let's say, the hidden or not so hidden depths of public opinion and political symbolization, of popular political thought, we find phenomena like the self-hatred and internalized self-contempt of the working class, the sense people have that they face chaos if certain things change.

LIFTON: In the mid-1950s when I did work with Chinese intellectuals, older Chinese intellectuals who had been converted to Communism between the two wars, I was very struck by the way in which what we might call critical theory in China (even if viewed by some American scholars as a corruption of Marxism) was extremely viable and forceful in getting people to transform themselves very rapidly. People I interviewed gave very dramatic descriptions of how they had felt suffocated in their families, by the society, by suppressive influences of many kinds. They told of how critical ideas not only liberated them from these things but also gave them a chance to cease doing all the hypocritical things they were doing. Intellectuals who had been contemptuous of human labor were able to transform their relationship to less privileged sectors of society, and people who go to China now are still very impressed by this. There is something about critical theory that has taken hold, that is in a very simple way transformative. We talked about transformation among the autoplastic side of the counterculture, but it's no less so in political terms, or in the terms of critical theory you're describing. One difficulty in American life is that there is a need for transformation without the transformative ideas, ideas that begin to tell you that your life has been hypocritical, and that sufficiently convince you of that to release a new plane of imagery which carries you into a real transformation.

LIEBERT: Related to that is the general question of why one should study other people at all. Cohn-Bendit understood the need on the part of the people whom he led to experience this spontaneous release of energy, this kind of anarchistic rebellion free of programs, free of instructed ideology. We need to know more about the relationship between the existential anxieties of all human beings and those historically transient ideologies which derive from the social and technological structure. And if one understands those, which certainly our New Left does not, one can formulate some rational program.

KENISTON: It seems to me that Norman is correct in saying that many of the most insidious forms of exploitation and domination become internalized, are unconscious, become voluntary—whatever words we want to use. And we are in a better position to reverse this process if we understand how it comes about. Now it turns out that this process is extremely complex. It is not simply an absorption of corrections from the outside. It is a complex interactive process involving transactions between the inborn developmental potentials of the child and his broadening universe. It is a very active process whereby we willingly accept and even seek subjugation. As we understand this process better we become more able to interrupt it at points of vulnerability. This is not to say that the only way to create political change is to start with children, which I think is a kind of copout, but it is to say that we can do more about domination if we understand the process by which people accept it.

SENNETT: I want to know precisely how if we study the crisis of generativity—from Erik's model of human development—and learn something about what happens in that crisis, how does that kind of study help me to understand a social process in which power is becoming harder and harder to locate as something tangible?

MARCUS: I think part of what Dick is saying is that if, for example, you take the analysis of the British socioeconomic system that is put forth in *Das Kapital,* that that is at a higher level of penetration and understanding than anything we can manifest in relation to our society today.

Norman cited three major structural changes in capitalism. The first is the pervasive bureaucratization and the fusion of state and society; second, the complicity of social imperialism and the national community; third, the industrialization of culture. Take the whole development of Marxism, add these three things to it, and you still don't have a representation of society today which is as penetrating, analogically, as Marx's representation in 1868.

SENNETT: Norman seems to be suggesting that we will get to that high level by applying these insights not simply to the life of one particular individual, but to the social system as a whole. That I don't understand. I don't understand how you would go about it.

BIRNBAUM: It seems to me that before that can be done we have to take account of a methodological peculiarity of both Marxism and Freudianism. Remember Erik's citation from Freud, that education can only develop or work with what is given. Marx held that socialism was inevitable because the inner contradictions of bourgeois or capitalist society tended in this direction, and that socialism was the seizure of the inner movement of reality. It seems to me that what we need is the completion of the liberating, humanly therapeutic dimensions of Freudian theory, an abandonment of its stoic renunciation to some degree. We need to know from the psychohistorians, the critical psychologists and psychoanalysts, what is given in human nature, what are its capacities for growth, development, liberation, its capacity to free itself from its multiple, internalized, secreted tyrannies. Unless we know that, no project in the sense of a model of the future, a social utopia, will be viable. It becomes a gratuitous exercise in speculation. Now, that is a long initial detour but, I think, an important one, and that seems to me to be the task of psychohistory, of the critical theorists in a very general sense, because no other competence will respond to these questions.

PHILLIPS: Do you think that is knowable?

BIRNBAUM: Probably.

KENISTON: I think that is a point. The paradox may be that just at the point where one turns to the critical psychoanalysts for insight, one finds that they're—

LIFTON: They're lost.

KENISTON: They're lost for the very same reasons that other social theorists are lost, namely, that we all draw on the experience of the decade preceding, when what we're really interested in are the decades ahead. It is precisely those elements of novelty which we cannot know simply by empirical or psychoanalytic or clinical inquiry that have the greatest interest, are of the greatest concern. What is possible that has never happened before?

LIFTON: Couldn't that be overcome if the psychological component of the psychohistorical theory were increasingly process-oriented so that a change in a decade or five years or whatever wouldn't be catastrophic to the intellectual force of that theory?

KENISTON: I think that there is a very deep paradox here, in the nature of the future. We gain that kind of certainty only by being so general that we're not of much use.

BIRNBAUM: I still have to deal with Dick's question. It seems to me that it is easy enough to give you a series of methodological devices, intergenerational panel studies, retrospective psychohistorical studies, of the kind you yourself have done. We could develop a new concept of public opinion which would show up as derisory and superficial the one that is elicited by present conventional polling techniques. The question you ask, however, is not technical, a matter of technique or method in a narrow sense.

ERIKSON: We have not been able to come up with a new concept that could be as central to our own theory as alienation was to Marx. But we might begin to ask a slightly different question. We might ask about the ways in which an adult would be alienated simply by virtue of being an adult, simply because he has the care of—what the Hindus call the maintenance of—the world.

An adult has to settle, has to take care of his children, to take care to keep this going. Then I think we could connect with ideas of mortality and immortality, and these ideas would be theory. To what extent is an adult, simply by being an adult and involved in the crisis of generativity, unable to think about death? It is almost as if nature has put something into the human condition—call it numbing or denial—that prevents this.

BRENMAN-GIBSON: A filtering and scanning process.

KENISTON: Selective inattention.

We suffer on the one hand from a surfeit of information, stimuli which are available, visible in the number of things unread, communications not responded to, notes, papers, books—especially books—as they pile up. We have a sense, all of us, of missing whole areas of intellectual experience. It is a conceptual deprivation, personal in the sense of impoverishing our abilities to do serious work. It isn't, however, quite a quantitative one; it has other dimensions.

We are all asking whether there are new unifying concepts which we could discover or invent which would play a role analogous to or equivalent to the concept of alienation in Marxist thought, possibly of repression in Freud's thought. Is our deficiency in this sense a conceptual deficiency which, once resolved, would somehow enable us to put together this surfeit of information, to interpret it selectively according to new criteria of significance? Or is this difficulty not part of a much more complex historical difficulty, which in the political sphere expresses itself through the inchoate shape of the agencies of positive historical transformation? That lack of historical certainty about our capacity to transform the world may well express itself in the absence of any clear notion of the inner developmental tendencies of our society. Did not the British anthropologist Edmund Leach write of a world gone wild, a world running out of control, a world which in its inner mechanisms escapes our vision? We do not grasp those mechanisms, we do not understand our world. And that, in some measure, reflects the way in which humanity has been dwarfed, humiliated, by its own history.

ERIKSON: You notice that discussions are apt to get stuck in adolescence, and rarely reach beyond young adulthood. What you might learn, if you want to go at this, is what is an adult and what is in the condition of adulthood.

LIFTON: If the projection is partly utopian, maybe we can produce an adult who can think about death, even a young adult.

ERIKSON: Something like that is what Freud and Marx had in mind.

SYMBOLIZATION AND FICTION-MAKING

PETER BROOKS

Edited reconstruction of taped presentation at Wellfleet meetings, August 28, 1972

PARTICIPANTS: Norman Birnbaum, Peter Brooks, Kenneth Keniston, Robert Jay Lifton, Steven Marcus, Alexander Mitscherlich, Margarete Mitscherlich, William Phillips, Richard Sennett

I am going to suggest one possible approach or model for thinking about some of the questions of "symbolization" that have been raised in our discussions. This is not anything I've formulated in writing, though I have explored its possibilities in undergraduate teaching. What I say will be rather simplistic and schematic, but perhaps it will provide a framework for reflection. I will not follow Bob's lead and approach the question through symbolic forms, myths or symbols—through Cassirer, Langer, or Eliade. This can no doubt usefully be done, but I prefer to outline a process of reflection starting from a concept of fiction-making. I begin by asking myself, What compels someone to write about the world outside him? Or, to extend the question, Why does he make sculptures or build model railroads? And why do we more or less constantly daydream? What kind of play of the hand and the mind is involved, and what is it about our relation to the world "out there" that makes us need such play? The processing of the world by human consciousness I will call fiction-making because the word "fictions" (cf. *fingere*: to fabricate, to feign) usefully compounds the fabricated and the feigned, the "made-up" in the two senses that interest me.

To get myself going, I need two quotations. The first is from the French poet Paul Claudel, who said: "The world is before us like a text to be deciphered." The other is from Wallace Stevens, from "Notes Toward a Supreme Fiction." These three lines:

From this the poem springs: that we live in a place
That is not our own and, much more, not ourselves
And hard it is in spite of blazoned days.

Claudel's statement, though chronologically it belongs to the twentieth century, really expresses a traditional and religious view of the function of symbolism, where the symbol is token of a revealed truth. Claudel is a Catholic poet, and he can therefore see the world as a sacred text. It is a text because it is composed of sacred metaphor: that is, every detail of reality refers us to revealed truth, to a spiritual center of things, if we know how to read it correctly. In analogous manner, Emerson said, more or less: "Words are signs of natural facts, and natural facts are signs of spiritual facts." Emerson was writing in quite a different tradition, but there is, provisionally and ideally at least, the same factor of belief. If the world is such a coherent and all-signifying text, that is because it is animated by belief. One could take off from here to define the difference between (sacred) myth and fiction as I understand it.

I think that there is a type of modern symbolism that strives toward the status of the Claudelian symbol: that of the Symbolist movement and of Modernism, of someone like Yeats. But there is always this difference, at least with its most lucid practitioners: the realization that symbolism has necessarily become a kind of as-if thinking. There is an awareness that the cognitive and emotional value of the symbol is in fact created by the poet and the poem itself, that it cannot ultimately be the emblem of a revealed truth. I think basically that the system of symbolism referred to by Claudel became impossible for most men when man moved out from under the mantle of the sacred, when the Christian idea of the sacred ceased to be an operative force in life and thought.

Stevens, I believe, expresses the central modern (Romantic and post-Romantic) tradition: that man is consciousness living in a world of nonconsciousness, in a world that is not mind and does not belong to mind. And that this is hard, as he says, "in spite of blazoned days," in spite of the natural beauty. Stevens implies that man is defined by his essential difference from the world he inhabits. He *is* the difference in the world. And he uses this "difference"—his self-consciousness—to process phenomena, in an attempt to understand his place in the world, its meaning to him, his meaning to it. Art, symbolization, is called forth by the fact that we are not what we live amidst. Fictions originate at the intersection of consciousness and a primary otherness (which in another model could be the unconscious); we make up in order to make sense of, in order to get a grasp on something that would otherwise remain incomprehensible, alien, unassimilable.

To talk a little more technically about what goes on in the processing of what is nonmind, I would suggest the importance of the act of transfer or displacement which enables mind to turn phenomena into something it can discourse of. And here I would think that the basic trope, and in fact the root fiction of all fictions, is really metaphor, in the sense of a carrying over or transfer (*meta-pherein*: to transport, to carry across)—that process taking place as things are accommodated to the system of mind and language. Now, our simplest (and many of our oldest) fictions often are little more than a naming of the world, an inventory of its elements, a "putting into language" of its things. You remember that in Genesis God brings the animals to Adam and he gives them names, and they enter into human history. This naming is itself a metaphoric process: through naming, things are transferred from the realm of pure phenomenal existence into language. I. A. Richards calls metaphor a "transaction between contexts." Without this transaction or transference, one could not speak of the world outside mind, and there could be no meaning. Language itself may then be fundamentally metaphor, it is this process of transfer or displacement.

Here I'd like to refer to a somewhat mad text of Rousseau's which I think has great symbolic importance, his "Essay on the Origins of Language." For Rousseau, language is a product of man's desires, his subjective reactions, not his needs, and he claims that language begins in figure and displacement (though he doesn't use the latter word). He says that primitive man (this is one of his imaginary scenarios) goes out and meets another man, and he's scared of him, this great big thing coming over the horizon. So he says "giant." Later on, when he finds that what he has really discovered is someone like himself, he invents another name, and the word "giant" is assigned to describe a different category of beings. That is: naming always begins by displacement, im-proper naming, figure, as-if thinking. We could say that language is always founded in this displacement from sense impression or visual image, to use the terms Erik Erikson was using in talking about children. It's the transference that enables mind to discourse of the world, and even more: that enables mind to live in the world. Mind couldn't live in the world otherwise, because it would be surrounded by nothing but undifferentiated phenomena.

Metaphor as the root fiction is that playing room, that leeway in the world—I found Erikson's terms completely congruent with my own thinking here—that allows man to be at home in the world. Another poetic instance of this comes in Valéry's "Le Cimetière Marin." At the moment of still perfection in the world, the world at noon when the sun is at the meridian and everything is in a kind of deathlike perfection, he says to the universe: "I am the secret changing in you" (*Je suis en toi le secret changement*). In other words, he, his consciousness, is the one principle of free play in the mechanism, in what is all too perfect, exclusive of man. I would propose that man is essentially and by his nature a fiction-maker: by his invention of language, by his invention of signs in order to make sense. He is *Homo signiferens,* the bearer of sense-making sign systems.

If we want to ask how this sense-making sign system functions, probably the most useful place we can go is to the workings of language itself, to the laws of language that have been discovered by linguistics. Here we would probably have to begin with Saussure, who is really the cornerstone of modern linguistics. Saussure, as you know, divided the sign into signifier/signified; the sign is like the two sides of a sheet of paper, the signifier being the top side, the signified the underside. The point to emphasize is that language is systematic: the signifier is subject to sets of laws that have nothing to do with reference to an outside world, nothing to do with nomenclature, but with phonetics, grammar, syntax. The sign doesn't operate in a vacuum. One of the chief lessons of Saussure in terms of sense-making is that sense is not produced alone: it is relational, produced from oppositions, of phonemes and then words, and from spacings. Using the functioning of the linguistic sign as a model, we can say that sense is always a kind of web, or piece of lace, a text or tissue of relational meanings. This is something we might want to come back to. There is also Jakobson's discovery that there are really just two basic polar processes of language, which are metaphor and metonymy. These can usefully be connected with Freud's two procedures of the dream work, condensation and displacement.

Another consequence of working from Saussure comes out in anthropology, in Lévi-Strauss, where he talks about the sense-making of primitive man, in kinship systems for instance. We discover that all meaning comes into existence simultaneously. That is, since meaning is relational, created through bipolar oppositions and spacings, once you have set up your system of relations the whole of meaning comes into existence simultaneously, and everything can be placed within the system. This is man's trace on nature, if you will, this system of sense-making where everything is brought into significant relation with everything else: where the world becomes man's text.

A possible next stage, I think (here I depart from structuralism, which has largely been concerned with the synchronic rather than the diachronic), is the organization of these signs and their relations, these metaphors and metonymies, in time and in history. Moving from the model of metaphor, a next step might be into plot, in the good old Aristotelian sense of beginnings, middles and ends. And here it seems to me that the first term to examine might be the end, or at least the end in relation to the beginning.

I can illustrate this with a passage from Sartre's novel *Nausea*. His hero, Roquentin, is thinking about the term "adventure" and how nothing that could be called an adventure ever happens in his life, whereas in a novel all is different. The novel begins by telling you that a guy is out walking on a beautiful night, and there seems to be nothing particular or exceptional about the situation, he's thinking of his money troubles and so on. But, says Roquentin, since it's a novel, since it's a fiction, you know that nothing stated is innocent: it is all information to be stored away for future use. And the reason it isn't innocent is that this beginning is transformed and illuminated by the end lying in wait. The novelistic person must live these seemingly insignificant details as "promises and annunciations" of what is to come. In other words, the end is already there, and because it is there it confers significance on all the words you are reading, from the beginning.

If we try to specify the nature of this end, I think we discover that it is always a form of death—a literal death (as so often in the nineteenth-century novel), the closing of a cycle in life, or (as in much contemporary fiction) simply the death of the reader in the text. It is more difficult to specify the operative force of the beginning. The best term I have been able to find is desire: our fictions act out over and over again all varieties of desire, and desire is the motor or impulsion of plot, what makes not only the hero but the text itself move toward the chosen object. And then—skipping over all that should be said here in the analysis of desire itself, its problems in determining its object and achieving its goal—one could say that this desire is ultimately desire *for* the end. Here I find the Freud of *Beyond the Pleasure Principle* most suggestive, because the desire that informs plot appears to me ultimately to be a desire for the *proper* end, a desire to find and achieve the *right* end. The whole plot, through its various detours and mistaken choices and risks of short circuit, is a series of repetitions which serve to "bind" mobile libidinal energy in order to bring it to a final discharge, which is that end that consummates and confers significance on life. Plot would thus be a series of metaphors and metonymies, repeated in variation, to achieve the correct end. In this connection, I recommend to you the splendid essay by Walter Benjamin on "Leskov the Storyteller," where Benjamin argues that death is the sanction of everything that the storyteller has to tell. It is only at the moment of death that life achieves significance, transmissible meaning. Yet knowledge of our own death is denied to us. This, then, is what we seek in fictions: knowledge of death, knowledge, says Benjamin, that is like a candle from which we warm our shivering lives.

To sum up briefly what I have said so far: it seems to me that sign- and sense-making, considered first, starting from a somewhat phenomenological model, as necessary for the survival of consciousness in the world, can then be considered, on a more psychoanalytic model, as the working out of man's fundamental desire to achieve proper integration in the course of life and death.

What might be the implications of all this for psychohistory? It seems to me that the "psychic numbing" that Bob was talking about might be a kind of impairment of this sign-making function itself, and could imply a kind of psychically defenseless man who is overwhelmed by what has become for him an undifferentiated and insignificant reality. The breakdown of symbolization described by Bob would be the incapacity to imagine that necessary leeway in existence, an overacceptance of the literality of existence. None of us accepts the literality of existence, and we can't. We would die. As Nietzsche says, we have fictions in order not to die of the truth. I also think that this overliteralization could result in the acceptance of certain dominant fictions, the fictions of "the others," if you will, as myths. Historically, this would seem to recur when people lose their sense of leeway; they accept a dominant fiction, such as the master race, as a myth. They come to believe that the world has once again become the sacred text, where everything is explained and justified in terms of a monolithic fiction.

As Frank Kermode says in *The Sense of an Ending,* if you let your fictions degenerate into myths you end up sending people to the gas chambers in their name. This may be a partial explanation of why so much modern fiction of the Borges–John Barth type has always insisted (to the annoyance of the average reader) on its status as fiction. It has insisted on its fictionality and has sought to resist the temptation of myth that an earlier generation frequently surrendered to, with disastrous results.

PHILLIPS: The split between Coleridge and Arnold reflects these two streams. I think you are part of a project which is trying to bridge the division between the Arnoldian emphasis on the moral aspect of literature, the truth aspect of literature, the continuity with normal experience; and the Coleridgian idea that literature is a construct.

BROOKS: I think that a lot of people who grew up in the New Criticism that derived from Coleridgian bases feel that it led to a bind, to something excessively disconnected from reality.

PHILLIPS: And there was an emphasis on formalism, despite all their qualifications and reservations. What you are saying represents recent developments in attempting to get out of the bind created by thinking of fictions as formal structures. You retain the value of the New Criticism, which indicated the autonomy of a fiction and its formal qualities. At the same time you're asking questions about its sources and its values.

One of the difficulties the New Critics got into was the problem of judgment. How do you judge the poem? To be consistent, a New Critic had to have formal structural criteria. Second, everyone knew there was something there in a work beyond formal structure, but all that was avoided because the New Critics talked about poetry, not about fiction. When you talk about fiction, then, you obviously have some relationship to experience. When you stay with poetry, with music, or with the formal aspects of painting and sculpture, you have fewer problems.

But the reasons you have fewer problems is that we have no

terminology for designating the meanings within music and painting which might be comparable or similar to the meanings in literature which are verbal and therefore partake of the essence of or simply have the feel and the look of ordinary experience—what I'm trying to say is, you seem to have moved toward bridging that gap and it's a very intriguing point of view. Still, it seems to me we don't have the connection. My own guess is that we don't have the critical terminology, the conceptualization, to make that link.

On the one hand we use terms that emphasize the autonomous and purely creative aspects of these fictions: we use terms like "structure," "form," "symbol," "myth." On the other side we use terms like "express," "communicate," "meaning." So we're in a terminological bind, and I believe terminological binds are really conceptual binds.

BROOKS: To put it another way, we make very little sense of the psychological correspondences to formal structure. That wouldn't be the only place you could look for correspondences, but it's a good place and it's one reason that I've been pushed back to reading a lot of Freud.

KENISTON: I think there are two issues here which are intertwined and also confused. One is the primal nature of symbolization or conceptualization at a very rudimentary level. That is, the extent to which when we see a tree we say "tree" and have a concept of a tree. This seems a much more elemental level than the issues of fiction and myth, which take for granted a whole set of elaborate concepts, and conceptualizations (however we define them and however they're arrived at) and then go on to explore the way these things are put together.

With regard to the first, there are at least three viable views on the way by which internal structures are developed. None of these is a simple mirror view. These three are the psychoanalytic view, the Piagetian, and the structuralist.

Both Freud and Piaget accept some kind of tension between the inner and the outer as the crucible in which symbols are formed. Both see symbolization as *functional,* as enabling man to bridge, relate and organize the world in a way without which he would not be a man. But this process is problematic. For both men this process doesn't *necessarily* happen; it requires a set of conditions which may be absent. Here Lévi-Strauss and Chomsky can be grouped together as having a kind of "calling-forth" view in which the whole apparatus is present in the child's head, and it's more a matter of getting the process started.

The functional and the structuralist developmental views have different political and ideological implications. For example, one reading of Piaget is that since higher levels of internal structures are developed by a problematic and complex interaction of the individual and social world, since there are hierarchies of development, and since there are differences in the ages at which these emerge, then one can end up not only with a developmental hierarchy but also with a societal hierarchy. That is, some people are "more developed" than others, and some societies may be better than others in that they have more people who are "more developed." Higher levels are implicitly "better" than lower levels. Kohlberg is an extreme of this: recall his paper on "Why Stage Six Is the Best." He ends up with a Platonic view of justice and mankind.

One could conclude that what we should do is try to get everyone to the higher levels. Or one could say that the conditions that activate these higher levels are rare and always will be, and that some people will always be better than others.

The Lévi-Strauss/Chomsky view doesn't have this implication. I think Piaget is more likely correct. But the great virtue of the structuralist view is that it says everyone is the same; the only things that differ are the *objects* of thought. Primitive thought is fully as complex as Western thought.

MARCUS: Let me say how I think what Ken said is connected. Emerson said, "I dreamed last night that the world is an apple; and I ate it." You're saying that essentially the human activity is the provision of meaning.

One of the things that gets left behind in a theory of fiction-making is the older notion of *mimesis*. In the seventeenth and eighteenth centuries the representation within yourself of a Roman or a Greek had *moral* value. I don't think this is defensible, but I'm sorry to see it go.

I am interested in looking at the *cognitive* value of literature. If one takes a neo-Kantian or positivist position and says it has no cognitive value, then one can only defend literature as amusement.

One can say that literature is fiction-making, and literature is the creation and provision of meaning, and this is the major cognitive activity of human beings. We can say it's true of philosophy; but we can also say it's true of science and technology. But to what degree is it true in these fields? At what point does the idea of science and technology as fictions cease to carry a payoff? How would this compare with trying to see what's going on in the science itself?

KENISTON: The Piagetian view stresses symbolization as a vital form of adaptation and change. Communication—in both the Freudian and Piagetian schemes—is seen as instrumental. One is very interested in what's going on *between* the person and his world. This leads to a view of literature as a form of enlightenment, instruction and potential change. One is not simply tickling another person's structure which is the same as one's own. One can communicate and change other people.

In contrast, the structuralist view is not at all interested in language as functional. It is interested in the *structure* of language. Nor is there interest in communication, since we all have the same basic structures. At the *deepest* level there is no problem in communication, all men have the same *deep* structures. This view would see literature as evoking certain collective structures which would be common to all men in all societies.

BROOKS: I limit my own work to self-conscious fictions, fictions which are aware of their status as fictions. It is not useful past a certain point to see science as a fiction.

LIFTON: I want to try to connect some of what Peter has been saying to psychohistory.

Looking historically, there is a whole category of people, which would include Piaget and Chomsky, Cassirer, Langer, and Jakobsen, who represent an emerging current of twentieth-century thought that Freud half began and yet spoke of in the language of mechanism. Freud is transitional in this, because he moves toward meaning and yet he speaks in the language of mechanism. The term "fiction" has dubious value in psychological thought, because it suggests falsehood. But the principle of fabrication is very important and central.

Incidentally, the overall idea in all these twentieth-century thinkers has to do, I think, with transformation.

We place stress on psychic representation, but yet there is a distinct gap between psychic representation and what we think to be the larger cause or influence. That's part of the problem, for instance, when Freud says death has no psychic representation. I think that is quite true: it's very hard to represent death psychically. And yet I would maintain that death has enormous influence, and I would say causative influence, on ordinary psychic life.

Freud also had ambivalence about the extent to which instinct could be psychically represented. Sometimes instinct is so deep in the biology of the organism that it's merely the engine of the psychic fragments that appear in the unconscious or in the conscious mind. At other times Freud speaks of instinctual representations. This ambivalence was Freud's way of dealing with this problem of the distance between psychic representation and causation.

I believe we have to think of a hierarchy. I prefer the idea of inchoate image to that of instinct; the infant has a direction. When there is a releasing mechanism it's really a direction of the organism which is released in some degree by the environment.

This inchoate image is physiological at first, meaning that it is a direction of the organism. Boulding's work is important here. From inchoate image there develops a more formed image that becomes pictorial. This happens in the human infant in the first year. Later this becomes more symbolized, and has to do with symbolic forms. This means inner re-creation of experience in a way that is more complex than simply pictorial representation.

Still, it is difficult to find a language to speak of the psychic action of all this. I find Freud's language here very inadequate. And that fits together with what William said about not quite having the terms to take us further along lines we sense to be true. The mind is dealing with the world, but is always working on itself. The mind takes materials from the world. This creates the problem of a language adequate to talking about mind working on itself but still dealing with large historical transformations. That is a problem for psychohistory.

The point about desire moving toward an end is that the movement is toward an end that one perceives during one's life as animating, life-giving or vital. And what is ultimately life-giving is that which connects with other desires. And that's where symbolic immortality comes in, the sense of being connected with principles beyond oneself.

Peter described numbing as the absence of a signifying capacity in the face of an overwhelming actuality of the environment. That would be the absence of symbols or inner forms with which to connect in this symbolic or transformative way. But this impairment in symbolic function can arise either through *absence* of inner forms or the *blocking and impairment* of the forms where they do exist. This differentiation between absence and blocking may be a separation of function that's important to make. Then, interpreting the world literally really means that one is no longer able to perform one's basic human function of re-creation. When that is so, the world becomes deathlike and static. It's not simply that our fictions become *myths*. It's that what was once a living and an animating idea is rendered into a static, almost inorganic entity. When one does this one takes the world and oneself as something that is static and doesn't end, doesn't die, and because it doesn't end and doesn't die it doesn't live either.

Finally, the issue of meaning, which is a new twentieth-century emphasis. Freud is transitional in this, because he did speak of meaning, but always in terms of mechanism—that was the only language he had. Actually it's amazing what he did with that language as a result of his being so committed to the issue of meaning and signification. But his disciples in this process of literalization reified this, using the language of mechanism but without Freud's animating intent, and in the end they were caught *in* mechanism.

The task of psychohistory in all this is to create languages of meaning, particularly if we take seriously history with its constant *shifts* in meaning.

MARGARETE MITSCHERLICH: Actually Freud had a lot of different kinds of languages, such as his emphasis on the representation of the drives in imagination.

Psychoanalysis has been much concerned with the motivation for inner representation. The dog, for example, can remember something when he is hungry or has an outer sign. But the child starts between one and a half and two to remember something without either of these.

Freud was wrong in not recognizing this human capacity for inner representation without either outer sign or inner drive. And Freud's views on this led to the mistakes he made about women. Freud thought that because women lack the penis they never fully internalize the prohibitions of the parents and never develop the inner superego functions that make possible abstract thinking.

SENNETT: We're struggling to get an understanding of the role of consciousness, and what the energy for consciousness is.

I have been using the term consciousness to mean the kicking into being of a fiction by a previous act of unintended failure. That failure is first processed as guilt and then results in a fiction.

LIFTON: That really has to do with *change* in moral consciousness.

MARCUS: The first use of the word "consciousness" in English is usually traced to Hobbes. And it's important that the greatest work of political philosophy in the English language is epistemology.

BIRNBAUM: And Marx said Hobbes was the father of us all.

SENNETT: That means Freud's idea of consciousness was very weak.

KENISTON: And yet your model is isomorphic with Freud; that is, hallucinatory wish fulfillment as a model for ideation. Ideas appear *after* frustration, or failure. Freud talked about mental representations as appearing when the infant is frustrated.

BIRNBAUM: We have had a marvelous series of presentations: Peter's portrayal of the state of modern aesthetic argument and its historic background, William's critical remarks, Ken's explanation of the modern theory of mind, Steve's statement on literature and the position of science in all this, Bob's effort to integrate this with his own theory of symbolism, and Dr. Mitscherlich's remarks on the internal difficulties of Freud's original theory.

All of this seems to indicate that we're on to something: that is, a metatheory in which particular theories could be couched or phrased. It's almost as if concrete discourse has to stop until certain philosophical problems are solved. It reminds me of the early Marx letter to his father in which he said that without philosophy you can't go further.

Two specific points interest me: the antagonism in art between its aesthetic, pleasure-giving function and its moral, narrative or exemplary function. Maybe one could say that the aesthetic function is there precisely because of the inevitable failure of its moral function. Since the fitting end which art tries to teach never comes, the aesthetic function gives at least the pleasure of having posed and resolved certain purely aesthetic tensions. If art did not take on this moral burden (which is doomed to fail), paradoxically it would not have any aesthetic value or success.

BROOKS: I think the split that you're talking about and that William described can be bridged. Freud assigns literary pleasure to forepleasure in terms of the artist's function being wish fulfillment. Aesthetic form becomes simply forepleasure. But if you look at art as striving for the *right* end, the *proper* death, then you can look at form as play with *improper* ends. The protagonist in a Dickens novel, for instance, is always faced with all sorts of choices which would lead to the wrong end.

MARGARETE MITSCHERLICH: Freud's view of sublimation is not *only* forepleasure. Sublimation has its own object. Defense always has a countercathexis, but sublimation does not. The entire energy of the drive flows into it.

BROOKS: I was thinking mainly of the essay on "The Relation of the Poet to Daydreaming," where Freud tends to dissolve aesthetic form mainly into forepleasure.

ALEXANDER MITSCHERLICH: Actually it is remarkable that Freud, using the language of nineteenth-century science in a kind of metaphorical way, was able to describe psychic processes as well as he did, and was able to discover so much. And aren't we in danger, as we shift to a new language which is not designed to describe motion, of losing the capacity to describe the psychic process?

LIFTON: One of the things Erikson says in his essay about Freud ("The First Psychoanalyst") is that the innovator uses the language and ideas of his own tradition to the point of absurdity. He *has* to rely on that older science, or he won't make the breakthrough.

Freud invested so much moral energy in what he was doing that he was able to emerge with a discipline in then being able to talk about psychic representations—which *are* issues of meaning.

But I don't think we need the mechanistic language to get a sense of psychic process. But you're right; we don't yet have a language adequate to deal with *both* meaning and process.

KENISTON: We reject the physicalist language, but we are hard put to come up with an alternative. Psychoanalysis remains the best thing we've got at this point.

Birnbaum: In Paris now a group of analysts, philosophers, literary theorists, and linguists are working on this problem of transmuting psychoanalysis—Lacan and others. They're arguing that the mechanical language of Freud *can* be transformed into a language of meaning derived from linguistics. Then they argue that of course we communicate with others and with ourselves through language, so that language is of course constitutive of our being.

Brooks: They treat Freud much more as a philosopher than as a doctor. Lacan's discovery was really that the unconscious is organized as a language, and linguistic material—that is, *what the patient says*—is the only thing we have to work with. So to understand the functioning of the unconscious and then the functioning of mind we have to understand language.

Phillips: In this process of taking concepts from one field to another there is a problem of the criteria of verifiability. Can we verify things in fictions the same way we would in psychology or history? In these other disciplines (nonliterary) there is a question of reference to the outer world. And terms in these other disciplines have a specificity of reference.

Brooks: Henry James once said (*contra* Flaubert), "Even if we're so strangely constituted as to be nine-tenths literary, there's still the other one-tenth that made us want to walk over and pick up the book and read it in the first place."

Art *always* reflects on human experience; and our failure has been the failure to study the relationships between aesthetic forms and psychological forms.

Phillips: I'm just saying that writing a novel is very different from what Freud did.

Keniston: But by suggesting these are *absolutely* different you close off the examination. We know they're different. But are there lines of contact, whether psychological, motivational or structural? This is one question we need to discuss.

Brooks: I would insist that a novel does have some kind of complex verifiability; we wouldn't be interested otherwise. And the sort of verifiability in psychoanalysis itself is very complex.

MARGARETE MITSCHERLICH: What happens in psychoanalysis is that we—my patient and I—find a lot of interesting and fruitful things together.

BROOKS: Right; it's animating and enriching and you can work with it.

PHILLIPS: The point is that no one reads a poem in the same way or for the same reasons that one reads Freud.

KENISTON: One of the criteria by which one judges psychoanalysis is its ability to *make sense* out of a whole realm of experience. This point of making sense out of experience is very different from narrow verifiability, and is much closer to what happens in a novel. It becomes an issue of the capacity of a point of view to *illuminate* experience.

MARCUS: We're saying literature has some kind of truth value; what that truth value is, is very difficult to define.

KENISTON: To go further, there *is* a kind of demand that one makes upon a work of fiction in terms of its relationship to experience.

MARCUS: And I think that this "demand" *is* in a continuum with the kind of truth value which we expect of social theory. I think there is a differentiation, but not a break.

LIFTON: In psychohistory if you take the two models—the great man in history and the shared themes—you do try to get empirical data. But there is still a leap of imagination that is necessary to connect that work with something else in a way that feels true and will seem true to others. If I talk about themes of survival in Hiroshima, or Erikson talks about conscience in Luther, there *is* a leap of imagination.

KENISTON: In my work it is necessary not only that the interviews I do tickle my imagination and that I generate hypotheses, but also that I then return to the interviews to determine the relevance of my hypotheses. I can be called to account for this. I agree with William that this demand *is* a different sort of demand than that placed on a writer of fiction.

SENNETT: To return to the idea of consciousness. In my interviews with working-class people I discovered that there was a lack of agency—a use of the passive voice to talk about actions that win praise from other people. They don't say, "I did . . ." The reason for this is that the penalty for praise is loss of fraternity. This removal of a sense of agency is a contemporary form of class consciousness. There is created a divided self—an active and passive self. These people remove the consciousness of themselves as actors in order to ward off a war between fraternity and individual achievement. So the word "consciousness" is a confusing word in that sense.

When we have a case history, we have no laws for how to interpret it. How are we to discover anything that is new in an interview or in our data? It's a question of how we perceive variation and discrepancy.

BIRNBAUM: The question Dick raises is whether the language of ideology can still be applied now in the traditional way. The alternative, of course—in the best traditions of empirical sociology—may be that we abandon the evidence instead. . . .

STRUGGLES OVER THEORY

STUART HAMPSHIRE

Edited reconstruction of taped presentation at Wellfleet meetings, August 22, 1969

PARTICIPANTS: Margaret Brenman-Gibson, Lawrence Chisolm, Erik H. Erikson, Stuart Hampshire, Kenneth Keniston, George Klein, Robert Jay Lifton, Steve Marcus, Frederick Wyatt

The question raised by the enterprise called psychohistory is how the fusion of the two disciplines, psychology (usually meaning psychoanalytic psychology) and history, is to be brought about. The difficulty is to see how they can be brought together in a system of explanation which applies not only to individual behavior but to social change. Presumably a psychohistorical study must be a study of social change.

Two remarks that Erik Erikson made earlier in this conference made clearer to me what some of the difficulties are. He said, for example, that "we" is not a concept of psychoanalysis. Secondly, there was Erik's use of the word "prophetic," which seemed to be precisely the right word for what he wanted to say. But that word itself raises for me the question of how one brings together the universal biological, which has its home in the psychoanalytic study of individuals, and explanations of social change, which bring in the culture of the group and specific local currents.

I thought that, at the risk of being very heavy-handed, I would consider first the two distinct kinds of explanation given in these disciplines to see if there is any incompatibility in bringing them together. The two kinds of explanation are psychoanalytic explanation in its day-to-day and classical application in therapy, and social explanation—explanation of social change—as we inherit it from the nineteenth-century thinkers who first made it precise.

In our earlier discussions we more or less agreed (in that nobody violently objected) that psychoanalytic explanation in the individual classical case is intentional explanation. That is, it explains the behavior or thoughts (or both in combination) of the patient or subject by reference to the patient's or subject's thoughts. And it is of utmost importance in this process of explanation that thoughts should be reproduced in their pristine form, exactly as they occur to or are acceptably formulated to the subject or patient. It is the meaning of the symptom, and of the thought that accompanies the symptom, which is of greatest importance.

Secondly, it was agreed, particularly when there was a stress on the role that transference and countertransference play in the ordinary analytical situation, that the therapist is not primarily an observer. In consequence one does not look for or find very generally stated laws which specify initial conditions or "input" and yield predictions about symptoms or behavioral patterns or indeed about sentences and thoughts themselves. On the contrary, the criteria of understanding—in the sense in which "explanation" means explaining something to somebody—are to be found in an interpersonal situation. There are various tests as to whether or not this understanding has been achieved. But in no case is the explanation sought an explanation of high generality. It is not an explanation of the form that, given specified inputs and a specified situation, a specified result is to be anticipated or predicted, and specified manipulations will alter the situation in specified ways.

The psychoanalytic mode of explanation is historical in two senses. First, it is characteristic of conventional history that you distinguish it from sociology in virtue of its narrative form or quasi-narrative form. One doesn't look in conventional history for overarching generalizations. Rather, one is concerned with the development of an individual society or set of societies. So there is a sense in which the absence of aim at generality makes psychoanalytic explanation (where the explanation is something presented in a paper, or given in a case history, or presented to colleagues) analogous to the sort of explanation given in conventional history. But in a more interesting sense it is a historical method in that it exhibits the weight of the past or an attachment to the past as the determining factor. The arrow of explanation points to the past. The past is thought of as having a certain weight that has to be borne and has to be dealt with. Again, this is one way of looking also at conventional history. And the ideal of understanding is very closely connected with the ideal of being able to go on from there. The patient is to be enabled to go on with his story having understood and assimilated the past, to *use* the weight of the past and not feel it as a burden.

To introduce a term such as "prophetic" is to make, it seems to me, a very important contribution to Freud's thought as it is ordinarily interpreted. The term "prophetic" adds a normal time dimension to the employment of psychoanalytical concepts. Freud clings to the notion of determinism, not, I think, because he has in mind the idea of strict causal explanation in the natural sciences, but rather because he wants to stress the weight of the past as the explanatory factor. Freud looked at the developmental past as pointing forward in a teleological function, but not simply as a solution of a past logjam, as an outcome, as if a lot of logs had fallen together in a certain shape in which one looks to the past to see how they got there. He introduced a biological metaphor which points in another way. Freud's thought is deeply historical in its emphasis upon looking to the past as the ideal of what it is to understand a particular phase.

All the terms we've been using—"crisis," "recapitulation," "developmental set," "prophetic" (in its secular usage), and the concept of development itself, which contrasts with that of mere maturation and socialization—have their original home in classical nineteenth-century social theory and historiography. Hegel, Marx, Comte and Taine all thought of the explanation of successive phases of society not as solely emerging from the past but as receiving their meaning in pointing toward the future. There is the implication that societies have a life cycle. There is a historical sociology that begins with Vico which models the life cycle of society on an analogy with the individual life cycle. In this tradition, explanation is inseparable from a modicum of prediction. The social theory arose out of a need for social action and an attempt to give a rational basis to political action. These theories were intended to provide practical guidance toward what could be done and what could not be done politically. The notion of explaining was tied up with the problem of elucidating future courses of action and saying what is likely to happen.

We've discussed the youth movement at some length. Now ordinary people who want to understand the youth movement are in part asking a question about the *future* of the youth movement. They are concerned with what the youth movement is likely to yield in terms of what will happen to it and what range of social change, if any, will result from it. Or is it a surface phenomenon which will entail no great social change? They want to ask a question about the historical function of the youth movement, a question which cannot be answered without a modicum of prediction.

But of course you can take "understanding" in the strictly psychoanalytical sense. You can ask yourself, how is it that a group of persons at this time had these behaviors, exhibit these symptoms, gather together in these ways? What is the function of the youth movement *for them as individuals?* This is the approach which Erik Erikson has taken in speaking of the contrast between the inverted dissenters who are liable to find themselves under treatment and the institutional dissenters who "solve" individual problems by joining a movement which has as its function the institutionalization of their neuroses, allowing them to act them out, finding a partial solution for them and relieving them.

Philip Rieff's objection to this kind of explanation was that it would be widely accepted, and in a hostile sense. One of the reasons it would be accepted in a hostile sense is that it exhibits what looks like a movement with a future as a movement which is in fact constituted by a mere collection of individual needs. And indeed, this is the ordinary liberal historian's sense of where psychoanalytical explanation fits into conventional historical explanation. I think if you asked ordinary working historians who are in no way concerned with an enterprise called psychohistory they would say that what one expects from psychoanalytic enlightenment is that it enables one to make far more sensitive, accurate and careful diagnoses of individual motives and their summation in social movements. What happens is that a group of persons come together, driven by motives (as they would be called in that framework of explanation) which would be more sensitively understood. Therefore the functioning of institutions would also be understood more sensitively because of the inclusion of a psychological dimension otherwise missing when other forms of institutional analysis—anthropology or sociology—are attempted.

That kind of explanation, it seems to me, in no way constitutes a separate enterprise. It fits very conveniently into ordinary functional social theory in which one exhibits certain tensions in the society as having a solution through certain institutions. And if one is asked to demonstrate this, the demonstration is made by looking into a series of personal histories, and this justifies making the claim. But the important thing about this is that it still treats the movement or group as a collection of individuals with converging psychic histories which, taken together, hope to explain group behavior. What is missing here, from the point of view of the ordinary inquirer who wants to understand the youth movement and its significance, is that so far nothing is said about the coherence of the youth as a social movement, whether it really is a movement with an identity of its own and distinct social force. The issue is not addressed as to whether it is the kind of thing that can be an agent of social change, whether it is an element in the history of a society, or not. Is it a genuinely coherent social group as, for example, Marx believed a social class properly defined to be?

This is a question that youth themselves don't know how to answer. So they naturally tend to believe that the youth movement *does* have a historical and revolutionary role. The question for them is whether this is a false consciousness or not, in Marxist terms. Is there something properly called the youth movement in addition to a number of people scattered all over the world who for certain reasons which could be separately analyzed in terms of individual histories and cultural pressures have come together? Or, on the other hand, is there a possibility that they really do form a movement in the sense that they will cohere, they will act together, and they will bring about or help in bringing about some form of social change?

One could not answer this question of whether the youth movement is an effective social agent except by adding some general social theory which had some independent warrant. One would have to look outside the range of individual psychology in order to have a view one way or the other on this question of group identity. After all, in no identity crisis short of psychotic break is there not *some* sense of self. But the question of group identity, which is the central issue for social theory, can be answered only by social theory. Therefore, it is no accident that "we" is not a concept of psychoanalysis. The answer to whether a collection of individuals really does belong together and will act together has got to be obtained from somewhere else. And traditionally this question has been answered in rational terms using the concept of identity of interest, so that if you identify certain common interests then you've identified a genuine "we" or group.

If one sees psychohistory as a program distinct from any other method of study (rather than merely adding a complexity and a sensitiveness to ordinary accounts of individual motives in ordinary historical writing), then one has to apply psychoanalytical terms to an apparent social group which is picked out by some independent social theory. Otherwise we are not necessarily studying genuine group phenomena but perhaps studying simply a casual confluence of individual histories. I'm not sure what counts as having access to the thoughts or fantasies of the group *qua* group—themes which are genuinely group themes and which arise by virtue of the group being a group as opposed to themes which arise in individuals who, subject to common pressures and having a common biopsychological base and instinctual structure, have reached a common point. Now, it's clear that in history people have given rise to a group imagery, imagery which serves to hold the group together and is an expression of its "groupness" and wouldn't be there were it not for the group. But there is nothing in psychoanalysis as such which provides one with criteria for picking out genuine social groups.

KENISTON: I have spoken about youth as a "developmental set" in order not to have to talk about a group, which suggests interrelatedness, shared culture, and so on. The question, then, is at what point a set—which is simply a collection of individuals who have certain objective things in common—becomes a group.

HAMPSHIRE: A developmental set would *describe* a collection of people, but one would not be prepared to say that if somebody was in specified circumstances or had a specified history he would exhibit this set in virtue of being attached to the group. It doesn't permit you to go beyond the actual set.

One possible way around these problems is the great-man-in-history model, for the great man can be taken not only as just great, but as exemplary and representative of the confluence of an individual history in relation to a restricting culture around him. In this case the psychoanalytic terms can be put to their full use without losing touch with their original ground in psychology. Within the study itself you don't need to introduce a general theory of social change, because you don't attempt to indicate how Luther differed from the little Luthers of his time. This very largely avoids the methodological problem.

KLEIN: But it doesn't help the historian.

HAMPSHIRE: Well, it confines the work to a biographical mode.

KLEIN: The problem for the historian would be how to use a concept developed in the context in exploring the vantage point of the individual to characterize a flow of events, like Hofstadter referring to the "paranoid style" in American life. There he takes a concept drawn from individual psychology to characterize a social movement.

HAMPSHIRE: But he uses that term descriptively, and doesn't derive an explanation from it—it's simply a *style.*

KLEIN: The psychoanalyst, in order to call someone paranoid, makes use of what has been called cognitive identification. So what is the historian empathizing with in the nature of an organism that he can apply a concept like paranoid that has its origin in the individual?

HAMPSHIRE: Yes, it's very hard to get rid of the explanatory theory that comes along with the word. To use it just impressionistically can be very misleading.

WYATT: Hofstadter has an "as if" before "paranoid," and he means to refer to analogical ways of thinking. I do not think he intended to be explanatory. He is speaking of certain common qualities of behavior which, for the want of a better word, he calls paranoid.

MARCUS: Stuart, would you say that even the method of looking at the great man in history contains within it implicit notions of social change?

HAMPSHIRE: Yes I would; it's almost unavoidable. To continue: I take it that the youth who are asking whether they are a social group with a function in society are really asking whether what unites them qualifies them or disqualifies them from being effective agents of social change. Behaviors and rituals which might be retrogressive in individual life histories might be prophetic socially, or the reverse. It seems to me that youth themselves are very much aware of this, that behavior that is prophetic in one way might not be prophetic in the other. And this is for them a great problem. And it is important for any interpreter of the youth movement to decide whether or not what they create is some form of community, because if it is it would be a rival or a substitute for what exists.

There is one unit which is at one and the same time a social element which is studied by anthropologists and sociologists, and which is the focus of an immense body of social theory and is also *the* topic of most psychoanalytical investigation. The topic of psychoanalytic investigation, as it is seen by its subjects, is the family. As Freud constantly stresses, this is the unit which is at once subjectively studied in terms of the picture of family relationships, but it is socially variable and its structure is externally studied. As behaviors, no one can doubt that family roles are subject to ordinary rational analysis and the mechanisms of change as sociologists, social anthropologists or historians study them. And no one will doubt that fantasies of family roles make up the larger part of intrapsychic history. The family is, therefore, the point of intersection where we have both theories focused on what we can regard as a single object, so one would expect what indeed happens, that the political imagery of any radical movement is shot through with metaphors from the family.

There is a long history of looking at institutional change—change in role distribution, change in property distribution, change in types of authority—through analogues in family relationships. This has been done by people who have tried to understand the less conscious links that make a community. In this sense I think what is important about the youth movement is the styles of parenthood that it might foreshadow.

Starting this way, from thinking of the family as the point of junction, one must conclude that the universal biological base isn't really a universal biological base. What is universal biological is the *conflict* between the roles allotted within the family—whatever the culture determines these roles to be—and the individual fantasies that a person has about what his role might be or should be. This conflict is universal, but not the actual roles, nor even the fantasies which are in conflict within the roles. The existing roles are always in conflict with fantasies of what the roles might be; the prohibitions are universal biological.

WYATT: What would you say about the incest taboo? As far as I know it is universal in society. It rests on biological conditions such as man's long latency in growing up, but the universal is a societal matter, and in itself not biological.

HAMPSHIRE: Yes, but that it is universal would be established by reference to social anthropology. Incest is a behavior, and you would in fact discover that all societies have the incest taboo. But at that point you would not be using incest taboo as a psychological term. What I'm attempting to do is to give an example of something that could come only from a distinctive psychohistorical method. Specifically, I'm suggesting that the psychohistorical approach is ideally suited to examine what happens in the transition to adulthood when suddenly new roles are imposed which are experienced as being premature. That is, premature specialization might be one of the things that the youth movements have been protesting against.

It is intrinsic to individual history that there is a crisis of specialization of role at the time of assuming competency and parenthood. There are special cultural factors associated with industrial civilization which made a degree of specialization that is greater than ever before seem mandatory. Our analysis here derives from a long tradition of social thought going back to Schiller which takes a psychological model of the life cycle as a basis for social theory. This tradition emphasizes the extreme forms of specialization that modern technology requires, and asserts that this imposes a greater burden than people can bear and will produce madness unless it is relieved by play. Then you get a whole theory of play and art. So here you get a confluence by putting together a developmental stage required for individual psychological purposes and a highly abstract idea of social alienation. And combining these two things really does seem to me to show something of why the youth movement may indeed be thought of as an historically efficacious group.

The real question is not why youth dissent, which is only too obvious: there's so much to dissent to. The real question is why they dissent under this generational banner. This is what requires to be explained. After all, they might have dissented as socialist radicals or something else. So here one is able to understand by the use of a psychohistorical method what it is that does make them cohere as a group, and what gives them the potential for making a contribution to social change. The combined use of these terms taken from individual psychology and the family, especially the concept of adulthood, and the traditional analysis of alienation by specialization of function and all that went with it in Schiller and Marx—this really does explain contemporary phenomena or at least makes them intelligible in a way that they could not otherwise be. Here the connection between the cultural and the intrapsychic is really illuminating about the future. It does show where the dynamism comes from. Under this description an external evil, or what is felt as such, is challenged under the right heading. There is a general pressure for specialization of function (which in the classical theory arises out of the division of labor), and this leads to alienation. And what we now see in response is a contemporary form of dissent taking place with great generational consciousness and challenging the idea of adulthood as the renunciation of wholeness, psychic numbing, etc. This is exactly what social theory predicted, but social theory underpredicts the form in which this would become conscious. The idea of specialization of function may be a useful bridge between social and psychological analysis. Around this idea the two points of view genuinely come together, each with their separate ancestries.

MARCUS: Would you press the analogy between the kind of differentiation of function that goes on in the family and that which goes on in society?

HAMPSHIRE: I understood one of the points Erik Erikson was making earlier in this conference to be an idea that has been constant in the youth phenomenon—that adulthood is one closing of a box. It is the time when potentialities subjectively felt to be there are foreclosed once and for all by the assuming of an adult role. This can be seen from a social point of view as resistance to bureaucratization and specialization of function. But quite apart from the social development there are independent reasons for thinking of the transition to adulthood as entailing this possible sense of loss. This is a natural kind of imagery for this period of history, and one would predict its appearance in individual psychology.

KENISTON: I want to return to an earlier point, the contrast between the psychoanalytic mode of explanation, which seeks individual motives in explaining individual history, and the social theoretical mode of analysis, which has a socially predictive component. Your view, as I understand it, is that the family is an institution that can provide a connecting link between these two modes.

I think one might reverse the whole question and ask: How on earth did we ever get into a position where we have to explain the connection between individuals and the social order? Might one not start from a completely different point of view and say that it is obvious at every stage of life—in dealing with every possible intrapsychic structure—that we are dealing with a continual inner–outer transaction? From the time of the earliest mother–child transaction in the womb we see, in a steadily widening orbit of the social world, that the outer becomes inner and the inner becomes outer. An individual can be defined as he who works upon the social material which is given him and can operate only with that as his medium. The family—and identifications that take place with the family (Oedipus complex, incest taboo, etc.)—is only one of a great series of ways in which the individual is profoundly connected to groups and society from the very start. Every psychic structure involves this connection. The superego is an obvious example; the ego, equally, is to a large extent a social creation. And instinctual life is never expressed except in social forms.

One might look upon the whole question of the relation of man and society as a peculiarly nineteenth-century, romantic question: one has isolated individuals on one side and institutions on the other. In the twentieth century this question is usually phrased as self versus society.

HAMPSHIRE: The problem for me is the modes of combinations of individuals. From the standpoint of an individual who is acting—whether it is in a family or in a larger group—the nature of the coherence of the group (what holds the group together) is the problem. People have always looked for microscopic laws of group action. And they've looked for guidance as to how, if you're writing history or studying society, you are to go about picking out the genuinely dynamic elements which enter into relationship with one another without which you just have an inchoate herd of individuals. The result is that you might latch upon the totally nonpsychological category of a social class (defined in terms of role in production) and seek for an understanding of the change in society through laws formulated in terms of social class.

In all writing on social progress you require some assumption for the selection of the units which are to be studied in explaining some phenomenon such as the youth movement or unrest in universities. And that presupposition—which specifies the elements to be mentioned, the possible forces—won't be directly derivable from the set of terms which are given for the understanding of individual histories. Psychoanalytical explanation, when it is crudely done, simply takes the idea of the "family past" and makes that the variable for the explanation of both individual and collective action. But it is precisely that crudity which everyone objects to.

ERIKSON: In the great-man-in-history approach the biography is a way of getting at the historical process. Could one speak of the complementarity between identity and ideology? We know that every person needs an identity. We also know, from Piaget, that every young person in adolescence goes through a particular kind of thinking which lends itself very well to an ideological orientation. Then one also knows that both of these things are activated—the need for an identity and ideological conflict—during periods of history when society does not provide the correlates in which all these individuals together can orient themselves.

I would never say that this joint orientation can be explained on the basis of individual psychology. But it could be explained on the basis of there being something in the social process which works for rejuvenation, and which always has and needs youth for its own rejuvenation.

KLEIN: You said "*it* would be explained," and "which always has and needs youth for *its* own rejuvenation." The problem is in defining what you mean by the "it" and the "its"—specifying the unit we're talking about.

ERIKSON: Societies have a tendency to create ideological universes which correspond exactly to what youth needs. There is a complementarity between what happens to the individual and what happens to the ideology. The complementarity is that if you look at it from the point of view of the individual, then he is the one who is looking for an identity in relation to an ideological universe. If you look at it from the point of view of the society, it is the society that creates the ideological universe.

BRENMAN-GIBSON: Or the ideological vacuum.

ERIKSON: Right; I mean society tries to create this ideological universe. This is the tendency. It never completely fits. This doesn't mean that any ideology is complete. But this is the way these things approximate each other, work on each other.

Only after describing all this can one talk about the great man. The great man is the person with a particular life history which, as I say in *Young Man Luther,* can resolve his own identity only by resolving that of others too. By doing this for a communality, he becomes a leader and becomes great in the eyes of others. Is that a social theory or isn't it?

HAMPSHIRE: I think, in fact, there is an implicit social theory that goes with that.

MARCUS: When you finished up, Stuart, you had the family on one side and the job or specialization on the other. And the bridge between them is the specialization of function and the resistance to this. The implicit social theory here is the one that was beginning to be articulated in the *Paris Manuscripts of 1844* of Marx. And it therefore may be no coincidence that these *Manuscripts* are just those that are read by the young people and these seem to answer a certain need for them.

HAMPSHIRE: Yes, and I think there is in Erik's writing an implicit social theory about where these ideologies come from. I think there can easily be a confusion—into which I may have fallen—between speaking from the standpoint of a theorist studying a phenomenon and speaking from the standpoint of those within the phenomenon being studied. I was struck in what Ken was saying and what Erik was saying that what was reproduced, especially when socialization was being discussed, was almost an exact duplication of Rousseau on inequality and the social contract. Rousseauesque ideas on the family, the community, and state recur, and this is a phenomenon one has to take account of. I don't want to suggest that we will gain anything by retrogressing to "On Patriarchy," but I do think we gain from grasping the family imagery and understanding why it's there in radical movements, why these Rousseauesque theories of breaking down the community recur. And this is a psychological question—why this theoretically indefensible attempt recurs to break down the work that's been done by Marx and other critics of Rousseauesque thought.

The idea of development is central to what we've been discussing. And the idea of development is tied to the idea of phases and to the idea that some phases have elements in them that are prophetic of the next phase. And if a crisis isn't past, there is a relapse.

This set of ideas, of the reintegrative or synthesizing phase, where certain elements come together in a new unity and where some of those elements have to be seen as prophetic of the next phase and you may fail to turn certain crucial corners in development—this whole set of ideas is present both in Comte and in Marx. But if you just take prediction in the scientific sense, this would be the wrong sense of prediction to apply to Marx. The way the idea of development has been used in psychology is derived from a body of social theory plus this idea of a crisis which can lead either to a lapse, to a dead end or to an advance. The trick of the thing is to pick out those elements which point forward and those things that point back.

KENISTON: Parenthetically we should note that this stress on development and phases is increasingly drawn from ethological work. It starts from the Hegelian idea of thesis-antithesis-synthesis, but increasingly also emphasizes critical stages in development derived from ethological studies. This latter influence is certainly most conscious in developmental theorists as they talk about the life cycle.

LIFTON: Much of Stuart's presentation raises the problem of defining or even coping with a group theoretically, as opposed to an individual, the question of how one even knows a group exists as a group. But what about the idea of groups as created by history, at least in considerable degree? Ken speaks of youth as a stage of life created by history. More dramatically, the group of Hiroshima survivors whom I interviewed were sought out by me only because they had been through a dreadful historical experience, which immediately did create them as a group. How important they are as a group for various theoretical and conceptual purposes of understanding can be debated. But nonetheless they were created as a group by a specific historical event, both in their own awareness and others' awareness of them.

If one has this idea of groups as created by history—that is, that certain numbers of people have a feeling of having much in common with one another, of being like one another because of certain historical circumstances—then your argument about turning away from the study of a group because it gets no further than the study of an individual doesn't seem to me to be satisfactory. It's true that if you go back to the study of an individual person, say the great man, you are truer to psychoanalytic roots. But it may be that our problem should not be that of how to be true to psychoanalytic roots, but rather to think in terms of radical innovation and departure from psychoanalytic roots while still being true to the early spirit of psychoanalysis.

Unless one does this I think one is caught in another kind of bind. It is terribly hard to define or even to locate in your theorizing those elements that might be new or changing. For example, even so large and important a subject as the family, which cannot be left out of psychohistorical studies, may blind us to the fact that family imagery in youth movements may be of some significance but may not be the only or main thing that matters. By picking up on the family imagery, focusing upon that and then insisting upon the family as the organizing bridge or continuum, one would enormously prejudge the group one was studying.

My general point is that one needs to try to understand what is new in relationship to what is old in history, or what groups are created by history and then in turn themselves help to re-create history. History has indeed been changed by such groups. This is similar to Ken's point that young militants are partly created by history—the life-cycle stage of youth itself has been created by history—and then exert an influence upon history. Unless one struggles toward some such approach to a group, however difficult that struggle is theoretically, one becomes bound to prejudgements that may blind one to historical developments.

HAMPSHIRE: I ought not to have implied that it is difficult from the point of view of the observer to find a group that makes a distinct entity for study. My point was rather that if you yourself are a member of a group that has a program of social action and thinks of itself as acting on the basis of that which constitutes it as a group, then you need guidance through a theory to tell you whether or not this group will hold together as an effective social force. And that theory must come from beyond the immediate situation.

LIFTON: What Stuart has said, I think, is that the shared-themes approach deals essentially with a group of individuals. But then the innovation for us as investigators is to determine how one can supplement that kind of data by creating concepts that emerge from themes that occur in a number of people who have been through the same historical experience, as well as from other data outside of that. This other data need not be immediately dependent upon the individuals one studies, and such data are always used, though not as systematically as they should be.

HAMPSHIRE: We were talking about identity. And identity is a question of descriptions under which people see themselves as acting in a moral sense in society, as having a position, a program, a place. Now, it might very well be that survivors see themselves as survivors and see themselves as held together by a common identity of survivorhood. And it may be that in virtue of seeing themselves as survivors they have an ideology and want to act as members of a group with this common bond which they attribute to themselves. Now, it could be that they are mistaken . . .

KENISTON: But what are they mistaken about? They're not mistaken with regard to all being survivors. They are mistaken with regard to the future success of their movement?

HAMPSHIRE: Well, there are two ways they could be wrong; one is causal and the other is not. It might be that what held them together is not what they thought held them together. For example, those who oppose the youth movements might say that what holds these youth together is a common neurosis arrived at in their individual histories. And acting as they are as young radicals under the heading of "youth and radicalism" is a misdescription of how they came to be in the business of dissent. And, of course, if it is a misdescription this will emerge as they go along. They will have suffered a deception, and nothing will come of their movement. This is where theoretical prediction comes in.

LIFTON: Isn't that where the psychohistorical investigator, by being both empathically involved with them (and in that sense *of* them) and at the same time outside of them as an investigator—isn't that where he can make a judgment as to whether they are, so to speak, right or wrong in their view of their actions or their status? Or at least suggest factors they are not taking into account?

HAMPSHIRE: Yes, but in doing so he does invoke general social theories.

KENISTON: I think it's important to break that down. The judgment *does* involve general social theory when one comes to prophecy or prediction, as for example if one is going to say about young radicals that they will or will not succeed, they will make a revolution or they will collapse. The fact that perhaps they all hate their fathers and that this is the common neurotic origin of their radicalism may or may not be relevant to a judgment about their future. That is, one need not have a predictive social theory in order to decide what unites them as a group. One needs a social theory only if one goes on to say, "Ah, but we know on the basis of our social theory that neurotic motives are very poor motives on which to base a political movement."

Stuart said that the fact that a group is retrogressive from a psychological point of view says nothing one way or another about its social role of prophecy. In fact, one could argue that certain retrogressive groups are the most prophetic. And one might say of radical youth that even if what unites them is their neuroticism they may still constitute a prophetic group, though maybe not in the way that they think they do. It's only when one comes to the question of the future, as to whether they will be effective or not, that one requires additional theory.

ERIKSON: What I wanted to say in my paper is that people who become neurotic in the clinical sense and want help harbor the same conflicts as everybody in their time, including those who harbor them only latently.

LIFTON: Maybe implicit social theory can evolve from this kind of psychological beginnings rather than its usual beginnings in social thought. And then a lot of work has to be done in refining that theory. And a related point is that ability to predict is not the only criterion of theory, social or otherwise; there is also the capacity to illuminate or in some degree explain events and behavior. Most psychohistorical theory tends toward the latter and not the former.

HAMPSHIRE: I want to reply to Ken's point. There is a question of group identity, so the issue comes up for a group acting under a common label of what their social role is as they see it. This question is for them quite distinct from accounts of how each individual entered the group. The painful question for them is whether they are hanging together as a group of people who would be unhappy elsewhere, to put it simply, or whether they have a program which gives a sense of their group identity. Now, they could be deceived in this, because of attempting to make their private pictures fit the group's sense of itself. They could be systematically misreading their actual situation in society, the way in which they are viewed by others and what actions they evoke from others. They could be deceived and in Marxist terms serve a very different role from what they thought they were serving.

So the prophetic element could be taken in two ways: either crudely predictive from their point of view (what *they* think they're going to do), or from the point of view of a theoretical social analysis.

To continue now with my answer to Ken. I said that the first way in which a group could be wrong about their own interpretation of themselves is in wrongly analyzing what it is that holds them together. Second, the group will draw on the theories around in the culture for a description of themselves, in somewhat the way Marcuse describes. In using theories they may distort them and mean by them something very unlike what the theories intended. And there may be deeper reasons why they change and distort various theories in the process of adopting them.

KENISTON: Perhaps this goes back to what we mean by a group in the first place. One can think of a group of people, all of whom have certain shared themes. I once studied such a group, all of whom had in common their opposition to American society. This was at a time when such views were not popular, and other people did not readily join with them. So unless one takes a paradoxical definition of group, they formed no group except in my eye and that of other observers. They were a set: they had shared themes. They were like the Hiroshima survivors who never got together and who did all they could to avoid each other. They were tainted with survivorhood, and that was formative for their lives, and they were not a group.

CHISOLM: Our whole discussion assumes that there are social theories to which we are heir that can in fact illuminate the kinds of issues that have been raised, or our situation. I'm highly skeptical of that. It seems to me that where one begins, almost as axiomatic, is that the social theories that we've inherited bear the stamp of the cultural matrices of their origins. They simply are not comprehensive enough in terms of the kinds of evidence we want to look at. And they tend always to skew our discussion in terms of these dualisms like self and society.

It seems that our problem is how to take these inherited vocabularies and use them without thereby being led into the stylized selections of evidence and the canonical commentaries on the past which evade the unthinkable possibility, which is that we are out of control. Which is to say we have no social theories which are adequate enough to illumine our situation.

When I look at social scientific writings, they do not illumine the world for me in almost any significant way. And I think that Bob's recommendation that we begin from a psychological direction certainly connects with our situation. One way of understanding the reluctance of the young, and not only the young, to apprentice themselves to traditional disciplines is that the young deny the epistemological assumptions of most of these disciplines as to what constitutes the minimum framework of relevant evidence which has to be considered in order to render any satisfactory account of an event.

CHISOLM: It seems to me that one of the things that has to be part of the working through of a given disciplinary training is a systematically self-critical attitude toward the discipline itself, in terms of an examination of the cultural origins of the master theorists. And this is simply not part of the framework in which the social theory is used.

LIFTON: As you get large numbers of people who feel a profound kind of dislocation and can identify this with a number of historical and personal events, beginning again has a very valid kind of importance for them. This has to do with the whole theme of death and rebirth especially in youth, and with crisis generally. Now, beginning again doesn't mean you jettison everything from the past, but it may mean that as you struggle with ideas from the past and, indeed, take them very seriously ideally, and examine them very critically—meaning learning them, reading them—your relationship to them may be different from what is generally assumed. It may be that as coherent theories for us in our disciplines, as for the youth in another way in action, they are only partially useful. It may be that they are so loaded with the presuppositions of the times in which the theories were put forward that taking them as the basis from which one starts would lead one to grief as any sort of approximation of the current situation.

MARCUS: There is something of a discrepancy here. We don't speak this way about psychoanalysis itself; we don't say that we don't need theory or don't have to know the theory. In fact we assume that the more we are in command of it, the more we are capable of applying it or dealing with it critically. In psychoanalysis the knowing of theory and the practice of it are really inseparable.

I think what Stuart is saying is that not only is social theory necessary to solve certain problems fully, but it's there all the time anyway and we're using it whether we know it or not. Now, it seems to me that there is great intellectual danger in using a theory which is only there implicitly.

LIFTON: I agree. Therefore one should make the theory explicit and should deal explicitly with social theory. But, first, the social theory that I am using, that Erik is using, and that Ken is using, is not exactly that of any classical social theory. It draws upon classical theory in fragments and it must continue to do that. Perhaps the most useful social theory for this kind of enterprise will be rather different from any previous social theory and will emerge just by dint of its psychological beginning. The social theory inseparable from that psychological work will take a different shape from the classical form. And this is true of a lot of endeavors now in terms of coming to grips with traditional theory.

HAMPSHIRE: I've been talking about social groups and their coherence and their programs of social agency. I'm aware in speaking this way that this is language really derived from old-fashioned ideas of interest groups and the notion of a program and the relation of a program to a sense of identity. In the minds of the people we've been discussing—youth, students—these may be an inapplicable set of ideas, drawn in my mind from a simplified set of Marxist ideas. The ideas of a program, of social action, or even being responsible for one's actions may be alien to them. Certainly I derive all these ideas from Marxist sources really.

LIFTON: What I'm saying, what I think Larry was saying and Erik and Ken were saying in different ways, is that if one lays out classical social theories—about alienation, the family or whatever—and says this is what must be used, then one may, in taking that step, eliminate or impair one's theoretical grasp of terribly confusing, in some ways unprecedentedly confusing, social and psychological events that we are in the midst of. The only alternative that I can pose to that is to take traditional psychological and social theory seriously; that means "be scholarly" while at the same time keeping open the idea that the very process of putting together theory may be changing. As one struggles to build one's appropriate theory, one may borrow certain fragments and do it as a scholar. But the theory-making process itself may be undertaken in new ways. That's the kind of point I'm making. And that's in keeping with a lot of processes which have happened historically, which have dislocated both theorists and the people one theorizes about.

KENISTON: As I listen to this discussion I find very little real disagreement but a good deal of energy. Much of this may have to do with our individual sense of our relationship to the past, that stance or posture toward it that we find most productive for our own work. And I think there are major differences in our styles in this regard.

KLEIN: I think we shouldn't lose sight of what I took to be Stuart's essential message here. Stuart started with the problem of explanation, and the necessity of knowing what you are explaining. He alluded to a very important danger in diagnosing that which looks like psychological explanation but which hides a problem in social theory. This was touched on a bit yesterday when Erik said, "Ken, you've been brainwashed." What he was suggesting was that Ken was buying the group's definition of itself as youth. And he said, now let's not just accept that. Not accepting it means standing back and looking at it from the standpoint of a theoretical matrix which allows you to distinguish the conception of the group as itself from what it is as a social process which has an impact and a future.

That's a very important distinction. And it is true that people working with youth today constantly buy all self-justifying definitions of youth. And I think this is an important distinction. For us it's a problem of where our explanatory focus has to be.

MARCUS: What Stuart has done is bring to articulation the genuine problems that we face and the border we have not yet crossed. His comments really provide the next step for real deliberation. He has provided us with the subjects for a series of seminars in which real collaborative work would have to take place.

WYATT: From the beginning of these meetings we have assumed that many things could take place. We have always made the same mistake in assuming that the presentations would be brief and succinct, we would discuss them and then proceed to the next subject. This is not the first time that we have found ourselves stepping over something that has greater depth than we first thought and which, in the minds of some of us, needs further exploration, because of the substantive wealth of the problem. We should also recognize that at such an occasion certain personality needs and personality problems will be acted out here so that we have to leave some room for that. In the future we should not be so presumptuous about time. We should have fewer topics and be prepared to stick to them.

LIFTON: There's one special characteristic of this summer's meetings. This is the first time in the four summers that we have really talked only about theory the whole time. I think that's one of the sources of the tension. When we talk extensively about data there's a kind of group immersion into that data from which lots of things can happen rather readily. Theoretical differences or unresolved theoretical positions can be either glossed over or just less intensely felt. But when you talk about theory the whole time, with virtually no research data presented as such, I think we're learning that that creates a very special set of tensions, and perhaps not without considerable value.

KENISTON: I think very much with their value. For four years, over and over we have said that there are limitations to a psychological approach. Perhaps agreement on that is why we're here. That point has now come to a head in this discussion. By discussing theory in this way we have become more aware of the implicit social theory which has been smuggled in and yet left unanalyzed.

BRENMAN-GIBSON: Is it not likely, Ken, that if we are to discover the implicit social theory it would take place best around presented data rather than simply on the level of generalization?

KENISTON: In the three previous years I felt frustrated because there was so much data and very little theoretical discussion. I think there has been a good progression from the empirical to the theoretical.

CHISOLM: There's one theme which I, not being fully initiated into the psychoanalytic tradition, have been surprised has not been developed more than it has. That is the theme of the absolutely essential dimension of the autobiography to the understanding of any idea, any encounter, any kind of phenomenon. Autobiography is something which is continually in process and is part of participant observation requirement for us as investigators. Bob Coles confessed last year that the preface in *Children of Crisis,** which is essential and is part of the quality of the book, was added at the suggestion of his wife. He was reluctant to put in the preface. And I know that my students in reading your work, Bob, want to know more about your experience in interviewing, for example, the people in Hong Kong.

There's kind of insistent contextualism that includes now, on the part of any kind of audience, this sense of the total life history of the participants in the act of investigation, and in reporting a study. What gave Erik's remarks this morning their special quality, I thought, was just this dimension of personal history. He dropped a casual remark that when he came to the United States in the 1930s he felt submissive to the dominant culture and that these were the ideals he could believe in. Well, that smuggles in a great deal. The United States in the 1930s and the 1960s: what does that mean for an identity concept? These are important aspects of the Eriksonian theory.

MARCUS: There's a whole social theory in that remark.

CHISOLM: Don't we need to take that into account in some systematic way, in identifying our own personal pasts and in being self-skeptical?

WYATT: I like what you say, but I think it goes even further. We have also been talking about our own salvation in these three days under the guise of youth. We really want to know where we stand. Are we worth anything or should what we have to offer be discarded and instead, should we run along with youth and identify with them? We really were talking about our own salvation. In that sense there is merit in the idea that perhaps we should sometimes have more remote topics for our joint effort.

BRENMAN-GIBSON: We have to talk about what we're interested in.

KLEIN: As a first-time attendant of these meetings I find it extremely involving, informative, enriching. Call it brain-picking if you like.

*Vol. I.

There's a lot of pejorative terms for which one could substitute other terms that would emphasize the uniqueness of these meetings. It becomes deplorable if that's not what you wanted it to be. If this is what you expect, I think quite positive values can be associated. My criterion is whether I'm a little different for having been at this conference. And I think I am.

KENISTON: It's not as if we alone had chosen this form. It is *the* academic form, although here it has been modified in rather pleasant ways. The alternatives—which one can easily caricature—are finding a boring subject which no one knows about or is interested in, or avoiding the apocalyptic mood that we bring into the room. These would be very difficult to set up logistically.

MARCUS: What we are looking for is a subject which does have its apocalyptic possibilities in the sense that it's not dead historically but current today, and which can be dealt with from a variety of points of view—historical, theoretical—and to which empirical data can be brought. We're not interested in a subject which is purely historical and which has ceased to exist in contemporary reference. We want a subject with adequate thickness so that the various analytical skills that we have can meet and out of which our deficiencies which Stuart describes will arise and be met.

LIFTON: As a group we've wavered between ambitions (and I mean ambition in a positive way) toward creating a new institution that would help create a new field of thought, and on the other hand not wanting to do that work. It would require a great deal of work that we have all been reluctant to undertake—the Academy* has encouraged us in the direction of a more time-consuming institutional commitment. All of us resisted that approach, but not without ambivalence. Why, then, have we stayed this way? Partly because it's been easy and comfortable. Erik and I first took the initiative, also Ken, and then with Philip, Bruce Mazlish and others we fell into a pattern. That included meeting here regularly for from four to six days. A second reason is that we know that we do not have either the theory or the agreement to start a "new field," so each of us has been guarding his or her own individual struggles in which this group has played a part, but which remained individual, the struggles we each have alone in our own studies. Changing to a more

*The American Academy of Arts and Sciences.

collective or shared struggle would be a major innovation in our way of doing things.

Some of the group's impatience has to do, I think, with the depth of our commitment to our own intellectual course. That is very much in all of us. The paths that we have carved out have rather complex connections to traditions and to friends and colleagues. But these are mostly by now rather firm courses. They're not without great struggle and pain, but they're well under way. We have what we have to contribute partly because each of our individual courses is well under way. We come together in various ways, but there's a deep push in each of us individually toward developing these individual courses further. I think that's a fair statement.

KENISTON: I think it is, too, and I think it reflects what happens. If we analyzed a transcript of any given day's proceedings we would find, essentially, a number of virtuoso long statements. By and large we proceed by presentations interrupted by other presentations. Many of the comments, while brilliant and important, move to another realm or are not precisely to the point at issue. They're in part connected; they start from and they often go back to the main presentation. But they are expressive as well as instrumental, self-presentational as well as analytic. Which is the charm and excitement of this group; it couldn't exist unless it were that way. At the same time, that points to the fact that this is a group of people who are solo virtuosi in many respects. If one were looking for a group which was *not* task-oriented in a strict sense, a group which has *not* said, "OK, let's get to the bottom of this," we are it. Certainly this is the way this group has proceeded over the course of twenty days now spread over four years.

In thinking about what we might do in the future we have to think about the way this group has taken shape in the past and the way each of our characters is reflected in this. Even though we're frustrated and each of us would like to get to what we consider to be the bottom of each issue, we have to ask whether, even if we did closet ourselves together for six months, we could get to the bottom of this. I for one think I would find myself feeling very frustrated and very confined. What I'm trying to point to is a particular kind of individual solo quality that many of the people here have. And many of us are the kind of people who pick up cards and shuffle them into our own deck. Can we do anything else?

Klein: Doesn't the "anything else" occur between conferences? Isn't one of the spurs that come out of the conference a heightened awareness of insufficiency in certain areas of our own work? I now feel I have a lot to do that was in the periphery of my consciousness before. The things that Stuart deplores as dangers I find hard to see as dangers except as they become so in the context of our own inadequacies which would be there despite the form of the conference. One may come out of this a better or worse scholar, but the conference form alone does not decide that. We do.

Lifton: Incidentally, we've never really thought of this as a conference so much as meetings.

Chisolm: The other point that Bob has made is that it's premature to assert that there is a body of theory which exists and which would make a great deal of sense out of a wide and comprehensive set of phenomena. Erik's gone much further than others in this, but it will take quite a while before the resources of the group could reach this stage in which we could all address ourselves to the leading problems.

Lifton: Bringing in younger people may be rather essential for the kinds of things we want to do.

THE INABILITY TO MOURN

ALEXANDER AND
MARGARETE MITSCHERLICH

The war was lost: though the mountains of rubble it left behind were enormous, there is no denying that we did not allow this fact fully to penetrate our consciousness.

Mourning is the mental process by which the individual copes with a loss. Henry Lowenfeld[1] has rightly pointed out that a disturbance of this work of mourning in the individual hampers his mental development, his interhuman relations, his spontaneity and creativity. Transferring such individual experiences to a large group must lead to considerable difficulties, because here the great variety of living circumstances and characters adds new and unknown factors. The authors are well aware that their attempts at generalization, or rather their description of reactions that take an identical course in persons of otherwise very different characters, are based chiefly on hypotheses. Their concern is to draw attention to these processes and perhaps to stimulate empirical studies of their thesis; they contend that there is a determining connection between the political and social immobilism and provincialism that prevail in the Federal Republic of Germany and the stubbornly maintained rejection of memories, in particular the blocking of any sense of involvement in the events of the past that are now being denied.

This sociopsychological analysis is based, not on any systematic investigation, but on spontaneous observations wherever behavior came to light which could be said to represent not just an individual reaction, but one that was widespread and frequently observable. We shall describe two patterns of behavior that seem to us to be so ubiquitous that they can be regarded as representative. One can be summed up under the heading of "defense mechanisms against the Nazi past." Something of this mental attitude appears in the denial of defeat by an enemy who was felt to be greatly inferior in "race" and culture. It is important to note that defeat does not seem to have brought about much change in this negative evaluation. At all events, until recently the German Government and the official and unofficial spokesmen of our country have done little to bring about a better understanding and thus diminish the deep gulf of estrangement that exists between us and our Eastern neighbors.

The second trend is far more difficult to describe. It has to do with a slowness of reaction discernible throughout our political and social organism. The insights that are here warded off with the help of psychic barriers are related to unresolved or insufficiently understood problems of our contemporary society. Where we should expect the greatest involvement, we find indifference. This diffuse indifference is particularly striking when one bears in mind the rapid change in our material environment. Lively interest in technical problems contrasts with the apathy that prevails in regard to basic political rights. Participation in everything that should be of the greatest concern to an enlightened public opinion is relatively slight. The rapid advance of industrialization, the concentration of population in industrial focal points, the increase in nonindependent work, the perpetual restructuring of all the techniques of production, the problems of the transmission of knowledge in such a changed and complex society, and the effect of all this on that related pair, human drives and human morality, should stimulate efforts to achieve an adequate understanding of what is happening. A new world is coming into being before our eyes. But most people in our country show little interest in acquiring reliable information, in penetrating the manipulations to which their values are being continually subjected, and, in general, in forming a coherent picture of the forces that are influencing the course of history in our lifetime.

Here a specifically German way of behaving coincides with a general contemporary one. The boundless and ever accelerating increase in our knowledge, the growing trend for the individual to become a mere cog in the wheels of big productive or administrative conglomerates, his specialization involving an ever narrower field of action, have a crippling effect on initiative everywhere. Every country affected by the process of industrialization is more and more urgently confronted with the vital question of how to secure the political involvement of the masses in the processes that decisively affect their future and their social environment, issues which, under present conditions, they are less and less able to influence. The processes of concentration of power in a few places, the extremely indirect influence of multiply dependent specialists, exclude the masses from the politically really important decisions for different reasons but just as effectively as in the past. Here lies one of the roots of an ossifying national egotism. In our time the problem of political apathy (accompanied by simultaneous intense stimulation of feeling in the consumer field) presents special aspects. Among the masses on whom apathy has been imposed by social processes, outbreaks of irrational, destructive behavior continually occur. Also, masses have never before existed on the present scale, and never before have political decisions affected so many people.

These ubiquitous difficulties of societies limited by national boundaries and undergoing industrialization were very convenient for us Germans after the end of the war. So far as the phenotype was concerned, we changed from a backward, aggressive nation under Nazism into one that was nonpolitical and conservative. It is relatively easy to demonstrate this by our lack of curiosity. We have shown a minimum of psychological interest in why we became followers of a leader who led us to the greatest material and moral catastrophe in our history, though, rationally, this ought to have been the most burning problem in our minds. We have also shown a minimum of interest in the new ordering of our society. Instead, with a spirit of enterprise that arouses admiration and envy, we concentrated all our energies on the restoration of what was destroyed and the extension and modernization of our industrial potential—down to and including our kitchen equipment. The monomaniac exclusivity of this effort cannot be overlooked. It has caused the political life of our country gradually to ossify into administrative routine, a development which we take as a matter of course. But that is certainly wrong. Instead, what is really required is an examination of the motives of this one-sided behavior.

It is the very absence of traditions, that is, of identifications that have remained intact and effective, that makes the slogan "No experiments," which sums up the present state of affairs, contrast so strikingly with German social history. At an earlier stage in the industrial era the initiative for tackling oppressive social conditions came from our country. In the last third of the nineteenth century we produced the world's most powerful Socialist movement, which imposed a notable compromise in social legislation on the conservative forces under Bismarck. But after the end of the Third Reich there was no trace of any such revolutionary, forward-looking idea. The country seems to have exhausted its capacity to produce politically effective ideas, as most of its citizens accepted the Nazi ideas of racism and world domination.

After living in the illusion that social problems could be dealt with in the style of the "final solution," it was not to be expected that the return to everyday life would be easy. In 1945 there were no authorities in German public life that had not been compromised. This applied to the remnants of feudalism and to the liberal bourgeoisie. Also, apart from a vague hope of European integration, there were no political ideas that an anti-Nazi resistance movement might have produced to fall back on. Instead, it was necessary to reach back still further to a man who had been formed under the governmental system—long since dead and gone—of Imperial Germany. The reign of a very aged father figure began. It was left to him to represent the "State," while, as we have said, libidinal energy was concentrated in the economic field. The "State" took over the role of preserving the economy from clashes that might have resulted from criticism of our pre-1945 national aims. And to a large extent such criticism did not arise. Instead of a political working through of the past, as a minimal attempt at making amends, the explosive development of German industry began. Hard work and its success soon covered the open wounds left by the past. Where building and development took place, it was carried out almost literally on the same foundations, but not in any considered connection with tradition. This applies not only to building but also to what was taught in our schools, to the legal system, to municipal administration, and to a great many other things as well. The economic restoration was accompanied by the growth of a characteristic new self-esteem. Neither the millions of lives lost in the war nor the millions of Jews slaughtered can prevent the feeling that we have had enough of being reminded of the past. Above all, there is no sense that an effort should be made—from kindergarten to the university—to incorporate the catastrophes of the past into our stock of experience, not just as a warning but as a specific challenge to our national society to deal with the brutally aggressive trends these disasters had revealed.

Our hypothesis views the political and social sterility of present-day Germany as resulting from the denial of the past. Defense against collective responsibility and guilt—guilt whether of action or of toleration—has left traces in our character. When psychic defense mechanisms such as denial and repression play an excessive role in the solution of conflicts, whether on the individual or the collective level, it can regularly be observed that perception of reality narrows and stereotyped prejudices spread. In reciprocal reinforcement the prejudices in turn preserve the process of repression or denial from disturbance. When social problems have been treated in the style of the "final solution," this cannot be followed by an effortless transition to civilized "normality" without a split in consciousness occurring.

No matter how much our conscious minds may be dominated by a sense of breach with the past, estrangement from it, the sense of a new beginning from zero hour, if what came after is to be understood it must be considered in conjunction with what happened before. It is obvious that the murder of millions cannot be "mastered." This is illustrated in symbolically condensed form by the impotence of our courts when faced with the perpetrators of crimes dating from that period; the very scale of those crimes is baffling. But such a narrowly legal interpretation cannot do justice to the real meaning of what we call the unmastered past. Rather, by "mastering" we mean a sequence of steps in self-knowledge. Freud called them "remembering, repeating, working through." [2] The content of unique memories, even when they are accompanied by violent feelings, quickly fades. Repetition of inner conflicts and critical analysis are necessary to overcome the instinctive and unconscious self-protective forces of forgetting, denying, projecting, and similar defense mechanisms. The therapeutic effect of such remembering and working through is familiar to us from clinical practice. In political practice this knowledge takes us not a single step forward: only a patient whose symptoms cause him suffering greater than the gain he gets from repression is willing, step by step, to relax the censorship preventing the return to consciousness of what has been denied and forgotten. But we are asking that this therapy be carried out by a society that, at least materially, is on the whole better off than ever before. It feels no incentive to expose its interpretation of the recent past to the inconvenient questioning of others; for one thing, because the manic defense of using the economic miracle to obliterate the past has been very successful, and the world, whatever else it may think about the Germans, acknowledges the German virtue of industriousness; for another—and this is no less important—because the military and moral victors over the Third Reich have since shown, in "limited" wars such as those in Algeria or Vietnam, that they too are capable of grave acts of inhumanity.

Thus we need a fuller explanation of the leap that so many made from yesterday to today. It was a lightning change, of which one would not have supposed people so easily capable. For years the Nazi leaders' conduct of the war and their war aims had been accepted with a minimum of inner detachment; certainly any reservations remained without effect. But after the total defeat, the theory of enforced obedience sprang up; suddenly it was only the undiscoverable or convicted leaders who were responsible for carrying out the genocide. All levels of society, and in particular the leading sections—the industrialists, the judges, the university teachers—had given the regime their definite and enthusiastic support, but with its failure they regarded themselves as automatically absolved from personal responsibility.

In retrospect the great majority of Germans now feel that the Nazi period was like the obtrusion of an infectious illness in their childhood, even though the collective regression in which they engaged while under the Führer's care was mainly pleasurable—it was magnificent to be a chosen people. For a great many people, this belief, while shaken, has still not been disproved. The nationalism that Germany shows today is relatively mild in comparison with that of other Western countries, and very definitely mild in comparison with that of the Eastern and developing countries. Nevertheless many observers feel threatened and alarmed by it, because for an unforeseeable time ahead the memory of Auschwitz and Lidice will be connected with German national feeling; the lightning change of scene to peaceful and busy industriousness and the rapidly accumulated prosperity only show how quickly everything in this country can change.

A very considerable expenditure of psychic energy is necessary to maintain this separation of acceptable and unacceptable memories; and what is used in the defense of a self anxious to protect itself against bitter qualms of conscience and doubts about its own worth is unavailable for mastering the present. Moreover, the fewer really productive solutions are found or succeed, the more sensitively does the general public react to those "malicious" persons who are unwilling to forget, and who feel that our so carefully warded-off past is a reality that is in fact still at work.

Hence the "intellectual task" must be, first of all, cautiously to expose for what they are the self-deceptions that are substantially contributing to the creation of a new self-image. Perhaps Freud's observation that neurosis does not deny reality, but merely wants to know nothing about it, applies also to the collective efforts that we see around us. Of course, defense mechanisms of this kind not only dominate the German scene, they are a universal form of human reaction. Nevertheless, what is decisive is the way individuals and groups manage to become aware of the specific self-deceptions they nourish and learn to overcome them.

Few twinges of conscience break through, for in these outbreaks of destructive aggression religious arguments can be used to show that the victims are human only in appearance, while in reality they are diabolical. The loathing of the Jews that Nazi propaganda sought to inculcate was in keeping with these tactics. The Jews were regarded as "vermin"; killing vermin is no crime and can be carried out without conflict. The dictator's only task is thus, with the aid of this dehumanization, to turn conscience "upside down." Himmler did this in a speech to SS leaders. He assured them of the gratitude of the nation and of humanity for their self-sacrifice in having undertaken the horrible but unavoidable task of exterminating millions of Jews. "Most of you," he said, "will know what it means to see a hundred corpses, or five hundred, or a thousand, lying before you. Having stood up to that and—apart from some exceptional cases of human weakness—having remained decent has made us hard. This is an unwritten and never to be written page of glory in our history." [3]

What is a society to do that finds itself confronted with the inescapable realization that in its name six million people have been killed for no reason other than its own aggressive urges? It has hardly any choice but to continue to deny its motives or *retreat into depression*. As it turned out, however, Nazi officials who were not arrested until twenty years later—Eichmann, for instance—did not show signs of serious psychic disturbance. Also, not everyone was directly criminally associated with the genocide, and so did not have to feel a direct share in the guilt; accordingly, with denial and whitewashing, innumerable ways out of the calamity were found. Depressive reactions, self-reproach, despair at the extent of the guilt one had assumed, were far rarer.

The most important collectively practiced defense is to withdraw cathecting energies from all the processes related to enthusiasm for the Third Reich, idealization of the Führer and his doctrine, and, of course, actual criminal acts. The use of this psychic defense tactic makes the memory of the twelve years of Nazi rule dim and ghost-like. When recent history in all its crude brutality is again brought to our notice—by the trial of a Nazi criminal, for instance—the avoidance is continued, and the page of the newspaper on which the trial is reported is quickly turned. When, however, the past is forced on our attention it is in no way acknowledged as part of our own history, our own identity. It is to be presumed that those who are thus "unaffected" think in exactly the same way when they are by themselves. Consequently the tangible suffering that brings the neurotic patient to analytic treatment, and thus to a working through of the repressed, does not arise. So far as we are concerned, bygones shall be bygones without there being any occasion for remorse.

We can now sum up as follows. The inability to mourn the loss of the Führer is the result of an intensive defense against guilt, shame and anxiety, which could be achieved by the withdrawal of previously powerful libidinal cathexes. The Nazi past was de-realized, made unreal. The occasion for mourning was not only the death of the real Adolf Hitler but above all his disappearance as the representation of the collective ego-ideal. He was an object on which one depended, to which one transferred responsibility, and he was an internal object. As such, he represented and gave new life to the ideas of omnipotence that we carry over from infancy; his death, and his devaluation by the victors, also meant the loss of a narcissistic object and thus an ego- or self-impoverishment and devaluation.

To avoid these traumas must be regarded as the immediate reason for the suppression of the memories. Defense against mourning for the innumerable victims of Hitler's aggression—an aggression which, in our identification with him, we had so willingly and unresistingly shared—came only in second place. Once the order of priority of these psychic processes has been recognized, the reasons become clearer for the difficulties in mutual understanding between the Germans and the rest of the world after the end of the war. Our victorious opponents had experienced a reinforcement of their ego-ideal, while we Germans had experienced a crushing humiliation. The victors could acknowledge reality without feelings of devaluation and could mourn for the victims of the war, while the Germans had received a blow to the very core of their sense of their own worth, and the most urgent task for their psychic apparatus was to ward off the experience of a melancholy impoverishment of the self. Thus the moral duty to join in mourning for the victims of our ideological aims—which for the rest of the world was self-evident—could not for the time being be anything but a superficial psychic process for us. The mechanisms concerned here are emergency reactions, processes very close to if not actual psychic correlates of biological survival processes. Thus it is pointless to make a reproach of these immediate postcollapse reactions. The real problem is that even later on no adequate work of mourning was done for the millions of our *fellow men* slaughtered by our doing. In other words, if the victors had pursued a policy of an eye for an eye, and slaughtered millions of Germans, there would have been historical precedents for it. But the population, whose insane goals and the gruesome crimes to which they had led had been thus exposed, was in a state of shock; in such a situation, it would be wrong to expect that they could be concerned with anything but themselves.

A period of maximum self-glorification now turned out to have been inseparably associated with the greatest crimes. The motivation for feelings of unreality associated with this period was thus not only fear of punishment and defense against guilt, but also defense against the admission that one was now powerless and worthless and had to renounce primitive mechanisms of gratification, the pleasure, namely, of acting out infantile fantasies of omnipotence. We probably are not going astray if we connect the ever recurrent cult of stainless national honor with our narcissism—that is to say, with a very early infantile self-love.

To millions of Germans the loss of the "Führer" (for all the lack of traces left by his downfall and the rapidity with which he was renounced) was not the loss of an ordinary person. Identifications that had filled a central function in the lives of his followers were associated with him. He had, as we have said, become the embodiment of their ego-ideal. The loss of an object so highly cathected with libidinal energy, one about whom no one had doubts, nor dared to have doubts even when the country was being reduced to rubble, was indeed a reason for melancholia. Not only did our ego-ideal lose its support in outside reality, but in addition our Führer was exposed by the victors as a criminal of truly monstrous proportions. With this sudden reversal of his qualities, the ego of each and every individual suffered a central devaluation and impoverishment. Thus at least the prerequisites for a melancholic reaction were created.

This is the point to introduce our working hypothesis: The Federal Republic did not succumb to melancholia. Instead, the community of those who had lost their "ideal leader," the representative of a commonly shared ego-ideal, managed to avoid self-devaluation by breaking all affective bridges linking them to the immediate past. This withdrawal of affective cathecting energy, of interest, should not be regarded as a conscious, deliberate act; it was an unconscious process, with only minimal guidance from the conscious ego. The disappearance from memory of processes that had previously been highly stimulating and exciting must be regarded as the result of a self-protective mechanism triggered off, as it were, like a reflex action. By this rejection of inner involvement in one's own behavior under the Third Reich, a loss of self-esteem that could hardly have been mastered, and with it an outbreak of melancholia, were avoided in innumerable cases. The consequence of this unusual psychic effort of self-defense, which has by no means ended, is the present psychic immobilism in the face of the acute problems facing our society. Because of the persistence of this autistic attitude, a large number if not the majority of the inhabitants of our country have not succeeded in identifying themselves with anything in our democratic society beyond its economic system.

In view of these meager indications of any inner burden that could not be coped with by normal means, one might have gathered the impression that Germany had never been Nazi and that in 1945 it had at most lost a group of Nazi, that is to say foreign, "occupiers."

This striking lack of any signs of inner crisis requires an explanation. We find it in the fact that, while a neurosis in childhood prepares for the reappearance of neurotic illness under conditions of stress in later years, to those involved in the Third Reich and living in it in 1945 the present stress arose not so much from individual inner conflicts as from processes that shook the whole of society. It makes a great deal of difference, for example, whether a massive clinical persecution mania develops in a single individual because of conflicts in his childhood and in his later personal life, or whether within a society a compulsion to conform leads to a similarly massive aggressive delusional projection onto a persecutor who appears to be equipped with mysterious powers. A delusion of this kind can also, so long as it persists, paralyze the critical intervention of the ego. But obviously such a delusional system can break down more rapidly, leaving fewer traces, as soon as the manipulated external pressure is relaxed. The ego is then faced with a new task: that of coping with the guilt accumulated during the phase of collective delusion. This can consist in accepting and remorsefully realizing what has happened or in resorting to defense mechanisms against the menacing reality, such as we used in childhood against the fear of punishment; significant among these mechanisms is the denial of guilt. The absence of genuinely felt remorse for what happened under the Third Reich shows us that a new phase of the neurotic process has set in, the chief feature of which is no longer the acting out of destructive fantasies with the permission of an "upside-down" conscience, but a denial of these drivelike impulses and a detached indifference to the crimes committed.

It must also be pointed out that defense against a collectively incurred guilt is easy when it too is carried out collectively, for here a universal consensus determines the degree of guilt. Normally, a guilt-laden individual is isolated from society, but in a group, being one among many, he does not endure this fate.

One of our patients, a man of forty who had been called up for war service after membership in the Hitler Youth, manifested an extraordinary lack of feeling in connection with memories of his activities during the war. One might say that the patient remembered them as if he had been turning the pages of an old photograph album and had come across some forgotten snapshots of a forgotten trip. He had to make an effort to revive the memories concerned; the pictures were remote and unmeaningful, and as he continued to turn the pages everything was again forgotten. The attempt to make plain to him the defense mechanism at work behind his casual attitude to these memories, his lack of interest in and feeling about them, failed. In view of his normally acute sensibility, this was very striking. At this point in the treatment we were no longer dealing with his individual resistance to the appearance of feelings of unpleasure, but with a collectively approved resistance. He was withdrawing libidinal cathexis from an experience belonging to a period from which his whole environment had inwardly detached itself. Thus the episodes concerned relapsed into the realm of the unreal. In his case—and it is to be expected that the same applies to many others—tacit agreement with the collectively practiced denial reinforced a defense mechanism that was ready and waiting: he regularly reacted with such a withdrawal of affect to memories associated with disappointments about himself or with the reactivation of guilt feelings established in infancy. This attitude was not without a more general connection with his "bourgeois" origin—"bourgeois" in this context implying a far-reaching denial of the basic drives. But the power of these collective prejudgments can hardly be overestimated. If a whole society absolves itself of responsibility on the ground that it has merely been obedient, even individuals who try to remain free of these collective views or beliefs are affected.

Though more than three decades have since passed, the number of those able to orient themselves to political reality on the basis of a general recognition of guilt remains minimal. The shock produced by the threat of a total loss of worth has not yet worn off. But so long as we do not "at last take note" of the guilt or "the mass crimes carried out with indescribable horror," not only is the life of the mind condemned to stagnation in our country, but there can be no genuinely felt reconciliation with our former enemies, even though we may be bound to them by political alliances and flourishing trade relations. Rather, we are in constant danger of using complicitory alliances to cover up the contempt for us which, while it is no longer so frequently verbalized, is still unchanged.

In the case of every aggression the rationalizing self-justification was: we were not looking for personal power or personal gain. The guilt feelings deriving from the murderous aggressivity are allayed by the fact that the father, at whom originally the aggression is actually aimed, is felt in the end to be an object to whom one has dedicated oneself, for whom one has sacrified oneself: it was all done only for the Führer and the Fatherland. Here we can see one of the psychological roots of a patriotism capable of such blind aggression; it must produce enemies, so that the intolerable tension of the ambivalence to one's own paternal authority can be diverted onto a relationship with an object outside the group. A correlation is always to be noted between the fanaticism of this patriotism and the degree of severity with which the father demands unconditional subjection to his authority, according to the role pattern for such behavior that he finds existing in his society.

We have argued that, had it not been counteracted by these defense mechanisms—of denial, isolation, transformation into the opposite, and above all withdrawal of interest and affect, that is to say of rendering memories of the whole period of the Third Reich devoid of feeling—a condition of extreme melancholia would have been inevitable for a large number of people in postwar Germany, as a consequence of their narcissistic love of the Führer and the ruthless crimes committed in his service. Because of the narcissistic identification with the Führer, his failure was a failure of our own ego. Though defense mechanisms did prevent an outbreak of melancholia, they could only imperfectly ward off a "tremendous impoverishment of the ego." This seems to us the key to understanding the psychic immobilism and the inability to tackle the problems of our society in a socially progressive fashion.

We paid not ungenerous compensation to the surviving European Jews whom we persecuted but did not manage to kill. But emotionally we have not yet visualized the real human beings whom we were ready to sacrifice to our master race. They have remained part of the de-realized reality. Many of the medical evaluations, for instance, of physical and mental damage sustained by victims of Nazi persecution betray a terrifying lack of empathy. The medical evaluator is still completely on the side of and unconsciously identified with the persecutors. He cannot imagine what it means when the fourteen-year-old daughter of a textile merchant in a country town in Baden is suddenly seized by the power of a police state, carried off by uniformed, well-fed, self-confident men and treated as a kind of vermin. He cannot imagine that this might have happened to his own fourteen-year-old daughter. He cannot put himself into the state of mind of a girl whose parents were gassed in the same camp in which she was also confined, and in which she was then left behind alone, herself ultimately escaping extermination only by chance. Are such experiences supposed to leave no scars behind?

We cannot bring the dead back to life. But until we manage to free ourselves from the stereotyped prejudices of our history—the Third Reich represented only a recent phase—in relation to the living, we shall remain chained to our psychosocial immobilism as to an illness involving symptoms of severe paralysis.

"The collective responsibility of a nation for a chapter of its development," George Lukács writes:

> is something so abstract and intangible that it borders on absurdity. And yet a period such as the time of Hitler can be regarded as over and done with in our own memory only if the intellectual and moral

> outlook that filled it, gave it movement, direction and shape, has been radically overcome. Only then does it become possible for others—for other nations—to trust in the conversion and to feel that the past is really past.[4]

But an outlook can be "radically overcome" only on the basis of knowledge firmly anchored in consciousness, even though at first the knowledge be painful, since what happened could happen only because that consciousness was corrupted. What censorship has excluded from our consciousness, as a memory too painful to bear, may return unbidden from the past; it has not been "mastered"; it does not belong to a past that has been grappled with and understood. The work of mourning can be accomplished only when we know what we must free ourselves from. And only by slowly freeing ourselves from lost object relations—whether to human beings or ideals—can a relationship to reality and to the past be meaningfully maintained. Without the painful work of recollection this cannot be achieved. And without it the old ideals, that with National Socialism led to the fatal turn taken by German history, will continue to operate unconsciously.

Psychologically, it would not be impossible to admit in retrospect what we did under the Third Reich, and to move from the narcissistic type of love toward a recognition of our fellow men as human beings having the same rights as ourselves. To correct our false and restricted consciousness in this way, to discover our capacity to pity people whom we had never before seen clearly behind our distorting projections, would give us back our ability to mourn.

We are demanding empathy in relation to events the very scale of which makes empathy impossible. Thus we cannot hope for total understanding. However, we can hope for at least a gradually growing recognition that the Third Reich brought back to the very center of our civilization a dictatorship of contempt for humanity; this was something we believed had been overcome, but instead it has been imitated in many parts of the world.

THE SENSE OF IMMORTALITY: ON DEATH AND THE CONTINUITY OF LIFE

ROBERT JAY LIFTON

I

Serious concern with the way in which people confront death leads one to question the nature of death and the nature of life in the face of death. In my work in Hiroshima I found that studying an extreme situation such as that facing the survivors of the atomic bomb can lead to insights about everyday death, about ordinary people facing what Kurt Vonnegut has called "plain old death." I feel that our psychological ideas about death have been so stereotyped, so limited, so extraordinarily impoverished, that any exposure to a holocaust like Hiroshima, or My Lai, or, in fact, the entire American involvement in Indochina, forces us to develop new ideas and hypotheses that begin to account for some of the reactions that we observe. I want to suggest a few such principles that are both psychological and historical.

My basic premise is that we understand man through paradigms or models. The choice of the paradigm or model becomes extremely important, because it determines what might be called the "controlling image" or central theme of our psychological theory. Human culture is sufficiently rich that a great variety of paradigms are available to serve as controlling images, including those of "power," "being," "instinct and defense," "social class," "collective unconscious," "interpersonal relations," etc. These paradigms are by no means of equal merit, but each can be used to illuminate some aspect of human experience.

At the end of my study of Hiroshima, *Death in Life,* I stated that sexuality and moralism had been the central themes confronted by Freud in developing psychoanalysis, but that now unlimited technological violence and absurd death have become more pressing themes for contemporary man.[1] During the Victorian era, when Freud was evolving his ideas, there was an overwhelming repression of sexuality but a relatively greater openness to the reality of human death. The extent of sexual repression is revealed by the Victorian custom of putting doilies on table legs because these were thought to be suggestive of the human anatomy. There has been a historical shift, and the contemporary situation is one in which we are less overwhelmed by sexual difficulties but more overwhelmed by difficulties around death. One can characterize the shift as from covering the legs of tables with doilies to the display of hotpants; and from the grim reaper as public celebrity to the Forest Lawn syndrome. The fact that Freud's model of libido and repression of instinctual sexual impulses was put forth during the late Victorian era, at a time when society was struggling with these issues, does not invalidate the generalizability of his ideas: their power lies precisely in that generalizability. But it does raise the important point—not only for Freud but for our own work now—of the influence of historical forces on the psychological theories we choose to develop. If we now begin to build psychological theory around death, it is because death imposes itself upon us in such unmanageable ways.

In my own psychological work on extreme historical situations involving ultimate violence and massive death, I have preferred to speak of a process of psychic numbing rather than repression. Repression occurs when an idea or experience is forgotten, excluded from consciousness, or relegated to the realm of the unconscious. Repressed childhood memories and repressed instinctual impulses are illustrations of this process. Repression is part of a model or controlling image characterized by drives and defenses and refers to the compensatory effort of the organism to cope with innate or instinctual forces that dominate emotional life. The original idea was to analyze these forces and thereby bring the patient to cure.

Psychoanalysis has been changed significantly by the development of ego psychology, by various neo-Freudian modifications, and by many new influences, including ethology. But I think that psychoanalytic theory is still bedeviled by its traditional imagery of instinct, repression, and defense. This imagery yields limited and distorted insight when one approaches the subject of death and the relationship of death to larger contemporary experience. The concept of psychic numbing, in contrast, suggests the cessation of what I call the formative process, the impairment of man's essential mental function of symbol formation or symbolization. This point of view is strongly influenced by the symbolic philosophy of Cassirer and Langer.[2] Psychic numbing is a form of desensitization; it refers to an incapacity to feel or to confront certain kinds of experience, due to the blocking or absence of inner forms or imagery that can connect with such experience.

The importance of this kind of phenomenon was impressed upon me very profoundly by my work in Hiroshima. It would appear that the technology of destruction has had a strong impact on the spread of psychic numbing. But my assumption is that psychic numbing is central in everyday experience as well, and may be identified whenever there is interference in the "formative" mental function, the process of creating viable inner forms. The "psychoformative" perspective would stress that a human being can never simply *receive* a bit of information nakedly. The process of perception is vitally bound up with the process of inner re-creation, in which one utilizes whatever forms are available in individual psychic existence.

Within this psychoformative perspective the central paradigm I wish to develop is that of *death and the continuity of life.* In elaborating this paradigm I will speak first of a theory of symbolic immortality, then of an accompanying theory of evolving death imagery, and finally discuss the application of this paradigm in clinical work and psychopathology.

I want to emphasize at the beginning that this approach to psychology and history is impelled by a sense of urgency about our present historical predicament, and by a strong desire to evolve psychohistorical theory adequate to the dangerous times in which we live. In this approach it is necessary to make our own subjectivity as investigators clear and conscious, to try to understand it and use it as part of the conceptual process. I have elsewhere suggested possibilities for going even further and making our forms of advocacy clear, forthright and, again, part of the conceptual process.[3] In presenting this paradigm of death and the continuity of life I also assume a sense of urgency in our intellectual and professional lives. A crisis exists in the psychiatric profession, and in other professions as well, that has to do with despair about the adequacy of traditional ideas for coping with new data impinging from all sides.

In his book *The Structure of Scientific Revolutions* [4] Thomas Kuhn describes a sequence that occurs in the development of scientific thought when the data can no longer be explained by prevailing theories. Kuhn observed that when this happens the usual reaction among scientists is to cling to the old theories all the more persistently. At a certain point the incongruity between the theory and data becomes so glaring—and the anxiety of those defending the theory so great—that the whole system collapses and the paradigm changes. I think we are at a point something like that now, and that a new depth-psychological paradigm is required. Ironically, the paradigm of death and the continuity of life is actually man's oldest and most fundamental paradigm.

Psychiatrists and psychoanalysts have for the most part left the question of death to philosophers. Freud's theory legitimized this neglect when he said:

> It is indeed impossible to imagine our own death: and whenever we attempt to do so we can perceive that we are in fact still present as spectators. Hence the psychoanalytic school could venture on the assertion that at bottom no one believes in his own death, or, to put the same thing in another way, that in his unconscious, every one of us is convinced of his own immortality.[5]

Freud viewed all interest in immortality as compensatory, as a denial of death and a refusal to face it unflinchingly. Freud insisted that we look at death squarely, that we cannot psychologically afford the consequences of denial. But Freud had no place in his system for the *symbolic* significance of the idea of immortality as an expression of continuity. For this reason I call Freud's approach "rationalist-iconoclastic."

Jung's approach was very different: he took the mythological and symbolic aspects of death and immortality very seriously. He emphasized the enormous significance of the idea of immortality on the basis of the map of the human psyche, and especially of the unconscious, provided by mythology. But he also said: "As a physician I am convinced that it is hygienic to discover in death a goal toward which one can strive; and that shrinking away from it is something unhealthy and abnormal"; and "I . . . consider the religious teaching of a life hereafter consonant with the standpoint of psychic hygiene."[6] In such statements it becomes unclear whether Jung is talking about the literal idea of a life after death or a more symbolic one. He surrenders much of the scientific viewpoint, however broadly defined, that man has struggled for so painfully over the last few centuries. We can thus call Jung's approach "hygienic-mythical."

Both of these views are important; neither is completely satisfactory. Freud's attitude has the merit of unflinching acceptance of death as a total annihilation of the organism. Jung's view has the merit of stressing the symbolic significance of universal imagery around death and immortality.

A third perspective—which I shall call "formative-symbolic"—draws upon both Freud and Jung but takes into account the increasing awareness of symbol formation as a fundamental characteristic of man's psychic life. I should emphasize that I am speaking of an ongoing *process of symbolization,* rather than of particular symbols (the flag, the cross, etc.). In classical psychoanalysis the focus tends to be in symbols as specific equivalents—pencil for penis, sea for mother, etc.—and much less upon the more fundamental process of creation and re-creation of images and forms that characterize human mentation.

II

I would hold, in the context of this psychoformative view, that even in our unconscious lives we are by no means *convinced* of our own immortality. Rather we have what some recent workers have called "middle knowledge"[7] of the idea of death. We both "know" that we will die and resist and fail to act upon that knowledge. Nor is the need to transcend death *mere* denial. More essentially, it represents a compelling universal urge to maintain an inner sense of continuous symbolic relationship, over time and space, with the various elements of life. In other words, I am speaking of a *sense* of immortality as in itself neither compensatory nor pathological, but as man's symbolization of his ties with both his biological fellows and his history, past and future. This view is consistent with Otto Rank's stress on man's perpetual need for "an assurance of eternal survival for his self." Rank suggested that "man creates culture by changing natural conditions in order to maintain his spiritual self." [8] But this need for a sense of symbolic immortality, interwoven with man's biology and his history, is for the most part ignored by individually biased psychological theory.

The sense of immortality can be expressed in five general modes. The first and most obvious is the biological mode, the sense of living on *through* and *in* one's sons and daughters and their sons and daughters. At some level of consciousness we imagine an endless chain of biological attachments. This mode has been a classical expression of symbolic immortality in East Asian culture, especially in traditional China, with its extraordinary emphasis on the family line: In Confucian ethics, the greatest of all unfilial acts is lack of posterity. But this mode never remains purely biological; it becomes simultaneously biosocial, and expresses itself in attachments to one's group, tribe, organization, people, nation or even species. Ultimately one can feel at least glimmerings of a sense of immortality in "living on" through and in mankind.

A second expression of the sense of immortality is the theological idea of a life after death or, more importantly, the idea of release from profane life to existence on a higher plane. The literal idea of an afterlife is not essential to this mode and such a notion is not present in many religions. More basic is the concept of transcending death through spiritual attainment. The power of spiritual life to in some way overcome death is exemplified in all the great religious leaders around whom religions have been founded: Buddha, Moses, Christ, Mohammed. Within each of the religious traditions there has been a word to convey the spiritual state in which one has transcended death: the Japanese word *kami;* the Polynesian term *mana;* the Roman idea of *noumen;* the Eskimo concept of *tungnik* and the Christian doctrine of *grace*. All these words describe a state in which one possesses spiritual power over death, meaning, in a symbolic sense, that one is in harmony with a principle extending beyond the limited biological life span.

The third mode of symbolic immortality is that achieved through "works": the mode of creativity, the achievement of enduring human impact; the sense that one's writing, one's teaching, one's human influences, great or humble, will live on; that one's contribution will not die. The therapeutic efforts of physicians and psychotherapists are strongly impelled, I believe, by an image of therapeutic impact extending through the patient to others, including the patient's children, in an endless potentially beneficent chain of influence. The "therapeutic despair" described so sensitively by Leslie Farber [9] as an occupational hazard of the psychiatrist treating schizophrenic patients might well result from the perception that one's strenuous therapeutic endeavors are not producing these lasting effects, that one's energies are not animating the life of the patient and cannot therefore symbolically extend the life of the therapist.

A fourth mode is the sense of immortality through being survived by nature itself: the theme of eternal nature. This theme is very vivid among the Japanese, and was one of the most important kinds of imagery for survivors of the atomic bomb. It is strong not only in Shinto belief, but in the European Romantic movement and in the Anglo-Saxon cult of the great outdoors—indeed in every culture in one form or another.

The fifth mode is somewhat different from the others in that it depends solely upon a psychic state. This is the state of "experiential transcendence," a state so intense that in it time and death disappear. When one achieves ecstasy or rapture, the restrictions of the senses—including the sense of mortality—no longer exist. Poetically and religiously this has been described as "losing oneself." It can occur not only in religious or secular mysticism, but also in song, dance, battle, sexual love, childbirth, athletic effort, mechanical flight, or in contemplating works of artistic or intellectual creation.[10] This state is characterized by extraordinary psychic unity and perceptual intensity. But there also occurs, as we hear described in drug experiences, a process of symbolic reordering. One feels oneself to be different after returning from this state. I see experiential transcendence and its aftermath as epitomizing the death-and-rebirth experience. It is central to change or transformation and has great significance for psychotherapy. Experiential transcendence includes a feeling of what Eliade has called "continuous present" that can be equated with eternity or with "mythical time." [11] This continuous present is perceived as not only "here and now" but as inseparable from past and future.

The theory of symbolic immortality can be used to illuminate changes in cultural emphasis from one historical period to another. We can think of historical shifts as involving alterations in the stress given to one or another mode or combinations of modes. The Darwinian revolution of the nineteenth century, for example, can be seen as entailing a shift from a predominantly theological mode to a more natural and biological one. The continuous transformation in China over the last few decades involves a shift from a family-centered biological mode to a revolutionary mode, which I have written about elsewhere[12] as emphasizing man's works but as including also elements of other modes with periodic emphasis upon experiential transcendence.

Following the holocaust of World War II the viability of psychic activity within the modes has undergone something of a collapse, at least in the West. We exist now in a time of doubt about modes of continuity and connection, and I believe this has direct relevance for work with individual patients. Awareness of our historical predicament—of threats posed by nuclear weapons, environmental destruction, and the press of rising population against limited resources—has created extensive imagery of extinction. These threats occur at a time when the rate of historical velocity and the resulting psychohistorical dislocation has already undermined established symbols around the institutions of family, church, government, and education. Combined imagery of extinction and dislocation leave us in doubt about whether we will "live on" in our children and their children, in our groups and organizations, in our works, in our spirituality, or even in nature, which we now know to be vulnerable to our pollution and our weaponry. It is the loss of faith, I think, in these four modes of symbolic immortality that leads people, especially the young, to plunge—sometimes desperately and sometimes with considerable self-realization—into the mode of experiential transcendence. This very old and classical form of personal quest has had to be discovered anew in the face of doubts about the other four modes.

III

In postulating a theory of symbolic immortality on such a grand scale, one must also account for the everyday idea of death, for the sense of *mortality* that develops over the course of a lifetime. Freud's notion of the death instinct is unacceptable, could in fact be viewed as a contradiction in terms in that instinctual forces are in the service of the preservation of life. Nor is death an adequate goal for life. Yet as is generally the case with Freud when we disagree with him, the concept, whatever its confusions around the instinctual idiom, contains an insight we had best retain concerning the fundamental importance of death for psychological life. Hence, the widespread rejection of the death instinct poses the danger not so much of throwing out the baby with the bath water but perhaps the grim reaper with the scythe.

Freud himself faced death heroically and understood well the dangers involved in denying man's mortality. But at the same time Freudian theory, insisting that death has no representation in the unconscious, has relegated fear of death to a derivative of fear of castration. Freud also seemed ambivalent about whether to view death and life within a unitary or dualistic perspective. His ultimate instinctual dualism opposed death and life instincts. Yet the notion of life leading inevitably toward death is a unitary vision, and it is this unitary element that I think we should preserve. This unitary perspective on death would insist upon its overall consistency as an absolute infringement upon the organism (as opposed to certain contemporary efforts to subdivide death into a number of different categories); and as an event anticipated, and therefore influential, from the beginning of the life of the organism.

I believe that the representation of death evolves from dim and vague articulation in the young organism's inchoate imagery to sophisticated symbolization in maturity. I rely partly here on Kenneth Boulding's work on the image,[13] in which he has stressed the presence in the organism from the very beginning of some innate tendency or direction which I call an *inchoate image*. This image is at first simply a direction or physiological "push." But inchoate though it may be, the image includes an *interpretative anticipation of interaction with the environment.* Evidence for the existence of innate imagery can be drawn from two sources; one is ethology and the other is observation of rapid eyeball movements (REM) in sleep studies.

Work in ethology has demonstrated through the study of "releasing mechanisms" the existence of what I am here calling an image. The newborn organism is impelled innately toward certain expected behavior on the part of older (nurturing) organisms, which, when encountered, acts as a releasing mechanism for a specific action (such as feeding) of its own. Sleep studies also suggest the presence of images in some form from the beginning of life, possibly during prenatal experience, that "cause" or at least provide some basis for the rapid eyeball movements observed in various species. Rather than demonstrating the presence of pictorial images, these two areas of research suggest the presence at birth of primordial images or precursors to later imagery.

In the human being the sequence of this process is from psychological push (or direction of the organism) to pictures of the world (images in the usual sense) to symbolization. Within this theory of evolving imagery we can understand the elaboration of the inner idea of death from earliest childhood in terms of three subparadigms or polarities. These are: connection versus separation, integrity versus disintegration, and movement versus stasis. The inchoate imagery of the first polarity is expressed in a seeking of connection, what John Bowlby has described as "attachment behavior" around sucking, clinging, smiling, crying and following.[14] The organism actively seeks connection with the nurturing or mothering person. First this quest is mainly physiological, then is internalized in pictorial image formation, and finally becomes highly symbolized. The organism's evolution is from simple movement toward the mother to a nurturing relationship with her, and eventually toward connection with other people, with groups, with ideas, with historical forces, etc. Where this striving for connection fails, as it always must in some degree, there is the alternative image of separation, of being cut off. This alternative image of separation forms one precursor for the idea of death.

In a similar way one can look at the idea of integrity versus disintegration. As indicated in the work of Melanie Klein on the infant's fear of annihilation,[15] there is from the beginning some sense of the organism's being threatened with dissolution, disintegration. The terms of this negative image or fear are at first entirely physiological, having to do with physical intactness or deterioration; but over the course of time integrity, without entirely losing its physiological reference, comes to assume primarily ethical-psychological dimensions. At those more symbolized dimensions one "disintegrates" as one's inner forms and images become inadequate representations of the self–world relationship and inadequate bases for action.

The third mode, that of movement versus stasis, is the most ignored of the three; but it has great clinical significance and is especially vivid to those who deal with children. An infant held tight and unable to move becomes extremely anxious and uncomfortable. The early meaning of movement is the literal, physiological idea of moving the body or a portion of it from one place to another. Later the meaning of movement takes on symbolic qualities having to do with development, progress and change (or with a specific collectivity in some form of motion). The absence of movement becomes a form of stasis, a deathlike experience closely related to psychic numbing.

One could illustrate in detail the evolution of these polarities over the course of the life cycle. But it is clear that rather early, or earlier than is usually assumed, death achieves some kind of conscious meaning. By the age of three, four, and five children are thinking and talking, however confusedly, about death and dying. And over the course of the next few years something in that process consolidates so that the idea of death is more fundamentally learned and understood. At every developmental level all conflicts exacerbate, and are exacerbated by, these three aspects of what later becomes death anxiety—that is, disintegration, statis or separation. These death-linked conflicts take on characteristic form for each developmental stage and reach a climax during adolescence. During young adulthood there occurs a process partly described by Kenneth Keniston around the term "youth,"[16] and partly described in my own work around the concept of the "Protean style."[17] I see the continuing search characterizing the Protean style as a constant process of death and rebirth of inner form. The quest is always for images and forms more malleable and inwardly acceptable at this historical moment than are those available from the past. Sometime in early adulthood one moves more fully into the realm of historical action and one then connects with the modes of symbolic immortality.

Later, in middle adulthood, one becomes impressed that one will indeed die. It becomes apparent that the limitations of physiology and life span will not permit the full accomplishment of all one's projects. But even with this fuller recognition of mortality the issues of integrity, connection and movement remain salient. Old people approaching death look back nostalgically over their whole lives. This "life review," as it is sometimes called, has to do with a process of self-judgment, of examining one's life around issues of integrity, but also of connection and movement; and for evidence of relationship to the modes of symbolic immortality.

IV

How do these principles apply in mental disturbance? I want to suggest the clinical applicability of this paradigm of death and the continuity of life for various categories of psychopathology. Psychiatrists have turned away from death, as has our whole culture, and there has been little appreciation of the importance of death anxiety in the precipitation of psychological disorder.

What I am here calling the sense of immortality is close to what Erik Erikson calls basic trust.[18] Erikson emphasizes the issue of basic trust as the earliest developmental crisis and he sees the legacy of this earliest time as having vital importance for adulthood. But the establishment of trust itself involves confidence in the integrity, connection and movement of life, prerequisites for a viable form of symbolic immortality. Where this confidence collapses psychological impairment ensues.

The principle of impaired death imagery—or, more accurately, of impaired imagery of death and the continuity of life—is a unitary theme around which mental illness can be described and in some degree understood. I see this kind of impairment as being involved in the etiology of mental illness but not as causative in the nineteenth-century sense of a single cause bringing about one specific effect. Rather, impaired death imagery is at the center of a constellation of forms, each of which is of some importance for the overall process we call mental disturbance. Here I would point to three relevant issues central to the process of mental illness. The first is death anxiety, which evolves in relation to the three polarities I have described. The second is psychic numbing, which I see as a process of desymbolization and deformation. The image which accompanies psychic numbing is that "if I feel nothing, then death does not exist; therefore I need not feel anxious about death either actually or symbolically; I am invulnerable." A third principle is what I call "suspicion of counterfeit nurturance." This is the idea that if death exists, then life is counterfeit. Ionesco's question "Why was I born if it wasn't forever?" illustrates the relation of this theme to the quest for immortality. But it is a very old question.

Death anxiety can be seen as a signal of threat to the organism, threat now understood as disintegration, stasis or separation. All anxiety relates to these equivalents of death imagery, and guilt too is generated insofar as one makes oneself "responsible" for these processes. In other writing I have distinguished between static (either numbed or self-lacerating) and animating guilt, and have emphasized the importance of the latter in the process of self-transformation.[19]

One can take as a model for much of neurosis the syndrome which used to be called "traumatic neurosis" or "war neurosis." It is generally described as involving the continuous reliving of the unconscious conflicts aroused by the traumatic situation. More recently emphasis has been placed on imagery of death aroused by the trauma, rather than the trauma *per se*. Thus the syndrome has been called by some observers "death anxiety neurosis."[20] I see this process in terms of the psychology of the survivor as I have elaborated that psychology in my work on Hiroshima and more recently with antiwar veterans. My belief is that survivor conflicts emerge from and apply to everyday psychological experience as well. When one "outlives" something or someone, and there are of course many large and small survivals in anyone's life, the specter of premature death becomes vivid. Simultaneously one begins to feel what I came to call in my Hiroshima work "guilt over survival priority"—the notion that one's life was purchased at the cost of another's, that one was able to survive *because* someone else died. This is a classical survivor process and is very much involved in traumatic neurosis. In describing traumatic neurosis, earlier observers spoke of "ego contraction."[21] This is close to what I call psychic numbing, also very marked in the survivor syndrome and in neurosis in general.

A great number of writers (including Stekel, Rank, Horney, and Tillich) have emphasized patterns closely resembling psychic numbing as the essence of neurosis. Stekel, in 1908, spoke of neurotics who "die every day" and who "play the game of dying."[22] Otto Rank referred to the neurotic's "constant restriction of life," because "he refuses the loan (life) in order to avoid the payment of the debt (death)."[23] The neurotic thus seeks to defend himself against stimuli in a way Freud described in a little-known passage in *Civilization and Its Discontents*. Freud observed:

> No matter how much we may shrink with horror from certain situations —of a galley slave in antiquity, of a peasant during the Thirty Years' War, of a victim of the Holy Inquisition, of a Jew awaiting a pogrom—

> it is nevertheless impossible for us to feel our way into such people, to divine the changes which original obtuseness of mind, a gradual stupefying process, the cessation of expectations and cruder or more refined methods of narcotization have produced upon their receptivity to sensations of pleasure and unpleasure. Moreover, in the case of the most extreme possibility of suffering, special mental protective devices are brought into operation.[24]

It is strange that Freud turned away from his own argument at this point and concluded that it was "unprofitable to pursue this aspect of the problem any further." For that argument contained the core of the idea of psychic numbing in extreme situations. The holocausts described by Freud have become almost a norm, a model for our times. But in lesser degree, what Freud called narcotization and I am calling psychic numbing is associated with the individual "holocausts" and survivals around which neurosis takes shape.

Let me now make some preliminary suggestions about the significance of these struggles around death imagery for the classical psychiatric syndromes. I am exploring these relationships more fully in work in progress,[25] and my hope is that others will as well.

If we view neurosis in general as an expression of psychic numbing—shrinking of the ego and diminished capacity for experience—we can see in depression specific examples of impaired mourning, impaired symbolization, and the impaired formulation of the survivor. Where a known loss triggers the process, as in reactive depression, the depressed person acts very much like a survivor, and psychic numbing becomes very prominent. He often expresses the feeling that a part of him has died, and that he "killed" the other person in some symbolic way by failing to sustain the other's life with needed support, help and nurturance. The idea of either having killed the other person or of having purchased one's own life at the cost of another person's is fundamental. Such feelings are also related to Freud's explanation of guilt, in that earlier ambivalent feelings toward the other person included hate and death wishes, which now become attached to the actual loss. The whole issue of grief and its relation to mental disturbance is too complex to examine fully here. I can only say here that grief is of enormous importance in the experience of survival and in its residuum of mental and physical disturbance related to psychic numbing.

In character disorders, and in the related phenomenon of psychosomatic disorders in which one speaks through the "language of the body," there are lifelong characterological patterns of deadening or numbing of various aspects of the psyche. This numbing may involve moral sensitivity or interpersonal capacities. However the numbing is expressed, there is a situation of meaninglessness and unfulfilled life, in which the defensive psychological structures built up to ward off death anxiety also ward off autonomy and self-understanding.

Turning to hysteria, the "psychic anesthesia" emphasized in early literature suggests the centrality of stasis, deadening, or numbing. Freud's case of Anna O., for example, is properly understood as a mourning reaction.[26] The hysteria followed very quickly upon the death of Anna's father and had much to do with her reaction to that death. Her conception of being alive became altered in such a way that merely to *live* and *feel*—to exist as a sexual being—was dangerous, impermissible, and a violation of an unspoken pact with the dead person. Whether or not there is a mourning reaction directly involved, hysteria tends to involve either this form of stasis or its seeming opposite, exaggerated movement or activity that serves as a similar barrier against feeling and living. These patterns again resemble those I encountered among Hiroshima survivors.

In obsessional neurosis and obsessive-compulsive styles of behavior the stress is upon order and control. One tries to "stop time," to control its flow so as to order existence and block spontaneous expression, which is in turn felt to be threatening and "deadly."

Much of Freudian theory of phobia evolved from the case of little Hans. In this case Freud interpreted castration fears as being displaced and transformed into a fear of horses—the inner danger being transformed into an external one.[27] But I would say that little Hans's experience could also be understood in terms of fear of annihilation and separation. His castration fear epitomized but was not the cause of his general death anxiety. Rather than viewing this death anxiety as secondary to castration anxiety, as psychoanalytic literature has done ever since, we do better to reverse our understanding and interpret the castration anxiety as an expression of more general death anxiety.

Finally I want to turn to psychosis and to an application of this theoretical position to schizophrenia. One is appalled by the degree to which death imagery has been observed in schizophrenic persons without being really incorporated into any conceptual scheme. As with more general psychiatric concern with death, the situation is changing. Harold Searles writes at some length about the problems a schizophrenic person has with the "universal factor of mortality." Searles says that the schizophrenic patient doesn't really believe he is living, doesn't feel himself to be alive, feels life passing him by, and feels stalked by death. Thus the patient employs a variety of techniques to defend himself against death anxiety, and yet in another sense feels himself already dead, "having therefore nothing to lose through death."[28] And what Ronald Laing calls the "false self" is very close to what I am calling a numbed or "dead self." Laing goes on to "translate" from what he calls "schizophrenese" and describes "the desire to be dead, the desire for a nonbeing" as "perhaps the most dangerous desire that can be pursued," and the "state of death-in-life" as both a response to "the primary guilt of having no right to life in the first place, and hence of being entitled at most only to a dead life" and "probably the most extreme defensive posture that can be adopted," in which, "being dead, one cannot die, and one cannot kill."[29] What Searles and Laing describe in schizophrenics is directly reminiscent of the process I observed among survivors in Hiroshima, and is similar to the *Musselmänner* phenomenon that occurred in Nazi concentration camps: so extreme was the state of psychic numbing that, as one observer put it, "one hesitates to call their death death."[30] These were people who had become robots.

The schizophrenic experiences a pathetic illusion of omnipotence, a despairing mask of pseudo-immortality because he is blocked in the most fundamental way from authentic connection or continuity —from what I have been calling a sense of symbolic immortality. He therefore fantasizes omnipotence and pseudo-immortality. But the productions of the schizophrenic are infused with death: again like the Hiroshima survivors at the time the bomb fell, he sees himself as dead, other people around him as dead, the world as dead.

Wynne, Lidz, and others who have studied family process in schizophrenia emphasize the transmission of "meaninglessness, pointlessness, and emptiness," of "irrationality," of "schism and skew."[31] Bateson's "double bind" theory of conflicted messages received by the child also stresses the difficulty faced by the child in establishing a coherent field of meaning.[32] All of these theories represent a transmission of "desymbolized" or "deformed" images, which cannot cohere for the child and which leave him overwhelmed with death anxiety and suspicion of counterfeit nurturance. In the child's experience nurturance is dangerous: he flees from it into isolation, stasis, a "safer death" of his own.

It may require several generations to produce a schizophrenic person. But one can say that, however the inheritance mechanism may operate, whatever the contribution of genetic legacy, the early life of the schizophrenic is flooded with death anxiety, and the result is thought disorder and impairment of reality sense. The schizophrenic's behavior and symptoms represent alternate tendencies of surrender to death anxiety and struggle against it. The near-total suspicion of counterfeit nurturance which characterizes the schizophrenic's emotional life renders his psychic numbing more extensive and more enduring than in any other form of psychiatric disturbance. Although one sometimes sees in acute forms of schizophrenia an exaggerated response to stimuli, the general and long-range process is one of profound psychic numbing. To the schizophrenic as to certain survivors of mass holocausts, life is counterfeit, inner death predominant, and biological death unacceptable. Because the schizophrenic's existence has been a series of unabsorbable death immersions and survivals, he ultimately settles for a "devil's bargain": a lifeless life.

The paradigm of death and continuity of life I have elaborated here—together with psychoformative and psychohistorical perspectives—can help keep psychiatry and psychoanalysis close to their biological origins without imposing on them an instinctual determinism. The paradigm recognizes the scope of man's symbolization and provides a link between his biology and his history, a link essential to make if either is to be sustained.

I close with a few quotations. The first is a slogan from an eighteenth-century guild—very simply: "Remember to die." Ostensibly it was a reminder to make advance funeral arrangements through the guild, but, however inadvertently, it conveys much more. The next is from the playwright Peter Weiss, who said, "Once we thought a few hundred corpses would be enough, then we said thousands were still too few; today we can't even count all the corpses everywhere you look." Finally, Yeats:

> Man is in love and loves what
> vanishes,
> What more is there to say?

REVOLUTION OR COUNTERREVOLUTION?

KENNETH KENISTON

No issue today divides the public or intellectual community so deeply as does the "counterculture," the "new culture," "Consciousness III"—what I will call the new youthful opposition. Hawks and doves on the youth question debate campus unrest with an intensity and heat generally reserved only for the weightiest ideological matters. The mildest criticism of the youthful romance with violence or the gentlest critique of radical mindlessness evokes epithets like "reactionary," "counterrevolutionary," or, worst of all, "liberal" from the passionate defenders of the youthful opposition. But, conversely, hawks on the youth question feel that the expression of guarded optimism about the decency of students or the claim that most young people act from idealistic motives makes the speaker a sycophant, a Pied Piper, or an "apologist."

Merely to deride this debate would blind us to the real importance of the issues raised. However fashionable it has become to laud or lambaste the dissenting young, serious issues lie hidden behind the current polemics in little magazines. For the debate about the oppositional young ultimately involves a debate about the nature of man and society, and requires that we examine our basic assumptions about both. I suspect that this debate, which crosscuts and confounds the traditional distinctions between conservatives and liberals, may well define the basic terms of intellectual inquiry, controversy, and creativity during the decades ahead.

The debate is important because no event is quite so interesting theoretically as an event that we were led to believe could not occur. A scientific experiment that confirms a prediction is ultimately of far less importance than an experiment that fails. For if our predictions are merely confirmed, we are only reinforced in our attachment to the ways of thinking that led us to anticipate correctly what was going to happen. But when prediction fails, we are obliged to re-examine the theories upon which the prediction was based, so as to explain, at least in retrospect, the events we failed to anticipate.

The emergence of a youthful opposition is an instance of a historical event that was predicted by no one twenty years ago. Marxist theorists either continued to cherish hopes of a working-class revolt in the capitalist nations or else devoted their theoretical energies to explaining how monopoly capitalism had successfully co-opted the potentially revolutionary spirit of the working class. Even the most sophisticated neo-Marxists did not predict that those who apparently benefited most from capitalist societies would help lead a new attack upon them. In a comparable way, what I will group together as "liberal theories" not only failed to anticipate the emergence of the youthful revolt, but predicted that such a revolt would become progressively *less* likely as affluence and higher education spread. To understand the theoretical importance of the current debate over the meaning of the youthful opposition therefore requires us to examine in broad outline the widely shared theoretical assumptions of liberal thinkers in the 1950s and early 1960s.

The "Liberal" Analysis

Liberal theories of man have usually started from the malleability or plasticity of human nature. The cultural anthropologists' discovery of the enormous variety of human belief and behavior in primitive cultures led to the view that man was almost totally adaptable to his social environment. Even psychoanalysis, with its heavy initial emphasis upon innate biological factors in development, was modified so as to place far greater stress on environmental influences in shaping the child's personality, and to minimize the importance of innate developmental sequences.

Given this implicit or explicit assumption of human plasticity, psychology as a field concentrated upon the processes by which human beings are influenced, shaped, and molded. For example, among the most highly developed areas in social psychology are the study of attitude change and small-group behavior. Attitude-change studies stressed the way convictions, beliefs, and values could be changed through experimental manipulation. Small-group studies explored how groups influence their members. In general, psychologists attempted to discover the "laws" that governed the molding and alteration of men's feelings, beliefs, convictions, and behavior.

If liberal psychology emphasized human plasticity and the techniques by which human conviction and behavior can be molded and modified, liberal social theories stressed equilibrium, stability, and the mechanisms of social control. The basic model of human society was the model of the "social system," constantly seeking to reach "dynamic equilibrium." The major theoretical effort of liberal sociologists went into explaining precisely *how* this equilibrium, harmony, lack of conflict, or absence of revolution had been guaranteed.

Many of the most powerful liberal theories in politics and economics can also be understood as efforts to explain the mechanisms of social equilibrium. Political theorists emphasized the stabilizing effects of competing interest groups, each with "veto power" over the others. The importance of pluralistic tolerance, of "democratic consensus," and of "liberal personality" was extensively studied. Still others examined how social conflicts are routinized—channeled into institutional forms that minimize social disruption and encourage compromise and reconciliation. For their part, some economists have emphasized the "countervailing powers" that prevent the domination of the economy by any one set of monopolistic interests. Even Keynesianism can be seen as an effort to define the means whereby a stable economy might be guaranteed. Experts on labor relations scrutinized the way highly organized trade unions and the institutions of collective bargaining minimized class struggle, promoting peaceful "conflict resolution." In virtually all areas of scholarly endeavor, then, the major theoretical emphasis was upon explaining that stability which was considered the goal and norm of societal existence.

The liberal assumptions of human plasticity and sociopolitical equilibrium were joined explicitly in the theory of socialization and acculturation. Malleable man was said to be related to stable society through a series of special socializing institutions like the family and the education system, whose primary function was to "integrate" the individual into society. Specifically, families' and schools' chief job was to teach children the social roles and cultural values necessary for adult life in that society. Key societal norms, symbolic systems, values, and role models were said to be "internalized" during the socialization process, and their internalization resulted in adults who were "adjusted"—who "functioned" with the symbols, values, and roles expected by their society.

The family is seen as the primary socializing and acculturing institution. But with the advent of early and prolonged schooling, formal education has increasingly supplemented the family as an agency of socialization. In highly industrialized states, it was argued, prolonged education is inevitable, for the skills required to operate a complex industrial state take many years to learn. Similarly, each of the higher vocations, occupations, and professions has its own set of specialized norms and ethics, its own methods and techniques, its own body of knowledge. So even the far reaches of higher education—graduate and professional school—have generally been described in terms of "professional socialization." Indeed, a generation of studies of the impact of higher education on students has been almost exclusively organized around the single concept of socialization.

Liberal social theorists did not naïvely confuse stability with stasis. A society in a state of basic equilibrium might still be a society that was changing rapidly: the equilibrium could be "dynamic." Social change created social strains and psychological stresses; but if all went well, it did not finally upset the basic social equilibrium. Between social strain and social disequilibrium stood a series of "mechanisms of social control," ranging from the police force to the practice of psychotherapy, which served to reduce societal tension by resocializing or isolating deviant individuals and by encapsulating or co-opting deviant social movements. The ideal kind of social change was seen as incremental—slow, quantitative, gradual and nonrevolutionary. Indeed, some social changes like rising economic prosperity or increasing education were believed to increase the stability of the societies in which they occurred. Increasing prosperity meant that more human needs could be met by society, while prolonging education provided more individuals with a lengthier and more thorough socialization experience.

Nor were liberal social theorists ignorant of the fact that revolutions, social convulsions, and dramatic upheavals abound in history. But convulsive social upheavals were almost always seen as symptoms of a breakdown of the system of social control, and as regressive or destructive in their consequences. "Meaningful social change" was thought most likely to occur through "gradualism" and "piecemeal social reform." Nor have liberal theorists blinded themselves to the existence within every society of murderers, artists, radicals, racists, inventors, crackpots, and geniuses—i.e., of "unsocialized" or "deviant" men and women. But individual behavior that deviated markedly from the norm was seen as the result of aberrant or deviant socialization, generally during the years of early childhood.

In principle, there is no reason why functional failures—e.g., breakdowns in mechanisms of social control—should be deemed undesirable. Nazi Germany abounded with mechanisms of social control, from the Gestapo on down. Had they failed from a functional point of view, we might well have deemed this failure ideal from a broader ethical or political point of view. Nor is there any logical reason why societal equilibrium should be maintained: it is conceivable in principle that sudden and dramatic revolutions might result in human betterment. Similarly, there is no *a priori* reason to equate individual "deviance" with sin or pathology. In fact, individual "deviants" are the wellsprings of art, philosophy, religion, and all constructive ideological innovation: one might applaud rather than deplore "deviance."

But in practice, liberal social theories have tended to identify functional "failures" with undesirable moral failures. The collapse of the French Revolution into Bonapartism or of the Russian Revolution into Stalinism was used to demonstrate the general undesirability of revolutions, and to confirm the implication that social change involving naked conflict was the undesirable result of a "breakdown" in the system of social control. Similarly, the study of psychological deviance has largely been a study of criminals, psychopaths, delinquents, or other "desocialized" or "unsocialized" individuals whose behavior resulted in patently undesirable consequences.

The internal logic of liberal theories thus pushes them toward psychological explanations of both individual deviance and social revolution. At an individual level, criminals, artists, and rebels are seen as the products of anomalies in childhood experience. Psychoanalytic theory was extensively adapted in order to explain—and to explain away—radicalism, innovation, creativity, homosexuality, delinquency, and so on in terms of their alleged childhood origins. But since, by definition, the deviant individual must be the product of deviant socialization, the sophisticated liberal never blamed the deviant himself for his deviance. Instead, he blamed the deviant's early environment—especially his family—and aimed his reformist efforts at changing the family circle that was said to produce deviance. Thus, for example, one characteristic liberal solution to racial tensions was to reform the "inadequate" Negro family, which allegedly bred so much suffering and crime. At a collective level, mass revolutionary movements like fascism, Nazism, or Communism were often traced to the special conditions of childhood socialization in the nations where these movements prospered. Psychological "strains" transmitted to individuals through their families were thought to culminate in bizarre or irrational collective behavior: e.g., the authoritarian German family led indirectly to Nazism; early swaddling contributed to the totalitarian Russian character, and so on.

In looking to the future, liberal theorists naturally enough foresaw and inevitable: more industrial productivity, more technologization, more of what their theories led them to view as normal, desirable, more piecemeal reform, higher education, more stability, and more effective management. Admittedly, problems were anticipated—for example, the problem of avoiding political apathy when most major social and ideological problems had been solved. Most liberal writers urged that new ways must be found to involve the young in the political future of their nation, and most deplored the "privatism" of the "silent generation" of the 1950s. Other problems were also foreseen: the problems of mass culture, of the lonely crowd, of the use of leisure time, of the organization man, of rapid job obsolescence, and so on. But compared with the old problems of scarcity, economic depression, class warfare, and ideological conflict, these new problems seemed minor. It was persuasively argued by writers like Daniel Bell, Seymour Martin Lipset, and Edward Shils that the age of ideology was over, and that the remaining problems of Western civilization could be defined as largely instrumental—as problems of "how" and not of "what." As a result, it was believed that these problems would eventually yield to scientific knowledge, professional expertise, and technical know-how.

Theories like these attempted to explain—indeed, they *did* explain—the relative domestic stability of the Western democracies in the 1950s, along with the general acceptance, acquiescence, or apathy of educated youth. But in retrospect, they were too airtight and too historically parochial. We can now see that they took a particular historical moment—one that today seems abnormal in its tranquillity—and constructed theories that elevated this particular moment into the natural state of affairs. And among other things, this liberal system of ideas—it would be fair to call it an ideology—effectively prevented us from anticipating, much less understanding, what was increasingly to happen among a growing minority of the young during the 1960s. Like Marxist theories, liberal theories demonstrated the *impossibility* of wide-scale dissent by the educated, privileged young in the highly industrialized democracies.

We cannot, however, simply deprecate the achievements, the usefulness, or the enduring power of the diverse points of view that share what I have called "liberal" assumptions. Men and women are indeed malleable in many ways, and readily influenced. Societies do often exhibit stability and employ powerful resources to preserve equilibrium. And men and women are indeed socialized to the society in which they live from the moment they draw their first breath. It is easy to caricature, criticize, and mock liberal social thought, but it will be the work of a generation to develop a view of the world that does a better job. In the meanwhile, we had best admit that we are all at least partly liberals in our theoretical bases, sometimes the more so as we insist on our radicalism.

Yet in its treatment of the relationship of youth to society, liberal social thought, like Marxism, predicted precisely the opposite of what has actually happened. And that fact alone should impel us to question and redefine the basic assumptions from which liberalism began. The emergence of a youthful opposition, then, demands new theories not only of youthfulness, but of human nature, of society, and of their relationship. Theoretically, this is perhaps the prime significance of the youthful revolt.

Two Current Theories

Given the failure of liberal theories to anticipate the growing disaffection of the affluent young, it was inevitable that other views would emerge. Most of these views are not worthy of serious consideration: they select some single factor like parental permissiveness, the war in Vietnam, the idealism of youth, faculty instigation, Communist conspiracy, or the Oedipus complex as satisfactory explanations of what is happening. But two new analyses of the youthful opposition are emerging that have theoretical depth, scope, and profundity: they properly attempt to understand the new opposition in terms of a broader theory of man and society. The first theory, which is an adaptation of liberal theories, asserts in essence that the youth movement in the industrialized nations is historically a counterrevolutionary movement, a reaction against the more basic forces involved in the growth of a new technological society. The second theory counters by claiming that the dissenting young are true revolutionaries, a historical vanguard that is defining a new and better society. It is worth examining each theory in greater detail.

Youth as a counterrevolutionary force. Consider first the "counterrevolutionary" theory of youth. The most thoughtful proponents of this view are men like Zbigniew Brzezinski, Lewis Feuer, and, in very different ways, Raymond Aron, Daniel Bell, Alvin Toffler, Bruno Bettelheim, and Herman Kahn. These thinkers differ on a great many key issues, and it does each an injustice to group them together without also underlining their differences. But they are usually in essential agreement on several major points.

First, they agree that we are in the midst of a major social transformation that is taking us out of an industrial society into the post-industrial, technological, postmodern, superindustrial, or, in Brzezinski's terms, "technetronic" society of the future. The new society will be highly rationalized. It will be characterized by high productivity, automation, increased leisure time, more individual choices, better social planning, greater opportunities for the expression of individual interests, rapid rates of social change, more rational administration, and the demand for enormously high levels of education among those who occupy positions of leadership. It will be a society of complex large-scale organizations, global communications, and a basically technical approach to the solution of human problems. In this society, power will lie increasingly not with those who possess economic capital, but with those who possess educational "capital." In the technetronic society, the "knowledge industry," centered above all in the professoriate and in the universities, will be the central industry of society and the central motor of historical change.

The second assumption common to the counterrevolutionary theory of youth is that periods of basic historical transition are inevitably marked by social disturbances. The introduction of factories in Europe and America in the nineteenth century was marked by growing class conflict and the Luddite movement, which led displaced agricultural workers to try to destroy the factories that were depriving them of work. Today, the transition into the technetronic age is marked by an equally violent revulsion by those whose skills and values are made obsolete by the new social revolution.

Specifically, a postindustrial society imposes what Daniel Bell terms a heavy "organizational harness" upon the young: it requires them to study for many years, to acquire highly specialized technical skills, to stay in school, and to postpone gratification well into biological adulthood. Equally important, this new society renders obsolete a large number of traditional values, skills, and outlooks. A technetronic society above all needs skilled executives, systems analysts, computer programmers, trained administrators, and high-level scientists. Those who possess these skills are in the forefront of historical change: their talents are needed; their outlooks are valued. But those identified with "traditional" fields like the humanities and the social sciences find that their values and skills are becoming increasingly unnecessary, irrelevant, and obsolete; they are today's neo-Luddites. The ideals of romanticism, expressiveness, and traditional humanism may dominate the contemporary youth culture, but they do not dominate the social structure—the specific institutions that are changing our lives. One consequence, then, is what Bell terms the disjuncture between the culture—specifically the adversary culture of intellectuals and many students—and the dominant social structure of large-scale organization, technology, mass communications, and electronics.

The conclusion that the revolt of the young is essentially counterrevolutionary follows from the first two points. According to this theory, the humanistic young are rebelling because of their latent awareness of their own obsolescence. The "organizational harness" around their necks is too tight and heavy for them to endure. An ever-larger group of young men and women feel that they have no place in the modern world, for they lack salable skills, basic character styles, and value orientations that are adaptable to the emergent postindustrial society. They are, as Bruno Bettelheim puts it, "obsolete youth." They rebel in a blind, mindless, and generally destructive way against rationalism, intellect, technology, organization, discipline, hierarchy, and all of the requisites of a postindustrial society. Sensing their historical obsolescence, they lash out like the Luddites against the computers and managers that are consigning them into the "dustbin of history." It is predictable that they will end with bombing, terrorism, and anarchy, for the obsolete young are desperately pitting themselves against historical forces that they cannot stop. But students of engineering, business administration, and so on —students in the fields most rewarded in the technetronic society—do not protest or rebel; instead, it is the obsolescent humanist and social scientist who lead the counterculture.

Although theorists differ as to precisely *which* unconscious forces are expressed in student dissent, the logic of the counterrevolutionary argument makes a recourse to psychologism almost mandatory. For if the manifest issues of student unrest are seen as pseudo-issues, disguises, and rationalizations, then we are forced into the realm of the not-conscious in our search to locate the "real" motives behind the youthful opposition. And in today's post-Freudian age, such explanations are likely to involve recourse to concepts like unconscious Oedipal feelings, adolescent rebellion, castration anxiety, and the "acting out" of feelings that originate in the early family.

As a result, the counterrevolutionary view of youth is associated with an interpretation of psychoanalysis that sees Oedipal urges as driving forces for student rebellion. To be sure, theorists do not agree about the exact nature of the Oedipal forces that are acted out. Some like Feuer see a simple reenactment of the jealous child's hatred of his powerful father; others see a blind striking out against surrogates for a father who was not powerful *enough* to inoculate his son against excessive castration anxieties; another psychoanalyst has pointed to insufficient parental responsiveness as a causative factor in radicalism; early family permissiveness or failure to set limits has also been blamed. But whatever the precise irrational forces behind the youthful revolt are said to be, the counterrevolutionary theory, by denying the validity of the youth movement's own explanations of its acts, is forced to hypothesize unconscious motivations as the "real" motives behind the revolt.

A final conclusion follows from this argument: no matter how destructive the revolt of the young may be in the short run, that revolt is historically foredoomed to failure in the long run. The technetronic society, the postindustrial world, the superindustrial state—these forces are unstoppable. The liberal democratic state is being basically transformed, but the rantings and rampagings of the young, devoted to obsolescent ideas of self-expression, anarchism, romanticism, direct democracy, liberation, and the expansion of consciousness, cannot stop this transformation. The revolt of the young may indeed be, in Daniel Bell's phrase, the emergent "class conflict" of postindustrial society. But from Bell's analysis it follows that students are a neo-Luddite, counterrevolutionary class, and that their counterrevolution will fail. Increasingly, power will be held by those who have more successfully acquired the capital dispensed by the knowledge industry. The counterculture is, in Brzezinski's words, the "death rattle" of the historically obsolete.

The counterrevolutionary theory of the youth revolt is a reformulation of liberal theory, modified to make room for the convulsions of the last decade. Within any social-equilibrium theory there must be room for the possibility that the system will temporarily get "out of balance." The assumption of thinkers like Brzezinski is that we have entered a period of imbalance that accompanies the transition from an industrial to a technetronic society. In this transitional period, traditional mechanisms of social control, older forms of integration between social structure and culture, and previous forms of socialization have ceased to function adequately. But in the future, it is assumed, equilibrium can once again be regained. Upon arrival in the technetronic society, the postindustrial society, or the world of the year 2000, the temporary storm squalls on the weatherfront between industrial and postindustrial society will have dissipated, and we will once again be in a state of relative social equilibrium. If we can only wait out the transition, maintaining and repairing our basic institutions, we can build a new equilibrium—one that will grind under the youthful opposition just as triumphant industrialism destroyed the Luddites. In the meanwhile, we must fight to preserve decency, civilization, rationality, and higher education from the depredations of the mindless young.

Youth as a revolutionary force. The second major theory holds that the dissenting young are historically a revolutionary force. This theory views the counterculture as a regenerative culture, and interprets those forces that oppose it as ultimately counterrevolutionary. This view is expressed in different forms in the works of Theodore Roszak and Charles Reich, in the writings of members of the counterculture like Tom Hayden and Abbie Hoffman, and, most convincingly of all, by Philip Slater. Let us consider the basic assumptions of the revolutionary view of the youth culture.

First, this theory also accepts the notion that industrialized societies are in a period of major cultural, institutional, and historical transition. But it alleges that the thrust of the liberal democratic state has exhausted itself. What is variously termed "corporate liberalism," the "Establishment," or the "welfare-warfare state" is seen as fundamentally bankrupt. Admittedly, industrial states have produced unprecedented wealth. But they have not been able to distribute it equitably, nor have they found ways to include large minorities in the mainstream of society. Furthermore, their basic assumptions have led directly to disastrous "neoimperialistic" wars like the American involvement in Southeast Asia. Corporate liberalism has produced a highly manipulated society, in which "real" human needs and interests are neglected in the pursuit of political power, the merchandising of products, or the extension of overseas markets. Large-scale organizations have dehumanized their members, depriving men of participation in the decisions that affect their lives. The electronic revolution merely provides the rulers of the corporate state with more effective means of manipulating the populace. Corporate liberalism has today revealed its bankruptcy.

The second assumption of this theory is that the economic successes and moral failures of liberal industrial societies today make possible and necessary a new kind of consciousness, new values, new aspirations, and new life styles—in short, a new culture. The old industrial state was founded upon the assumption of scarcity. It was organized to reduce poverty, to increase production, to provide plenitude. But today it has largely succeeded in this goal, and, as a result, a new generation has been born in affluence and freed from the repressed character structure of the scarcity culture. In an era of abundance, the niggardly, inhibited psychology of saving, scrupulosity, and repression is no longer necessary. Alienated relationships between people who view each other as commodities are no longer inevitable. The "objective consciousness" of the scientist or technician is becoming obsolete. In brief, the material successes and moral failures of corporate liberalism permit and require the emergence of a new and truly revolutionary generation with a new consciousness, a postscarcity outlook, and a new vision of the possibilities of human liberation.

It follows from this analysis that the new oppositional culture is not an atavistic and irrational reaction against the old culture but a logical outgrowth of it—an expression of its latent possibilities, a rational effort to remedy its failings, in some sense its logical fulfillment. If the central goal of the old culture was to overcome want and if that goal has been largely achieved, then the counterculture stands on the shoulders of the old culture, fulfilling, renewing, and expressing that culture's latent hopes. Far from being historical reactionaries, the counterculturists are the historical vanguard. Their alleged anarchism and anti-intellectualism are but efforts to express the desire for human liberation whose roots lie in the postponed dreams of the old culture. As the British philosopher Stuart Hampshire has recently suggested, the dissenting young are not against reason, but only against a constricted definition of reason as a quantitative calculus that ignores human values and needs.

The revolutionary theory of youth also entails a definite view of the psychology of young rebels and revolutionaries. It asks that we take them completely at their word when they state the reasons for their protests, disruptions, dropouts, or rejections. The dissenting young are seen as miraculously healthy products of the irrational, dangerous, and unjust world they inherited. Their motives are noble, idealistic, and pure, while their statements of their goals are to be taken at face value. They are not animated by their childhood pasts, but by a vision (which they may, however, find it difficult to articulate) of a freer, more peaceful, more liberated, and more just society. As for the Oedipus complex, to discuss the psychological motives of the members of the youthful opposition at all is seen as a typically "liberal" way of distracting attention from the real issues. Thus, even if the dissenting young behave in an undemocratic, dogmatic or violent way, one "understands" their behavior by discussing the undemocratic, dogmatic, and violent society to which they are objecting.

This view of the psychology of the youthful opposition follows logically from the assumption that the young are in the historical vanguard. In general, historical vanguards must be endowed with extraordinary wisdom and prescience, and with a special freedom from that gnawingly irrational attachment to the personal or historic past that plagues most nonvanguard groups. In the views of one theorist, "radical man" is the highest possible form of human development; another political theorist has argued that only rebellion can attest to human freedom, and that among today's young, only those who rebel are truly free. The argument that the youthful revolt arises from psychopathology is here encountered by its opposite—by the claim that the new opposition springs from the extraordinary insight, maturity, high consciousness, and "positive mental health" of its members.

Finally, as is by definition true of any historical vanguard, the triumph of this vanguard is seen as ultimately inevitable. With rising abundance, new recruits to the counterculture are being created daily. It is the old, then, who are obsolete, not the young. The locomotive of history, so to speak, has the youth movement sitting on the front bumper, scattering its opponents in a relentless rush into the future. Eventually the opponents of progressive change will be defeated or will die of old age—only then will the truly liberating potentials of the postscarcity era be actualized in society.

In many respects the theory of the youth movement as revolutionary is embryonic and incomplete. The counterrevolutionary theory builds upon the highly developed resources of liberal social thought. But the "revolutionary" view, rejecting both liberalism and Marxism, presents us more with a vision of what the counterculture might be at its best than with a complex or thorough social analysis. Only in the work of Philip Slater do we have the beginnings of a critical examination of liberal theory, a task so enormous that it is obviously beyond the capabilities of any one man, much less one book. Other writers who view the counterculture as revolutionary largely limit themselves to a vision that is more literary than descriptive and that makes little attempt to connect the emergence of the counterculture to the structural changes emphasized by writers like Bell, Brzezinski, or Kahn. In this sense, the revolutionary theory of the new opposition remains more of a promise than a fulfillment.

The Limits of Both Theories

My presentation of two theories obviously does scant justice to the complexity of the specific theorists who have seriously considered the counterculture. There is no unity, much less membership in a "school," either among those who oppose or among those who support the youthful opposition. Among its critics, for example, Feuer and Bettelheim concentrate upon the psychopathology that allegedly animates its members, while Brzezinski or Kahn focuses upon the structural or social conditions that make the youthful opposition obsolete. Similarly, there is an enormous difference between the romantic portrait of "Consciousness III" presented by Reich and the more careful social-psychological analysis offered by Slater in his *The Pursuit of Loneliness.*

But no matter how oversimplified this account of the revolutionary and the counterrevolutionary theories, if either interpretation of youthful dissent were fundamentally adequate, this discussion could end. It therefore behooves us to examine each of these theories critically.

We should first acknowledge that each of these views has its highly persuasive points. Those who view the new opposition as historically counterrevolutionary are correct in underlining the increasing importance of technology, complex social organizations, and education in the most industrialized nations. They have pointed accurately to the new role of a highly educated and technologically trained elite. And they seem to help us explain why youthful dissenters are virtually absent among potential engineers, computer specialists, and business administrators, but disproportionately drawn from the ranks of social scientists and humanists.

Above all, however, the opponents of the youthful opposition are accurate in their criticism of that opposition. They rightly argue that the counterculture almost completely neglects the institutional side of modern life. Thus the call for liberation, for the expansion of consciousness, and for the expression of impulse has not been matched by the creation or even by the definition of institutions whereby these purposes could be achieved and sustained. Furthermore, in its cultural wing, the new opposition has often been callous to continuing injustice, oppression, and poverty in America and abroad. In its political wing, the counterculture has been vulnerable to despair, to apocalyptic but transient fantasies of instant revolution, to superficial Marxism, and to a romance with violence. Finally, the youthful opposition as a whole has never adequately confronted or understood its own derivative relationship to the dominant society. Perhaps as a result, it has too often been a caricature rather than a critique of the consumption-oriented, manipulative, technocratic, violent, electronic society that it nominally opposes. In pointing to the weakness of the counterculture, its critics seem to me largely correct.

Yet there is a deep plausibility, as well, in the theory that the youthful opposition is in historical terms a revolutionary movement. In particular, the "revolutionary" theorists accurately capture the growing feeling of frustration and the increasing sense of the exhaustion of the old order that obsess growing numbers of the educated young in industrialized nations. Furthermore, they correctly recognize the irony in the fact that the most prosperous and educated societies in world history have generated the most massive youthful opposition in world history. And in seeking to explain this unexpected opposition, the revolutionary theory understands well its relationship to the "systemic" failings of corporate liberalism—its failure to include large minorities in the general prosperity, its exploitative or destructive relationship to the developing nations, its use of advanced technology to manipulate the citizens in whose interest it allegedly governs, its neglect of basic human needs, values, and aspirations in a social calculus that sees men and women as merely "inputs" or "outputs" in complex organizations.

The strengths of each theory, however, are largely negative: in essence, each is at its best in pointing to the flaws of the culture or the social system defended by the other. But judged for its positive contribution, each theory tends to have parallel weaknesses: each disregards the facts at odds with its own central thesis. In order to do this, each operates at a different level of analysis: the counterrevolutionary theory at the level of social institutions, the revolutionary theory at the level of culture. As a consequence, each theory neglects precisely what the other theory correctly stresses.

The counterrevolutionary theory of the new opposition starts from an analysis of social institutions, modes of production, and the formal organization of human roles and relationships. Despite its emphasis upon the psychopathology of the new rebels, it is fundamentally a sociological theory of institutional changes and technological transformations. It stresses the importance of applied science, the growth of new educational institutions, and the power of the new elite that dominates the "knowledge industry." In defining the future, it emphasizes the further development of rational-bureaucratic institutions and the revolutionary impact of new electronic technology upon social organization, communication, and knowledge. But it tends to forget consciousness and culture, treating ideas, symbols, values, ideologies, aspirations, fantasies, and dreams largely as reflections of technological, economic, and social forces.

Theorists who argue that the new opposition is historically revolutionary operate at a quite different level of analysis. For them, the two key concepts are culture and consciousness. What matters most is feelings, aspirations, outlooks, ideologies, and world views. Charles Reich's recent analysis of three kinds of consciousness is explicit in asserting that institutions are secondary and in the last analysis unimportant. Most other revolutionary theorists also start from an analysis of a "new consciousness" to argue that the decisive revolution is a cultural revolution. How men view the world, how they organize their experience symbolically, what their values are—these are seen as historically determining. Institutional changes are said to follow changes in human aspirations and consciousness.

Daniel Bell has written of the disjuncture of social structure and culture in modern society. We need not accept his entire analysis to agree that this disjuncture is reflected in theories about youthful dissent. For on closer examination, they turn out to be talking about either social structure *or* culture, but rarely about both. The key weakness of the counterrevolutionary theory is its neglect of consciousness and culture, its assumption that social-structural, technological, and material factors will be decisive in determining the future. The parallel weakness of the revolutionary view of youthful dissent is its disregard of the way organized systems of production, technology, education, communication, and "social control" influence, shape, and may yet co-opt or destroy the youthful opposition. In fact, then, these two theories are not as contradictory as they seem: in many ways, they are simply talking about two different aspects of the modern world.

A second limitation of both theories is their assumption that the trends they define are historically inevitable. In this respect, both theories are eschatological as well as explanatory. The postindustrial, or technetronic, view assumes the future inevitability of a postindustrial, technetronic, technocratic society. Given this assumption, it follows logically that anyone who opposes the technetronic society is historically counterrevolutionary. Brzezinski, for example, writes in *Between Two Ages:*

> The Luddites were threatened by economic obsolescence and reacted against it. Today the militant leaders of the [student] reaction, as well as their ideologues, frequently come from those branches of learning which are more sensitive to the threat of social irrelevance. Their political activism is thus only a reaction to the more basic fear that the times are against them, that a new world is emerging without either their assistance or their leadership.

Brzezinski's claim that the youth revolt constitutes a counterrevolutionary force clearly rests upon the assumption that the technetronic society is inevitable.

Exactly the same assumption of historical inevitability is made by supporters of the counterculture. Reich is very explicit about this in *The Greening of America:*

> [The revolution] will originate with the individual and with culture, and it will change the political structure only as its final act. It will not require violence to succeed, and it cannot be successfully resisted by violence. It is now spreading with amazing rapidity. . . . It is both necessary and inevitable, and in time it will include not only youth, but all people in America.

Given Reich's assumption that history is on the side of the counterculture, it follows automatically that those who oppose it are actually counterrevolutionary.

But this claim that the future is in fact predetermined by blind historical forces is open to major question. In retrospect, most previous claims about the historical inevitability of this or that trend have turned out to have been mere expressions of the wishes of those who made these claims. It makes equal or better sense to believe that "history" is on the side neither of the technetronic revolution nor of the counterculture. In fact, we may deny that history is on anyone's side, arguing that history is simply made by human beings, acting individually and in concert, influenced by the institutions in which they live *and* by their consciousness and culture.

If we reject the assumption of historical inevitability, both the counterrevolutionary and the revolutionary theories must be understood in part as efforts to justify a set of special interests by attributing historical inevitability to them, and perhaps ultimately as exercises in the use of prophecy to convince others of the truth of the prophecy and thereby to make the prophecy self-fulfilling. Andrew Greeley has compared Charles Reich with the ancient Hebrew prophets. The similarities are vivid. Although the more academic prose of Brzezinski, Feuer, or Bettelheim does not lend itself so readily to comparisons with the Old Testament, the same prophetic tendencies are there as well. But in either case, the claim that God or His modern-day equivalents—history, technology, and culture—are on our side is best understood as a claim that men make to rally support and persist despite adversity.

What both theories fail to comprehend is the extent to which the emergence of a new youthful opposition requires us to embark upon a critical reexamination of concepts of man, society, and their interrelationship that we have heretofore taken largely for granted. This inability to come to grips with the theoretical challenge posed by the new opposition is seen clearly in each theory's attitude toward education. Neoliberals who view student dissent as largely counterrevolutionary are committed to a view of education as socialization. Given this view, it follows that a postindustrial society characterized by prolonged higher education should be a society where youthful dissent is rare. The eruption of wide-scale disaffection among the most educated products of the most industrialized societies thus requires neoliberal theories to posit wide-scale "deviant socialization," or else to argue that higher education is failing to "do its job." In fact, however, the extensive evidence concerning the backgrounds of young dissenters provides little support for the "deviant socialization" interpretation of the new opposition. And paradoxically, those institutions of higher education that liberals have traditionally seen as doing the "best job" seem to be the breeding grounds for the greatest disaffection.

Those who view youthful disaffection as a revolutionary phenomenon are faced with the same dilemma. They tend to see higher education as a way of "integrating" or "co-opting" youth into the existing society. It therefore comes as a surprise that higher education seems to promote disaffection and to be closely related to the emergence of a youthful counterculture. But those who view the youth movement as revolutionary have so far failed to offer any adequate explanation of why many young men and women in so many nations have escaped the net of socialization.

The fact that theorists of neither persuasion can explain the contemporary correlation between higher education and dissent indicates the need for a critical analysis of our prevailing assumptions concerning human malleability, social equilibrium, and socialization. To undertake this reexamination will be the task of many years; it will necessarily be the work of a generation, not of an individual. But it is impressive that, for all of the talk today about "radical thought" and the "New Left," the basic assumptions of liberalism have been subjected to so little fundamental criticism.

What follows is not an attempt to provide this critical reanalysis, or even to outline it. Rather, it is an agenda, or, more precisely, some items on an agenda which, if accomplished, might move us toward a better understanding of the meaning of the new opposition and of contemporary society. This agenda is presented tentatively, and largely as an indication of the theoretical problems that have been opened up by a decade of dissent. Since it is easier to point out the flaws in the views of others than to propose unflawed alternatives to them, even these items for an agenda are bound to be anticlimactic.

But not to run the risks of at least suggesting an agenda would be even worse.

In brief, the work I believe needs to be done falls into three broad categories. First, there must be a critical reanalysis and reformulation of the theoretical assumptions with which we attempt to understand man and society. Second, we must begin to come to terms with the characteristics of modern society and modern man in their own right, and not in terms of strained analogies to the past. Third, a revised theoretical framework and a better understanding of contemporary man in society should help define a new political agenda.

Plasticity, Equilibrium, and Socialization

The first assumption to be reanalyzed critically is the assumption of virtually limitless human malleability and influenceability. Without denying that men can adapt to most surroundings, that they often conform to the pressures of their peers, or that they internalize social norms and cultural concepts, we need to rediscover and emphasize those elements in "human nature" that make men less than totally plastic.

I believe that the most fruitful line of inquiry will involve an intensive study of the sequences and stages of human development, and especially of those developmental processes that remain more or less constant regardless of historical era or social context. We need to return to Freud's concept of human development as not simply a smooth process of internalizing societal expectations, but rather as the arduous work of mastering internal conflict, without which psychological growth could not occur. Equally relevant is the developmental psychology of Jean Piaget, who insists that the child's growth proceeds through psychologically necessary stages and sequences that cannot be short-circuited. In the developmental process as defined by both Freud and Piaget, the imprint of the social environment is assimilated and interpreted through the steadily changing internal structures of personality, which has its own laws and imperatives.

To trace the full implications of a developmental view of personality for a theory of man and society would be the topic of a lengthy work. Here it should suffice to note that a developmental approach clearly contradicts the almost exclusively environmental view of psychological change that has dominated liberal thought.

Critically interpreted, the work of Freud and Piaget may help us understand man not merely as an adjusting and adapting animal, but as a creature whose growth has both important societal prerequisites and a dynamic of its own. We can then think of man as possessing a "human nature" that can be "violated" by social expectations; we may then be better able to see man as possessing innate potentials for autonomy and integration that may at times lead him into conflict with his society.

We will also need to explore in detail the ways in which these developmental potentials may be actualized or frustrated by any given social or historical context. Recent studies that demonstrate the existence of developmental potentials that are not actualized in most men and women under contemporary conditions point to sociohistorical influences upon adult personality of a kind that have not heretofore been studied. I have elsewhere argued that one important factor in the emergence of a new opposition is the unfolding, on a mass scale, of developmental potentials that in the past were actualized, if at all, only in a tiny minority of men and women.

A related task should involve a critical scrutiny of the large body of studies of attitude change, group pressures, and interpersonal influence. We will need to distinguish, for example, more sharply than we have done so far between attitudes and belief systems on the one hand and the cognitive frameworks or developmental levels within which any given attitude or belief is held. William James long ago contrasted the once-born and the twice-born: the once-born are those who unreflectively and "innocently" accept the convictions of their childhoods; the twice-born are those who may adhere to exactly the same convictions, but who do so in a different way after a protracted period of doubt, criticism, and examination of these beliefs. Viewed as attitudes, the beliefs of the once-born and the twice-born may be identical: but the mind-set, cognitive framework, or developmental level of the once- and twice-born are extremely different. In other words, we need to examine not only the beliefs men hold, but the *way* they hold them—the complexity, richness, and structure of their views of the world. Politically and socially, it may be more important that members of a given subculture possess a relativistic view of truth than that they are conservatives or liberals.

Finally, the role of conflict in human development needs to be reexamined. Liberal psychology has tended to minimize the catalytic importance of conflict in growth: conflict was seen as neurotic, undesirable, and productive of regression. But there is much current evidence that individuals who attain high levels of complexity in feeling, thinking, and judging do so *as a result of* conflict, not in its absence. Students of cognitive development, like observers of personality development, find that disequilibrium, tension, and imbalance tend to produce growth. If this is true, then the absence of psychological conflict or tension may be as pathological as the overabundance of conflict, and the liberal view of the ideal man as smoothly socialized and conflict-free may need to be discarded.

To add further items to this agenda for psychology would take us to still more technical topics. The point is that, in ways we have not yet understood, our theories of human nature, our psychological research, and our methodologies have all been influenced by the largely unstated assumptions of human plasticity and smooth accommodation to pressures of the social environment. We need not deny that men are in some ways plastic and influenceable in order to consider anew everything in man that makes him unmalleable, uninfluenceable, and resistant to socialization.

Turning to broader theories of society, a comparable critical reexamination of basic assumptions seems in order. Above all, the utility of the equilibrium model of society must be examined. Increasingly, critical sociologists have begun to suggest that a "conflict" model of society and of social change may be more suited to the facts of contemporary history than a theory of societal balance. Just as we should appreciate the catalytic role of conflict in human development, so the critical importance of conflict in social change must be acknowledged. Both human and social development, I believe, are best viewed as dialectic processes, involving force, counterforce, and potential resolution; thesis, antithesis, and potential synthesis. At a societal level, such a view would require us to start from change, struggle, revolution, and transformation as the basic "natural" state of affairs rather than viewing them as unfortunate exceptions that require special explanation.

This view of society would put social change in the first chapter, not in the last chapter as one of the unexplained problems of our theory. It would see conflict between individuals, groups, and historical forces as a necessary and vital component of historical change, not as a result of a "failure" of the "mechanisms of social control." It would also entail that any given "resolution" of conflicting historical forces should in turn generate new antithetical forces which will oppose that resolution, thus continuing the dialectic of change. A sociology based on the theory of conflict would especially attempt to understand the processes by which new conflicts are generated out of apparent equilibrium, rather than focusing solely upon how equilibrium is maintained.

Such a view of society obviously moves us away from liberalism and toward Marxism. But Marxism too must be examined critically. Just as we today should reject the nineteenth-century biology and physics upon which Freud based his psychological determinism and many of his specific views of personality, so we need not continue to accept the nineteenth-century economism and millennialism of Marxist thought. Marx's view that the critical historical conflict was class conflict, although it reflected the facts of the mid-nineteenth century, may less clearly reflect the realities of the late twentieth century. And the nineteenth-century optimism which led Marx to believe that historical conflict would ultimately be progressively resolved, like his millennial view of the classless state as the end of historical conflict, seems today unwarranted. Finally, we must question whether the historical dialectic in fact "stopped" at the end point defined by Marx, or whether it continues today in ways that Marx could not have foreseen.

However we reinterpret Marx, one corollary of a dialectic view of social change is that the historical significance of a group, institution, social force, or ideology will inevitably change as historical conditions change. A group that is progressive during one historical era may become reactionary at a later period. Marx emphasized that during its struggle against feudalism, the bourgeoisie was a progressive force, although during the nineteenth century the triumphant bourgeoisie had become reactionary in its opposition to the demands of the revolutionary working class. Following the logic of a dialectic analysis would lead us to expect that the once revolutionary proletariat might in its turn become defensive and opposed to progressive social change. And especially as the rate of historical change accelerates, the transformation of social groups from progressive to reactionary, from revolutionary to counterrevolutionary, may well occur during the lifetime of their members.

If we reexamine critically both the concept of malleable man and the concept of stable society, then we must also reexamine the concept of socialization as the key process whereby the individual is joined to society. We need not deny that socialization occurs in order to point to other processes of equal or greater importance that connect the individual and society in more complex ways. For example, as Erik Erikson has noted, every society must accommodate itself to the developmental needs of the growing child. By attending more carefully to the inborn developmental schedules and potentials of the child, adolescent, youth, and adult, we may better understand the constraints upon society's capacity to "integrate" individuals of any given age. Just as it is not possible for the seven-year-old to comprehend hypothetico-deductive reasoning, so it may not be possible for the highly educated, relativistic youth to accept his society's norms and precepts without criticism. Instead of emphasizing only how society molds the individual to meet social needs, we must also consider how human needs and developmental processes set outer limits on what societies can reasonably expect of their members.

If we abandon the notion of society as a stable and homogeneous entity, then the process whereby individuals and their societies interrelate becomes vastly more complex. For if every society contains within it important internal conflicts, then growing children are exposed not to a stable, self-consistent set of social expectations and cultural values, but to social and cultural contradictions. Intrapsychic conflicts and social contradictions will thus be mutually related, although never in a simple one-to-one fashion. Furthermore, in times of rapid historical change, the societal conflicts to which one generation is exposed will differ from those of the previous generation; partly for this reason, individuals of different historical generations will typically differ from each other in basic personality.

The full agenda for the reexamination of our understanding of the relationship between men and societies will be lengthy. But as we examine our theoretical assumptions, it will not suffice simply to reject out of hand what I have termed "liberal" views. The goal must be more ambitious; it must be to analyze these views critically, preserving what is valid in them while complementing them with new understanding of the inherent logic of human development, of the central role of conflict in social change, and of the forces in man that militate against acquiescent acceptance of the existing social order.

Contradictions Within the Knowledge Sector

The second, related theoretical task is to understand in detail the special characteristics of modern personality and modern society.

Even if a critical analysis of the basic assumptions of liberal thought were completed, the substance of a more adequate account of what is unique about our own era would still be lacking. Here, once again, I can only indicate the general lines of thought that seem most likely to be worth pursuing.

If we start from a dialectical view of historical change, but admit that Marx's juxtaposition of a revolutionary proletariat and a reactionary bourgeoisie did not necessarily mark the last stage in the dialectic, then we must entertain seriously the possibility that the conflicts about which Marx wrote have been largely resolved and that new conflicts have today begun to emerge. I believe it is useful and accurate to consider the corporate liberal state as embodying to a large extent the synthesis of the class conflicts that preoccupied Marx. In this respect, liberal theorists were correct in arguing that earlier conflicts between capitalist entrepreneurs and exploited workers had been softened and essentially reconciled by the growth of powerful bureaucratic trade unions able to negotiate with large but publicly regulated corporations. The "welfare state" indeed mitigated many of the most vicious exploitations of unrestrained nineteenth-century capitalism. The "liberal consensus" of the mid-twentieth century tolerated a wide spectrum of political opinion and many forms of deviant behavior. Furthermore, if "ideology" is narrowly defined to mean Stalinism, fascism, and Nazism, then it was largely accurate to say that the age of ideology was dead.

In the period before and after the Second World War, then, the dominant class conflicts of the nineteenth and early twentieth centuries were increasingly resolved, reconciled, or synthesized in the liberal-democratic-capitalist or socialist states in Western Europe, America, and, after the war, Japan. These new industrial states proved themselves immensely productive economically and immensely inventive technologically. Older problems of mass poverty increasingly disappeared, while the proportion of workers involved in primary and secondary production dwindled to a decreasing minority. First in America, and then increasingly in Western Europe and Japan, the middle class grew to be the largest class, the working class became increasingly prosperous, and both classes became more and more committed to the preservation of the existing society. Especially during the years of the Cold War, a domestic equilibrium was reached in the liberal democracies, and this equilibrium provided the empirical ground upon which liberal social thought grew and by which it seemed confirmed. To be sure, like all historical syntheses, this one was far from complete: large minorities were excluded from the general prosperity; problems of poverty amidst affluence continued; subtle forms of imperialism replaced the earlier forms, and so on. Yet, all things considered, the decades from 1945 to 1965 were remarkable for the absence of basic social conflict in all of the highly industrialized non-Communist nations.

The ascendancy of the corporate liberal state, however, did not mark an end to social conflict or to the dialectic of history. The successes of the emergent technological society were purchased at an enormous moral and ecological price. Fulfilling the promises of liberalism was far from complete, and it became apparent that the liberal program itself would not suffice to fulfill them. Increases in national productivity were not enough to include in the mainstream of affluence those whose poverty was "structural" rather than merely economic. Racism persisted in America despite a century's public commitment to end it. Effective political power remained in the hands of a small minority of the population. It is therefore incorrect to say that the traditional economic, social, and political conflicts of industrial societies were totally "solved." It is more accurate to say that for the first time in history the day could be foreseen when with the techniques at hand they *might* be solved, but that liberal social thought and liberal reformism proved largely ineffective in solving them.

The inability of liberalism to complete its own agenda was one of the new contradictions that became apparent only with the advent of the corporate liberal society. The second contradiction was in some ways more profound, and even more directly related to the emergence of a youthful opposition. The liberal democratic states in America, Western Europe, and Japan provided a large proportion of the people with material goods, social security, cultural opportunities, and relative political freedom, all of which had been the goals of previous generations. There thus arose a new generation that took for granted the accomplishments of corporate liberalism, expressing neither gratitude nor admiration for these achievements. To this new generation, what were instead important were, first of all, the inabilities of a liberal society to fulfill its own promises, and, second, the surfacing of a set of cultural and psychological goals that had previously been deferred in the liberal society. These newly surfaced aspirations had to do above all with the quality of life, the possibilities for self-expression, full human development, self-actualization, the expansion of consciousness, and the pursuit of empathy, sentience, and experience.

I have elsewhere tried to outline in more detail some of the emergent aspirations of the new youthful opposition. Here it should be enough to reiterate that the roots of this new opposition lie precisely in the success of liberalism—e.g., its success in extending to most of the population the material and social benefits it had promised, but its inability to complete the process or to define goals beyond abundance. To the new generation, and specifically to the most affluent, educated, and secure members of this generation, the historical successes of the corporate liberal state were less important than its moral, ecological, psychological, and cultural failures.

To understand the new conflicts in corporate liberal society, I believe we must above all examine the role of the "knowledge sector." For the liberal-democratic and industrialized nations are increasingly dominated neither by capitalists nor by workers, but by a vast new "intelligentsia" of educated professionals who exert unprecedented influence on both public policy and private practice. In some ways their contemporary role is analogous to the traditional role of intellectuals, artists, and Bohemians in earlier historical eras. But because of their increasing numbers and influence, they occupy an altogether different place in technological societies. What they share is that the enterprises in which they are engaged depend upon extensions, manipulations, or applications of knowledge and ideas. The knowledge sector thus includes not only universities, scientific laboratories, research institutes, and the world of creative artists, but a much broader set of enterprises including corporate research and development, the communications industry, data analysis and data processing, the major higher professions, advertising, merchandising, administrative science, personnel management, entertainment, systems analysis, and so on. So defined, the knowledge sector is clearly that sector of contemporary industrialized societies that has grown most rapidly in size and power.

Neo-Marxist theorists have tended to see this knowledge sector as a "new working class" or "technical intelligentsia"—merely the handmaiden of the capitalist managers and politicians assumed to exercise real power. Theorists of the postindustrial states, in contrast, have emphasized the dominance of the knowledge sector in advanced societies, viewing academics as the key professionals and universities as the key institutions of the postindustrial society. Still others, operating in a more traditional liberal framework, have seen the knowledge sector as one of many "interest groups" competing in the process of defining social and political policy.

But in the end, none of these characterizations seems quite adequate to define the unique role of the knowledge sector in the technological societies. Only by remote analogy can workers in this sector be considered a true "working class," for only rarely are they the direct or indirect victims of capitalist exploitation. On the face of it, the argument of Bell, Brzezinski, and others that the knowledge sector constitutes the dominant sector of technological societies seems closer to the truth. But this view in turn tends to exaggerate the power of the academic profession and the indispensability of such institutions as universities to technological society. It is also tempting to accept the liberal analysis of the knowledge sector as merely one of many interest groups; but this view, too, fails to acknowledge the very special powers that today accrue to those who possess knowledge and the visible tokens of its possession: higher degrees, recognition in the knowledge community, access to the mass media, and so on.

Rather than define the knowledge sector as a new working class, as a ruling group, or as another interest group, we would do better to start by assuming that its relationship to the rest of society cannot be adequately understood in historical analogies. To try to define the relationship between the knowledge sector and the rest of society in terms of capitalist-worker analogies is like attempting to define the capitalist-worker relationship as a kind of lord-vassal relationship. Often exploited yet more often manipulating, immensely influential yet vastly vulnerable, an interest group but one that possesses unprecedented power, the role of the knowledge sector in modern society must be defined as unprecedented, new, and *sui generis*. Indeed, one of the major theoretical tasks ahead is the careful definition and explication of the relationship between this new sector and the remainder of society.

Spokesmen for the knowledge sector have tended to define this sector as relatively value-free and "objective" in its approach to human and social problems. The plausibility of this view rests upon the propensity of the knowledge sector to invoke "scientific" analyses of problems, to define rationality in quantitative terms, and to attempt to exclude "irrational" feelings or "sentimental" moral considerations from decision-making. The main agents of the knowledge sector have usually presented themselves as neutral, cool, and technical servants of others, as less concerned with ultimate moral ends than with efficiency, accuracy, rationality, and the levelheaded consideration of the costs and benefits of alternative courses of action. One of the chief characteristics of the knowledge sector, even as it has moved toward increasing influence, has been to publicly proclaim its "neutrality"—its indifference to the major moral, psychological, and political questions of the day.

Yet in the last decade it has become clear that the "value-free" self-definition of the knowledge sector masks an important ideology, an ideology increasingly recognized and challenged by the new opposition. This ideology can be termed "technism," that is, a set of pseudo-scientific assumptions about the nature and resolution of human and social problems. Most highly articulated in various forms of systems analysis, technism insists that the highest rationality involves measurement and consigns the incommensurable (feelings, values, "intangibles") to a lesser order of rationality and reality. Military policies are therefore judged in terms of quantitative indices like body counts, kilotonnage, sorties flown, megadeaths, planes lost, or enemy dead per dollar. Education is seen as a complex form of human "processing," with freshmen as "inputs," graduates as "outputs," dropouts as "wastage," and efficiency measured in terms of "Ph.D. production" or "lifetime income increments." Technism further assumes that innovation is desirable, that growth is imperative, that whatever is technically possible should be done, and that large quantities are preferable to small ones. Drawing heavily upon the mystique of science, technism adds to true science a series of further assumptions that qualify it as an ideology, albeit one that prefers not to recognize itself or be recognized as such.

Paradoxically, however, it is from within the knowledge sector that today there also emerges the most astringent critique of technism. Institutions of higher education, once predicted to become the central institutions of postindustrial society, have indeed become the prime exemplars of a technist approach to problems of government, business, and social planning; but they have also become the prime generators of the antitechnist, romantic, expressive, moralistic, anarchic humanism of the new opposition. Rejecting technism, this opposition stresses all those factors in human life and social experience that do not fit the technist equations. If "value-free," objective technism is the dominant voice of the dominant knowledge sector, then expressive, subjective anarchism is the subversive voice. Theodore Roszak's eulogy of the counterculture is illustrative, for Roszak abhors above all what he calls "objective consciousness"—the technist consciousness of the scientist or program analyst. The new opposition can thus be seen as the ideological reflection of an emergent contradiction *within* the knowledge sector, as the new antithesis to the knowledge sector's technism, as embodying a counteremphasis upon people, upon "creative disorder," upon the nonquantifiable, the subjective, and the qualitative. Increasingly, this contradiction between objective technism and subjective anarchism defines the key ideological polarity of our time.

The intimate relationship between the knowledge sector and the new opposition is also apparent when we examine the social origins of the members of the opposition. For the core of the counterculture consists not of the children of the working class or of the lower middle class, but of the children of the knowledge sector. I have elsewhere insisted that the new opposition is not monolithic, and that we must distinguish its "political" from its "cultural" wing. Available evidence suggests that members of the political wing tend to be recruited disproportionately from among the children of professors, social workers, ministers, scientists, lawyers, and artists. These young men and women are the most concerned with institutional, social, and political change, and are also most likely to express solidarity with the basic values of their parents. Recruits to the cultural, expressive, aesthetic, or "hippie" wing of the counterculture, in contrast, tend to be drawn to a much greater degree from the families of media executives, entertainers, advertising men, merchandisers, scientific administrators, and personnel managers. These young men and women are more concerned with the expansion of consciousness, the development of alternative life styles, and the pursuit of communal ways of living. As a rule, they reject not only the conventional values and institutions of American society, but the values and life styles of their parents. The parents of the "politicals" are thus the more established members of the knowledge sector, while the parents of the "culturals" are the "newly arrived," whose membership in the knowledge sector is more tenuous and ambivalent. If we accept the analogy between knowledge in technological society and capital in industrial society, the parents of the political wing of the opposition are more often the holders of "old money," while the parents of the cultural wing are more often "*nouveaux riches.*"

A variety of factors within the knowledge sector clearly cooperate to generate its own opposition. Among these, for example, are the ambivalences of the parents of youthful dissenters toward the very knowledge sector in which they are employed. But no factor is of greater importance than the impact of higher education upon its recruits. Higher education bears a paradoxical relationship to the knowledge sector. On the one hand, higher education is essential for the maintenance and growth of the knowledge sector; but on the other hand, higher education provides many of the catalysts that push students to develop a critical consciousness which leads them to become part of the youthful opposition, and thus to oppose the dominant ideology of the knowledge sector.

To explore this paradox fully should again be the topic of a lengthy essay. Here I can only emphasize the obvious fact that technological societies require extremely high levels of knowledge and education of their members. "Knowledge societies" like our own must expose millions of young people to ideas, and in such a way as to encourage a critical analysis of these ideas. For only up to a point can higher education as a technological society be narrowly technical. By definition, technical education attempts to teach the student a given body of knowledge, along with methods for applying that knowledge to the solution of problems. But when, as today, existing bodies of knowledge change rapidly, and when existing techniques for applying knowledge to the solution of problems become quickly obsolete, then a system of higher education that remains exclusively technical teaches obsolescence. To avoid this, higher education must encourage students to examine ideas critically, to take multiple points of view in looking at a particular problem, and to become familiar with contrasting ways of looking at the world. Higher education must therefore attempt to produce in students a "critical" approach to a particular area or subject matter.

But once a student has acquired the ability to approach one subject critically, it is hard to prevent him from applying the same critical orientation to other areas of life and society. Given the discovery that there are many distinct perspectives on "truth" in natural science, engineering, or literature, the student is likely to become a relativist in moral and ideological matters as well. Taught to challenge traditional beliefs in a narrow academic arena, at least some students will move quickly to challenge traditional moral codes in society. What can be thought of as a "critical consciousness"—a mind-set disposed to question, examine, probe, and challenge—tends to generalize from the area where it was first learned to other areas, and finally to all of life. The result is, increasingly, an across-the-board relativization of knowledge, a pervasive individualization of morality.

Precisely because a technological society cannot rely exclusively upon a narrowly technical system of higher education, it must foster a high degree of critical consciousness among its most educated products, and this critical consciousness is readily turned against the dominant assumptions and practices of the technological society. In a way not often acknowledged by educators but increasingly sensed by the general public, higher education today is "subversive" in that it is helping to create youth who challenge many of the basic assumptions of their society. Prolonged mass higher education is a major factor in "producing" millions of young dissenters from the social order that creates them.

This argument indicates that higher education is a key process whereby the contradictions of technological society are being generated. To be sure, higher education also has a socializing function, as pointed out by liberal theories, and for many of those who are exposed to it, socialization remains its primary result. Especially when higher education remains narrowly technical, and when students by previous inclination or present experience reject alternative views of the world and accept conventional definitions of morality, then education performs the function currently assigned it by most liberals and radicals, namely, the function of integrating the individual into society. But increasingly, higher education conspires with the mass media and the juxtaposition of cultures within modern societies to create millions of young men and women who are unwilling to accept the existing social order uncritically.

These notes on contemporary society are obviously incomplete, sketchy, and doubtless often wrong. They should indicate, however, my conviction that, in analyzing contemporary technological societies, we do well to start from one of the central points emphasized by the "counterrevolutionary" theorists, namely, the ascendancy of the knowledge sector. But an analysis of the meaning of this sector, I believe, leads not to the conclusion that it will inevitably triumph, but rather to the realization that the knowledge sector is riven through with basic contradictions, and that it is generating its own critics on a mass scale.

A New Politics

The connection between social theory and political action is exceedingly complex. No matter how refined, precise, and detailed a theory, it does not necessarily or automatically lead to a political agenda. Yet, on the other hand, political action in the absence of social theory tends to be random, haphazard, trial-and-error, and empirical in the worst sense. Such is the case with much of what today passes as "radical politics": lacking any grounding in critical social theory, it tends to consist in *ad hoc* reactions of moral indignation, to lack any long-range direction, to fritter away the best energies of its members in internecine battles, or to adopt programs inspired by a pop-Marxist analysis of guerrilla warfare in some far-off ex-colonial nation.

The alternative is to try to think seriously about the basic issues and forces in contemporary industrialized societies. The arguments outlined above indicate my basic agreement with the counterrevolutionary theorists of youth that we are in a period of transition "between two ages," in Brzezinski's phrase, and that this transition is likely to be prolonged and difficult. This analysis also suggests, however, that the emergence of a new opposition is a sign of the surfacing of new contradictions within the dominant knowledge sector of technological society, and specifically, that youthful dissent is the expression of a historically revolutionary trend.

Several general political implications follow from this line of reasoning. For one, it follows that visions of immediate social or political revolution are based on a flawed social and historical analysis. The processes of sociohistorical change in which we are living are long-term, secular processes, which will take at least a generation to work themselves out. Those who have a serious interest in effecting meaningful social change must therefore be prepared to devote decades, and even a lifetime, to this enterprise; those whose energies flag after a week, a month, or a year will be of little help.

If we view the youthful opposition as reflecting emerging contradictions within the dominant knowledge sector of technological societies, then we would be wrong to ally ourselves politically with either the "value-free" technism that I have defined as thesis in this conflict or with the subjective anarchism that I have defined as the antithesis. In the long run, what will be called for will be a synthesis of technism with anarchism, of "scientific objectivity" with the romantic expressiveness of the counterculture. It would therefore be a political mistake to embrace unreservedly the future of either the systems analyst or the tribal communard. Instead we should work toward a future that could bring together the enormous power placed in man's hands by his technology and the vision of human liberation proclaimed by the counterculture. A politics that aligns itself with either the thesis or the antithesis will be a politics tnat settles for too little.

Another corollary of the views outlined here concerns the need to support a particular kind of higher education. Those who bitterly oppose the new opposition are already eager to limit higher education to technical education, eliminating or deemphasizing its critical component. This strategy, if successful, could well reduce the numbers of those who possess that critical consciousness which seems vital for membership in the new opposition. It is therefore important for all who sympathize with the opposition to seek to extend higher education that is truly critical. The current radical attack upon higher education is, I think, misguided when it fails to discriminate between technical and critical education. Higher education in the broad sense not only has been but should continue to be the nursery for the new opposition. And the possibility that the new opposition might eventually generate enough political power to create major social change depends in large part on the continuing creation, through education, of an ever larger minority (and eventually even a majority) who share the basic orientations of that opposition. This process will take, at the very least, a generation. But it will not occur at all unless higher education as critical education is nurtured.

It also follows from these comments that those who today argue that the working class in the highly industrialized nations retains its revolutionary potential are incorrect. If we insist that the dialectic of social change did not cease with Marx's death, then it makes theoretical sense that groups like the working class, which once were revolutionary, might have become largely counterrevolutionary. Empirical evidence supports this proposition: the new "revolutionary class" appears to be a subsector of the knowledge sector, while the working class constitutes a conservative and at times a reactionary force. No political program today can or should neglect the real interests of the dwindling and often still exploited working class. But political programs based on the assumption that the working class in the industrialized nations can be exhorted to assume its "true" revolutionary role are built upon a historical mirage.

The proposition that social forces that begin as progressive generally end as reactionary obviously applies to the youthful opposition itself. As the youthful opposition ceases to be youthful, it must constantly guard against further evolution into a reactionary force. Already we can envision how this could occur: the collectivism of the counterculture could readily become an insistence upon the abrogation of individual rights; the tribalism of Consciousness III could well portend a society of coercive group membership; the counterculture's opposition to technism could degenerate into a mindless hatred of reason, science, intellect, reflection, and accuracy. Today the youthful opposition is so weak politically that none of these dangers seems socially or politically important. But should the opposition gain in strength, its own reactionary potentials might well unfold.

In essence, then, a politics consistent with this agenda must be one that rejects both the "value-free" technism of corporate liberalism and the subjective anarchism of the counterculture, attempting instead the painful and slow work of creating a synthesis of the institutions of technological society with the culture of oppositional youth. That synthesis must ultimately entail the creation of a culture where the concept of liberation is not merely a facile slogan, but a commitment to the hard work of creating institutions within which genuine human relatedness may be attained. That synthesis must attempt to combine new-culture participation with old-culture competence, Consciousness III enthusiasm with Consciousness II professionalism—and all of this in ways that have hardly begun to be imagined, much less tried. It must involve an effort to turn modern technology around so that it facilitates man's liberation instead of encouraging his manipulation, so that it makes wars less possible rather than more likely, so that it helps men understand each other rather than oppose one another.

It is easy to call for a synthesis in general terms; it will be difficult to achieve it in practice. Nor do I believe that such a political synthesis is inevitable or even highly probable. We are indeed at a historical juncture, a turning point, a cultural and institutional crisis. And the youth revolt, the counterculture, the new opposition—these define one pole, one catalyst, one ingredient in that crisis. But history is not necessarily on the side of progress, synthesis, or the good. What happens in the next decades will depend not upon blind institutional and cultural forces, but upon the intelligence, good will, and hard work of countless individual men and women. It is possible today to begin to imagine a society far better than any society men have known—a society where technology serves man, where abundance makes possible higher levels of human development, where men and women attain new freedom not only from hunger, injustice, and tyranny, but from the inner coercions of greed, powerlust, and envy. The political agenda should be to move toward these goals, and to do so even in the absence of certainty that history is on our side.

APPENDIX

EXCERPTS FROM SIGMUND FREUD'S *Moses and Monotheism** DEALING WITH FREUD'S APPROACH TO HISTORY

. . . To deprive a people of the man whom they take pride in as the greatest of their sons is not a thing to be gladly or carelessly undertaken, least of all by someone who is himself one of them. But we cannot allow any such reflection to induce us to put the truth aside in favor of what are supposed to be national interests; and, moreover, the clarification of a set of facts may be expected to bring us a gain in knowledge. [p. 7]

. . .

Now, we should have expected that one of the many people who have recognized that "Moses" is an Egyptian name would also have drawn the conclusion or would at least have considered the possibility that the person who bore this Egyptian name may himself have been an Egyptian. In relation to modern times we have no hesitation in drawing such conclusions, though nowadays people bear not one name but two—a family name and a personal name—and though a change of name or the adoption of a similar one in fresh circumstances is not beyond possibility. . . . Nevertheless, so far as I know, no historian has drawn this conclusion in the case of Moses—not even any of those who, like Breasted himself (1934, 354), are ready to assume that "Moses was learned in all the wisdom of the Egyptians."

[p. 9]

. . .

In 1909 Otto Rank, who was at that time still under my influence,

*In Vol. XXIII of *The Complete Psychological Works of Sigmund Freud*, Standard Edition, ed. James Strachey (London, 1964).

published, following a suggestion of mine, a book bearing the title *Der Mythus von der Geburt des Helden.* It deals with the fact that "almost all the prominent civilized nations . . . began at an early stage to glorify their heroes, legendary kings and princes, founders of religions, dynasties, empires or cities, in brief their national heroes, in a number of poetic tales and legends. The history of the birth and of the early life of these personalities came to be especially invested with fantastic features, which, in different peoples, even though widely separated by space and entirely independent of each other, present a baffling similarity and in part, indeed, a literal conformity. Many investigators have been impressed with this fact, which has long been recognized." . . . [p. 10]

. . .

Rank's researches have made us acquainted with the source and purpose of this myth. I need only refer to them with some brief indications. A hero is someone who has had the courage to rebel against his father and has in the end victoriously overcome him. Our myth traces this struggle back as far as the individual's prehistory, for it represents him as being born against his father's will and rescued despite his father's evil intention. The exposure in a casket is an unmistakable symbolic representation of birth: the casket is the womb and the water is the amniotic fluid. The parent–child relationship is represented in countless dreams by pulling out of the water or rescuing from the water. When a people's imagination attaches the myth of birth which we are discussing to an outstanding figure, it is intending in that way to recognize him as a hero and to announce that he has fulfilled the regular pattern of a hero's life. In fact, however, the source of the whole poetic fiction is what is known as a child's "family romance," in which the son reacts to a change in his emotional relation to his parents and in particular to his father. A child's earliest years are dominated by an enormous overvalution of his father; in accordance with this a king and queen in dreams and fairy tales invariably stand for parents. Later, under the influence of rivalry and of disappointment in real life, the child begins to detach himself from his parents and to adopt a critical attitude toward his father. Thus the two families in the myth—the aristocratic one and the humble one—are both of them reflections of the child's own family as they appeared to him in successive periods of his life. [p. 12]

. . .

We will borrow from Sellin his hypothesis that the Egyptian Moses was murdered by the Jews and the religion he had introduced abandoned. This allows us to spin our threads further without contradicting the authentic findings of historical research. But apart from this we shall venture to maintain independence of the authorities and to "proceed along our own track." The Exodus from Egypt remains our starting point. A considerable number of people must have left the country with Moses; a small collection would not have seemed worthwhile to this ambitious man with his large aims in view. The immigrants had probably been living in Egypt long enough to have grown into quite a large population. But we shall certainly not be going wrong if we assume, with the majority of the authorities, that only a fraction of what was later to be the Jewish people had experienced the events in Egypt. In other words, the tribe that returned from Egypt joined up later, in the stretch of country between Egypt and Canaan, with other kindred tribes, which had been settled there for a considerable time. . . . [p. 37]

. . .

Jewish history is familiar to us for its dualities: *two* groups of people who came together to form the nation, *two* kingdoms into which this nation fell apart, *two* gods' names in the documentary sources of the Bible. To these we add two fresh ones: the foundation of *two* religions—the first repressed by the second but nevertheless later emerging victoriously behind it, and *two* religious founders, who are both called by the same name of Moses and whose personalities we have to distinguish from each other. All of these dualities are the necessary consequences of the first one: the fact that one portion of the people had an experience which must be regarded as traumatic and which the other portion escaped. Beyond this there would be a very great deal to discuss, to explain and to assert. Only thus would an interest in our purely historical study find its true justification. What the real nature of a tradition resides in, and what its special power rests on, how impossible it is to dispute the personal influence upon world history of individual great men, what sacrilege one commits against the splendid diversity of human life if one recognizes only those motives which arise from material needs, from what sources some ideas (and particularly religious ones) derive their power to subject both men and peoples to their yoke—to study all this in the special case of Jewish history would be an alluring task. To continue my work on such lines as these would be to find a link with the statements I put forward twenty-five years ago in *Totem and Taboo* [1912–1913]. But I no longer feel that I have the strength to do so. [pp. 52–53]

. . .

The Latency Period and Tradition

We confess the belief, therefore, that the idea of a single god, as well as the rejection of magically effective ceremonial and the stress upon ethical demands made in his name, were in fact Mosaic doctrines, to which no attention was paid to begin with, but which, after a long interval had elapsed, came into operation and eventually became permanently established. How are we to explain a delayed effect of this kind and where do we meet with a similar phenomenon? [p. 66]

. . .

There is no difficulty in finding an analogy in the mental life of an individual corresponding precisely to this process. Such would be the case if a person learned something new to him which, on the ground of certain evidence, he ought to recognize as true, but which contradicts some of his wishes and shocks a few convictions that are precious to him. Thereupon he will hesitate, seek for reasons to enable him to throw doubts on this new thing, and for a while will struggle with himself, till finally he admits to himself: "All the same it *is* so, though it's not easy for me to accept it, though it's distressing to me to have to believe it." What we learn from this is merely that it takes time for the reasoning activity of the ego to overcome the objections that are maintained by strong affective cathexes. The similarity between this case and the one we are endeavoring to understand is not very great.

The next example we turn to appears to have even less in common with our problem. It may happen that a man who has experienced some frightful accident—a railway collision, for instance—leaves the scene of the event apparently uninjured. In the course of the next few weeks, however, he develops a number of severe psychical and motor symptoms which can only be traced to his shock, the concussion or whatever else it was. He now has a "traumatic neurosis." It is a quite unintelligible—that is to say, a new—fact. The time that has passed between the accident and the first appearance of the symptoms is described as the "incubation period," in a clear allusion to the pathology of infectious diseases. On reflection, it must strike us that, in spite of the fundamental difference between the two cases—the problem of traumatic neurosis and that of Jewish monotheism—there is nevertheless one point of agreement: namely, in the characteristic that might be described as "latency." According to our assured hypothesis, in the history of the Jewish religion there was a long period after the defection from the religion of Moses during which no sign was to be detected of the monotheist idea, of the contempt for ceremonial or of the great emphasis on ethics. We are thus prepared for the possibility that the solution of our problem is to be looked for in a particular psychological situation. [pp. 67–68]

. . .

The phenomenon of latency in the history of the Jewish religion, with which we are dealing, may be explained, then, by the circumstance that the facts and ideas which were intentionally disavowed by what may be called the official historians were in fact never lost. Information about them persisted in traditions which survived among the people. As we are assured by Sellin, indeed, there was actually a tradition about the end of Moses which flatly contradicted the official account and was far nearer the truth. The same, we may assume, also applied to other things which apparently ceased to exist at the same time as Moses—to some of the contents of the Mosaic religion, which had been unacceptable to the majority of his contemporaries. [p. 69]

. . .

The Analogy

The only satisfying analogy to the remarkable course of events that we have found in the history of the Jewish religion lies in an apparently remote field; but it is very complete, and approaches identity. In it we once more come upon the phenomenon of latency, the emergence of unintelligible manifestations calling for an explanation and an early, and later forgotten, event as a necessary determinant. We also find the characteristic of compulsion, which forces itself on the mind along with an overpowering of logical thought—a feature which did not come into account, for instance, in the genesis of the epic.

This analogy is met with in psychopathology, in the genesis of human neuroses—in a field, that is to say, belonging to the psychology of individuals, while religious phenomena have of course to be reckoned as part of group psychology. We shall see that this analogy is not so surprising as might first be thought—indeed, that it is more like a postulate.

We give the name of *traumas* to those impressions, experienced early and later forgotten, to which we attach such great importance in the aetiology of the neuroses. We may leave on one side the question of whether the aetiology of the neuroses in general may be regarded as traumatic. The obvious objection to this is that it is not possible in every case to discover a manifest trauma in the neurotic subject's earliest history. We must often resign ourselves to saying that all we have before us is an unusual, abnormal reaction to experiences and demands which affect everyone, but are worked over and dealt with by other people in another manner which may be called normal. When we have nothing else at our disposal for explaining a neurosis but hereditary and constitutional dispositions, we are naturally tempted to say that it was not acquired but developed.

But in this connection two points must be stressed. Firstly, the genesis of a neurosis invariably goes back to very early impressions in childhood. Secondly, it is true that there are cases which are distinguished as being "traumatic" because their effects go back unmistakably to one or more powerful impressions in these early times—impressions which have escaped being dealt with normally, so that one is inclined to judge that if they had not occurred the neurosis would not have come about either. It would be enough for our purposes if we were obliged to restrict the analogy we are in search of to these traumatic cases. But the gap between the two groups [of cases] appears not to be unbridgeable. It is quite possible to unite the two aetiological determinants under a single conception; it is merely a question of how one defines "traumatic." If we may assume that the experience acquires its traumatic character only as a result of a quantitative factor—that is to say, that in every case it is an excess in demand that is responsible for an experience evoking unusual pathological reactions—then we can easily arrive at the expedient of saying that something acts as a trauma in the case of one constitution but in the case of another would have no such effect. [pp. 72–73]

• • •

Application

Early trauma—defense—latency—outbreak of neurotic illness—partial return of the repressed. Such is the formula which we have laid down for the development of a neurosis. The reader is now invited to take the step of supposing that something occurred in the life of the human species similar to what occurs in the life of individuals: of supposing, that is, that here too events occurred of a sexually aggressive nature, which left behind them permanent consequences but were for the most part fended off and forgotten, and which after a long latency came into effect and created phenomena similar to symptoms in their structure and purpose.

We believe that we can guess these events and we propose to show that their symptomlike consequences are the phenomena of religion. Since the emergence of the idea of evolution no longer leaves room for doubt that the human race has a prehistory, and since this is unknown—that is, forgotten—a conclusion of this kind almost carries the weight of a postulate. When we learn that in both cases the operative and forgotten traumas relate to life in the human family, we can greet this as a highly welcome, unforeseen bonus which has not been called for by our discussions up to this point.

I put forward these assertions as much as a quarter of a century ago in my *Totem and Taboo* and I need only repeat them here. My construction starts out from a statement of Darwin's (1871, II, 362 f.) and takes in a hypothesis of Atkinson's (1903, 220 f.). It asserts that in primeval times primitive man lived in small hordes, each under the domination of a powerful male. No date can be assigned to this, nor has it been synchronized with the geological epochs known to us: it is probable that these human creatures had not advanced far in the development of speech. An essential part of the construction is the hypothesis that the events

I am about to describe occurred to all primitive men—that is, to all our ancestors. The story is told in an enormously condensed form, as though it had happened on a single occasion, while in fact it covered thousands of years and was repeated countless times during that long period. The strong male was lord and father of the entire horde and unrestricted in his power, which he exercised with violence. All the females were his property—wives and daughters of his own horde and some, perhaps, robbed from other hordes. The lot of his sons was a hard one: if they roused their father's jealousy they were killed or castrated or driven out. Their only resource was to collect together in small communities, to get themselves wives by robbery, and, when one or the other of them could succeed in it, to raise themselves into a position similar to their father's in the primal horde. For natural reasons, youngest sons occupied an exceptional position. They were protected by their mother's love, and were able to take advantage of their father's increasing age and succeed him on his death. We seem to detect echoes in legends and fairy tales both of the expulsion of elder sons and of the favoring of youngest sons.

The first decisive step toward a change in this sort of "social" organization seems to have been that the expelled brothers, living in a community, united to overpower their father and, as was the custom in those days, devoured him raw. There is no need to balk at this cannibalism; it continued far into later times. The essential point, however, is that we attribute the same emotional attitudes to these primitive men that we are able to establish by analytic investigation in the primitives of the present day—in our children. We suppose, that is, that they not only hated and feared their father but also honored him as a model, and that each of them wished to take his place in reality. We can, if so, understand the cannibalistic act as an attempt to ensure identification with him by incorporating a piece of him.

It must be supposed that after the parricide a considerable time elapsed during which the brothers disputed with one another for their father's heritage, which each of them wanted for himself alone. A realization of the dangers and uselessness of these struggles, a recollection of the act of liberation which they had accomplished together, and the emotional ties with one another which had arisen during the period of their explusion, led at last to an agreement among them, a sort of social contract. The first form of a social organization came about with a *renunciation of instinct*, a recognition of mutual *obligations*, the introduction of definite *institutions*, pronounced inviolable (holy)—that is to say, the beginnings of morality and justice. Each individual renounced his ideal of acquiring his father's position for himself and of possessing his mother and sisters. Thus the *taboo on incest* and the injunction to *exogamy* came about. A fair amount of the absolute power liberated by the removal of the father passed over to the women; there came a period of *matriarchy*.

Recollection of their father persisted at this period of the "fraternal alliance." A powerful animal—at first, perhaps, always one that was feared as well—was chosen as a substitute for the father. A choice of this kind may seem strange, but the gulf which men established later between themselves and animals did not exist for primitive peoples; nor does it exist for our children, whose animal phobias we have been able to understand as fear of their father. In relation to the totem animal the original dichotomy in the emotional relation to the father (ambivalence) was wholly retained. On the one hand the totem was regarded as the clan's blood ancestor and protective spirit, who must be worshiped and protected, and on the other hand a festival was appointed at which the same fate was prepared for him that the primal father had met with. He was killed and devoured by all the tribesmen in common. (The totem meal, according to Robertson Smith [1894].) This great festival was in fact a triumphant celebration of the combined sons' victory over their father. [pp. 80–83]

. . .

If our account of primeval history is accepted as on the whole worthy of belief, two sorts of elements will be recognized in religious doctrines and rituals: on the one hand fixations to the ancient history of the family and survivals of it, and on the other hand revivals of the past and returns, after long intervals, of what has been forgotten. It is this last portion which, hitherto overlooked and therefore not understood, is to be demonstrated here in a least one impressive instance. [p. 84]

. . .

It is worth specially stressing the fact that each portion which returns from oblivion asserts itself with peculiar force, exercises an incomparably powerful influence on people in the mass, and raises an irresistible claim to truth against which logical objections remain powerless: a kind of "*credo quia absurdum.*" This remarkable feature can only be understood on the pattern of the delusions of psychotics. We have long understood that a portion of forgotten truth lies hidden in delusional ideas, that when this returns it has to put up with distortions and misunderstandings, and that the compulsive conviction which attaches to the delusion arises from this core of truth and spreads out on to the errors that wrap it round. We must grant an ingredient such as this of what may be called *historical* truth to the dogmas of religion as well, which, it is true, bear the character of psychotic symptoms but which, as group phenomena, escape the curse of isolation. [p. 85]

. . .

The reestablishment of the primal father in his historic rights was a great step forward, but it could not be the end. The other portions of the prehistoric tragedy insisted on being recognized. It is not easy to discern what set this process in motion. It appears as though a growing sense of guilt had taken hold of the Jewish people, or perhaps of the whole civilized world of the time, as a precursor to the return of the repressed material. Till at last one of these Jewish people found, in justifying a politico-religious agitator, the occasion for detaching a new—the Christian—religion from Judaism. Paul, a Roman Jew from Tarsus, seized upon this sense of guilt and traced it back correctly to its original source. He called this the "original sin": it was a crime against God and could only be atoned for by death. With the original sin death came into the world. In fact this crime deserving death had been the murder of the primal father who was later deified. But the murder was not remembered; instead of it there was a fantasy of its atonement, and for that reason this fantasy could be hailed as a message of redemption (*evangelium*). A son of God had allowed himself to be killed without guilt and had thus taken on himself the guilt of all men. It had to be a son, since it had been the murder of a father. . . .

[p. 86]

. . .

Difficulties

Perhaps by what I have said I have succeeded in establishing the analogy between neurotic processes and religious events and in thus indicating the unsuspected origin of the latter. In this transference from individual to group psychology two difficulties arise, differing in their nature and importance, to which we must now turn.

The first of these is that we have here dealt with only a single instance from the copious phenomenology of religions and have thrown no light on any others. I must regretfully admit that I am unable to give more than this one example and that my expert knowledge is insufficient to complete the inquiry. From my limited information I may perhaps add that the case of the founding of the Mohammedan religion seems to me like an abbreviated repetition of the Jewish one, of which it emerged as an imitation. It appears, indeed, that the Prophet intended originally to accept Judaism completely for himself and his people. The recapture of the single great primal father brought the Arabs an extraordinary exaltation of their self-confidence, which led to great wordly successes but exhausted itself in them. Allah showed himself far more grateful to his chosen people than Yahweh did to his. But the internal development of the new religion soon came to a stop, perhaps because it lacked the depth which had been caused in the Jewish case by the murder of the founder of their religion. The apparently rationalistic religions of the East are in their core ancestor worship and so come to a halt, too, at an early stage of the reconstruction of the past. If it is true that in primitive peoples of today the recognition of a supreme being is the only content of their religion, we can only regard this as an atrophy of religious development and bring it into relation with the countless cases of rudimentary neuroses which are to be observed in the other field. Why it is that in the one case just as in the other things have gone no further, our knowledge is in both cases insufficient to tell us. We can only attribute the responsibility to the individual endowment of these peoples, the direction taken by their activity and their general social condition. Moreover, it is a good rule in the work of analysis to be content to explain what is actually before one and not to seek to explain what has *not* happened.

The second difficulty about this transference to group psychology is far more important, because it poses a fresh problem of a fundamental nature. It raises the question in what form the operative tradition in the life of peoples is present—a question which does not occur with individuals, since there it is solved by the existence in the unconscious of memory traces of the past. . . . [pp. 92–93]

. . .

The immediate and most certain answer is that it consists in certain [innate] dispositions such as are characteristic of all living organisms: in the capacity and tendency, that is, to enter particular lines of development and to react in a particular manner to certain excitations, impressions and stimuli. Since experience shows that there are distinctions in this respect between individuals of the human species, the archaic heritage must include these distinctions; they represent what we recognize as the *constitutional* factor in the individual. Now, since all human beings, at all events in their early days, have approximately the same experiences, they react to them, too, in a similar manner; a doubt was therefore able to arise whether we should not include these reactions, along with their individual distinctions, in the archaic heritage. This doubt should be put on one side: our knowledge of the archaic heritage is not enlarged by the fact of this similarity.

Nevertheless, analytic research has brought us a few results which give us cause for thought. There is, in the first place, the universality of symbolism in language. The symbolic representation of one object by another—the same thing applies to actions—is familiar to all our children and comes to them, as it were, as a matter of course. We cannot show in regard to them how they have learned it and must admit that in many cases learning it is impossible. It is a question of an original knowledge which adults afterward forget. It is true that an adult makes use of the same symbols in his dreams, but he does not understand them unless an analyst interprets them to him, and even then he is reluctant to believe the translation. If he makes use of one of the very common figures of speech in which this symbolism is recorded, he is obliged to admit that its true sense has completely escaped him. Moreover, symbolism disregards differences of language; investigation would probably show that it is ubiquitous—the same for all peoples. Here, then, we seem to have an assured instance of an archaic heritage dating from the period at which language developed. But another explanation might still be attempted. It might be said that we are dealing with thought connections between ideas—connections which had been established during the historical development of speech and which have to be repeated now every time the development of speech has to be gone through in an individual. It would thus be a case of the inheritance of an intellectual disposition similar to the ordinary inheritance of an instinctual disposition—and once again it would be no contribution to our problem.

The work of analysis has, however, brought something else to light which exceeds in its importance what we have so far considered. When we study the reactions to early traumas, we are quite often surprised to find that they are not strictly limited to what the subject himself has really experienced but diverge from it in a way which fits in much better with the model of a phylogenetic event and, in general, can only be explained by such an influence. The behavior of neurotic children toward their parents in the Oedipus and castration complex abounds in such reactions, which seem unjustified in the individual case and only become intelligible phylogenetically—by their connection with the experience of earlier generations. It would be well worthwhile to place this material, which I am able to appeal to here, before the public in a collected form. Its evidential value seems to me strong enough for me to venture on a further step and to posit the assertion that the archaic heritage of human beings comprises not only dispositions but also subject matter—memory traces of the experience of earlier generations. In this way the compass as well as the importance of the archaic heritage would be significantly extended.

On further reflection I must admit that I have behaved for a long time as though the inheritance of memory traces of the experience of our ancestors, independently of direct communication and of the influence of education by the setting of an example, were established beyond question. When I spoke of the survival of a tradition among a people or of the formation of a people's character, I had mostly in mind an inherited tradition of this kind and not one transmitted by communication. Or at least I made no distinction between the two and was not clearly aware of my audacity in neglecting to do so. My position, no doubt, is made more difficult by the present attitude of biological science, which refuses to hear of the inheritance of acquired characters by succeeding generations. I must, however, in all modesty confess that nevertheless I cannot do without this factor in biological evolution. The same thing is not in question, indeed, in the two cases: in the one it is a matter of acquired characters which are hard to grasp, in the other of memory traces of external events—something tangible, as it were. But it may well be that at bottom we cannot imagine one without the other.

If we assume the survival of these memory traces in the archaic heritage, we have bridged the gulf between individual and group psychology: we can deal with peoples as we do with an individual neurotic. Granted that at the time we have no stronger evidence for the presence of memory traces in the archaic heritage than the residual phenomena of the work of analysis which call for a phylogenetic derivation, yet this evidence seems to us strong enough to postulate that such is the fact. If it is not so, we shall not advance a step further along the path we entered on, either in analysis or in group psychology. The audacity cannot be avoided.
[pp. 98–100]

. . .

And lastly a remark which brings up a psychological argument. A tradition that was based only on communication could not lead to the compulsive character that attaches to religious phenomena. It would be listened to, judged, and perhaps dismissed, like any other piece of information from outside; it would never attain the privilege of being liberated from the constraint of logical thought. It must have undergone the fate of being repressed, the condition of lingering in the unconscious, before it is able to display such powerful effects on its return, to bring the masses under its spell, as we have seen with astonishment and hitherto without comprehension in the case of religious tradition. And this consideration weighs heavily in favor of our believing that things really happened in the way we have tried to picture them or at least in some similar way.*
[p. 101–02]

*[The discussion of the "archaic heritage" in this section is by far the longest in Freud's writings. The question of the relative parts played in mental life by heredity and experience was, of course, a repeated topic for discussion from the earliest times. But this particular point of the possibility of the inheritance of actual ancestral experiences had appeared relatively late in Freud's writings. The problem of the transmission of ancestral experiences was necessarily raised in *Totem and Taboo* (1912–1913). "What are the ways and means," Freud asks there, "employed by one generation in order to hand on its mental states to the next one?" (Standard Ed., XIII, 158.) His reply in this passage is non-committal, though he seems to suggest that the process can be accounted for by conscious and unconscious communication from one generation to another. But it is not difficult to see that even then he had other ideas at the back of his mind. Indeed, the possibility of the inheritance of an "archaic constitution as an atavistic vestige" is explicitly mentioned there in connection with ambivalence (*ibid.*, XIII, 66), and, in this same connection, the term "*archaisches Erbteil*" (translated "archaic inheritance") appears in "Instincts and their Vicissitudes" (1915*c*) (*ibid.*, XIV, 131). It seems probable that these ideas were precipitated (like so much else) in connection with the "Wolf Man" analysis and particularly

The People of Israel

If we are clear in our mind that a procedure like ours of accepting what seems to us serviceable in the material presented to us and of rejecting what does not suit us and of putting the different pieces together in accordance with psychological probability—if we are clear that a technique of this kind can give no certainty that we shall arrive at the truth, then it may justly be asked why we are undertaking this work at all. The answer is an appeal to the work's outcome. If we greatly tone down the strictness of the requirements made upon a historico-psychological investigation, it will perhaps be possible to throw light on problems which have always seemed to deserve attention and which recent events have forced upon our observation anew. As we know, of all the peoples who lived round the basin of the Mediterranean in antiquity, the Jewish people is almost the only one which still exists in name and also in substance. It has met misfortunes and ill-treatment with an unexampled capacity for resistance; it has developed special character traits and incidentally has earned the hearty dislike of every other people. We should be glad to understand more of the source of this viability of the Jews and of how their characteristics are connected with their history.

We may start from a character trait of the Jews which dominates their relation to others. There is no doubt that they have a particularly high opinion of themselves, that they regard themselves as more distinguished, of higher standing, as superior to other peoples—from whom they are also distinguished by many of their customs. At the same time they are inspired by a peculiar confidence in life, such as is derived from the secret ownership of some precious possession, a kind of optimism: pious people would call it trust in God.

We know the reason for this behavior and what their secret treasure is. They really regard themselves as God's chosen people, they believe that they stand especially close to him; and this makes them proud and confident. Trustworthy reports tell us that they behaved in Hellenistic times just as they do today, so that the complete Jew was already there; and the Greeks, among whom and alongside of whom they lived, reacted to the Jewish characteristics in the same way as their "hosts" do today. . . .

On the basis of our earlier discussions, we may now assert that it was the man Moses who imprinted this trait—significant for all time—upon the Jewish people. He raised their self-esteem by assuring them that they were God's chosen people, he enjoined them to holiness and pledged

---

with the topic of "primal fantasies." This analysis was actually in progress while Freud was writing *Totem and Taboo* and his first draft of the case history was written in 1914. . . .—J.S.]

them to be apart from others. Not that other peoples were lacking in self-esteem. Just as today, so in those days each nation thought itself better than any other. But the self-esteem of the Jews was given a religious anchorage by Moses: it became a part of their religious faith. Owing to their especially intimate relation to their God they acquired a share in his grandeur. And since we know that behind the God who has chosen the Jews and freed them from Egypt stands the figure of Moses, who had done precisely that, ostensibly at God's command, we venture to declare that it was this one man Moses who created the Jews. It is to him that this people owes its tenacity of life but also much of the hostility it has experienced and still experiences.

. . .

The Great Man

How is it possible for a single man to evolve such extraordinary effectiveness that he can form a people out of random individuals and families, can stamp them with their definitive character and determine their fate for thousands of years? Is not a hypothesis such as this a relapse into the mode of thought which led to myths of a creator and to the worship of heroes, into times in which the writing of history was nothing more than a report of the deeds and destinies of single individuals, of rulers or conquerors? The modern tendency is rather toward tracing back the events of human history to more concealed, general and impersonal factors, to the compelling influence of economic conditions, to alterations in food habits, to advances in the use of materials and tools, to migrations brought about by increases in population and climatic changes. Individuals have no other part to play in this than as exponents or representatives of group trends, which are bound to find expression and do so in these particular individuals largely by chance.

These are perfectly justifiable lines of approach, but they give us occasion for drawing attention to an important discrepancy between the attitude taken up by our organ of thought and the arrangement of things in the world, which are supposed to be grasped by means of our thought. It is enough for our need to discover causes (which, to be sure, is imperative) if each event has *one* demonstrable cause. But in the reality lying outside us that is scarcely the case; on the contrary, each event seems to be overdetermined and proves to be the effect of several convergent causes. Frightened by the immense complication of events, our investigations take the side of one correlation as against another and set up contradictions which do not exist but have only arisen owing to a rupture of more comprehensive relations. Accordingly, if the investigation of a particular case demonstrates to us the transcendent influence of a single personality, our conscience need not reproach us with having by this hypothesis flown in the face of the doctrine of the importance of the general and impersonal factors. There is room in principle for both. In the case of the genesis of monotheism, however, we can point to no external factor other than the one we have already mentioned—that this development was linked with the establishment of closer relations between different nations and with the building up of a great empire.

Thus we reserve a place for "great men" in the chain, or rather the network, of causes. But it may not, perhaps, be quite useless to inquire under what conditions we confer this title or honor. We shall be surprised to find that it is never quite easy to answer this question. A first formulation—"we do so if a man possesses to a specially high degree qualities that we value greatly"—clearly misses the mark in every respect. Beauty, for instance, and muscular strength, however enviable they may be, constitute no claim to "greatness." It would seem, then, that the qualities have to be mental ones—psychical and intellectual distinctions. [pp. 105–8]

. . .

For the moment, then, we are inclined to decide that it is not worthwhile to look for a connotation of the concept of a "great man" that is unambiguously determined. It seems to be only a loosely used and somewhat arbitrarily conferred recognition of an overlarge development of certain human qualities, with some approximation to the original literal sense of "greatness." We must recollect, too, that we are not so much interested in the essence of great men as in the question of the means by which they affect their fellow men. We will, however, keep this inquiry as short as possible, since it threatens to lead us far away from our goal.

Let us, therefore, take it for granted that a great man influences his fellow men in two ways: by personality and by the idea which he puts forward. That idea may stress some ancient wishful image of the masses, or it may point out a new wishful aim to them, or it may cast its spell over them in some other way. Occasionally—and this is undoubtedly the more primary case—the personality works by itself and the idea plays a quite trivial part. Not for a moment are we in the dark as to why a great man ever becomes important. We know that in the mass of mankind there is a powerful need for an authority who can be admired, before whom one bows down, by whom one is ruled and perhaps even ill-treated. We have learned from the psychology of individual men what the origin is of this need of the masses. It is a longing for the father felt by everyone from his childhood onward, for the same father whom the hero of legend boasts he has overcome. And now it may begin to dawn on us that all the characteristics with which we equipped the great man are paternal characteristics, and that the essence of great men for which we vainly searched lies in this conformity. The decisiveness of thought, the strength of will, the energy of action are part of the picture of a father—but above all the autonomy and independence of the great man, his divine unconcern which may grow into ruthlessness. One must admire him, one may trust him, but one cannot avoid being afraid of him, too. We should have been led to realize this from the world itself: who but the father can have been the "great man" in childhood? [pp. 109–10]

. . .

It may encourage us to inquire whether the religion of Moses brought the people nothing else besides an enhancement of their self-esteem owing to their consciousness of having been chosen. And indeed another factor can easily be found. That religion also brought the Jews a far grander conception of God, or, as we might put it more modestly, the conception of a grander God. Anyone who believed in this God had some kind of share in his greatness, might feel exalted himself.

. . . And, since one can scarcely claim to assist God in the administration of the world, the pride in God's greatness fuses with the pride in being chosen by him.

Among the precepts of the Moses religion there is one that is of greater importance than appears to begin with. This is the prohibition against making an image of God—the compulsion to worship a God whom one cannot see. In this, I suspect Moses was outdoing the strictness of the Aten religion. Perhaps he merely wanted to be consistent: his God would in that case have neither a name nor a countenance. Perhaps it was a fresh measure against magical abuses. But if this prohibition were accepted, it must have a profound effect. For it meant that a sensory perception was given second place to what may be called an abstract idea—a triumph of intellectuality over sensuality or, strictly speaking, an instinctual renunciation, with all its necessary psychological consequences. [pp.112–13]

. . .

The Mosaic prohibition elevated God to a higher degree of intellectuality, and the way was opened to further alterations in the idea of God which we have still to describe. But we may first consider another effect of the prohibition. All such advances in intellectuality have as their consequence that the individual's self-esteem is increased, that he is made proud—so that he feels superior to other people who have remained under the spell of sensuality. Moses, as we know, conveyed to the Jews an exalted sense of being a chosen people. The dematerialization of God brought a fresh and valuable contribution to their secret treasure. The Jews retained their inclination to intellectual interests. The nation's political misfortune taught it to value at its true worth the one possession that remained to it—its literature. . . . [pp. 114–15]

Renunciation of Instinct

It is not obvious and not immediately understandable why an advance in intellectuality, a setback to sensuality, should raise the self-regard both of an individual and of a people. It seems to presuppose the existence of a definite standard of value and of some other person or agency which maintains it. For an explanation let us turn to an analogous case in individual psychology which we have come to understand.

. . . In the course of an individual's development a portion of the inhibiting forces in the external world are internalized and an agency is constructed in the ego which confronts the rest of the ego in an observing, criticizing and prohibiting sense. We call this new agency the *superego.* Thenceforward the ego, before putting to work the instinctual satisfactions demanded by the id, has to take into account not merely the dangers of the external world but also the objections of the superego, and it will have all the more grounds for abstaining from satisfying the instinct. . . .

. . . The ego feels elevated; it is proud of the instinctual renunciation, as though it were a valuable achievement. We believe we can understand the mechanism of this yield of pleasure. The superego is the successor and representative of the individual's parents (and educators) who had supervised his actions in the first period of his life; it carries on their functions almost unchanged. It keeps the ego in a permanent state of dependence and exercises a constant pressure on it. Just as in childhood, the ego is apprehensive about risking the love of its supreme master; it feels his approval as liberation and satisfaction and his reproaches as pangs of conscience. When the ego has brought the superego the sacrifice of an instinctual renunciation, it expects to be rewarded by receiving more love from it. . . .

What help does this explanation of the satisfaction arising from instinctual renunciation give us toward understanding the processes that we want to study—the elevation of self-regard when there are advances in intellectuality? Very little, it seems. The circumstances are quite different. There is no question of any instinctual renunciation and there is no second person or agency for whose sake the sacrifice is made. We shall soon feel doubts about this last assertion. It can be said that the great man is precisely the authority for whose sake the achievement is carried out; and, since the great man himself operates by virtue of his similarity to the father, there is no need to feel surprise if in group psychology the role of the superego falls to him. So that this would apply, too, to the man Moses in relation to the Jewish people. [pp. 116–17]

. . .

. . . The religion which began with the prohibition against making an image of God develops more and more in the course of centuries into a religion of instinctual renunciations. It is not that it would demand sexual *abstinence*; it is content with a marked restriction of sexual freedom. God, however, becomes entirely removed from sexuality and elevated into the ideal of ethical perfection. But ethics is a limitation of instinct. The Prophets are never tired of asseverating that God requires nothing other from his people than a just and virtuous conduct of life—that is, abstention from every instinctual satisfaction which is still condemned as vicious by our morality today as well. And even the demand for belief in him seems to take a second place in comparison with the seriousness of these ethical requirements. In this way instinctual renunciation seems to play a prominent part in the religion, even if it did not stand out in it from the first. [pp. 118–19]

. . .

Let us return to the more modest problem which has occupied us hitherto. We wanted to explain the origin of the special character of the Jewish people, a character which is probably what has made their survival to the present day possible. We found that the man Moses impressed this character on them by giving them a religion which increased their self-esteem so much that they thought themselves superior to all other peoples. Thereafter they survived by keeping apart from others. Mixtures of blood interfered little with this, since what held them together was an ideal factor, the possession in common of certain intellectual and emotional wealth. The religion of Moses led to this result because (1) it allowed the people to take a share in the grandeur of a new idea of God, (2), it asserted that this people had been chosen by this great God and were destined to receive evidences of his special favor and (3) it forced upon the people an advance in intellectuality which, important enough in itself, opened the way, in addition, to the appreciation of intellectual work and to further renunciations of instinct. [p. 123]

. . .

. . . The religion of Moses did not produce its effect immediately but in a remarkably indirect manner. This does not mean to say simply that it did not work at once, that it took long periods of time, hundreds of years, to deploy its full effect, for that is self-evident when it is a question of the imprinting of a people's character. But the restriction relates to a fact which we have derived from the history of the Jewish religion or, if you like, have introduced into it. We have said that after a certain time the Jewish people rejected the religion of Moses once more—whether they did so completely or retained some of its precepts we cannot guess. . . .

The religion of Moses, however, had not disappeared without leaving a trace. A kind of memory of it had survived, obscured and distorted, supported, perhaps, among individual members of the priestly caste by ancient records. And it was this tradition of a great past which continued to work in the background, as it were, which gradually gained more and more power over men's minds, and which finally succeeded in transforming the god Yahweh into the god of Moses and in calling back to life the religion of Moses which had been established and then abandoned long centuries earlier.

. . .

The Return of the Repressed

It has long since become common knowledge that the experiences of a person's first five years exercise a determining effect on his life, which nothing later can withstand. Much that deserves knowing might be said about the way in which these early impressions maintain themselves against any influences in more mature periods of life—but it would not be relevant here. It may, however, be less well known that the strongest compulsive influence arises from impressions which impinge upon a child at a time when we would have to regard his psychical apparatus as not yet completely receptive.

. . . What children have experienced at the age of two and have not understood, need never be remembered by them except in dreams; they may only come to know of it through psychoanalytic treatment. But at some later time it will break into their life with obsessional impulses, it will govern their actions, it will decide their sympathies and antipathies and will quite often determine their choice of a love object, for which it is so frequently impossible to find a rational basis.

. . . The ego fends off the danger [deriving from the pressure of instinctual demands] by the process of repression. The instinctual impulse is in some way inhibited; its precipitating cause, with its attendant perceptions and ideas, is forgotten. This, however, is not the end of the process: the instinct has either retained its forces or collects them again, or it is reawakened by some new precipitating cause. Thereupon it renews its demand, and, since the path to normal satisfaction remains closed to it by what we may call the scar of repression, somewhere, at a weak spot, it opens another path for itself to what is known as a substitutive satisfaction, which comes to light as a symptom, without the acquiescence of the ego, but also without its understanding. All the phenomena of the formation of symptoms may justly be described as the "return of the repressed." Their distinguishing characteristic, however, is the far-reaching distortion to which the returning material has been subjected as compared with the original.

[pp. 124–27 *passim*]

. . .

Historical Truth

. . . We understand how a primitive man is in need of a god as creator of the universe, as chief of his clan, as personal protector. This god takes his position behind the dead fathers (of the clan), about whom tradition still has something to say. A man of later days, of our own day, behaves in the same way. He too remains childish and in need of protection, even when he is grown up; he thinks he cannot do without support from his god. That much is undisputed. But it is less easy to understand why there may only be a *single* god, why precisely the advance from henotheism* to monotheism acquires an overwhelming significance. . . .

Pious believers, however, know how to fill this obvious gap in motivation adequately. They say that the idea of a single god produced such an overwhelming effect on men because it is a portion of the eternal *truth* which, long concealed, came to light at last and was then bound to carry everyone along with it. We must admit that a factor of this kind is at last something that matches the magnitude both of the subject and of its effect.

We too would like to accept this solution. But we are brought up by a doubt. The pious argument rests on an optimistic and idealistic premise. It has not been possible to demonstrate in other connections that the human intellect has a particularly fine flair for the truth or that the human mind shows any special inclination for recognizing the truth. We have rather found, on the contrary, that our intellect very easily goes astray without any warning, and that nothing is more easily believed by us than what, without reference to the truth, comes to meet our wishful illusions. We must for that reason add a reservation to our agreement. We too believe that the pious solution contains the truth—but the *historical* truth and not the *material* truth. And we assume the right to correct a certain distortion to which this truth has been subjected on its return. That is to say, we do not believe that there is a single great god today, but that in primeval times there was a single person who was bound to appear huge at that time and who afterward returned in men's memory elevated to divinity.

We had assumed that the religion of Moses was to begin with rejected and half forgotten and afterward broke through as a tradition. We are now assuming that this process was being repeated then for the second time. When Moses brought the people the idea of a single god, it was not a novelty but signified the revival of an experience in the primeval ages of the human family which had long vanished from men's conscious

*[The word has not been very clearly defined. It is used to mean the belief of a community in one particular god of its own, and also to mean the belief in the dominance of one particular god over a hierarchy of other gods. In neither case does the belief imply that the god in question is the *only* god.—J.S.]

memory. But it had been so important and had produced or paved the way for such deeply penetrating changes in men's life that we cannot avoid believing that it had left behind it in the human mind some permanent traces, which can be compared to a tradition.

We have learned from the psychoanalyses of individuals that their earliest impressions, received at a time when the child was scarcely yet capable of speaking, produce at some time or another effects of a compulsive character without themselves being consciously remembered. We believe we have a right to make the same assumption about the earliest experiences of the whole of humanity. One of these effects would be the emergence of the idea of a single great god—an idea which must be recognized as a completely justified memory, though, it is true, one that has been distorted. An idea such as this has a compulsive character: it *must* be believed. To the extent to which it is distorted, it may be described as a *delusion*; insofar as it brings a return of the past, it must be called the *truth*. Psychiatric delusions, too, contain a small fragment of truth, and the patient's conviction extends over from this truth on to its delusional wrappings. [pp. 128–30]

. . .

The Historical Development

I cannot here repeat the contents of *Totem and Taboo* in greater detail. But I must undertake to fill up the long stretch between that hypothetical primeval period and the victory of monotheism in historical times. After the institution of the combination of brother-clan, matriarchy, exogamy and totemism, a development began which must be described as a slow "return of the repressed." Here I am not using the term "the repressed" in its proper sense. What is in question is something in a people's life which is past, lost to view, superseded, and which we venture to compare with what is repressed in the mental life of an individual. We cannot at first sight say in what form this past existed during the time of its eclipse. It is not easy for us to carry over the concepts of individual psychology into group psychology; and I do not think we gain anything by introducing the concept of a "collective" unconscious. The content of the unconscious, indeed, is in any case a collective, universal property of mankind. For the moment, then, we will make shift with the use of analogies. The processes in the life of peoples which we are studying here are very similar to those familiar to us in psychopathology, but nevertheless not quite the same. We must finally make up our minds to adopt the hypothesis that the psychical precipitates of the primeval period became inherited property which, in each fresh generation, called not for acquisition but only for awakening. In this we have in mind the example of what is certainly the "innate" symbolism which derives from the period of the development of speech, which is familiar to all children without their being instructed, and which is the same among all peoples despite their different languages. What we may perhaps still lack in certainty here is made good by other products of psychoanalytic research. We find that in a number of important relations our children react, not in a manner corresponding to their own experience, but instinctively, like the animals, in a manner that is only explicable as phylogenetic acquisition.

The return of the repressed took place slowly and certainly not spontaneously but under the influence of all the changes in conditions of life which fill the history of human civilization. I cannot give a survey here of these determinants nor more than a fragmentary enumeration of the stages of this return. The father once more became the head of the family, but was not by any means so absolute as the father of the primal horde had been. The totem animal was replaced by a god in a series of transitions which are still very plain. To begin with, the god in human form still bore an animal's head; later he turned himself by preference into that particular animal, and afterward it became sacred to him and was his favorite attendant; or he killed the animal and himself bore its name as an epithet. Between the totem animal and the god, the hero emerged, often as a preliminary step toward deification. The idea of a supreme deity seems to have started early, at first only in a shadowy manner without intruding into men's daily interests. As tribes and peoples came together into larger unities, the gods too organized themselves into families and into hierarchies. One of them was often elevated into being supreme lord over gods and men. After this, the further step was hesitatingly taken of paying respect to only one god, and finally the decision was taken of giving all power to a single god and of tolerating no other gods besides him. Only thus was it that the supremacy of the father of the primal horde was reestablished and that the emotions relating to him could be repeated.

The first effect of meeting the being who had so long been missed and longed for was overwhelming and was like the traditional description of the law-giving from Mount Sinai. Admiration, awe and thankfulness for having found grace in his eyes—the religion of Moses knew none but these positive feelings toward the father-god. The conviction of his irresistibility, the submission to his will, could not have been more unquestioning in the helpless and intimidated son of the father of the horde—indeed, those feelings only become fully intelligible when they are transposed into the primitive and infantile setting. A child's emotional impulses are intensely and inexhaustibly deep to a degree quite other than those of an adult; only religious ecstasy can bring them back. A rapture of devotion to God was thus the first reaction to the return of the great father.

[pp. 132–34]

The further development takes us beyond Judaism. The remainder of what returned from the tragic drama of the primal father was no longer reconcilable in any way with the religion of Moses. The sense of guilt of those days was very far from being any longer restricted to the Jewish people; it had caught hold of all the Mediterranean peoples as a dull malaise, a premonition of calamity for which no one could suggest a reason. Historians of our day speak of an aging of ancient civilization, but I suspect that they have only grasped accidental and contributory causes of this depressed mood of the peoples. The elucidation of this situation of depression sprang from Jewry. Irrespectively of all the approximations and preparations in the surrounding world, it was after all a Jewish man, Saul of Tarsus (who, as a Roman citizen, called himself Paul), in whose spirit the realization first emerged: "the reason we are so unhappy is that we have killed God the father." And it is entirely understandable that he could only grasp this piece of truth in the delusional disguise of the glad tidings: "we are freed from all guilt, since one of us has sacrificed his life to absolve us." In this formula the killing of God was of course not mentioned, but a crime that had to be atoned by the sacrifice of a victim could only have been a murder. And the intermediate step between the delusion and the historical truth was provided by the assurance that the victim of the sacrifice had been God's son. With the strength which it derived from the source of historical truth, this new faith overthrew every obstacle. The blissful sense of being chosen was replaced by the liberating sense of redemption. But the fact of the parricide, in returning to the memory of mankind, had to overcome greater resistances than the other fact, which had constituted the subject matter of monotheism; it was also obliged to submit to a more powerful distortion. The unnamable crime was replaced by the hypothesis of what must be described as a shadowy "original sin."

[p. 135]

. . .

Only a portion of the Jewish people accepted the new doctrine. Those who refused to are still called Jews today. Owing to this cleavage, they have become even more sharply divided from other peoples than before. They were obliged to hear the new religious community (which, besides Jews, included Egyptians, Greeks, Syrians, Romans and eventually Germans) reproach them with having murdered God. In full, this reproach would run as follows: "They will not accept it as true that they murdered God, whereas we admit it and have been cleansed of that guilt." It is easy therefore to see how much truth lies behind this reproach. A special inquiry would be called for to discover why it has been impossible for the Jews to join in this forward step which was implied, in spite of all its distortions, by the admission of having murdered God. In a certain sense they have in that way taken a tragic load of guilt on themselves; they have been made to pay heavy penance for it.

Our investigation may perhaps have thrown a little light on the question of how the Jewish people have acquired the characteristics which distinguish them. Less light has been thrown on the problem of how it is that they have been able to retain their individuality till the present day. But exhaustive answers to such riddles cannot in fairness be either demanded or expected. A contribution, to be judged in view of the limitations which I mentioned at the start [p. 105], is all that I can offer.

[pp. 136–37]

NOTES

"SE" in these Notes refers to the Standard Edition of *The Complete Psychological Works of Sigmund Freud*, edited by James Strachey (London: Hogarth Press, 1953–1966).

ROBERT JAY LIFTON, *On Psychohistory*

1. Kardiner was aware of the problem, but precisely the historical complexities of advanced Western (specifically American) society proved refractory to the approach he had evolved in the study of primitive societies. Primitive societies too, of course, could have revealed very different insights had they been approached from the perspective of historical change. See especially Kardiner, *The Individual and His Society* (New York, 1939), and Kardiner and associates, *The Psychological Frontiers of Society* (New York, 1945).

2. See Philip Rieff, "The Meaning of History and Religion in Freud's Thought," in Bruce Mazlish, ed., *Psychoanalysis and History* (Englewood Cliffs, N.J., 1963). Discussions suggesting the significance of the Moses Event for Freud can be found in the Jones biography, *The Life and Work of Sigmund Freud* (New York, 1953, 1955, 1957); in James Strachey's introduction to *Moses and Monotheism,* SE, Vol. XXIII, and Freud's own elaborate series of introductory and prefatory notes and summaries interspersed throughout the study; and in Maryse Choisy, *Sigmund Freud: A New Appraisal* (New York, 1963). Rieff, Erik Erikson, and Kenneth Keniston contributed directly to my understanding of these matters in their comments following my presentation of much of this paper at our small working group in psychohistory.

3. William C. Bullitt and Sigmund Freud, *Thomas Woodrow Wilson, Twenty-eighth President of the United States: A Psychological Study* (Boston, 1967). Erik Erikson's review of the book in *International Journal of Psycho-Analysis,* Vol. XLVIII (1967), pp. 462-68, is itself an important statement on psychohistorical method.

4. New York, 1958. See also Erikson's *Gandhi's Truth* (New York, 1969), his early study *Childhood and Society* (New York, 1950), and his two more recent collections of essays, *Insight and Responsibility* (New York, 1964) and *Identity: Youth and Crisis* (New York, 1968).

5. Freud, SE, Vol. XXIII, p. 27.

6. See Keniston's two books, *The Uncommitted* (New York, 1965) and *Young Radicals* (New York, 1968), and Coles's *Children of Crisis* (Boston, 1967).

7. These studies are reported respectively in *Thought Reform and the Psychology of Totalism* (New York, 1961), *History and Human Survival* (New York, 1970), and *Death in Life: Survivors of Hiroshima* (New York, 1968).

8. José Ortega y Gasset, *What Is Philosophy?* (New York, 1960), pp. 32-39.

9. "The Young and the Old—Notes on a New History," *Atlantic Monthly* (September and October 1969), and in *History and Human Survival.*

10. I introduce the concept of symbolic immortality in my essay "On Death and Symbolism: The Hiroshima Disaster," *Psychiatry*, Vol. XXVII, August 1964, pp. 191-210, refer to it in a number of subsequent writings, and discuss in detail its general (and especially historical) ramifications in "The Sense of Immortality: On Death and the Continuity of Life."

11. "Protean Man," *Partisan Review*, Vol. XXXV, No. 1 (Winter 1968), pp. 13-27, reprinted with further commentary on the concept in *History and Human Survival.*

12. See Erik H. Erikson, "On the Nature of Psycho-Historical Evidence: In Search of Gandhi," *Daedalus*, Summer 1968.

ERIK H. ERIKSON, *On the Nature of Psychohistorical Evidence: In Search of Gandhi*

1. Erik H. Erikson, "The Nature of Clinical Evidence," *Evidence and Inference* (Boston, 1958); revised and enlarged in *Insight and Responsibility* (New York, 1964).

2. Erik H. Erikson, *Young Man Luther* (New York, 1958).

3. Sigmund Freud, "An Autobiographical Study," *The Complete Works of Sigmund Freud*, Vol. XX (London, 1959), p. 40.

4. Erik H. Erikson, "Gandhi's Autobiography: The Leader as a Child," *The American Scholar*, Autumn 1966.

5. Mahadav Desai, *A Righteous Struggle* (Ahmedabad).

6. M. K. Gandhi, *An Autobiography* (Ahmedabad, 1927), Part 5, Chaps. 20–22.

7. L. Fischer, *The Life of Mahatma Gandhi* (New York, 1950), p. 238.

8. Gandhi, *An Autobiography*, Part 4, Chap. 11.

9. William C. Bullitt and Sigmund Freud, *Thomas Woodrow Wilson, Twenty-eighth President of the United States: A Psychological Study* (Boston, 1967).

10. Erik H. Erikson, *The New York Review of Books*, Vol. VII (1967), No. 2; also *The International Journal of Psychoanalysis*, Vol. XLII (1967), No. 8.

11. "Psychoanalysis and Ongoing History: Problems of Identity, Hatred, and Non-Violence," *Journal of the American Psychiatric Association*, 1965.

12. S. A. Wolpert, *Tilak and Gokhale* (Los Angeles, 1962).

13. *Collected Works of Mahatma Gandhi* (Ahmedabad).

14. Victor Wolfenstein, *The Revolutionary Personality* (Princeton, 1967).

15. Ernest Jones, *Essays in Applied Psychoanalysis* (London, 1951), Vol. II.

16. Robert Jay Lifton, *Death in Life: Survivors of Hiroshima* (New York, 1967).

17. Translated by Leo O. Lee for my seminar at Harvard from *Lu Hsün ch'üan-chi* (*Complete Works of Lu Hsün;* Peking, 1956), Vol. II, pp. 261–62.

18. Erikson, "Gandhi's Autobiography: The Leader as a Child."

19. This paper was presented in outline to the Group for the Study of Psychohistorical Processes at Wellfleet, Mass., in 1966.

PHILIP RIEFF, *Freud and the Authority of the Past*

1. *Inhibitions, Symptoms and Anxiety,* SE, Vol. XX, p. 75.
2. Cf. Carl Gustav Carus, *Symbolik der menschlichen Gestalt* (Leipzig, 1853, 1858), Vol. XXX; Freud had both editions in his library, now housed at the New York State Psychiatric Institute; Hughlings Jackson, *The Croonian Lectures* (London: Royal College of Physicians, 1884); T. A. Ribot, *Diseases of Memory,* trans. W. H. Smith (New York, 1882); Pierre Janet, *L'Automisme psychologique: essais de psychologie expérimentale sur les formes inférieures de l'activité humaine* (Paris, 1889); Moritz Lazarus and H. Steinthal, *Einleitende Gedanken über Völkerpsychologie* (Berlin, 1859).

For a brilliant survey of this entire development, see "Der Aufbau der Persönlichkeit," in Gottfried Benn, *Essays* (Wiesbaden, 1951), pp. 71-90.

3. *The Interpretation of Dreams,* SE, Vol. V, pp. 548-49.
4. *The Question of Lay Analysis,* SE, Vol. XX, p. 71.
5. *Moses and Monotheism,* SE, Vol. XXIII, p. 128.
6. *The Question of Lay Analysis,* pp. 96-97.
7. *Totem and Taboo,* SE, Vol. XIII, p. 88. Cf. *ibid.,* p. 77. As early as 1750 the French philosopher Turgot asserted that the advance of our knowledge of nature proceeded by a gradual emancipation from those anthropomorphic concepts which first led humans to interpret natural phenomena after their own image as animated by minds like their own. This idea was later to become a leading theme in the positivist philosophy of history, and the earliest stage of thinking it described was first called "fetishism," and then "anthropomorphism" and "animism."
8. *Ibid.,* p. 90. My italics.
9. *Moses and Monotheism,* p. 186.
10. "Why War?" (1932), in Vol. V of *The Collected Papers of Sigmund Freud,* ed. James Strachey (London: Hogarth Press, 1950), p. 286.
11. G. Stanley Hall, *Life and Confessions of a Psychologist* (New York: D. Appleton and Co., 1927), p. 359. Hall, with James J. Putnam, was one of Freud's first sponsors in America, and was president of Clark University when Freud delivered his lectures there in 1909. Hall ended as a very respectful critic, but a critic nonetheless. What the Freudians thought man needed was more and more rational consciousness. Hall agreed. "True," he writes, in the introductory chapter of his autobiography, "consciousness is in itself in many ways, and to a far larger extent than we have ever dreamed before, remedial" (p. 12). But then he suggests an alternative remedy, one the Freudians have treated as part of the disease. Hall continues: "But it is the motives of shame and shocked modesty which I believe are the chief curative agents." Here is a serious, indeed Christian, rejoinder to Freud's rationalism, according to which what men need nowadays may be not more consciousness, but more guilt.
12. *Totem and Taboo,* p. 161.
13. "Constructions in Analysis" (1937), *Coll. Papers,* Vol. V, p. 370.
14. *Group Psychology,* SE, Vol. XVIII, p. 122.
15. SE, Vol. XIV, p. 292.
16. *Coll. Papers,* Vol. V, p. 274.
17. *Moses and Monotheism,* p. 159.
18. *Group Psychology,* p. 123.
19. *Totem and Taboo,* p. 144.
20. SE, Vol. IV.
21. *Moses and Monotheism,* p. 129.
22. *Civilization and Its Discontents,* SE, Vol. XXI, p. 59.

23. *Ibid.*, pp. 51–52. In his conjectural prototypes of work and first cultural possessions, Freud presumes a universal facility in perceiving subjective spatial analogies. The uses of a tool to form and shape materials, he says, are regularly "animized" as the relation of male to female. With regard to the infantile impulse to extinguish fire with a stream of urine, Freud asserted that "the legends we possess . . . and in the later fables of Gulliver in Lilliput and Rabelais' Gargantua . . . leave no doubt that flames shooting upwards like tongues were originally felt to have a phallic sense." As he symbolically equated penis with flame, from the grossest abstraction of maleness, he similarly inferred that dwellings, hearths, and all other spaces of enclosure—on the analogy of the womb—are female. Cf. *Coll. Papers,* Vol. V, pp. 283-94.

24. "Constructions in Analysis," *Coll. Papers,* Vol. V, p. 363.

25. *Moses and Monotheism,* pp. 204-5.

26. *Ibid.*, pp. 157-61.

27. *Ibid.*, pp. 204-5.

28. "Analysis Terminable and Interminable," *Coll. Papers,* Vol. V, p. 343. Cf. *Totem and Taboo,* SE, Vol. XIII, p. 158: "Without the assumption of a collective mind, which makes it possible to neglect the interruptions of mental acts caused by the extinction of the individual, social psychology in general cannot exist."

29. The remarkable, curious Lamarckianism of Samuel Butler can best be documented from his *Notebooks,* ed. Henry Festing Jones (London, 1912). On pp. 57-59: "The connection between memory and heredity is so close that there is no reason for regarding the two as generically different." And further, "all forms of reproduction . . . are based directly or indirectly upon memory." See also Butler's book *Life and Habit* (London, 1910), esp. Chap. XI: "Instinct as Inherited Memory."

30. *Moses and Monotheism,* p. 209.

31. *Ibid.*, p. 208.

32. *Ibid.*, p. 201.

33. William James, *The Principles of Psychology,* Vol. II (New York, 1890), p. 678. James's italics.

34. *Moses and Monotheism,* p. 126.

35. *Introductory Lectures,* p. 387.

36. *Civilization and Its Discontents,* pp. 23-24.

37. *Group Psychology,* p. 135.

38. "Why War?" *Coll. Papers,* Vol. V, p. 283.

39. J. W. von Goethe, "Briefe an Frau Stein," June 8, 1787, in *Goethes Briefe* (Leipzig, 1923), Vol. VIII, pp. 252 ff.

40. *Group Psychology,* p. 122.

41. *Ibid.*, pp. 135-37.

42. SE, Vol. XXI.

43. "Psychoanalysis," SE, Vol. XVIII, p. 242.

44. *Introductory Lectures,* p. 134.

45. *The Interpretation of Dreams,* SE, Vol. V, p. 352.

46. *Ibid.*, 352 fn. Darwin had "actions" not "things" in mind when discussing the origin of symbolism.

47. *Moses and Monotheism,* p. 205.

48. *Ibid.*, p. 113.

49. *Ibid.*, p. 114.

50. *Totem and Taboo,* pp. 28-29.

51. SE, Vol. XXIII.

52. SE, Vol. XIX.

53. *Moses and Monotheism*, p. 108.
54. *Ibid.*, p. 109.
55. "Obsessive Acts and Religious Practices" (1907), *Coll. Papers*, Vol. II, pp. 25, 33.
56. G. W. F. Hegel, *The Philosophy of History*, rev. ed. (New York, 1900), pp. 31-32.
57. Karl Marx, *Capital* (Chicago, 1906), Vol. I, p. 648.
58. *Moses and Monotheism*, p. 200.
59. *Beyond the Pleasure Principle*, SE, Vol. XVIII, p. 49. Cf. "The Libido Theory," SE, Vol. XVIII, p. 258.
60. *Moses and Monotheism*, p. 198.
61. *The Future of an Illusion*, p. 8.

ERIK H. ERIKSON, *Play and Actuality*

1. Erik H. Erikson, *Childhood and Society*, 2nd ed. (New York: W. W. Norton, 1963).
2. In *The Man-Made Object*, ed. Gyorgy Kepes (New York: Braziller, 1966).
3. Ascanio Condivi, *Vita di Michelangiolo Buonarotti* (Rome, 1553). Here translated by Alice Wohl.
4. Charles Seymour, *Michelangelo's David: A Search for Identity* (Pittsburgh: University of Pittsburgh, 1967), p. 7.
5. 1 Corinthians 13:12.
6. Creighton Gilbert, *Complete Poems and Selected Letters of Michelangelo* (New York: McGraw-Hill, 1965), p. 5.
7. Jacques Hadamard, *The Psychology of Invention in the Mathematical Field* (Princeton: Princeton University, 1945), pp. 142-43.
8. Quoted in Holton, "On Trying to Understand Scientific Genius," *The American Scholar*, Vol. 41, No. 1 (Winter 1971–72).
9. "A Discussion of Ritualisation of Behavior in Animals and Man," organized by Sir Julian Huxley, F.R.S., *Philosophical Transactions of the Royal Society of London*, Series B, No. 772, Vol. 251, pp. 337-49.
10. "Reflections on the Dissent of Contemporary Youth," *International Journal of Psychoanalysis*, Vol. 51 (1970), No. 11.
11. Robert Frost, "Two Tramps in Mud-Time."
12. Robert Tucker, *The Marxian Revolutionary Idea* (New York: W. W. Norton, 1969), p. 215.
13. Erik H. Erikson, *Insight and Responsibility* (New York: W. W. Norton, 1964), Chap. 5.

KENNETH KENISTON, *Psychological Development and Historical Change*

1. William L. Langer, "The Next Assignment," *American Historical Review*, Vol. LXIII (1968), pp. 285–86.
2. See especially Erik H. Erikson, *Young Man Luther: A Study in Psychoanalysis and History* (New York, 1958), and *Gandhi's Truth: On the Origins of Militant Non-Violence* (New York, 1969).
3. See especially Robert Jay Lifton, *Thought Reform and the Psychology of Totalism: A Study of "Brainwashing" in China* (New York, 1961); *Death in Life* (New York, 1967); Robert Coles, *Children of Crisis: A Study of Courage and Fear* (Boston, 1967); Joel Kovel, *White Racism: A Psychohistory* (New York,

1970); Robert Liebert, *Radical and Militant Youth: A Psychoanalytic Inquiry* (New York, 1971); John Demos, *A Little Commonwealth: Family Life in Plymouth Colony* (New York, 1970); David Hunt, *Parents and Children in History: The Psychology of Family Life in Early Modern France* (New York, 1970).

4. Wilhelm Reich, *The Mass Psychology of Fascism* (New York, 1946); Erich Fromm, *Escape from Freedom* (New York, 1941); David Riesman, *The Lonely Crowd* (New Haven, 1950); Margaret Mead, *New Lives for Old: Cultural Transformation* (New York, 1956).

5. For a critical review of the concept of national character, see Alex Inkeles and Daniel J. Levinson, "National Character: The Study of Modal Personality and Socio-Cultural Systems," in Gardner Lindzey and Elliot Aronson, eds., *Handbook of Social Psychology* (Cambridge, Mass., 1968).

6. Daniel Lerner, *The Passing of Traditional Society: Modernizing the Middle East* (New York, 1964).

7. On the sociology of age-grading, see S. N. Eisenstadt, *From Generation to Generation* (Glencoe, 1956).

8. The following account draws heavily upon Bärbel Inhelder, "Some Aspects of Piaget's Approach to Cognition" in *Monograph of the Society for Research in Child Development*, Vol. XXVII (1962), pp. 19-33; Laurence Kohlberg, "Stage and Sequence: The Cognitive-Developmental Approach to Socialization," in David A. Goslin, ed., *Handbook of Socialization Theory and Research* (Chicago, 1969). For a more general discussion of concepts of development, see Dale B. Harris, ed., *The Concept of Development: An Issue in the Study of Human Behavior* (Minneapolis, 1957).

9. Erik H. Erikson, *Identity: Youth and Crisis* (New York, 1968).

10. Bärbel Inhelder and Jean Piaget (trans. Anne Parsons and Stanley Milgram), *The Growth of Logical Thinking from Childhood to Adolescence* (New York, 1958).

11. For an authoritative summary of the psychoanalytic view of development, see Otto Fenichel, *The Psychoanalytic Theory of Neurosis* (New York, 1945), Chaps. IV–VI. Erikson's views are summarized in his "Identity and the Life Cycle," *Psychological Issues*, Vol. I (1959), pp. 18-164; Harry Stack Sullivan, *The Interpersonal Theory of Psychiatry* (New York, 1953). The best general introduction to Piaget's immense body of work remains John H. Flavell, *The Developmental Psychology of Jean Piaget* (New York, 1963). For Kohlberg's views, see Kohlberg, "Stage and Sequence," and "The Child as a Moral Philosopher," *Psychology Today*, Vol. II (1968), pp. 25-30; William G. Perry, Jr., *Forms of Intellectual and Ethical Development in the College Years* (New York, 1970).

12. *Normality and Pathology in Childhood: Assessments of Development* (New York, 1965).

13. See, e.g., the elaborate forms used to assess early child development by Sally Provence and her colleagues at the Developmental Unit of the Child Study Center at Yale Medical School.

14. See René Spitz, "Hospitalism," *The Psychoanalytic Study of the Child*, Vol. I (1945), pp. 53-75; John Bowlby, *Maternal Care and Mental Health* (Geneva, 1951); Sally Provence and Rose C. Lipton, *Infants in Institutions* (New York, 1962).

15. *Growth of Logical Thinking.*

16. Flavell, *Developmental Psychology of Jean Piaget*, p. 399.

17. Martin P. Deutsch, Remarks at Research Conference, Dept. of Psychology, Yale Medical School, 1968.

18. Kohlberg, "The Child as a Moral Philosopher."

19. Kenneth Keniston, "Student Activism, Moral Development and Morality," *American Journal of Orthopsychiatry*, Vol. XL (1970), pp. 577-92.

20. Kohlberg, "Child as a Moral Philosopher."

21. Stuart T. Hauser, *Black and White Identity Formation* (New York, 1971), demonstrates marked identity foreclosures in black working-class adolescents. Research done in other cultures also suggests different rates and patterns of development that depend on the sociocultural matrix. See Patricia M. Greenfield and Jerome S. Bruner, "Culture and Cognitive Growth," in Goslin, *Handbook;* Jerome S. Bruner, Rose S. Olver, and Patricia M. Greenfield, *Studies in Cognitive Growth* (New York, 1967), especially Chaps. 11-14; Flavell, *Developmental Psychology of Jean Piaget,* 379-402; John Jay and Michael Cole, *The New Mathematics and an Old Culture: A Study of Learning Among the Kpelle of Liberia* (New York, 1967).

22. Some observers of development after puberty have argued that "adolescence," as commonly defined, is extremely rare in American society as well: see Edgar Z. Friedenberg, *The Vanishing Adolescent* (New York, 1962); Elizabeth Douvan and Joseph Adelson, *The Adolescent Experience* (New York, 1966); Daniel Offer, *Psychological World of the Teenager: A Study of Normal Adolescent Boys* (New York, 1969). These works may be interpreted either to indicate a widespread "foreclosure" of development in early adolescence or to indicate that the concept of adolescence has been incorrectly defined.

23. Stanley M. Elkins, *Slavery: A Problem in American Institutional and Intellectual Life* (Chicago, 1968).

24. Philippe Ariès, *Centuries of Childhood: A Social History of Family Life* (New York, 1962); Hunt, *Parents and Children in History.*

25. Kenneth Keniston, "Youth as a 'New' Stage of Life," *The American Scholar,* Vol. XXXIX (1970), pp. 631-54.

ROBERT COLES, *The Method*

1. I ended Vol. I of *Children of Crisis* with a quotation from James Agee's *Let Us Now Praise Famous Men* (Boston: Houghton Mifflin, 1941). I can only mention that book again—and say that in rural Alabama it is still possible to find some utterly poor white yeomen like those Agee and Walker Evans saw and tried to understand, write about, and (in photographs) present to their readers. Nor is George Orwell's *The Road to Wigan Pier* (New York: Harcourt, Brace and World, 1958) altogether out of date. His descriptions of miners and the mines, of company towns, of men robust and weary, of women devoted and sad, of children lively and canny and fearful, still apply to parts of Appalachia. Before Orwell, we had Emile Zola's *Germinal* (New York: Boni and Liveright, 1924) with its vivid portrayal of miners; and long before Agee, Dostoevsky knew how to convey the gentleness and brutishness that exist side by side in "Poor People," published in *The Gambler and Other Stories* (New York: Macmillan, 1923), and *The Insulted and Injured* (New York: Macmillan, 1956). I mention such writers simply to remind all of us that social scientists have a larger historical past to summon than some of them (and the rest of us) may care to remember.

2. Southern writers, as Flannery O'Connor has insisted in *Mystery and Manners, Occasional Prose,* selected and edited by Sally and Robert Fitzgerald (New York: Farrar, Straus & Giroux, 1969), are not simply dealers in the grotesque and bizarre, though ignorant and self-righteous Northerners would have it so.

Writers like William Faulkner and Eudora Welty draw upon Mississippi rather as any novelist draws upon what is familiar—in order to illuminate larger, more universal themes. Both Malcolm Cowley in *The Portable Faulkner* (New York: Viking, 1946) and Cleanth Brooks in *William Faulkner: The Yoknapatawpha Country* (New Haven: Yale University Press, 1963) have stressed the "brooding love for the land" that one finds in *Sartoris*, in *Sanctuary*, in *The Hamlet*, in *As I Lay Dying*. Robert Penn Warren agrees, and in his fine essay "William Faulkner" takes particular pains to describe the surroundings Faulkner both knew and constantly evoked: "No land in all fiction lives more vividly in its physical presence than this county of Faulkner's imagination." See *Selected Essays* (New York: Random House, 1958). If Faulkner was among other things a nature poet in the tradition of Wordsworth (which Cleanth Brooks argues convincingly) he was also another Southerner who knew his kin, his neighbors, his land—and those places and situations and conditions no road, let alone map, ever reveals to an outsider. I believe Southern writers persist in capturing our interest and imagination because they really do have stories to tell, adventures to relate, mysteries to unfold which entice us urban people (who read all those books). And the tradition of concrete descriptive writing in the South, tied always to the land, whether in the form of essays or novels, goes way back. Augustus Baldwin Longstreet wrote *Georgia Scenes* in 1835; Alice Walker, a black woman born in Eatonton, Georgia, to sharecropper parents wrote *The Third Life of Grange Copeland* (New York: Harcourt Brace Jovanovich) in 1970.

3. Erik H. Erikson has struggled for many years to cross all sorts of professional boundaries, yet preserve intact his own particular outlook as a psychoanalyst. His *Insight and Responsibility* (New York: W. W. Norton, 1964) is an especially rich resource for those of us who try to remain loyal to our clinical training, yet learn how life goes for men and women and children who are by no stretch of the imagination "patients." In this regard, two of that book's essays, "The Nature of Clinical Evidence" and "Psychological Reality and Historical Actuality," are of landmark importance. I have gone into Erikson's influence on psychoanalytic and psychiatric "field workers" in *Erik H. Erikson: The Growth of His Work* (Boston: Atlantic–Little, Brown, 1970). In a paper I wrote about Anna Freud's work, "The Achievement of Anna Freud," *The Massachusetts Review*, Vol. VII (Spring 1966), I tried to indicate how she too has made every effort to observe children outside as well as inside the so-called "clinical situation." Her study, in collaboration with Dorothy Burlingham, of *War and Children* (New York: International Universities Press, 1944) shows what two psychoanalysts could do to make sense of the responses young English children demonstrated during the Second World War—when death fell down from the skies. And her book *Normality and Pathology in Childhood* (New York: International Universities Press, 1965) emphasizes something a clinician become social observer must never stop reminding himself: it is no easy, clear-cut task to distinguish the "normal" from the "abnormal." If that holds in clinics and hospitals and in the doctor's private office, one can only imagine how careful a doctor must be as he works in a particular neighborhood of a Southern town or up an Appalachian hollow.

4. In the midst of the work that preceded the writing of this book I found myself struggling with this issue, and wrote about it in "Psychiatrists and the Poor," *The Atlantic Monthly*, Vol. CCXIV (July 1964).

5. I refer the reader to a section on "Method" in Vol. I of *Children of Crisis*, subtitled *A Study of Courage and Fear* (Boston: Atlantic–Little, Brown, 1967). In that section I tell how I became involved with the children who initiated school desegregation in the South and with the youths who waged sit-ins and

freedom rides and more generally carried on a widespread social and political struggle.

6. The first report of that work was delivered to the American Psychiatric Association at its annual meeting in May of 1965 and published as "The Lives of Migrant Farmers" in *The American Journal of Psychiatry*, Vol. CXXII (September 1965). A somewhat different report was issued by the Southern Regional Council as a monograph titled "The Migrant Worker" in the fall of 1965.

7. I reported upon that work to the American Orthopsychiatric Association in the spring of 1967. The paper was published as "American Youth in a Social Struggle: The Appalachian Volunteers," *American Journal of Orthopsychiatry*, Vol. XXXVIII (January 1968).

8. If muckraking journalism and testimony before Senate committees qualify as an effort "to change things," I can cite "Peonage in Florida," *The New Republic*, July 26, 1969, and a long summer morning that same month before the U.S. Senate Subcommittee on Migratory Labor. (See U.S. Congress, Senate, Subcommittee on Migratory Labor, *Hearings*, "The Migrant Subculture," Washington, D.C., July 28, 1969.) I must admit that more emphatic pressure than any people like me are likely to muster may well be the only way those "things" I just mentioned will indeed change.

9. At times I believe the only way to do justice to the black man's language is through his music: his songs, his spirituals, his blues, his "hollering." I find myself fiddling with phrases and sentences and paragraphs—with a whole afternoon of conversation—and I realize that the "translations" I make for a book like this, the grammatical and idiomatic and metaphoric demands I make, may also be considered an insulting straitjacket. And what I come up with may be terribly misleading too, because the spirit and power and force of what I hear, the "soul," just doesn't make it across the barrier of language—hence, both writer and reader still do not understand, still get the wrong "message." In any event, let me recommend LeRoi Jones's *Blues People: Negro Music in White America* (New York: Morrow, 1963) for its analysis of the words and rhythms sharecroppers and tenant farmers have called upon over the centuries; also *American Negro Folklore* by J. Mason Brewer (Chicago: Quadrangle, 1968), and Paul Oliver's first-rate *The Story of the Blues* (Philadelphia: Chilton, 1969). Oliver recommends many records; I want to mention especially "The Sound of the Delta" (Testament Records T–2209), and George Mitchell's two unforgettable volumes, "Delta Blues" (Arhoolie 1041 and 1042). With respect to mountaineers the same problem holds. I strongly urge a look at Wylene P. Dial, "Folk Speech Is English, Too," *Mountain Life and Work*, Vol. XLVI (February 1970), and, by the same author, "The Dialect of the Appalachian People," a publication of the Appalachian Center of the University of West Virginia.

10. See "Students Who Say No: Blacks, Radicals, Hippies," in Vol. VII of *International Psychiatry Clinics*, Dana Farnsworth and Graham Blaine, eds. (Boston: Little, Brown, 1970); also "Serpents and Doves: Non-Violent Youth in the South" in *Youth: Change and Challenge*, Erik H. Erikson, ed. (New York: Basic Books, 1963); and "Social Struggle and Weariness," *Psychiatry*, Vol. XXVII (November 1964).

ALEXANDER AND MARGARETE MITSCHERLICH, *The Inability to Mourn*

1. In a personal communication.

2. Freud, "Remembering, Repeating, Working Through," SE, Vol. XII, p. 145.

3. Walter Hofer, ed., *Der Nationalsozialismus, Dokumente 1933–1945*, Fischer Bücherei No. 172 (Frankfurt, 1957), p. 114.

4. G. Lukács, *Von Nietzsche bis Hitler* (Frankfurt, 1966), p. 21.

ROBERT JAY LIFTON, *The Sense of Immortality: On Death and the Continuity of Life*

1. Robert Jay Lifton, *Death in Life* (New York: Random House, 1968), pp. 540-41.

2. See Ernst Cassirer, *An Essay on Man* (Doubleday Anchor, 1944), *The Myth of the State* (Doubleday Anchor, 1946), and *The Philosophy of Symbolic Forms* (New Haven: Yale Univ. Press, 1953–1957); and Susanne Langer, *Philosophy in a New Key* (Cambridge: Harvard Univ. Press, 1942), *Feeling and Form* (New York: Scribner's, 1953), *Philosophical Sketches* (Baltimore: Johns Hopkins Press, 1962), and *Mind: An Essay on Human Feeling* (Baltimore: Johns Hopkins Press, 1967).

3. Lifton, "Experiments in Advocacy Research," *Research and Relevance*, Vol. XXI of *Science and Psycho-analysis*, ed. J. H. Masserman, pp. 259-71. Also in the academy newsletter of The American Academy of Psychoanalysis, February 1972 (Vol. XVI, No. 1), pp. 8-13.

4. Thomas Kuhn, *The Structure of Scientific Revolutions* (Chicago: Univ. of Chicago Press, Phoenix Books, 1962).

5. Sigmund Freud, "Thoughts for the Times on War and Death," SE, Vol. XIV, p. 289.

6. Carl Jung, *Modern Man in Search of a Soul* (New York: Harcourt Brace, 1936), p. 129.

7. Avery Weisman and Thomas Hackett, "Predilection to Death: Death and Dying as a Psychiatric Problem," *Psychosomatic Medicine*, May–June 1961 (Vol. XXXIII, No. 3).

8. Otto Rank, *Beyond Psychology* (New York: Dover reprint, 1958), p. 64.

9. Leslie Farber, "The Therapeutic Despair," *The Ways of the Will* (New York/London: Basic Books, 2nd printing, 1966).

10. Marghanita Laski, *Ecstasy: A Study of Some Secular and Religious Experiences* (Bloomington: Indiana Univ. Press, 1961).

11. Marcea Eliade, *Cosmos and History: The Myth of the Eternal Return* (New York: Torchbacks, 1959).

12. Lifton, *Revolutionary Immortality: Mao Tse-tung and the Chinese Revolution* (New York: Random House, 1968), p. 10.

13. Kenneth Boulding, *The Image* (Ann Arbor: Univ. of Michigan Press, 1956).

14. John Bowlby, *Attachment and Loss*, Vol. I: *Attachment* (New York: Basic Books, 1969).

15. Melanie Klein *et al.*, *Developments in Psychoanalysis* (London: Hogarth, 1952).

16. Kenneth Keniston, *Young Radicals* (New York: Harcourt Brace & World, 1968).

17. Lifton, "Protean Man," *Partisan Review*, Vol. XXXV, No. 1 (Winter 1968), pp. 13-27; *History and Human Survival* (New York: Random House, 1970), pp. 311-31; and *Archives of General Psychiatry*, April 1971, 24:298-304.

18. Erik H. Erikson, *Childhood and Society* (New York: Norton, 1950).

19. Lifton, *Home From the War: Vietnam Veterans—Neither Victims Nor Executioners* (New York: Simon and Schuster, 1973).

20. Joseph D. Teicher, "'Combat Fatigue' or 'Death Anxiety Neurosis,'" *Journal of Nervous and Mental Disease,* 1953, 117:234-42.

21. Abram Kardiner, "Traumatic Neuroses of War," *American Handbook of Psychiatry,* Vol. I (1959), pp. 246-57.

22. Wilhelm Stekel, *Nervous Anxiety States and Their Treatment,* translated by Rosalie Gabler (New York: Dodd, Mead & Co., 1923), as cited in Jacques Choron, *Modern Man and Mortality* (New York: Macmillan, 1964), p. 131.

23. Rank, *Will Therapy* (New York: Knopf, 1950).

24. Freud, *Civilization and Its Discontents,* SE, Vol. XXI, p. 89.

25. Lifton, *The Broken Connection,* ms., chapter on "Death and Psychiatry."

26. George R. Crupp and Bernard Kligfeld, "The Bereavement Reaction: A Cross-Cultural Evaluation," *Journal of Religion and Health,* Vol. I (1962), pp. 222-46.

27. Freud, "Analysis of a Phobia in a Five-year-old Boy," SE, Vol. X, pp. 5-149.

28. Harold Searles, "Schizophrenia and the Inevitability of Death," *Psychiatric Quarterly,* 1961, 35:631–35.

29. R. D. Laing, *The Divided Self* (Baltimore: Penguin [Pelican], 1965), p. 176.

30. Primo Levi, *Survival in Auschwitz* (New York: Collier, 1961), p. 82.

31. See, for instance, various papers in Don B. Jackson, ed., *The Etiology of Schizophrenia* (New York: Basic Books, 1960).

32. *Ibid.*

INDEX